MAGIC IN MERLIN'S REALM

Belief in magic was, until relatively recent times, widespread in Britain, yet the impact of such belief on determinative political events has frequently been overlooked. In his wide-ranging new book, Francis Young explores the role of occult traditions in the history of the island of Great Britain: Merlin's realm. He argues that, while the enduring magus and artificer invented by Geoffrey of Monmouth was a powerful model for a succession of actual royal magical advisers (including Roger Bacon and John Dee), monarchs nevertheless often lived in fear of hostile sorcery, while at other times they even attempted magic themselves. Successive governments were simultaneously fascinated by astrology and alchemy, yet also deeply wary of the possibility of treasonous spellcraft. Whether deployed in warfare, rebellion or propaganda, occult traditions were of central importance to British history and, as the author reveals, these dark arts of magic and politics remain entangled to this day.

FRANCIS YOUNG holds a PhD in History from the University of Cambridge and is the author of fourteen books, including *Magic as a Political Crime in Medieval and Early Modern England* (2017). He is a fellow of the Royal Historical Society and routinely broadcasts for BBC Radio on history, religion and folklore.

'Learned, judicious and rich in entertaining detail. I haven't enjoyed a history book this much in ages.'
 – *Tom Holland, author of* **Dominion: The Making of the Western Mind**

'The history of magic – in comparison to the history of witchcraft in Britain – has been under-researched in the Anglophone academy. The relationship of occult traditions to the politics of the realm has thus far been virtually ignored. A ground-breaking study of the history of occult traditions – of 'high' magic (elite, literate, clerical and courtly) as compared to 'low magic' (popular, non-literate, non-clerical) – is therefore to be warmly welcomed. This book is full of fascinating and previously little-known vignettes on the significant influence of the role of magic and the occult in the history of British politics, most of which will be unknown to the non-specialist. It would be an excellent text for undergraduate and postgraduate programs in the history of the occult.'
 – *Philip C. Almond, Emeritus Professor of Religion, University of Queensland*

'A terrific book. Francis Young is quite correct to say that no such survey has been done before, and the evidence presented by him unequivocally demonstrates that politics in pre-modern Britain cannot be fully understood without some attention to the notion and practice of magic and the occult sciences in general, such as alchemy and astrology. The author has also brought together a tremendous amount of scholarship in this volume which is commendable in its own right.'
 – *Frank Klaassen, Associate Professor of History, University of Saskatchewan*

'This is an important and accomplished project which demonstrates that – contrary to received opinion, and in modernity as well as the past – magical beliefs are central to political, religious and social lives, as conventionally categorised. I think the book will provoke much interest and comment with its claim that magic is as important as religion, and think too that there are likely to be over the next few years a series of books and theses that render that claim stronger. Magic's time has indeed come – and in that development the book will lead from the front. It will be accessible to a wide range of readers, written as it is with a light and engaging touch. The scope and detail never overwhelm, while the author's definition of magic and his inclusions and exclusions are convincing.'
  – *Marion Gibson, Professor of Renaissance and Magical Literatures, University of Exeter*

Merlin Dreams by Alan Lee. A contemporary rendering of the great enchanter.

MAGIC IN MERLIN'S REALM

A History of Occult Politics in Britain

FRANCIS YOUNG

Shaftesbury Road, Cambridge CB2 8EA, United Kingdom

One Liberty Plaza, 20th Floor, New York, NY 10006, USA

477 Williamstown Road, Port Melbourne, VIC 3207, Australia

314–321, 3rd Floor, Plot 3, Splendor Forum, Jasola District Centre, New Delhi – 110025, India

103 Penang Road, #05–06/07, Visioncrest Commercial, Singapore 238467

Cambridge University Press is part of Cambridge University Press & Assessment, a department of the University of Cambridge.

We share the University's mission to contribute to society through the pursuit of education, learning and research at the highest international levels of excellence.

www.cambridge.org
Information on this title: www.cambridge.org/9781316512401
DOI: 10.1017/9781009067133

© Francis Young 2022

This publication is in copyright. Subject to statutory exception and to the provisions of relevant collective licensing agreements, no reproduction of any part may take place without the written permission of Cambridge University Press & Assessment.

First published 2022 (version 3, July 2023)

Printed in the United Kingdom by TJ Books Limited, Padstow Cornwall, July 2023

A catalogue record for this publication is available from the British Library

Library of Congress Cataloging-in-Publication Data
NAMES: Young, Francis (Francis Kendrick), author.
TITLE: Magic in Merlin's realm : a history of occult politics in Britain / Francis Young, independent scholar.
DESCRIPTION: Cambridge : Cambridge University Press, 2022. | Includes bibliographical references and index.
IDENTIFIERS: LCCN 2021054777 (print) | LCCN 2021054778 (ebook) | ISBN 9781316512401 (hardback) | ISBN 9781009065870 (paperback) | ISBN 9781009067133 (epub)
SUBJECTS: LCSH: Occultism–Political aspects–Great Britain–History. | BISAC: RELIGION / History
CLASSIFICATION: LCC bf1434.g7 y68 2022 (print) | LCC bf1434.g7 (ebook) | ddc 203.0941–dc23/eng/20211230
LC record available at https://lccn.loc.gov/2021054777
LC ebook record available at https://lccn.loc.gov/2021054778

ISBN 978-1-316-51240-1 Hardback

Cambridge University Press & Assessment has no responsibility for the persistence or accuracy of URLs for external or third-party Internet websites referred to in this publication and does not guarantee that any content on such websites is, or will remain, accurate or appropriate.

*In memory of a modern Merlin
Peter John Payne (1924–2019)
pioneer of computer-aided design*

CONTENTS

List of Plates	*page* xiii
Preface	xv
Introduction	1
Merlin's Magic	2
History and Occult Traditions	6
Politics and the Occult	14
British Magic	24
Scope of the Book	25
1 **'Britain Indulges in Magic': The Origins of Occult Traditions in Britain**	32
Druids and Curse Tablets: The Occult Arts in Ancient Britain	33
Imagined Twilight: The Age of Merlin	37
The Occult Arts and Christianity in Early Medieval Britain	41
The Varieties of Magic	50
Natural Magic: Harnessing Occult Properties	54
Ritual Magic: Summoning Spirits	60
Alchemy: The Art of Transmutation	64
Astrology: Reading the Stars	70
Secrets of the Future: Divination and Prophecy	76
The Problem of Witchcraft As an Occult Tradition	80
Conclusion	83

Contents

2 **The Secrets of the King: Occult and Royal Power in Medieval Britain** 85
   Occult Power and the Royal Court in the Twelfth Century 87
   New Merlins: The Rise of the Occult Royal Advisor 92
   Magical Panic in Fourteenth-Century England and Ireland 97
   Militarising the Occult Arts: The Hundred Years' War 102
   The Monarch As Magus: Richard II 109
   Paranoia, Prophecy and Sorcery: The Occult Arts under the Lancastrian Kings 118
   Magic As Political Character Assassination: The Trial of Joan of Arc 122
   Occult Traditions and the Wars of the Roses 124
   Conclusion 135

3 **Arthurian Dynasty: The Tudors and Occult Power** 138
   Political Sorcery and the Early Tudor Court, 1485–1558 141
   Massmongers and Witchmongers: Discrediting Catholicism 151
   Elizabeth's Merlin: John Dee 161
   An Occult Empire 169
   Occult Missionary or Magical Spy? Giordano Bruno in England 178
   The Turn against Occultism 183
   Conclusion 188

4 **House of the Unicorn: Stuart Monarchy and the Contest for Occult Authority** 190
   Occult Traditions in Scotland 191

Supernatural Paranoia and Reformation
in Sixteenth-Century Scotland 196
The Demonologist King: James VI and I's
English Reign 204
Sorcery and Corruption at the Jacobean Court 212
Towards an Occult Revolution 218
Conclusion 232

5 Politics and the Decline of Magic, 1649–1714 234
An Occult Republic, 1649–1660 238
Restoring the Magic of Monarchy, 1660–1685 247
The End of Witchcraft? 254
Occult Revolutions, 1685–1688 260
Goodwin Wharton: The Last Merlin 267
Conclusion 276

6 Emanations of Albion: Politics and the Occult in Modern Britain 278
Politics and the Occult in Enlightenment Britain 279
Occultism and Politics in the Romantic Era 286
The Occult during the Second World War 295
Politics and the Occult in Postwar Britain 307
Extreme Politics and the Occult 313
Occult Traditions and the Modern Monarchy 319
Conclusion 322

Conclusion 326
The Re-enchantment of Politics? 327
The Royal Occult Adviser 331
The Ruler As Benevolent Magus 334
The Ruler As Witch or Bewitched 335
Sorcery As Treason 337

Occult Weapons of War 339
Occult and Political Secrecy 340
Occult Prophecy and Magical Saviours 341
'Magical Quietism': The Cost of Occult Politics? 342

Bibliography 345
Index 369

The plate section is to be found between pages 174 and 175

PLATES

1. Vortigern hears red and white dragons fighting beneath his fortress
2. Merlin Ambrosius interprets a comet for King Uther
3. King Nectanebus enchanting ships through sympathetic magic
4. The coronation of Richard II in 1377
5. English artillery at the siege of Orléans in 1429
6. Margery Jourdemayne conjures a demon for Eleanor Cobham, duchess of Gloucester in Shakespeare's *Henry VI Part Two*
7. Detail of the Ripley Scroll (watercolour copy)
8. Astrolabe made for Edward VI with astrological information in 1552
9. Astrological sphere graffito in the Salt Tower, Tower of London by Hew Draper, 1561
10. John Dee (1527–1608/9)
11. Frontispiece of King James VI's *Daemonologie*, 1597
12. Frontispiece of a pamphlet depicting the witch of Newbury, 1643
13. William Lilly (1602–81), astrologer and supposed Parliamentarian 'wizard general'

List of Plates

14 'Devills in the Ayre Bewitching M[onmouth]'s Army', 1685
15 Aleister Crowley in a self-designed uniform as 'Baphomet', 1919

PREFACE

Understanding the religious, philosophical and ideological beliefs of people in the past is essential for making sense of political events, yet historians have sometimes given short shrift to beliefs about magic and the occult in the realm of politics. It should come as no surprise that magic and politics are closely linked in history; both, after all, are concerned with the exercise of power. This book seeks to restore occult traditions to the central place they often occupied in the history of British politics. Monarchs from Henry III to William III and Mary II received (and occasionally acted on) the advice of magicians, who often modelled themselves on the character of Merlin – the original royal magical adviser. To give just a few examples, accusations of magic played a key role in the accession of Richard III, the downfall of Anne Boleyn and the success of the English Reformation. The idea of a global British empire was born out of the magical imagination of John Dee, while mystical Kabbalism inspired Britain's first experiment in the toleration of followers of a non-Christian religion. No less than religious belief, belief in magic is inseparable from the political histories of England and Scotland: the kingdoms of 'Merlin's realm' of Great Britain.

The idea for this book emerged while I was writing an earlier book, *Magic as a Political Crime in Medieval and Early Modern England: A History of Sorcery and Treason*

(2017), which focussed specifically on hostile acts of magic (real or perceived) directed against England's monarchs. In February 2017, just as I was sending the final text of *Magic as a Political Crime* to press, reports emerged from the United States of a campaign by American witches and Neopagans to 'bind' President Donald Trump, using rituals remarkably redolent of ones I discussed in the book. I just had time to include a brief allusion to this phenomenon in the book before it went to press, but I was astonished that a book on what I then considered a rather abstruse dimension of medieval and early modern England suddenly seemed relevant to modern politics. It became clear to me that the entanglement of politics and occult thinking was far more important – and more enduring – than I had previously considered. A book dealing much more thoroughly with this theme was needed, not just for the advancement of historical knowledge but also to help navigate a new and unfamiliar landscape where talk of occult power was now part of political discourse.

As fevered political rhetoric has become ever more extreme (and, arguably, separated from reality) in an increasingly divided Europe and America, accusations of attempted thought control by infinitely evil adversaries and allegations of ritualistic Satanic conspiracies have become almost commonplace. Politics since 2016 has taken a turn into magical thinking that scarcely anyone would have foreseen a decade ago, leaving many political commentators incredulous and uncomprehending at the re-emergence of forms of political rhetoric that hitherto seemed more at home in the seventeenth century. For those who study the history of witchcraft and magic, however, these are familiar developments: time and time again in British history, extreme political stress and uncertainty has resulted in people resorting to supernatural claims. Indeed, in many parts of the world magic and politics have never ceased to be intertwined. In light of these developments, this book is a historical 'guide for the perplexed' for those seeking to understand the origins of ideas of occult political power and influence that, contrary to all expectations, remain important today.

I am immensely grateful to my publisher, Alex Wright, for keeping faith with the idea of this book and seeing it through to publication. I thank Dr Graham John Wheeler for kindly reading and commenting on several draft chapters; Dr Joanne Edge for her helpful pointers on several matters; and the reviewers appointed by Cambridge University Press for their thorough and constructive comments on the draft manuscript. I thank the ever-helpful staff of the British Library, Cambridge University Library and the Bodleian Library, and I gratefully acknowledge the permission of the Trustees of the British Library Board, the British Museum and the Royal Museums at Greenwich to reproduce images from their collections. I extend my special thanks to Alan Lee for permitting the use of his artwork in the cover design. Last but not least, I am grateful to my wife, Rachel, and daughters, Abigail and Talitha, for bearing with my frequent imaginative journeys into Merlin's realm.

Spelling has been lightly modernised in all quotations. Translations from Latin, Scots and other languages are my own unless otherwise stated. All dates are given as Old Style before 1752 and New Style thereafter, with the year starting on 1 January.

Introduction

The history of magic is intimately entwined with political history. The connection is embedded in the very language we use to talk about politics. Politicians are practitioners of the 'dark arts' and form 'cabals', while an individual politician might be a 'Svengali', a 'prince of darkness' or a 'witch'. Probing deeper into the language of politics, the Latin word *coniuratio* has the double meaning of a political conspiracy and a magical conjuration, while the Bible itself warns that 'rebellion is as the sin of witchcraft' (1 Samuel 15:23). But magic is far more than just a source of political metaphors; in past centuries – and even in more recent years – concerns about magic routinely impinged on political decision-making. As one historian has observed, 'Precisely because there was a mystical dimension to politics ... there was a political dimension to magic; both were modifications of the same world of thought'.[1] That world of thought had both negative and positive expressions, based on both fear and hope, and throughout British history the idea of a wise royal magical adviser based on the legendary figure of Merlin has been a persistent theme, while more than one ruler has aspired to the occult wisdom of King Solomon. Yet the political histories of England, Scotland and Great Britain have

---

[1] Clark, *Thinking with Demons*, p. 552.

not hitherto been comprehensively examined in association with the occult beliefs and behaviours of the actors in that history. Just as it is crucial to understand the religious beliefs and ideological commitments of people in history, so it is important to understand the influence of belief in (and fear of) magic and other occult arts. In an effort to restore that missing piece of the puzzle of British history, this book examines the relationship between the occult arts and politics in Merlin's realm – the island of Great Britain – from the dawn of recorded history to the present day.

Merlin's Magic

In the twelfth century new and dangerous forms of knowledge were beginning to trickle into medieval Britain. At first, they were confined to a small, learned elite. The new knowledge included secrets about the formulation of life-prolonging elixirs and the transmutation of base metals into gold; precise understanding of the movements and occult influences of the heavens, giving a lucky few advance notice of future events; and even methods that claimed to enable someone to summon and control immensely powerful and intelligent spiritual beings. All of these new forms of knowledge had in common a 'hidden' or occult character, requiring initiation into difficult specialist skill sets. Originating in the Islamic world (often mediated through French and Iberian cultural translations before reaching Britain), these occult traditions deeply unsettled the cultural status quo of a world based on reverence for the Christian faith and the memory of ancient Greece and Rome. An enterprising

Welsh writer, Geoffrey of Monmouth (c. 1095 to c. 1155), created a pseudo-historical character who embodied this dangerous revolution of learning: Merlin the prophet and artificer, 'the magus of the twelfth-century renaissance'.[2] Crucially, Merlin was a figure who belonged to an imagined British past, giving Geoffrey the opportunity to plant occult knowledge not only in the present, but also in a fabricated British past.

Yet magic and occult knowledge were hardly new to medieval Britain. As early as the first century BCE, the Roman author Pliny the Elder reported that the British rivalled the Persians in their addiction to magic. In the early Middle Ages, Britons, Gaels and the early English alike practised traditional forms of natural magic and divination, drawing on the supposed occult powers of plants and stones and the signs of the natural world. In the twelfth century, however, something changed; magic became more than just a technique for healing cattle or protecting crops with charms. In the character of Merlin, occult knowledge became a tool of high politics and began to promise almost limitless power. And, as might have been expected, this promise attracted the attention of the powerful – both with the desire to profit from magic and to suppress occult knowledge as a danger to the realm.

There is ample evidence that Britain's monarchs, from the Plantagenets to the Stuarts, 'sought wondrous help in moments of social and cosmic drama', including the assistance of magicians and diviners.[3] There is also overwhelming evidence that monarchs and their counsellors

---

[2] Lawrence-Mathers, *True History of Merlin*, p. 5.
[3] Lawrence-Mathers, *True History of Merlin*, p. 125.

also feared harmful magic as a major threat to their reigns.[4] This book reappraises the political significance of magic and the occult tradition to the kingdoms of England and Scotland, arguing that the entanglement of occult traditions with politics from the twelfth century onwards was a key factor in enabling rulers to manage political change. Both the portrayal of political opponents as engaged in harmful magic (or even vain 'magical thinking'), and the use of occult symbolism to project political power were ways in which historical actors drew on the power of magic. From the civil war of Stephen and Matilda to the twenty-first-century crises of Brexit and the COVID-19 pandemic, the idea of magic (quite apart from any questions about whether magic is really effective) exercises a cultural power every bit as impressive as the supernatural powers claimed by magicians themselves.

While the phrase 'magical thinking' is usually deployed as a pejorative today, it is not without its advantages for politicians. The vaguest and most unrealisable promises and proposals often seem to have the greatest popular appeal. Magical thinking, far from preventing any change from occurring, can be the way in which change is effected – not through actual magic, but by promoting enough faith in the inexplicable power of rulers to accomplish the preposterous that they encounter little difficulty in pushing through more modest changes. In cultures where the efficacy of occult practices is widely accepted – such as medieval and early modern Britain or

---

[4] On the theme of harmful political magic see Jones, 'Political Uses of Sorcery', 670–87; Kelly, 'English Kings and the Fear of Sorcery', 206–38; Young, *Magic as a Political Crime*.

contemporary Africa – it can serve rulers not only to propose vague and unrealisable policies but also to articulate them in explicitly magical terms.

It is often impossible to have any certainty that magical acts were ever actually attempted in the past, but rumour invariably clusters thickly around the idea of magic and the possibility that politics and the occult are entangled. Magic occupies a cultural space where real practices shade almost imperceptibly into smears and slurs; the invocation of magic or the occult in propaganda was often enough to achieve a desired political effect. This book is therefore focussed as much on political representations of magic as on magical acts (whose historical reality is often difficult to demonstrate). It is the argument of the book that occult beliefs need to be considered alongside more conventional religious beliefs, ideological commitments and personal ambitions as important factors in political decision-making and events. Traditions of occult knowledge guided the decisions and actions of both monarchs and of rebels. Fear of harmful magic and witchcraft produced paranoia and unease, while magic also lent monarchs a powerful set of symbols for projecting majesty. Some English monarchs even saw themselves as participants in the occult tradition, whether as magi, alchemists, demonologists or fulfillers of prophecy.

According to one definition, occult traditions represent 'a coherent intellectual stream' that attempts to make sense of the world via 'a complex structure of connections, sympathies and affinities', where some or all of the knowledge required to apprehend the truth is hidden from the senses. The occult tradition is accompanied by a conviction that knowledge of occult truths somehow enables the supernatural manipulation of reality – the set of practices we might call magic.[5] Until the eighteenth century, the word 'occult' simply meant 'hidden', and did not always carry supernatural connotations – although the Enlightenment natural philosopher's pursuit of 'occult qualities' was in many respects a direct continuation of medieval and early modern natural magicians' search for the occult virtues (or 'powers') of nature. The occult tradition was 'a type of thinking, expressed either in writing or in action, that allowed the boundary between the natural and the supernatural to be crossed by the actions of human beings'.[6] It is important to bear in mind that the occult is a modern category applied to the past, just as the term 'supernatural' has changed its meaning over time to refer to unexplained phenomena in general rather than just the workings of God.

History and Occult Traditions

There is a long tradition in England of arguing that occult and magical beliefs are essentially irrelevant to history. In 1584, Reginald Scot noted that magicians seemed unable to influence politics or war, in spite of the great power ascribed to them by demonologists:

[I]f that … should be true in those things that witches are said to confess, what creature could live in security? Or what needed such preparation of wars, or such trouble, or charge in that behalf? No prince should be able to reign or live in the land. For (as Danaeus saith) that one Martin a witch killed the

---

[5] Katz, *Occult Tradition*, pp. 1–2.
[6] Monod, *Solomon's Secret Arts*, p. 5.

Emperor of Germany with witchcraft: so would our witches (if they could) destroy all our magistrates. One old witch might overthrow an army royal: and then what needed we any guns, or wildfire, or any other instruments of war? A witch might supply all wants, and accomplish a prince's will in this behalf, even without charge or bloodshed of his people.[7]

Scot went on to argue that, if magic were really effective, princes would not scruple to make use of it in warfare – since they displayed no reluctance to violate other precepts of the Christian religion in time of war.[8] Scot was saying, in effect, that all the theological handwringing about magic in his own time was a fuss about nothing, because deep down no one really believed that magic could influence the course of events. If they did, then they would be even more frightened of witches and magicians than they really were. One possible conclusion to draw from Scot's argument was that rulers who did not really believe in magical power promoted the persecution of witches and magicians for cynical political reasons rather than out of genuine concern for national security.

In 1978, the historian Edward Peters complained that 'political sorcery' was 'badly understood by most political historians'.[9] Little has changed since then. Although supernatural beliefs have been a major area of enquiry in social, intellectual and medical history since the 1970s, no corresponding shift has yet taken place in political history, with few political historians being willing to consider the impact of occult beliefs, real or ascribed. The relegation

---

[7] Scot, *Discovery of Witchcraft*, p. 34.
[8] Scot, *Discovery of Witchcraft*, p. 35.
[9] Peters, *The Magician, the Witch, and the Law*, p. xvii.

of occult traditions to the margins of political history is all the more surprising in light of the central place now occupied by religious belief in political histories of medieval and early modern England. The insights of church historians routinely inform and permeate broader historical discussions about medieval and early modern Britain, and no one would now seriously maintain that religious disputes were a façade that merely provided convenient cover for social and political agendas. Yet supernatural beliefs not easily placed under the umbrella of conventional religion have been treated as 'curious exotica scattered through the more humdrum narrative of kings, battles and ecclesiastical affairs'.[10] Where the occult tradition impinges on politics, it often serves merely as a reminder of the distance between the worlds of the past and the present, meriting little discussion or explanation.

In the 1920s the pioneering anthropologist, Sir James Frazer, described the persistence of belief in magic in modern societies as 'a solid layer of savagery beneath the surface of society',[11] an assessment based on his belief that magic was religion at a 'savage' stage of evolution. Although Frazer's approach has been thoroughly discredited by anthropologists, the notion that magical and occult beliefs are 'barbaric' and therefore in some way unworthy of historical study may be one reason why historians consciously or unconsciously avoid discussing them. Furthermore, supernatural beliefs beyond (or even within) the sphere of conventional religion are difficult to make sense of from inside a contemporary materialist

[10] Watkins, *History and the Supernatural*, p. 3.
[11] Quoted in Stone, 'Nazism as Modern Magic', 205.

worldview, and when we look back to eras when magical thinking suffused all aspects of thought, it can become very hard to distinguish occult from non-occult beliefs. In response to the difficulty of comprehending occult supernatural beliefs, it is easy to succumb to temptation and assume that everyone in the past was hopelessly credulous; the study of esoteric belief is, on this view, a futile attempt to comprehend nonsense. Another temptation is to follow in the footsteps of Carl Jung by treating belief in magic and the occult as 'a universal category', a kind of anthropological constant that cannot and should not be studied historically because it is present in every human society. Universalising the occult in this way allows us to abdicate responsibility for considering seriously the specific historical significance of occult traditions in a particular time and place.[12]

Yet another temptation is to adopt a 'functionalist' approach to magic and the occult. This usually involves assuming that belief in magic and the occult somehow served a symbolic or theatrical social or political function, sometimes accompanied by the assumption that members of elites did not actually think magic 'worked' – they simply used the idea of magic as a tool to achieve their purposes. Likewise, those who favour a Marxist interpretation of history as class struggle may choose to see political magic as a last resort of the powerless against the powerful – or, in a feminist reading of history, as an act of resistance by women against patriarchal power. Much of the entanglement of politics and the occult was indeed about propaganda and misrepresentation. Yet there is also

[12] Monod, *Solomon's Secret Arts*, p. 2.

convincing evidence that governments sometimes made use of magical rites and imagery, or showed excessive fear of magic, when they felt vulnerable or under threat. Belief in magic might be written off as part and parcel of the paranoid outlook of medieval and early modern rulers, but it is also clear that rulers sometimes regarded occult claims in a more positive light. The idea that occult beliefs and practices were little more than a form of performance is just not credible, given the volume of evidence that survives for well-developed and coherent popular supernatural belief, as well as the effort that went into acting on those beliefs.

There is an element of truth in functional interpretations of occult beliefs; this is why such explanations are so enduring. People did deploy the idea of magic for other purposes. However, anthropological explanations in terms of function tend to make most sense in studies of small communities, and falter when the use of accusations of magic 'as a lever for statecraft and social control' is taken into account.[13] Furthermore, as one historian of magic has observed, arguing that rulers used accusations of harmful magic as an excuse to persecute marginalised groups is like arguing that health inspectors use the presence of rats as a pretext for closing down restaurants. Just as health inspectors close down restaurants because they consider rats bad, so medieval rulers considered harmful magic bad because they genuinely believed that its practitioners were in league with demons.[14] If accusations of magic were just an instrument of political control, and

---

[13] Zhao, 'Political Uses of Wugu Sorcery', 135.
[14] Kieckhefer, 'Specific Rationality of Medieval Magic', 829–30.

one tool among many to assert dominance, then magic is little more than a political construct. Yet, as one historian observes, 'even when prosecution for magic served as a means of asserting or establishing social or political control, it was effective largely because its legitimating conceptions were widely shared'.[15] People took magic seriously long before they decided to deploy accusations against people using harmful magic for political purposes.

The temptation to 'functionalise' is just one example of a broader desire to reductively 'explain away' occult beliefs in the past, perhaps because beliefs so alien to the expected norms of our own society cause us intellectual discomfort. Assessments of the political significance of occult beliefs and practices in British history have hitherto been based on studies of a particular period, incident, idea or practice.[16] This book, by contrast, offers an overview

---

[15] Kieckhefer, 'Specific Rationality of Medieval Magic', 835.
[16] For examples of such studies see Bellany & Cogswell, *Murder of King James I*; Bloch, *Royal Touch*; Brogan, *Royal Touch*; Carey, *Courting Disaster*; Devine, 'Treasonous Catholic Magic', pp. 67–94; Elmer, *Witchcraft, Witch-Hunting and the State*; Gaskill, 'Witchcraft, Politics, and Memory', 289–308; Goodare, 'Witch-Hunting and the Scottish State', pp. 122–45; Griffiths, 'Trial of Eleanor Cobham', pp. 233–52; Hart, *Art and Magic in the Court of the Stuarts*; Hughes, *Arthurian Myths and Alchemy*; Hughes, 'Politics and the Occult at the Court of Edward IV', pp. 97–128; Hughes, *Rise of Alchemy in Fourteenth-Century England*; Jones, 'Defining Superstitions', pp. 187–204; Jones, 'Political Uses of Sorcery in Medieval Europe', 670–87; Kelly, 'English Kings and the Fear of Sorcery', 206–38; Larner, *Witchcraft and Religion*; Leland, 'Witchcraft and the Woodvilles', pp. 267–88; Mendelsohn, 'Alchemy and Politics in England', 30–78; Peters 'Political Sorcery at the Turn of the Fourteenth Century', pp. 218–22; Steible, 'Jane Shore and the Politics of Cursing', 1–17; Van Patten, 'Magic, Prophecy, and the Law of Treason in Reformation England', 1–32; Young, *Magic as a Political Crime*.

of the entanglement of occult traditions with politics throughout British history, seeking thereby to avoid the danger of generalising principles from particular cases or eras. Specific cases may reveal that magical beliefs served a particular function in a situation, but this does not mean that occult belief in general can or should be 'explained away' in other terms. The historian must grapple with occult traditions just like any other troubling characteristic of the past.

Once we are prepared to take the impact of occult beliefs seriously, there remains the challenge of how to make sense of occult claims made by people in past societies. How, for example, should we evaluate the actions of a magician chiefly renowned in his own time for doing things that most people would no longer consider possible? Should we try to 'demythologise' magic, explaining the operation of magical belief in naturalistic terms? Or should we accept reports of magical acts as factual because they are an integral part of the narrative of the past? Both approaches are problematic. The first approach is patronising and unreliable, because it usually requires us to dabble in psychological speculation unsupported by any historical evidence. For instance, if we speculate that witnesses who reported seeing a magician raise a demon were experiencing a collective hallucination induced by intense expectation, this involves imposing modern psychology on the past. We simply have no way of knowing whether the interpretation is true. Meanwhile, the second approach – accepting magic as part of the narrative – potentially allows us to abdicate any responsibility to interpret anything. Whatever anyone reported is to be treated as factual, and it cannot be analysed any further; but surrendering the right to analyse surely makes for poor history.

Occult traditions, by their very nature, are frequently nebulous and ill-defined. A satisfactory definition of magic, in particular, is notoriously elusive.[17] One recent writer on magic has argued that magic is about a two-way relationship between humans and the world around them: magic is when 'people are open to the workings of the universe and the universe is responsive to us'.[18] While it is always possible to argue, in any individual case, that no meaningful distinction exists between magic and religion (and even between magic and science), these contested categories have remained durable in their usage. We continue to make use of the categories, not least in order to challenge them critically; and it is noticeable that, in spite of criticism of the term 'magic' as lacking in meaning, few people stop using it. There are no good reasons to suppose that all people who held occult beliefs in the past were any less 'rational' than ourselves. Time and again, magical beliefs express their own internal 'magical logic' based on suppositions about reality different from those held by most educated people in the contemporary Western world.[19] Throughout the Middle Ages, and for much of the early modern period, magic was a 'rationally explicable practice with objective rationality',[20] and the same is true of other occult traditions adjacent to magic, such as alchemy and astrology. Occult beliefs usually have their own internal consistency, often to an extremely complex and detailed degree.

[17] For an overview of the discussion see Otto and Stausberg, 'General Introduction', pp. 1–15.
[18] Gosden, *History of Magic*, p. 2.
[19] Maxwell-Stuart, *British Witch*, p. 376.
[20] Kieckhefer, 'Specific Rationality of Magic', 822.

Religion, in spite of its complex character and the subtle shades of adherence, is something that matters to history because religious commitments profoundly influenced events. The same goes for magic, which cannot simply be left to specialists to puzzle over; magic is part of the story, because perceptions of magic genuinely influenced the decisions of the powerful. It would seem absurd to suggest that people in the past can or should be studied apart from their religious beliefs. However, whereas church history is a well-established field of study which enriches our understanding of the religious context of a period and its political significance, detailed studies of the history of magic that tie magical beliefs into historical events have hitherto been virtually non-existent. It is also important to note that perceptions of magic could affect political action without the presence of actual belief in magic. Medieval and early modern monarchs were expected to show their strength against all threats, whether visible or invisible, real or fictitious; whether monarchs believed in them or not, magic, prophecies and portents were threats to the government because such things were widely believed in by the population at large.[21] As long as a significant proportion of the population believed in magic, magic remained politically important.

Politics and the Occult

The contention of this book is that no straightforward functionalist or reductive explanation of the relationship

[21] Watkins, *History and the Supernatural*, p. 149.

between occult beliefs and politics is either possible or desirable. Nevertheless, the prevalence of occult beliefs in any society has political ramifications; if people believe in occult power, then occult power becomes a perceived instrument of political action both for rulers and ruled. Quite apart from whether people believe in the reality of occult power, cultural factors determine the extent to which occult power is considered a significant means of acting politically. A good example of such cultural differences is the contrast between the direct politicisation of witchcraft in early modern Scotland, where witches were accused of treason, and England, where accusations of political crime against witches were vanishingly rare. This difference does not, of course, mean that English people believed any less in witchcraft than their Scottish counterparts. In England, an elite tradition of 'political sorcery', usually involving members of the court consulting astrologers or professional service magicians, was considered far more significant than any threats of witchcraft from below.

The centrality of the court to medieval and early modern government is one reason why politics and occult beliefs became intertwined in Britain from at least the thirteenth century onwards. The conditions of a royal court were the perfect breeding ground for a growth of interest in influencing events by occult means. While the 'affair of the poisons' at the court of Louis XIV between 1677 and 1682 is the best known court magical scandal, it was the last major scandal of its kind in Europe and stands at the end of a long line of similar incidents and panics, some of which occurred in Britain. To some people, at a court where patronage was governed by the favour of a fickle monarch to whom favourites controlled access by others, magical stratagems to influence the monarch may have seemed the only resort. Just as elaborate rituals of courtesy often concealed simmering and deadly court rivalries, so some turned to secret ritual acts in order to influence events. Royal mistresses (and would-be royal mistresses) turned to love magic to retain or gain the monarch's affections, or in the hope of conceiving a child fathered by the king that would secure their status. Favourites of both sexes tried to influence royal judgement by occult means – or thought they could discover and expose the magical influence already exercised by favourites who seemed to have bewitched the royal favour.

We should be alert to the occasions when we encounter allegations of magic or other occult misdemeanours in the course of political history, because an individual's decision to use magic (or the government's decision to deploy accusations of magic against that individual) is an indication of the extent to which he or she was prepared to achieve political aims by transgressing moral and theological norms. While magic was in theory 'action at a distance', in practice any attempt to deploy magic in the political sphere would require an individual to involve others, and therefore exposed someone who used magic to the same dangers as those who planned or committed political crimes such as sedition and armed rebellion. A person's decision to use magic against the government should not always be seen as a sign of desperation, however; such an interpretation presumes a modern worldview in which practical measures would always take precedence over occult action for most people. This was simply not the case in medieval and early modern Britain, where occult power was frighteningly real to many people, and consulting with magicians and other practitioners of the occult arts was sometimes a first rather than a last resort.

Consultations with courtiers and opponents of the government had the effect of bringing magicians and astrologers within the ambit of political influence. To provide such services was a dangerous act, rendering an individual a partaker in state secrets and a potential security threat. Providers of occult services became unwitting and unwilling political actors through the ways in which their clients made use of their services. Yet this entanglement of occultists with politics was also an opportunity for those daring enough to seize it. The legend of Merlin provided a template for an ideal royal adviser whose skills would include mastery of the occult secrets of nature, allowing individuals such as George Ripley, John Dee and Elias Ashmole to portray themselves as latter-day Merlins to their respective monarchs. Geoffrey of Monmouth's Merlin myth, along with the Biblical narrative of King Solomon as a possessor of occult wisdom, created a semi-legitimate space for occult traditions at court. However severe the monarch's personal or legislative stance towards magic, the symbolic association between the king and the Magi of Matthew's Gospel reinforced every year in Epiphany celebrations; the ceremony of touching for the 'king's evil', steeped in natural magic; and the importance of the chivalric myth of King Arthur's court, meant that the institution of monarchy in England was inevitably infused with perceptions of occult power.

Introduction

For some monarchs, such as Richard II and Elizabeth I, the projection of a personal image as a quasi-magical figure was central to their reigns; for others, such as Henry IV, magic was purely a source of fear. The personal relationship between monarchs and occult traditions has much to reveal about monarchs' attitudes to self-representation, their anxieties about their own legitimacy, and their future aspirations for their reigns. However, the magic of monarchy did not just lie in the overt adoption of ideas, rhetoric or imagery taken from or influenced by occult traditions. The notion that a single man or woman was capable of governing wisely and justly, with due regard for the needs of his or her humblest subjects, was arguably magical thinking in and of itself. The myth of monarchy concealed the bureaucratic, factional reality of medieval and early modern government, but it also made it possible for rulers to enact radical change without seeming to compromise the established order. When rulers *consciously* appealed to occult narratives and imagery, the possibility of using occult ideas to facilitate political change was only magnified. The inherently unstable concepts of magic and the occult, capable of subverting and inverting established views of the world, were frequently the mercurial element that enabled the alchemy of political change to occur in highly stratified medieval and early modern societies bound by tradition and religious dogma.

Geoffrey of Monmouth created the figure of Merlin at a time of deep political uncertainty, generated by the drowning of Henry I's son and heir in the White Ship in 1120. Geoffrey held out the possibility that rulers might tap into occult forces in order to predict the future and stabilise the present. Would-be rebels and monarchs seeking to secure the throne sought to access the same sources of power, and when coups and rebellions succeeded – as they did in 1399 when Henry Bolingbroke overthrew Richard II, and in 1483 when Richard III seized the throne from his nephew Edward V – accusations of magic made it possible both to excuse the usurped and legitimise the usurper as a purifier of corrupt practices. Accusations of magic were especially associated with low-born royal servants who enjoyed an uncertain status at court, and such individuals seem to have made accusations in an effort to secure their positions as well as being frequent targets of such allegations.[22]

It can be tempting to view occult beliefs, especially in the modern world, as a relic of the past and an indication of political and social conservatism. The vodun religion's cultural dominance in Haiti, for example, has been blamed for encouraging dysfunctional behaviour that contributes to Haiti's poverty.[23] Similarly, the anthropologist Bronislaw Malinowski and others viewed the rise of fascism in mid-twentieth-century Europe as a recrudescence of magical thinking, since Nazis and fascists were responsible for a 'concerted working of magical forces through their highly developed system of physical control in propaganda ... which allow[s] the mental uniformity essential to magical action to be achieved on the mystical level of discourse'.[24] However, the anthropological analysis of Nazism as 'magic' really amounted to

---

[22] Peters, *The Magician, the Witch, and the Law*, p. 121.
[23] Kieckhefer, 'Specific Rationality of Magic', 830.
[24] Quoted in Stone, 'Nazism as Modern Magic', 207.

the argument that Hitler appealed to emotion and mysticism rather than fact and rationality.[25] The broad characterisation of far-right populism as 'magical', whether in the 1930s or the contemporary world, says more about its perceived conflict with modernity and predilection for fancifully simple solutions to political problems than its actual use of coherent occult traditions.

While there are examples from British history of political conservatives apparently giving credence to occult ideas, there is also ample evidence of historic links between magic and political radicalism. It would be wrong to see interest in magic and the occult as confined to a reactionary rejection of 'modernity'.[26] For medieval Icelanders, stories of magical attacks on monarchs became a site of national popular resistance to distant kings in Norway and Denmark.[27] In seventeenth-century Russia, 'magical processes could be interpreted as interventions in domestic and international policy',[28] and magic was extensively exploited by the supporters of Stepan Razin in his 1670 rebellion against Tsar Alexis. Their use of magic empowered the rebels, making possible a 'unitary notion of a people made of free individuals conceiving of themselves as the source of legitimacy for political power'. In this particular case, magic facilitated the development of political modernity. Magic, uniquely, allowed the rebels 'to think their action into efficacy' and freed them from dependency on the ideas of religious and dynastic

---

[25] Stone, 'Nazism as Modern Magic', 214.
[26] Lachman, *Politics and the Occult*, p. xv.
[27] Meylan, *Magic and Kingship*, pp. 1–26.
[28] Nun-Ingerflom, 'How Old Magic Does the Trick for Modern Politics', 434.

legitimacy that traditionally underpinned rebellions.[29] The willingness of Razin and his rebels to deploy the idea of magic echoes the deployment of astrology by William Lilly and alchemy by John Pordage and Gerard Winstanley in support of the English revolution of the 1640s.

In modern Africa, the resurgence of witch-hunting and the use of magic and rumours of magic to frighten and intimidate the population has often followed a breakdown of civil society. One feature of South Africa's transition to democracy in the 1990s was the appearance of calls to legalise and re-instigate witch-hunting, thereby distancing the new South Africa from a colonial past in which European Enlightenment ideas about witchcraft were imposed on the population. In the eyes of some Africans, state institutions in Africa based on Western models have failed because they could not take account of the threat of witchcraft.[30] This situation might be compared with the willingness of English Puritans to witch-hunt in the 1640s once they were freed from the restrictive influence of royal power and Laudian bishops. In seventeenth-century Britain, as in contemporary Africa, the decline of the state was 'experienced as a collective trauma for which people have no explanation', and the result was that people turned to witchcraft as an explanatory mechanism.[31] Furthermore, when modern

---

[29] Nun-Ingerflom, 'How Old Magic Does the Trick for Modern Politics', 449–50.
[30] Harnischfeger, 'State Decline and the Return of Occult Powers', 57–8. On legal debates concerning witchcraft and the state in Africa see also Tebbe, 'Witchcraft and Statecraft', 183–236.
[31] Harnischfeger, 'State Decline and the Return of Occult Powers', 59.

Introduction

African states are too weak to regulate power, that power becomes unpredictable, and therefore liable to be linked with hidden, occult forces – again, a trend that is detectable during the Civil War period in Britain.[32]

In pre-colonial South Africa, 'Magic ... resided at the centre of competitive politics' between chiefs,[33] while in ancient China politically motivated accusations of magic were 'prevalent during periods of state-building, territorial expansion, hegemony, and imperial absolutism'.[34] Such examples can provide useful comparisons with medieval and early modern Britain, where both magic itself and accusations of magic were deployed as political weapons. In the 1530s, Thomas Cromwell achieved an apparently impossible inversion of established belief – re-designating traditional Catholicism as unacceptable belief while installing formerly heretical ideas as a national religion – by invoking the accusation of magic against the Catholic church itself, thereby discrediting a traditional framework of religious belief established in England for almost a millennium. The general lines of anti-magical polemic laid down in Henry VIII's reign would be followed in subsequent eras, most notably in the thirties and forties of the seventeenth century, when Puritans deployed the same rhetoric against supporters of episcopacy in the Church of England. Yet it would be a mistake to see the political role of magic and occult beliefs in British history as a purely negative one, serving only as fuel for accusations, denunciations and damaging rhetoric. The stronger the anti-magical

---

[32] Harnischfeger, 'State Decline and the Return of Occult Powers', 74.
[33] Crais, *Politics of Evil*, p. 50.
[34] Zhao, 'Political Uses of Wugu Sorcery in Imperial China', 143.

polemic a government adopted – whether in sixteenth-century England and Scotland or twentieth-century China – the greater the extent to which that polemic confirmed, in the eyes of some, that magicians and other occult practitioners possessed genuine power, and that power might be harnessed as well as protected against.

Official anti-magical campaigns were sometimes a matter of affirming licit forms of magic over illicit ones, rather than attempts to stamp out magic altogether. For example, the concerns of Elizabeth I's government about people magically abusing images of the queen in the 1580s and 1590s occurred at a time when Elizabeth was making every effort to project her image, including the use of positive occult symbolism. Occult imagery replaced the outlawed religious imagery of Catholic England, enabling monarchs to continue the same kind of visual propaganda as their medieval predecessors, albeit imbued with a different symbolism. The exposure of illicit love magic at the court of James I as part of the Overbury poisoning case occurred at a time when the Stuart court was engaged in legitimating itself through ritualised court masques full of Hermetic imagery. Perceptions of magic in the Old World were a lens through which English settlers in the New World experienced the strangeness of the religious practices of indigenous peoples, while occult philosophy allowed individuals rigorously indoctrinated in a hierarchical worldview to make sense of the new 'topsy-turvy' political world of the Interregnum. Occult interpretations also made it possible for committed radicals to accept the Restoration in 1660. The ambiguity of magic and the difficulty of defining it – as well as the option of denying that one was engaging in magic at all – made it the perfect instrument for orchestrating, managing and facilitating acceptance of political change. Occult thinking was a crucial ingredient in the worldviews of many medieval and early modern people that enabled them to come to terms with otherwise unthinkable turns of events.

British Magic

This book is about the entanglement of magic and politics in Britain from the earliest times to the present day. The political entity known as the United Kingdom of Great Britain has only existed since 1707, when Scotland and England were formally united, yet the two kingdoms existed in personal union under a single monarch from 1603. The use of the word 'Britain' in the book's subtitle is not an attempt to elide the important differences that existed between the kingdoms of England and Scotland when it came to the relationship between politics and magic, or to claim anachronistically that England and Scotland constituted a single cultural unit. If anything, from the sixteenth century onwards English and Scottish rulers and legislators adopted sharply contrasting approaches to magic. Rather, the reference to Britain is a recognition that the history of occult traditions in the island of Great Britain goes back to a time before England and Scotland existed, as well as extending into the period after the Act of Union. Perhaps it would be more accurate to say that the history of British occult traditions goes back to an *imagined* time before England and Scotland existed. Merlin, the archetypal magician whom medieval and early modern magicians strove to emulate, was a British figure who supposedly lived in the sixth century,

Scope of the Book

but was tied to a variety of locations in England, Wales and Scotland. Merlin's prophecies concerned the destiny of Britain, not the individual kingdoms of England and Scotland.[35] The 'Merlin tradition' that underlay much of the entanglement of occult traditions with politics in medieval and early modern Britain thereby acted as a unifying factor in an otherwise fractured island.

The inclusion of English-controlled Ireland in a book about British history is not meant to imply that Ireland is geographically or politically a part of Britain. Instead, it is a recognition that individuals who identified themselves as English and belonged to a broader English culture lived in Ireland in the Middle Ages. In this sense, the Irish Pale was 'English', in contrast to Gaelic Ireland. The history of English Ireland is both British and Irish history. For the same reason, this book does not ignore British colonial attitudes to magic, although its coverage of the colonial context of the British Empire is by no means comprehensive. The interactions between indigenous and colonial attitudes to and beliefs about magic are so complex as to require a separate study.[36] Yet it is impossible to tell the story of the interrelationship between politics and magic while ignoring the political significance of England's (and later Britain's) expansionist and colonial ambitions.

Scope of the Book

The first chapter deals with the ways learned occult traditions reached Britain in the High Middle Ages (from the

[35] Lawrence-Mathers, *True History of Merlin*, p. 72.
[36] See Loar, *Political Magic*.

twelfth century onwards), thereby setting the scene for the political significance that these new forms of knowledge would go on to have. The chapter considers the earliest sources for the political use of magic in ancient Britain, first recorded by the Romans, and highlights the centrality of the legendary figure of Merlin to the imagined self-understanding and self-fashioned traditions of British practitioners of the occult arts. Chapter 1 addresses the relationship between occult traditions and Christianity in early medieval Britain, the nature of occult practices in early England, and the varieties of new hidden knowledge that arrived in the twelfth century, including natural magic, alchemy, astrology and ritual magic. Finally, the chapter considers the arrival of Renaissance magic and knowledge of the Hebrew Kabbalah in late medieval England, and elucidates the distinction between learned occult traditions and witchcraft. The chapter concludes that elite and secret forms of knowledge were inevitably both attractive and repulsive to rulers – a paradox that characterises the history of political engagement with occult traditions.

The focus of Chapter 2 is the evidence for the political application and representation of occult knowledge in medieval Britain between the eleventh and fifteenth centuries. Medieval monarchs feared political sorcery as a form of treason, with political anxiety about sorcerers reaching fever pitch in England and English-controlled Ireland in the fourteenth century. However, monarchs themselves were also accused of using magic against their own subjects, and several kings became intensely interested in the financial potential of alchemy and the predictive possibilities of astrology in statecraft and warfare.

A succession of royal 'magical advisers', including Roger Bacon and George Ripley, took on the legendary mantle of Merlin, but one king, Richard II, was determined to define himself as a magus. Richard's reign brought to a head many of the anxieties surrounding the paradox of the monarchy's fascination with occult knowledge. Yet in spite of the apparent contribution of Richard II's occult interests to his downfall, Lancastrian and Yorkist monarchs continued to be simultaneously terrified of and intrigued by political sorcery. The chapter argues that royal suppression and control of magic and other occult arts was essential to the projection of royal power and legitimacy in medieval Britain.

Chapter 3 addresses the role played by occult traditions in the seismic changes of the sixteenth century, as government took a turn towards centralisation and monarchical absolutism and religious reform transformed the societies of England and Scotland. The House of Tudor's Welsh ancestry made Tudor monarchs conscious successors of King Arthur. Accusations and rumours of magic were rife at the court of Henry VIII and played a role in the downfall of Anne Boleyn as queen, but allegations of magic also swirled around Cardinal Wolsey in Henry's early reign. As the Henrician Reformation began in the 1530s, propagandists such as John Bale made strenuous efforts to redefine the boundaries of occult practices, recasting traditional Catholic ceremonies such as the mass as magic (or at least as no better than magic). Similar developments occurred in Scotland, and in both countries the reorientation of the relationship of church and state produced unprecedented legislation to criminalise the practice of magic. Elizabeth I embraced her 'Arthurian' identity to the extent of seeking the advice of a latter-day Merlin, a role eagerly fulfilled by John Dee. Although the political centrality of Dee as an advisor to Elizabeth was subsequently exaggerated by Dee himself, at the high point of Dee's influence a vision of British empire inspired by occult traditions briefly informed official policy under a queen so fascinated by the hidden arts that she personally practised alchemy. However, towards the end of Elizabeth's reign a reaction set in against the intellectual and spiritual explorations of her early years, and occult knowledge came once more to be seen solely as a threat.

The House of Stuart, which ruled Scotland from 1371 and England from 1603, was assailed by magical threats from the fifteenth century, with no Scottish monarch suffering more magical attacks than James VI and I. However, James's reputation as a demonologist obsessed with witchcraft conceals a more subtle approach to the occult, to which James responded with both fascination and scepticism. Chapter 4 disentangles James VI's complicated relationship with occult traditions and witchcraft during both his Scottish reign and his English reign as James I, as well as examining the reputational damage done to the Stuart monarchy by magical scandals at court between 1613 and 1628. Beginning with the Overbury Plot, these scandals culminated in the accusations levelled against the duke of Buckingham and his 'wizard', John Lambe, and ultimately undermined the monarchy as a guardian of godliness in the nation. The chapter concludes by showing how the outbreak of Civil War in England in 1642 unleashed damaging allegations of the political and military deployment of occult power on both sides.

Beginning with the execution of Charles I in 1649, which risked emptying the British monarchy of its mystical power, Chapter 5 explores the continuing entanglement of occult traditions and politics up to the end of the Stuart dynasty's rule in 1714. The republic that succeeded Charles's death witnessed a flowering of popular interest in magic, alchemy and astrology as censorship broke down in the 1650s. Occult ideas inspired several radical religious and political figures of the Interregnum. Belief in the magical significance of the return of the Jews to England would result in the informal re-establishment of a Jewish community in London in 1656. Restored to the throne in 1660, Charles II was perhaps more eager than any previous monarch to revive the magic of monarchy, and turned the ancient ceremony of touching for the 'king's evil' into a major effort to project royal power as natural magic, as well as reviving royal patronage of astrologers and alchemists. The crises associated with the Catholic King James II's accession to the throne and his overthrow in 1688 produced numerous rumours of the political use of sorcery, although William and Mary were the last British monarchs to receive counsel from a practising magician, the Whig politician Goodwin Wharton, who attempted unsuccessfully to reprise the role of Merlin and John Dee. However, political interest in occult practices and witchcraft steadily diminished as the continued existence of such activities came to be perceived as indications of unstable government. This disengagement of the ruling elite from the language of magic prepared the way for the almost complete decriminalisation of magical acts in the eighteenth century.

Chapter 6 traces the changing relationship between politics and the occult from the eighteenth century to modern times. The relationship almost completely faded from view in eighteenth-century Britain, as it became socially unacceptable in elite circles to entertain a public interest in the supernatural. However, the apparent support of some mystical prophets for the French Revolution re-engaged the government's interest, and a tradition of 'mystical nationalism' was born at this time (largely through the writings of William Blake) that would go on to influence British politics to the present day. Elite interest in ritual magic returned at the end of the nineteenth century, and was often connected with traditionalist and ultra-conservative political views. The notorious twentieth-century magician Aleister Crowley has been the focus of numerous more or less credible claims that he was active as a spy, and that he and others used magic against the enemy during the Second World War. Less controversially, the era of the Second World War saw the politically motivated conviction of the Spiritualist medium Helen Duncan under the 1735 Witchcraft Act, if it is indeed true that the government feared that Duncan might reveal military secrets in her séances.

There is even evidence that government interest in magic continued into the Cold War period, perhaps owing to the habitual secrecy of magical groups, and one of the stranger results of the 'Troubles' in Northern Ireland in the 1970s was the emergence of a politically charged moral panic about black magic. By the 1980s both far-right and far-left politics in Britain had a 'magical fringe'. The British far right, in particular, has drawn in recent decades on earlier traditions of 'mystical nationalism' associated with an occult interpretation of the British landscape. British royalty's fascination with occult knowledge likewise continued in the twentieth century, primarily through Diana, Princess of Wales's willingness to associate with astrologers, mediums and psychics. Even today, belief in magical ideas has not altogether vanished in British politics, testifying to the persistent and enduring association between politics and the occult.

I
'Britain Indulges in Magic'
The Origins of Occult Traditions in Britain

In 61 CE, in one of the most dramatic episodes of the Roman invasion of Britain, the Roman governor Suetonius Paulinus launched an amphibious assault on the island of Mona (later called Anglesey), separated from the mainland of North Wales by the waters of the Menai Strait. Mona was one of the last British holdouts against Roman rule, where (at least according to the Roman historian Tacitus) the druids had whipped up the British into a warlike frenzy to resist conquest. As the flat-bottomed boats carrying the Roman legionaries approached the shore, the Roman army was met with the full might of druidic magic, witnessing 'black-robed women with disheveled hair like Furies' and 'Druids, raising their hands to heaven and screaming dreadful curses (*preces diras*)'.[1] The soldiers held their nerve, defeated the druids, and cut down their sacred groves. Yet Britain's reputation as an island famous for its practitioners of the occult arts was just beginning.

Britain's singular magical reputation lingers on even today, not least as the setting for the most popular fictional portrayal of magic in history, the *Harry Potter* novels of J. K. Rowling. For others, Britain is the home

---

[1] Tacitus, *Annals*, p. 327 (14.30).

of the druids, of Stonehenge and other mysterious megaliths, or the setting for tales of Merlin, Arthur and the Isle of Avalon. People from around the world visit Britain seeking magic and enchantment both fictional and real. It is a feature of occult traditions that they are frequently (and often quite deliberately) shrouded in obscurity and woven into the fabric of legends of their own making, rendering any historical analysis of such traditions challenging. This chapter identifies the key strands of occult tradition that became politically significant in British history, in each case exploring when and how each aspect of occult practice reached Britain.

Druids and Curse Tablets: The Occult Arts in Ancient Britain

Britain's many enigmatic prehistoric monuments are mysterious, beautiful and thought-provoking, but any 'magic' they have is a later cultural accretion. The solidity of stone belies the often flimsy basis on which antiquarians, archaeologists and amateurs alike have attempted to ascribe belief systems to prehistoric Britons. It is only from the first century BCE onwards that we have historical evidence of the Britons, but the evidence comes only from one side: a Roman perspective on barbarians. In Roman eyes, because the Britons practised human sacrifice their beliefs could not be dignified by the name of religion (*religio*); they were, rather, superstition (*superstitio*), which in a Roman context usually meant morally perverted religion (in contrast to the modern sense of 'superstition' as irrational credulity). In reality, the Romans applied the term to any religious practice that was sufficiently unlike their own. This included some forms of magic, although official Roman religion included many practices, such as divination from entrails (haruspicy) and the flight of birds (augury) that later ages would class as occult arts.

There are good reasons to be sceptical of the Roman stereotype of the Britons as superstitious and addicted to magic. The attempt by male and female druids to curse the Roman army at Anglesey is told exclusively from a Roman perspective. The Romans had only a limited understanding of British religion, and Tacitus may also have been using dramatic licence, so we cannot be certain that the druids were really attempting to curse the Romans on this occasion. It is surely suspicious that the black-robed women (who are presumably meant to be female druids) are very similar to Roman stereotypes of witches, such as Horace's Canidia.[2] Just as many centuries later the English settlers in the New World would dismiss the religion of Native Americans as nothing more than witchcraft, so the Romans may have been determined to stereotype the religious beliefs of the Britons according to their own understanding of forbidden spiritual practices. In the rhetoric that accompanied their conquest of Britain, the Romans anticipated later politicisations of magic in the service of colonialism.

Pliny the Elder was convinced the British druids were the world's foremost magicians, surpassing even the Persian *magi* from whom the Romans (via the Greeks) derived their word *magia*: 'Even these days Britain indulges in magic, filled with awe, and doing so with such remarkable rituals (*caerimoniis*) that you would think

---

[2] Hooley, *Roman Satire*, p. 59.

Persia learned magic from them!'[3] For both Greeks and Romans the Persians were a byword for barbarism and unacceptable religion (*superstitio*), and it is clear that the *magia* Pliny thought the druids were practising was the abominable rite of human sacrifice rather than anything that we or later ages might consider to be 'magic'. The Romans generally distinguished between religion and forbidden magic not by function but by form; divination, for example, was perfectly acceptable and pious, provided it was done in the correct way. The British druids' divination by the entrails of human beings was evil *magia* because it was quite literally 'divination from the dead' (necromancy). Roman divination from a sheep's liver, by contrast, was true religion. Indeed, if the Roman historians are to be believed, the druids and their practice of human sacrifice were the aspect of native British culture the Romans most actively suppressed after the Claudian invasion of 43 CE.

Perhaps the earliest hint of political sorcery in British history is to be found in Tacitus' account (in *Annals* 12.40) of events in the 50s CE in what is now the north of England, when the pro-Roman Queen Cartimandua of the Brigantes ensnared (*intercepit*) the relatives of her ex-husband Venutius 'by cunning arts' (*callidis ... artibus*).[4] Powerful women were frequently stereotyped in Roman literature as willing to use magic, and that may be what Tacitus intended to convey by the phrase 'cunning arts'.[5]

---

[3] Pliny, *Natural History* 30.13, quoted in De la Bédoyère, *Gods with Thunderbolts*, p. 63.
[4] De la Bédoyère, *Gods with Thunderbolts*, p. 269.
[5] Aldhouse-Green, *Boudica Britannia*, p. 127.

Alternatively, Tacitus may simply have been saying that Cartimandua adopted a clever political strategy. We find a clearer allusion to British use of magic in warfare with Cassius Dio's claim that the rebel queen of the Iceni, Boudicca, used divination to guide her decisions, releasing a hare from a fold in her cloak before a battle and interpreting the direction in which it ran.[6] This sounds like a terrestrial version of the Roman practice of augury (interpreting the flight of birds). There is no reason to suppose, however, that Cassius Dio would have regarded this practice as illicit.

Much later legends attributed magical powers to fictional ancient British kings. Geoffrey of Monmouth reported that Bladud, the ninth king of Britain, tried to fly in the air by magic, but ended up falling on the temple of Apollo in the city of New Troy (London), where he was killed.[7] Yet if the real nature and uses of magic in Iron Age Britain are largely obscure, we are fortunate to have a great deal of evidence of one kind of magical practice from Roman Britain. These are the lead *defixiones* or 'curse tablets', usually thrown into bodies of water. The most famous collection of such tablets comes from the Roman city of Aquae Sulis (Bath), where people regularly called on the deity to punish individuals guilty of offending them in some way. Although ostensibly religious, curse tablets may be interpreted as crossing the boundary into magic on account of their sinister intent, covert nature and trivial content, which suggests a highly instrumental attitude to divine power more characteristic

---

[6] Aldhouse-Green, *Boudica Britannia*, p. 138.
[7] Hart, *Art and Magic in the Court of the Stuarts*, pp. 176–7.

of magic than traditional ideas of religion.[8] Whether curse tablets were frowned upon by some Romans for religious or other reasons we cannot know, but surviving curse tablets approach the gods in administrative language, petitioning for justice as from a human magistrate or patron.[9] However, no evidence survives that this form of magic ever held political significance, and those curse tablets we have reflect private grudges. If occult arts became entangled with politics in Roman Britain, no evidence survives that this was the case.

Imagined Twilight: The Age of Merlin

The loaded term 'dark ages' has long since been jettisoned by historians for the period after the withdrawal of Roman troops from Britain in around 410, but it remains true that Britain entered a period of historical obscurity for two centuries that still forces historians to rely largely on archaeology and myth. One of the best-known figures to emerge from the semi-mythical twilight of post-Roman Britain is Merlin, whose name would become a byword for magic and the occult arts, but the process by which Merlin came to be portrayed as King Arthur's court wizard is far from straightforward. In his earliest known incarnation, Myrddin (Merlin) was the chief bard of the sixth-century Cumbrian king Gwenddoleu. Myrddin was driven mad after witnessing Gwenddoleu's defeat by another British king in battle. A thirteenth-century chronicle identified this battle as that fought at

---

[8] On the Bath curse tablets see Adams, 'British Latin', 1–26.
[9] Tomlin, 'Cursing a Thief', p. 246.

Arfderydd (Arthuret, now close to the Anglo-Scottish border) in 573.[10] Myrddin fled to a forest somewhere in the 'Old North' (now the Lowlands of Scotland), becoming known as *Myrddin Wyllt* ('Wild Merlin'), sometimes called Merlin Sylvester or 'Merlin of the Woods'. Arfderydd was probably a historical battle, although the oldest Welsh sources mentioning Myrddin date from the early twelfth century; nevertheless, 'a slim historical nucleus' may exist for the figure of Myrddin/Merlin.[11]

Geoffrey of Monmouth, who was wise enough to sprinkle his imaginative fiction with just enough pre-existing tradition to make it convincing, cleverly manufactured the familiar figure of Merlin in the twelfth century.[12] In his *Vita Merlini* ('Life of Merlin'), Geoffrey combined the ancient British theme of the 'wild man of the woods' with British Christian traditions of the ascetic woodland hermit.[13] Geoffrey took a story from the eighth-century *Historia Brittonum* ('History of the Britons') by Nennius, in which a boy named Ambrosius is selected by the court magicians of the British King Vortigern as a sacrifice whose blood will ensure the stability of Vortigern's fortress in the mountains of Wales. Ambrosius was selected because he had no human father, having been conceived by an incubus. However, Ambrosius turned out to have prophetic powers and saw through the rock to see two fighting dragons beneath the

---

[10] Lawrence-Mathers, *True History of Merlin*, pp. 66–7.
[11] Thomas, 'Celtic Wild Man Tradition', 29–30.
[12] Lawrence-Mathers, *True History of Merlin*, pp. 15–39.
[13] Thomas, 'Celtic Wild Man Tradition', 34.

castle, which represented the Britons and Saxons contending for the island of Britain.[14]

Geoffrey's masterstroke was to identify the boy Ambrosius as Merlin ('Merlin Ambrosius') on the grounds that Carmarthen was *Caer Merddin* ('Merlin's fort').[15] However, the narrative migration of the figure of Merlin from the British kingdoms of Strathclyde to what is now Wales may have taken place before Geoffrey, as early as the 1060s.[16] Geoffrey's Merlin is instructed by the legendary poet and seer Taliesin, who was in turn a pupil of Gildas (a genuine historical figure), who was instructed by the 'most wise magician' Illtud.[17] Bards were considered a class of druid in ancient Britain, and a strong association between poetry and supernatural power seems to have survived the Christianisation of the Britons. Furthermore, voluntary separation from human contact, especially in wild places, imbues an individual with occult power in many cultures.

Geoffrey prefers to describe Merlin as a *vates* ('prophet/seer') than as a magus,[18] and even in the late Middle Ages Merlin was famous chiefly for the many prophecies attributed to him,[19] with the themes of Merlin as prophet and magician co-existing in the medieval romances.[20] Even in the sixteenth century, Merlin was known primarily as the

---

[14] Lawrence-Mathers, *True History of Merlin*, pp. 36–7.
[15] On Geoffrey's reinterpretation see Jarman, 'Merlin Legend', pp. 115–16.
[16] Goodrich, 'Introduction', p. 6.
[17] Thomas, 'Celtic Wild Man Tradition', 36.
[18] Carey, *Courting Disaster*, p. 29.   [19] Hughes, *Arthurian Myths*, p. 72.
[20] Zumthor, 'Merlin: Prophet and Magician', p. 139.

author of prophecies.[21] 'Prophecies of Merlin' circulated far beyond Britain; Merlin was just as important in Breton as in Welsh legend, and his reputation spread from Brittany into France, Spain and Italy.[22] However, in the twelfth century, Geoffrey already extended Merlin's powers beyond those of a sage and seer, ascribing miraculous feats of engineering to him and, crucially, portraying Merlin as a figure simultaneously close to political power yet not beholden to it. Geoffrey's Merlin is the builder of Stonehenge (albeit not by magic), and although Merlin's true father is an incubus (the source of his prophetic knowledge), Geoffrey never calls Merlin a magus.[23] Merlin's use of spoken enchantments to make the stones of Stonehenge weightless first appears in Layamon's *Brut*,[24] and it was not until the early fourteenth century that the chronicler Robert Mannyng stated unequivocally that Merlin used 'coniurisons' (conjurations) to erect Stonehenge.[25]

By this period the idea that anyone possessed of deep learning or 'artifice' was a magician had become commonplace,[26] primarily as a consequence of the mingled 'scientific' and occult learning pouring out of the Islamic world and into western Europe from the eleventh century onwards. Geoffrey's confection of the character of Merlin coincided with an elite hunger for the new knowledge reaching England from the Continent, with the

---

[21] Thomas, *Religion and the Decline of Magic*, p. 467.
[22] Von Franz, 'Merlin in the Grail Legend', p. 278.
[23] Knight, *Merlin*, pp. 28–9.
[24] Lawrence-Mathers, *True History of Merlin*, p. 129.
[25] Knight, *Merlin*, p. 100.
[26] Knight, *Merlin*, p. 52; Lawrence-Mathers, *True History*, p. 128.

result that Merlin's identity as a magician was received positively rather than negatively.[27] This was partly because, by the 1130s, the church had not yet developed a coherent response to magic – Merlin slipped into history just in time, as it were.[28] Furthermore, Merlin differed from contemporary magicians because, having been fathered by an incubus demon, the source of his power was his own semi-supernatural nature. Merlin was able to achieve the goal of necromancers – access to the vast knowledge possessed by demons – without any need to commit the blasphemous act of summoning demons.[29] In this respect Merlin contrasted with another confected character in Geoffrey's *History of the Kings of Britain*, King Bladud, who summoned demons and practised necromancy in order to fly – with fatal consequences.[30]

The Occult Arts and Christianity in Early Medieval Britain

By the middle of the fifth century CE, pagan Germanic peoples from northern Germany and Denmark had begun to settle southern, eastern and central Britain, absorbing the native population into their culture in a gradual process of cultural transformation, and bringing with them the Old English language. There is no archaeological or genetic evidence to support the old idea that the invaders killed or drove out native Britons.[31] It is

---

[27] Lawrence-Mathers, *True History*, p. 118.
[28] Lawrence-Mathers, *True History*, p. 119.
[29] Lawrence-Mathers, *True History*, p. 6.
[30] Lawrence-Mathers, *True History*, pp. 122–3.
[31] Oosthuizen, *Emergence of the English*, pp. 1–19.

likely that magic was an important aspect of life for these early medieval English pagans. One scholar has argued that the name of one people group, the Hwicce (whose kingdom covered today's Gloucestershire, Worcestershire and Warwickshire) corresponded to the Old English word *wicce*, the root of 'witch'. According to this speculative argument, the Hwicce gained their name from the triple goddess worshipped by the Romano-British Dobunni in the same region, whom the Hwicce attempted to accommodate within the framework of Germanic paganism. In the process, the Hwicce reinterpreted the Romano-British goddesses as the Germanic goddesses governing the fate (*wyrd*) of human beings, who were later called the Norns or '*wyrd* sisters' in Norse mythology.[32]

This is an interpretation that rests on the large assumption that the post-Roman inhabitants encountered by the Hwicce still retained some memory of their pre-Christian religion. Although there are hints of continuity in belief – such as the adoption into Old English of the Celtic word *púca* (later 'puck') as a name for fairies – there is not enough evidence to be sure that supernatural beliefs contributed to the assimilation of Romano-Britons into early English society. Yet at least one place-name hints at magical practitioners wielding political power in early England: Teversal in Nottinghamshire probably derives from Old English *tēafreres heald*, 'the sorcerer's stronghold'[33] – although the exact significance of this name is something we can only guess at.

---

[32] Yeates, *Tribe of Witches*, pp. 144–5.
[33] Ekwall, *Studies on English Place-Names*, p. 55; Ekwall, *Concise Oxford Dictionary of English Place-Names*, p. 464; Mills, *Dictionary of English*

More reliable evidence for the place of magic in early English society can be found in condemnations of magic thought necessary by Christian bishops in the eighth and ninth centuries, following the conversion of the English to Christianity in the sixth and seventh centuries. The evidence that runes were used as a form of magic and divination in early medieval England is unconvincing,[34] but many charms (some containing obviously pagan allusions) survive in Old English medical texts. Prohibitions of practices that might be classed either as magic or as pagan survivals occur in eighth-century law codes, tailing off in the ninth century. However, the Viking invasions at the end of the ninth century, which established a pagan kingdom at York, intensified Christian anxieties about magic and 'superstition' in northern England, and magic was again condemned in tenth- and eleventh-century penitentials (lists of sins forbidden by the church).[35]

It is difficult to be certain that the law codes of early medieval English kings that outlawed sorcery were prompted by real-world practices in the England of the time rather than generic opposition to sorcery as a practice condemned by the Christian faith. However, the evidence of penitentials hints at cultural practices distinctive to England.[36] Yet in spite of its condemnation by kings, there is little evidence that occult practices ever acquired much political significance in pre-Conquest Christian England. Brontology (the art of predicting the

Place-Names, p. 323; Watts, *Cambridge Dictionary of English Place-Names*, p. 605
[34] See Page, 'Anglo-Saxon Runes and Magic', 14–31.
[35] Hutton, *Pagan Religions of the Ancient British Isles*, pp. 297–8.
[36] Raiswell and Dendle, 'Demon Possession', pp. 749–50.

future based on when thunder is heard) was practised as a form of divination to predict the deaths of kings, but never seems to have been condemned for this reason or even considered magical.[37] The pre-Conquest attitude to magic is unsurprising in light of the church's approach to magic in early medieval Europe. The tenth-century canon known as *Episcopi* ('of the bishop'), influential across Europe, urged priests to eject workers of magic from their parishes but described belief in magic as a delusion inspired by the devil. It took several centuries for the belief that magicians were genuinely able to work wonders in league with the devil to become theologically accepted.[38]

The influential *Etymologies* of Isidore of Seville (d. 636), which were well-known in pre-Conquest England, identified magic as a breach of God's law but did not define magic or explain how it was supposed to work. Isidore's omission created ambiguity about whether magic was a merely human deception that was wrong because it misled the faithful and mocked God, or an actual use of forbidden preternatural power that was wrong because it involved trafficking with demons.[39] For several centuries the austere attitude of the Church Fathers to all forms of magic as regrettable relics of paganism, to be regarded as

---

[37] Chardonnens, *Anglo-Saxon Prognostics*, p. 257. On the status of pre-Conquest prognostic techniques as magical or non-magical, see Liuzza, 'What Is and Is Not Magic', 1–4.

[38] Hutton, *Pagan Britain*, p. 376.

[39] Parish, 'Magic and Priestcraft', pp. 401–2. In medieval theological terminology, 'supernatural' power ('above nature') was technically possessed only by God and his direct agents, the angels and saints; any other exercise of spiritual power (such as by magicians or the devil) was 'preternatural' ('beside nature').

fraud and punished with ecclesiastical penances, prevailed in Christian Britain. In 1102, the Synod of Westminster prohibited a long list of 'works of the devil', including sorcery and divination; and a penitential produced between 1161 and 1186 of Bartholomew Iscanus, bishop of Exeter, warned against the making of charms to cure cattle.[40]

The penitentials' denunciation of numerous practices as 'unchristian' did not always mean that these practices were pagan, and when paganism was mentioned this was often little more than a polemical strategy. Interpreting all or most instances of magic as lingering survivals of paganism into the Christian world is problematic, because it overlooks the considerable potential for new magical practices to develop within the framework of Christianity. The majority of occult beliefs and practices in medieval Britain cannot be shown to have a pagan origin, except in the sense that they sometimes derived ultimately from the writings of pagan Classical authors such as Pliny the Elder. Yet pagan practices did sometimes survive as magical practices, shorn of their religious significance. Animal sacrifice, for example, survived in the form of the slaughter of cattle for good luck in the Scottish Highlands, as well as perhaps in the deposition of animal corpses or body parts in the foundations and walls of buildings (a practice that endured well into the nineteenth and possibly even into the twentieth century).[41]

---

[40] Watkins, *History and the Supernatural*, p. 90.
[41] Hutton, *Pagan Religions*, p. 292.

Even if there were 'pagan survivals' among occult practices, these cannot be used as evidence for the survival of paganism unless there is evidence that people believed in the pagan religions from which the practices were originally derived. By and large, ordinary Christians showed little hesitation in integrating pagan practices into their everyday lives as magic.[42] Occult practices that developed in the context of one religion are often transposed into the context of another without implying any *religious* exchange. For example, no one assumes that medieval ritual magicians in Britain who included garbled Arabic conjurations in their books of magic must have been Muslims; in the same way, there are no grounds to assume that pre-Conquest English people who used relics of pagan magic in the Christian era were 'pagan' in any meaningful sense.

In an earlier era, when the religious prejudices of Victorian Protestant Christianity functioned as an unconscious background norm for many historians, the idea that pious Christians could engage in occult practices without compromising their faith seemed absurd. Yet positive evaluations of the hidden arts were always available to medieval Christians. The Old Testament appeared to authorise a form of divination by sacred lots (1 Samuel 14:41), while 'Magi' who are clearly identified as astrologers appear as important protagonists in the nativity narrative of Matthew's Gospel. Indeed, the Magi are the first Gentiles to receive knowledge of the Messiah, a fact that inspired apocryphal stories about similar

---

[42] Hutton, *Pagan Religions*, p. 295.

intimations being received by the Roman sibyl.[43] Perhaps most significantly of all, the New Testament advocated the use of the name of Jesus as a word of power to achieve supernatural results, especially in exorcism.[44] Exorcism would go on to be the most visible form of authorised 'Christian magic'.

From late antiquity, a tradition existed that the wisdom Solomon received from God (2 Chronicles 1:7–12) included knowledge about the conjuration of demons.[45] This tradition spawned a wealth of apocryphal literature claiming to embody the magical wisdom of Solomon. Similarly, Moses was 'learned in all the wisdom of the Egyptians' (Acts 7:22), as the magical contest between Moses and Aaron and Pharaoh's magicians demonstrated (Exodus 7:8–12).[46] Medieval mystery plays regularly portrayed Moses as a magician.[47] However, in the late Middle Ages occult skill was also ascribed to other biblical figures. The fifteenth-century Italian alchemist, Petrus Bonus, claimed that the Old Testament prophets had been alchemists. St John the Evangelist also had an occult reputation, and John de Rupescissa believed that the extreme longevity of the biblical patriarchs could be explained by their skill in alchemy.[48] Likewise, the author of the fourteenth-century Middle English poem *The Pearl* described the Prophet Daniel as a master of 'dark knowledge'.[49]

---

[43] See Comparetti, *Vergil in the Middle Ages*, p. 313.
[44] On Christian exorcism as a magical practice see Young, *History of Exorcism*, pp. 18–19.
[45] Page, 'Medieval Magic', 42.
[46] Maxwell-Stuart, 'Magic in the Ancient World', p. 6.
[47] Hughes, *Rise of Alchemy*, p. 50.   [48] Hughes, *Rise of Alchemy*, p. 54.
[49] Hughes, *Rise of Alchemy*, p. 71.

The occult arts were as much a part of the fabric of Christianity as they were practices condemned and suppressed by the church. After all, most occult traditions were part of the Classical inheritance of ancient Greece and Rome, and a medieval 'reflexive deference to antiquity' and ancient literature, which contained many accounts of magic, kept alive the possibility that magic might really work.[50] For example, medieval readers usually assumed that the transformation of the character Lucius into a donkey by witches in Apuleius' second-century novel *The Golden Ass* had really taken place.[51] Furthermore, medieval Aristotelian philosophy (Scholasticism) could be deployed to support as well as oppose magic, since it presented the properties of matter as essentially mysterious and non-reductive.[52] Astrological image magic derived from the writings of the Islamic philosopher Al-Kindi developed into an entire genre of Scholastic discussion.[53] While it would be an exaggeration to characterise medieval attitudes to the occult arts as uniformly positive, justifications for positive evaluations of magical practices could easily be drawn from ancient literature, philosophy and even the Bible. However, occult knowledge took many different forms, all of which were appraised slightly differently within the framework of medieval and early modern Christianity.

Just as later medieval writers projected their own ideas about occult traditions onto figures from the post-Roman British past, so they did so for pre-Conquest England. In

---

[50] Copenhaver, *Magic in Western Culture*, p. 287.
[51] Gaisser, *Fortunes of Apuleius*, p. 17.
[52] Copenhaver, *Magic in Western Culture*, pp. 102–26.
[53] Klaassen, *Transformations of Magic*, pp. 2–3.

the twelfth century, Geoffrey of Monmouth imagined that King Edwin of Northumbria (d. 633) had been advised by an entirely fictitious Spanish augur called Pellitus, who predicted the future by the flight of birds.[54] Similarly, by the late Middle Ages, Bede was regularly portrayed as a prophet with knowledge of the future.[55] Although the historical Bede was interested in the stars for the purpose of telling the time during the night (for the monastic offices), he rejected the use of the stars for prognostication.[56] Most famously of all, Dunstan, abbot of Glastonbury and later archbishop of Canterbury (909–88), was widely credited with skill in alchemy and magic throughout the Middle Ages. The tale of Dunstan grasping the devil's nose with a blacksmith's tongs, first recounted in Osbern's *Life of St Dunstan* (c. 1089),[57] became one of the most popular legends of any English saint. Although Osbern said nothing about Dunstan's skill in necromancy, the idea of mastery over the devil inevitably became associated with magical knowledge. Finally, King Edward the Confessor (c. 1003–66) was later reputed to have been the first English monarch to possess the power to heal skin diseases by touching the afflicted in a quasi-magical rite that would be repeated by English monarchs down to Queen Anne.[58] The royal touch would prove to be an enduring quasi-magical enactment of 'the "marvelous" element in the monarchical idea'.[59]

[54] Carey, *Courting Disaster*, p. 28.
[55] Carey, *Courting Disaster*, p. 97.
[56] Truitt, 'Celestial Divination', 213.
[57] Osbern, *Vita S. Dunstani*, p. 67.
[58] Sturdy, 'Royal Touch in England', p. 180.
[59] Bloch, *Royal Touch*, p. 3.

Such legends tell us more about perceptions of the early medieval past in the late Middle Ages than they do about the reality of magic in early medieval England. Appeals to an ancient tradition of magic in Britain usually involved the projection of contemporary ideas onto both legendary and historical figures such as Merlin, Bede and Dunstan. Although the genuine origins of most occult beliefs and practices in medieval England can be traced to the influence of the Islamic world on western Europe, occult practitioners often saw themselves as part of an indigenous tradition and appealed to their own vision of an ancient British or English past.[60]

The Varieties of Magic

In a classic study of ancient Greek religion, Rudolf Herzog concluded that it was impossible to distinguish magic from religion, remarking that 'Magic is always other people's faith'.[61] In the context of a study of classical Greece, the view of magic as 'foreign' religion makes particular sense. The root of the Greek words *magos* ('magician') and *mageia* ('magic') is the Persian word for a priest, and as early as the fourth century BCE, competing statesmen in ancient Greece accused one another of being a *goēs* (sorcerer) or *magos* (magician) as a generalised slur designed to evoke foreignness and charlatanism.[62] However, the perception of magic as foreign in ancient Greece and Rome was itself a distinctive phenomenon of

---
[60] Hughes, *Rise of Alchemy*, p. 7.
[61] Herzog, *Wunderheilungen von Epidauros*, p. 140.
[62] Stratton, 'Early Greco-Roman Antiquity', p. 91.

those cultures. In reality, something like magic exists in virtually every human culture, whether indigenous or borrowed from elsewhere.

The seventeenth-century French scholar Gabriel Naudé (1600–53), whose *History of Magick* was published in English translation in London in 1657, believed that magic could be defined quite straightforwardly as the drawing of magical circles and conjuring of demons. Some historians continue to adopt Naudé's approach to the history of magic, arguing for the existence of a narrowly definable tradition based on specific texts.[63] However, Naudé's definition and others like it presume that magic is always a *learned* tradition, when the reality is that magic has always existed in both learned and unlearned forms. The development of the disciplines of anthropology and sociology have made us aware that concepts are fluid (magic especially so) and that people's beliefs do not always sit comfortably beside their actions and ritual behaviour.

Although the possibility of producing a satisfactory definition of magic is much debated by anthropologists, this is arguably less important to the historian than identifying what people in the past *considered* to be magic. According to one definition, magic in the Middle Ages was either 'undesirable rituals' or 'phenomena that did not fit ... established theories of cause and effect'.[64] However, it is problematic to confine the historical study of magic *solely* to those beliefs and practices considered to be magic

---

[63] See Copenhaver, *Magic in Western Culture*, p. 24.
[64] Page, *Magic in Medieval Manuscripts*, p. 9.

by people in the past. Whether a particular practice was deemed to be magic varied from person to person and from moment to moment. Magic was sometimes considered something unqualifiedly evil; at other times people argued that it was morally neutral or even good, depending on how magic was being defined. Positive and negative cultural evaluations co-existed in tension with one another, alongside a tradition of arguing that various occult practices were not magical at all.

The term 'magic' often had markedly different connotations for those 'inside' and 'outside' magical practice. Outsiders, for example, were often willing to label as 'magic' practices that no one other than their fellow learned demonologists regarded as magical. For example, some theologians denounced games of chance as a form of divination and therefore forbidden magic – a position that would probably have baffled most gamblers then and now.[65] Insiders to magical practice, on the other hand, were often reluctant to call what they did magic, although this reluctance dissipated somewhat after 1500 in the wake of attempts to rehabilitate the word 'magic' by Renaissance philosophers. Yet it would be impossible to restrict the history of magic to 'sources that display the "insider" perspectives, performances, and theorizations of people who claimed to be practising "magicians"',[66] because self-identifying magicians have never been a representative sample of those who actually practise magic.

One notable obstacle to defining magic is that it is difficult (if not impossible) to draw a hard and fast

---

[65] Tomás, 'Outside Bets', 147–64.
[66] Belingradt and Otto, *Magical*, p. 6.

distinction between magic and religion in the medieval and early modern periods. This is because most attempted definitions of magic can be shown to be applicable to religion as well, while many religious practices are (or strongly resemble) magical ones. Whether a practice is defined as 'mystical religion' or 'magic' depends to a large extent on whether a historian of magic or a historian of religion is studying it.[67] The traditional distinction between religion as submitting to a deity and magic as attempting to control and manipulate spiritual powers seems to rest on the expectation that traditional Protestant Christianity is the normative form of 'religion'. However, as one historian of magic has observed, there is not much to be gained from going to the opposite extreme and eliding the conceptual distinction between religion and magic.[68] This simply makes it impossible to study magic as a separate category at all, and involves an ahistorical denial of the fact that people in the past were capable of telling the difference between religion and magic. Although the practice of magic has often been framed in religious terms, and magicians would style themselves as holy sages, it is also clearly separable from religion since followers of different religions frequently borrowed and made use of one another's magical practices without demur. Another historian has observed that occult beliefs share much in common with organised religion – apart from the fact they lack organisation.[69] It is perhaps in this way that occult practices can best be

[67] Fanger, 'Introduction: Theurgy, Magic and Mysticism', p. 26.
[68] Collins, 'Introduction', p. 6.
[69] Monod, *Solomon's Secret Arts*, p. 3.

distinguished from conventional religion – they were never underpinned by institutional structures.

For one of the more confident scholarly defenders of a distinction between religion and magic, magic is 'any formalised practices by human beings designed to achieve particular ends by the manipulation and direction of supernatural power or of spiritual power concealed within the natural world'.[70] Occultism in general might be defined as theoretical speculation on the hidden causes of unexplained phenomena; magic implies some practical application of supernatural technology, although it may still contain a strong speculative element.[71] A more cautious pair of scholars observe that 'In its many forms, magic explicitly foregrounds questions concerning the nature of the self and its boundaries, the capacities of the will, and the relation of the self to external powers'.[72] This more tentative definition suggests that magic shares many features with religion, but that its emphases and self-presentation are different; the swagger of the sorcerer contrasts with the piety of the priest.

Natural Magic: Harnessing Occult Properties

On one level, natural magic is universal to almost all human cultures, and can be defined as the belief that natural objects such as stones, herbs and the bodies of animals contain occult properties that, under the right conditions, can be released, harnessed and even

[70] Hutton, *Pagan Britain*, p. viii.
[71] Kieckhefer, *Magic in the Middle Ages*, p. 131.
[72] Bever and Styers, 'Introduction', p. 4.

manipulated by the magician. However, although practices present in Britain since the earliest times implied belief in natural magic – such as herbalism, the use of semi-precious stones as talismans and traditional medicine – the appearance of explicit 'academic attempts to understand and classify the properties of natural objects and bodies not easily explained by known laws of physics and logic' can be traced to the thirteenth century.[73] Phenomena that theorists of natural magic sought to explain included the magnet, the power of the basilisk to kill just be looking at someone, and other examples of 'action at a distance'.[74] The underlying assumption of most forms of natural magic is belief in a 'vitalist' universe in which all matter is in some sense 'alive'. Within a Christian context, natural magic is also underpinned by the belief that Adam and Eve possessed perfect knowledge of the properties of nature before the Fall. That knowledge became 'occult' (hidden) after the Fall as a result of human sinfulness, but (in theory) the natural magician might recover 'prelapsarian' knowledge (knowledge possessed by Adam and Eve before their expulsion from Eden).

Although the Church Fathers were generally suspicious of natural magic as a pagan legacy, from the thirteenth century onwards there was a 'partial rehabilitation' of natural magic by theologians, some of whom argued that it was morally permissible to seek out the secrets of nature, provided that great caution was exercised in avoiding aid from supernatural beings other than God.

---

[73] Page, *Magic in the Cloister*, p. 31.
[74] Page, *Magic in the Cloister*, p. 32.

This change was made possible by the demise of a perceived link between magic and paganism, as paganism receded from view even as a cultural memory. The shift was also made possible by the extreme demonisation of other forms of magic, especially ritual magic involving conjuration. The demonisation of certain kinds of magic put clear blue water between impermissible and permissible forms of magic, allowing certain practices to be portrayed as 'natural' and free from demonic influence.[75]

By the late Middle Ages the use of herbs and stones for their magical properties (herbalism and lithomancy) was widely tolerated by the church, even to the extent that canon lawyers permitted the carrying of stones and herbs as protection against demonic attack.[76] Furthermore, there were clear connections between natural magic and other occult arts that had gained a measure of respectability, including astrology and alchemy. Natural magicians often attributed the efficacy of their use of herbs and stones to astrological correspondences that existed between natural objects and their governing planetary influences. The connection between terrestrial natural magic and the stars was the foundation of astrological medicine. Alchemy, insofar it involved the manipulation of natural materials in order to release their occult properties, was also a form of natural magic.

Knowledge of the properties of natural things had sinister as well as positive applications. *Veneficium*, the art of poisoning, was a synonym for harmful magic (and, more controversially, witchcraft) throughout the Middle Ages

---

[75] Watkins, *History and the Supernatural*, p. 140.
[76] Young, *History of Exorcism*, p. 90.

because the ability of plants and chemicals to kill was believed to be an occult power until well into the seventeenth century.[77] Furthermore, natural magic could be used to harm a person since a 'sympathetic' magical relationship continued to exist between a person and items belonging to him or her, or parts of his or her body. A person's clothing, hair or nail-clippings could be abused in order to harm or even kill, and the resemblance between an effigy and a person might draw down on that person the same malign astral influences that were directed against the effigy.[78] Although these were techniques strongly associated with witchcraft, they were also practised by learned magicians.

From the 1460s onwards, natural magic began to change, as the traditional medieval wisdom began to be supplemented by Greek and Hebrew texts newly discovered in the Christian West. Most famously, the Florentine Neoplatonist, Marsilio Ficino, began translating into Latin the Greek *Hermetic Corpus*, and was inspired by his encounter with the learned magic of antiquity to advocate a purified form of magic, free from the corruptions of medieval necromancy, that would mirror the purified texts of Classical literature being produced by other Renaissance humanists. Ficino and other figures of the Italian Renaissance who followed him began to make a sharp distinction between the legitimate 'theurgy' (wonder-working by natural magic) of the true magus and the illegitimate sorcery of demonic

---

[77] Young, *Magic as a Political Crime*, pp. 10–11.
[78] Young, *Magic as a Political Crime*, p. 30.

magicians.[79] However, the Renaissance magicians' conception of natural magic went far beyond the medieval notion of taking advantage of the intrinsic virtues of natural things. They argued that human beings' original created dignity, forfeited by the Fall, was recoverable by magical means, and that boundless knowledge could be obtained by the magus attuned to the vital principles of a living universe.[80]

The magical project of Renaissance thinkers was based on the rediscovery of ancient texts believed to be much older than they really were, most notably the *Hermetic Corpus*, which actually originated in late Hellenistic Egypt but was long thought to be older than the Pentateuch. However, the Egyptian pagan origin of the *Hermetic Corpus* and some of the magic featured in it – notably a rite to draw down the influences of stars to animate statues – were highly controversial. The issue of the legitimacy of Hermetic magic divided philosophers, with some more conservative figures like Ficino distancing themselves from controversial elements. Others, most notably Giordano Bruno in the sixteenth century, embraced Hermetic magic to the point of regarding it as a superior religion to replace Christianity. The early influence of Renaissance magic in England was limited, although material drawn from Italian natural magicians such as Arnold of Villanova had begun to appear in English books of magic by the mid-sixteenth century.[81]

---

[79] On Ficino see Copenhaver, *Magic in Western Culture*, pp. 38–41.
[80] Copenhaver, *Magic in Western Culture*, p. 123.
[81] See Foreman, *Cambridge Book of Magic*, p. xxix.

The first significant self-proclaimed Renaissance magus in England was John Dee, and the arrival of the Italian magus, Giordano Bruno, in the country in 1583 further fanned elite interest in the new, purified magic.

Renaissance enthusiasm for the recovery of ancient texts extended to Jewish as well as Egyptian wisdom, resulting in the creation of a Christian version of the Jewish Kabbalah by Johann Reuchlin in 1514. Just as they believed the *Hermetic Corpus* to be extremely ancient, so Renaissance scholars assumed that medieval Jewish Kabbalistic works were written by (or even older than) Moses.[82] Although the Reformation cut off many of the more speculative enterprises of British Renaissance thought, interest in the Kabbalah survived the Reformation owing to the Protestant emphasis on the importance of the word of God, although some Catholics also retained an interest.[83] The Christianised Kabbalah fed into the early development of Freemasonry in sixteenth-century Scotland, and Kabbalistic prophecy influenced seventeenth-century Puritans who campaigned for the readmission of the Jews to England in order to hasten the apocalypse (a subject further explored in Chapter 5). Kabbalism teetered on the edge of what might be considered natural magic, insofar as it appealed to the idea of occult qualities hidden within God's creation, but also focussed on language and speech – elements of magic usually associated with the ritual magical tradition.

---

[82] On the development of Kabbalistic learning in England see Lloyd Jones, *Discovery of Hebrew*, pp. 168–74.
[83] Young, 'Sir Thomas Tresham', 145–68.

Ritual Magic: Summoning Spirits

Ritual magic, sometimes called ceremonial magic, necromancy, or demonic magic, was widely considered by its critics the most dangerous form of magic throughout the Middle Ages and the early modern period, because it involved summoning supernatural entities to perform the will of the magician. The original meaning of necromancy was, literally, 'divination by the dead', evoking the grisly practice of reanimating corpses in order to foretell the future, as described by Classical authors such as Horace and Lucan.[84] One of the earliest mentions of this kind of magic in England dates from 1222, when the chronicler Ralph of Coggeshall noted that a Jew was accused of necromancy by wrapping a boy in a dead man's skin so that the dead man could speak through the boy as an oracle.[85] It is no accident that the necromancer in Ralph's story was a Jew. Ritual magic involving the evocation of demons was associated in legend with King Solomon, and many therefore assumed that the Jews (especially Jews living under Muslim rule in Spain) were masters of this art.[86]

However, summoning and communicating with the spirits of the dead was only a small part of medieval necromancy. A sign that 'necromancy' was beginning to change its original meaning was the appearance of the word 'nigromancy', literally 'divination by the black art', which may have been a scribal mistranscription of 'necromancy' but more accurately described the actual range of

---

[84] Maxwell-Stuart, *British Witch*, pp. 67–8.
[85] Saunders, *Magic and the Supernatural*, p. 105.
[86] On the Solomonic legend see Butler, *Ritual Magic*, pp. 29–36.

practices involved in ritual magic. Although the invocation of spiritual beings other than God to cure disease and avert disaster had been commonplace since late antiquity, the notion of summoning spirits in order to gain something more positive from them took longer to develop, only crystallising in the twelfth century.[87] However, ritual magicians not only imitated Solomon by summoning spirits; they also relied on 'names of power' derived from the Hebrew Kabbalah to summon them. Although the original meaning of the Kabbalah as a mystical philosophy based on the Hebrew alphabet was lost in its adoption by magicians, it was an essential element in the ritual magical tradition.[88] The *Clavicula Solomonis* ('Key of Solomon'), a work with apparent Greek origins, had appeared in western Europe by the end of the thirteenth century, while the *Liber Razielis* ('Book of Raziel') was a heavily edited translation of a Hebrew manual of angel conjuring. The *Almandal* was a translated Arabic text but may have come from a Sanskrit original.[89] Yet these origins were almost completely unknown to the medieval practitioners who used such texts.

Ritual magic can be subdivided into theurgy (the attempt to work wonders, usually by contemplating divine names), angelic magic and necromancy, which differed from angelic magic only because necromancers conjured both angels and demons, gave less emphasis to spiritual preparation, and generally had less exalted goals than

---

[87] Butler, *Ritual Magic*, p. 32.   [88] See Butler, *Ritual Magic*, pp. 36–44.
[89] Klaassen, *Transformations of Magic*, pp. 116–17.

angel conjurers.[90] What most ritual magic had in common was its desire to summon, bind and then dismiss spiritual beings – whether these were understood as the spirits of the dead, demons, angels or even fairies.[91] The ultimate origins of ritual magic lay in Jewish legends about King Solomon, and while the banishment of the Jews from England in 1290 may have brought an end to Jewish magic in Britain, it certainly did not end interest in it. In subsequent centuries magical knowledge was often presented as Jewish wisdom, and magical diagrams continued to be adorned with more or less accurately copied Hebrew letters.[92] However, texts of ritual magic were not accompanied by elaborate theoretical justifications of their operations, as texts of astrological image magic so often were.[93] Ritual magic often claimed the validation of experience and was therefore frequently characterised by its instability.[94]

Because ritual magic relied so heavily on adapted portions of the church's liturgy, throughout the Middle Ages it was largely the preserve of a 'clerical underworld' of individuals literate in Latin: university students, schoolmasters, minor clerics, monks, friars and priests.[95] However, although many practised this kind of magic with self-centred motives as a shortcut to money, power or sex, others genuinely regarded magic as a path of spiritual illumination and saw themselves as the successors

---

[90] Klaassen, *Transformations of Magic*, p. 153.
[91] Young, *Magic as a Political Crime*, p. 20.
[92] Page, *Magic in Medieval Manuscripts*, p. 73.
[93] Klaassen, *Transformations of Magic*, pp. 86–7.
[94] Klaassen, *Transformations of Magic*, pp. 87–8.
[95] Kieckhefer, *Magic in the Middle Ages*, p. xi; Klaassen, *Transformations of Magic*, pp. 117–18.

of King Solomon, vindicating the supreme dignity of humanity redeemed by Christ by daring to command spirits.[96] Yet for most theologians, there was no question that ritual magic was morally and religiously unacceptable – not because ritual magicians bound or exorcised spirits, but because they had the temerity to summon them in the first place. One of the earliest and most extensive efforts to demarcate acceptable from unacceptable magic in England was made by John of Salisbury (c. 1120–80), who argued that it was acceptable to grind up dry human bones and consume them as a natural remedy, but never to make medicinal use of human blood. This was because blood was thought to contain and embody the life force, and its use smacked of necromancy.[97] Salisbury's *Policraticus*, written in around 1159, may have been aimed at the court of Henry II; if so, the author was concerned about courtiers' fascination with divination, although his arguments were directed against the effectiveness of astrology and other practices, and he did not attempt to demonise astrology.[98]

Ritual magic had considerable potential for exploitation in the political arena, and many accusations of political sorcery claimed that individuals had conjured demons to discover politically crucial information (usually the time of the monarch's death), to gain the favour of rulers, and even to kill them. Surviving books of ritual magic show that magicians conjured spirits associated with particular planets including Mars, which 'cause and stir up war, murder, destruction and mortality of people and all

[96] Foreman, *Cambridge Book of Magic*, p. xxxvi.
[97] Watkins, *History and the Supernatural*, pp. 139–40.
[98] Carey, *Courting Disaster*, pp. 29–30.

earthly things'.[99] Books of magic also contained detailed instructions on harming one's enemies,[100] and even conjurations 'to make battling armed knights appear'.[101] Rituals for constructing magical rings to gain the affections of judges and rulers are common in such texts.[102]

However, firm evidence for people in Britain actually attempting ritual magic for political ends is elusive, and in the majority of cases other practices became conflated with ritual magic. In one famous case, Eleanor Cobham, duchess of Gloucester, engaged astrologers to cast the horoscope of Henry VI in 1441, but the astrologers were accused of demonic sorcery and, in subsequent popular culture, Eleanor was invariably portrayed as a patron of necromancers.[103] Accusations of ritual magic must always be treated with caution, as they were often used as a slur against practitioners of other occult arts. The evidence of books of ritual magic is that magicians were more interested in making a living through finding stolen goods, thieves and buried treasure than in influencing politics.[104]

Alchemy: The Art of Transmutation

Alchemy in the medieval and early modern periods was rarely considered to be a branch of magic, but it was certainly an occult art in the sense that its practitioners

---

[99] Page, *Magic in Medieval Manuscripts*, p. 94.
[100] Young, *Magic as a Political Crime*, p. 20.
[101] Klaassen, *Transformations of Magic*, p. 128.
[102] Klaassen, *Transformations of Magic*, p. 144.
[103] On this case and its subsequent portrayal see Young, *Magic as a Political Crime*, pp. 35–46, 147–50.
[104] Klaassen, *Transformations of Magic*, p. 140.

appealed to hidden forces of nature and did their best to conceal secrets beneath elaborate symbolic language. Alchemy was not merely a primitive precursor to the science of chemistry, a reductive interpretation now rejected by historians of science for the obvious reason that very little of what alchemists were interested in had anything to do with modern chemistry.[105] Alchemists made a handful of chemical 'discoveries' by accident, but they did not recognise at the time that there was any distinction between these 'genuine' discoveries and the ongoing quest for the Philosophers' Stone.

The origins of alchemy can be traced to the Islamic world, whose learning began to seep into England in the twelfth century via scholars who travelled to study in European cities formerly under Muslim rule. These included Adelard of Bath (c. 1080 to c. 1152) and Robert of Ketton (d. c. 1160), the first Latin translator of the Qur'an.[106] The first English scholar to write on alchemy was Daniel Morley (d. c. 1210), who produced a treatise on the four elements and the fifth element, the alchemical 'quintessence'.[107] By the fourteenth century, however, a myth had begun to develop that alchemy originated in Britain. This can be traced back, in part, to Geoffrey of Monmouth's projection of rumours about a school of occult arts at Toledo onto King Arthur's alleged court at Caerleon.[108] However, it may also have been connected with Edward III's interest in alchemy. In his

---

[105] Láng, 'Why Magic Cannot be Falsified', p. 52.
[106] Parry, *Arch-Conjurer of England*, pp. 25–6.
[107] Parry, *Arch-Conjurer of England*, p. 26.
[108] Carey, *Courting Disaster*, p. 28.

dialogue *De lapide philosophorum et de auro potabile* ('Of the Philosophers' Stone and of potable gold') the fifteenth-century Italian alchemist, Fabri de Dya Fabri, praised Edward III for patronising Ramon Llull, Arnold of Villanova and John Dastin. This claim may have given rise to the legend that Edward imprisoned Ramon Llull in the Tower of London until he managed to transmute gold. In reality, Llull was never in England and was not an alchemist.[109]

Late medieval legends ascribing knowledge of alchemy to St Dunstan (909–88), abbot of Glastonbury between 940–60, may have been linked to an earlier legend about Joseph of Arimathea, who was supposed to have brought to Britain two silver vessels containing the sweat and blood of Jesus Christ. These were deposited in the earliest church at Glastonbury. The red blood and white sweat became symbols of red sulphur and white mercury, the two substances united in the alchemical work to create the Philosophers' Stone.[110] Furthermore, medieval alchemists applied an alchemical interpretation to Geoffrey of Monmouth's account of the young Merlin fighting red and white dragons under a tower built by King Vortigern. In addition to the traditional interpretation (the dragons represented the British and Saxon peoples), the alchemists claimed that the dragons represented red sulphur and white mercury; the resolution of their conflict was the completion of the alchemical work. Thus, 'England's national identity was bound up with the alchemical myth that the nation was born out of a resolution of a conflict

---

[109] Hughes, *Rise of Alchemy*, p. 32.
[110] Hughes, *Rise of Alchemy*, pp. 16–17.

between sulphur and mercury in the sixth century', and the alchemical secret of the nation's birth became linked with Glastonbury as the site where Joseph of Arimathea deposited the vessels containing Christ's sweat and blood and the supposed burial place of King Arthur.[111] It is even possible that when Edward III ordered a search for the body of Joseph of Arimathea in 1345 he was in search of these vessels and the power they contained.[112] Certainly, alchemists such as George Ripley and Thomas Norton did not hesitate to apply alchemical interpretations to contemporary political events.[113]

Although the goal of alchemy is popularly understood to have been the transmutation of base metals into gold by means of the Philosophers' Stone or 'powder of projection', alchemy also had an important medical dimension. Alchemists were as much interested in the potential health benefits that might be conferred by an 'elixir of life' as they were in the wealth generated by unlimited gold. Likewise, monarchs were often as much interested in the medical applications of alchemy to their own persons as in its benefits to the treasury. There are also strong grounds to consider alchemy a spiritual and mystical pursuit as much as a practical one, since many alchemists believed that the success of the 'great work' depended (at least in part) on the moral and spiritual worthiness of the operator, aided by prayer, fasting and celibacy – something that alchemy and magic had in common.[114]

---

[111] Hughes, *Rise of Alchemy*, p. 19.
[112] Hughes, *Rise of Alchemy*, p. 115.
[113] Maxwell-Stuart, *Chemical Choir*, p. 73.
[114] Hughes, *Rise of Alchemy*, pp. 59–60.

Alchemy's emphasis on the redemption of material nature constituted an optimistic alternative to the western church's traditional 'Augustinian' pessimism about human nature.[115] In the Middle Ages – and for a long time thereafter – alchemy was usually regarded as a respectable pursuit that was 'occult' only in the literal sense of 'secret'.[116] Owing to the potential financial gain to be made from a successful transmutation of a base material into gold, alchemy could not be public knowledge and consisted of secrets passed from teacher to disciple, often expressed in allegorical and symbolic form. Although alchemy was not taught in the universities, its underlying theory was largely grounded in the mainstream Scholastic-Aristotelian worldview the universities promoted,[117] and the study of Aristotelian philosophy often led to the practice of alchemy as 'a natural continuation'.[118]

By the seventeenth century, Elias Ashmole regarded Britain as the foremost treasury of alchemical knowledge, to the extent that the flag of England itself (a red cross on a white field) came to acquire an alchemical interpretation as the union of red sulphur and white mercury.[119] Medieval English interest in alchemy was indeed intense, and nearly 3,500 manuscripts of Latin translations of Arabic alchemical works and English alchemical works

---

[115] Hughes, *Rise of Alchemy*, p. 55.
[116] Pope John XXII condemned alchemy in a bull of 1317, but on the grounds that alchemists were forging gold rather than because alchemy was a form of natural magic (Hughes, *Rise of Alchemy*, p. 31).
[117] Hughes, *Rise of Alchemy*, p. 10.
[118] Parry, *Arch-Conjurer of England*, p. 9.
[119] Hughes, *Rise of Alchemy*, p. 16.

survive from the fourteenth, fifteenth and sixteenth centuries.[120] One much copied alchemical text was the *Liber Merlin*, which supposedly contained the wisdom revealed to Merlin when he was a disciple of the Arab alchemist Rhases (Mohammed ibn Zakariya al-Razi),[121] thereby linking Islamic alchemy to Arthurian Britain. Indeed, in the late Middle Ages Merlin was transformed into a symbol of alchemy itself. As one historian explains:

> [Merlin's] unnatural conception [by an *incubus*] linked him with the artificially created *homunculus*. He was seen as an unpredictable and powerful agent in the birth of Britain, fulfilling the function of the volatile mercury in the gestation of the philosopher's stone. Like mercury Merlin was an elusive shape shifter, an amoral reconciler of opposites including good and evil, and he, like mercury, was eventually imprisoned in matter either in glass or a rock, symbolic of the trapped energy of the primal substance.[122]

In addition to their mystical quest for transmutation, the alchemists were also preoccupied with the creation of potable (drinkable) gold, which they believed might serve as a universal medicine. Consequently, medieval monastic hospitals were often a focus of alchemical experimentation.[123] Gold, the noblest of metals, astrologically associated with the sun, was supposed to grant immunity from disease. Yet there was also a shadier side of alchemy, which periodically brought alchemists into disrepute. This was the counterfeiting of coinage, at which

---

[120] Hughes, *Rise of Alchemy*, p. 9.
[121] Hughes, 'Politics and the Occult', p. 105
[122] Hughes, *Rise of Alchemy*, pp. 17–18. On Merlin's importance to alchemy see also Stein, *Death of Merlin*.
[123] See Booth, 'Holy Alchemists', pp. 195–216.

alchemists were especially adept since they had mastered genuine chemical techniques of simulating the appearance of silver and gold.[124] English laws against counterfeiting targeted alchemists, but monarchs also had a perennial fascination with alchemy and regularly recruited them to perform feats of transmutation. Similarly, in broader English culture, 'Alchemists were mocked, and yet people still made use of their services'.[125]

From the late Middle Ages, alchemical language and symbolism seeped into the English language to the extent that some alchemical terms became part of the cultural vernacular. Alchemical language often lent itself to political use, although it would be misguided to see every use of a word or phrase derived from alchemy as evidence for a literal engagement between politics and alchemy in medieval and early modern England. Nevertheless, when authors on political subjects made extended and conscious use of alchemical language this was more than just a cultural idiom. For believers in alchemy, the 'great work' was integrated into the totality of a hierarchically ordered universe; the great work reflected the macrocosm, and the macrocosm (including the political health of the nation) reflected the great work. Alchemy was of political significance, and politics was of alchemical significance.

Astrology: Reading the Stars

In theory, the medieval church was opposed to any form of divination as a transgression against the law of God, as

---

[124] Hughes, *Rise of Alchemy*, pp. 35–6.
[125] Maxwell-Stuart, *Chemical Choir*, p. 67.

was the Protestant church after the Reformation, but in practice these theological objections were often set aside when it came to interpreting the stars.[126] The church seldom – if ever – questioned the principle that the stars could influence earthly events, but theologians did question whether it was possible for astrologers to *know* these influences accurately, and whether such knowledge of God's purposes was permitted. Theologians equivocated on the subject of astrology, opening a gap in which natural philosophers eager to speculate on the influence of the stars could flourish.[127] In one sense, astrology was anything but an *occult* art because the evidence on which astrologers drew their conclusions was manifestly visible to anyone looking at the night sky. However, the skills and training required to work as an astrologer meant that the profession retained considerable mystique, and the integration of astrological elements into both natural and ritual magic meant that astrologers were always liable to be suspected of involvement in magic, even when they had nothing to do with it.

In around 1000 the English monk Leofnoth copied a work on horoscopes, the *Mathesis* (a title that could mean either 'astral science' or 'divination') of Julius Firmicus.[128] By 1125, when William of Malmesbury composed his *Gesta regum anglorum* ('Deeds of the English kings'), scholars in England recognised a distinction between illicit knowledge of the future obtained through demons and permissible prediction obtained through astrological

---

[126] Carey, *Courting Disaster*, p. 11.
[127] Carey, *Courting Disaster*, p. 15.
[128] Truitt, 'Celestial Divination', 214.

calculation.[129] On the other hand, William also noted that Gerard of Hereford, archbishop of York (d. 1108), gained a reputation as a student of the black arts by reading Firmicus, to the extent that the canons of York Minster refused to bury him in consecrated ground.[130] This was a trend that would be repeated throughout the Middle Ages. Astrology was not a black art, but students of astrology were particularly vulnerable to the accusation of sorcery, especially at times of crisis.

The earliest surviving firm evidence of the practice of astrology in England is the compilation of astronomical tables in Worcestershire and Herefordshire in the mid-twelfth century.[131] The converted Spanish Jew, Peter Alfonsi (1062–1110), visited England in the last decade of the eleventh century, instructing the prior of Great Malvern, Walcher, in the composition of astronomical tables.[132] The earliest surviving English horoscope, of poor quality, may have been cast by either Adelard of Bath (c. 1080 to c. 1150) or Robert of Chester, and was drawn up between 1150 and 1151 in an effort to predict the outcome of the civil war for King Stephen.[133] One possible interpretation of the horoscope is that the astrologer was posing the question of whether Henry of Anjou would invade England, or perhaps what Henry would do if he invaded;[134] in the centre of one astrological diagram

---

[129] Truitt, 'Celestial Divination', 203–4.
[130] Truitt, 'Celestial Divination', 216.
[131] Carey, *Courting Disaster*, p. 27.
[132] Truitt, 'Celestial Divination', 216.
[133] Carey, *Courting Disaster*, pp. 30–1; Burnett, 'Bath, Adelard of', pp. 339–41.
[134] Kieckhefer, *Magic in the Middle Ages*, p. 121.

are the words 'On the question of the Norman army – the answer is that it will not come'.[135]

Astrological knowledge in the early medieval Western world was restricted to knowing the signs of the zodiac and which one the sun was in; which planet was close to that sign; and the phases of the moon. This allowed the determination of lucky and unlucky days, but little more.[136] However, at some point in the first two decades of the twelfth century, the English scholar Adelard of Bath went travelling in the Islamic world and learnt Arabic, translating many Arabic astrological works into Latin including the *Liber prestigiorum* ('Book of magical illusions') of the pagan Sabaean astrologer, Thabit ibn Qurra. Thabit's book described the manufacture of astrological amulets in order to draw down the power of the stars for the working of natural magic.[137] Adelard's interest in astral magic as an outworking of astrological practice anticipated later developments and formed an important link between natural magic and astrology.

Geoffrey of Monmouth's decision to include astrology as one of the skills possessed by Merlin is likely to have been motivated by a belief that the educated and powerful audience of his *Life of Merlin* would be interested in astrology's political possibilities. Certainly, the supernatural power that Geoffrey's Merlin inherently possesses as the son of an incubus means that he has no need for astrological skill in order to interpret the heavens.[138]

---

[135] Lawrence-Mathers, *True History*, p. 105.
[136] Lawrence-Mathers, *True History*, p. 102.
[137] Láng, *Unlocked Books*, pp. 285–6.
[138] Lawrence-Mathers, *True History*, p. 101.

However, Geoffrey's Merlin also has no need of instruments such as an astrolabe or astrological tables in order to accomplish his interpretation, thus setting him apart from genuine astrologers of the period.[139] Neither Matthew Paris nor Gervase of Tilbury, in spite of their interest in and technical knowledge of astrology, commented on the employment of astrologers by rulers,[140] perhaps because the church remained uncertain of the illegitimacy of astrology, and drawing attention to royal astrologers risked embarrassing the monarch.[141]

Astral magic, a branch of natural magic that claimed to take advantage of the 'celestial rays' that allowed the stars to influence events on earth, was an outgrowth of astrology (although by no means all astrologers practised, believed in, or endorsed astral magic). The celestial ray theory originated with the Islamic philosopher, Al-Kindi (801–73),[142] and extended to the idea that an inanimate object might even be animated by astrological influences if constructed with sufficient skill. Speculation about the power of astrological images as a class of *naturalia* was an established genre of Scholastic discussion by the beginning of the fourteenth century.[143] William of Malmesbury recounted how Gerbert of Aurillac (who reigned as Pope Sylvester II 999–1003) used astral magic to turn a bronze head into a talking oracle,[144] a story that

---

[139] Lawrence-Mathers, *True History*, p. 104.
[140] Lawrence-Mathers, *True History*, pp. 106–7.
[141] Lawrence-Mathers, *True History*, p. 108.
[142] Parry, *Arch-Conjuror*, p. 44.
[143] On medieval image magic see Klaassen, *Transformations of Magic*, pp. 17–56.
[144] Truitt, 'Celestial Divination', pp. 219–20.

later became associated with Roger Bacon and became a staple tale of wizards for many centuries. Astral magic quickly became entangled with ritual magic, since ritual magicians often sought to enhance the effectiveness of their operations by adding an astrological element, and this was one reason why astrologers were always vulnerable to accusations of sorcery. However, the two traditions of astral and ritual magic remained separate in the manuscript tradition until after 1500.[145]

The first truly skilled English astrologer was Robert Grosseteste, bishop of Lincoln (d. 1253).[146] In the reign of Edward III (1327–77), astrologers primarily attempted to make general predictions of war, famine and bad weather, owing to the church's hostility to questionary horoscopes that posed specific questions about events or persons. However, by the reign of Henry IV the English nobility, under the influence of the French court, had begun to demand the services of astrologers for more detailed predictions. Since courtiers were invariably interested in the king's future health and likely time of death, accusations of treason against astrologers were almost inevitable.[147] By the end of the fifteenth century, the advent of printing meant that astrologers multiplied well beyond the universities and the royal court; at the same time, the practice of astrology by the intellectual and noble elite declined, perhaps as a result of the grisly fates suffered by astrologers implicated in treason.[148]

---

[145] Klaassen, *Transformations of Magic*, p. 57.
[146] Carey, *Courting Disaster*, p. 32.
[147] Carey, *Courting Disaster*, p. 152.
[148] Carey, *Courting Disaster*, p. 154.

At one end of the spectrum, astrology might be an abstract mathematical pursuit yielding the sort of insights that made the development of the modern science of astronomy possible. At the other end it might exist purely to support magical practices. As one historian put it, 'Astrology can exist as a stable constituent of the intellectual world of scholarship, or it can synthesise within the cauldron of the court into a potent and noxious compound'.[149] Calculating a monarch's nativity was often seen as an activity only a step removed from conjuring demons to kill the monarch,[150] and in 1580 a law was passed specifically to outlaw this practice.[151] Astrology and politics were a dangerous mix, but horoscopes were a vital tool of propaganda for monarchs as well as a threat to their security. Monarchs insisted on astrologers calculating favourable days for their coronations and casting questionary horoscopes to determine the outcome of wars and other political decisions. Its central importance at court and in royal affairs meant that astrology was among the most politically significant of all occult arts.

Secrets of the Future: Divination and Prophecy

The recognition of one form of divination from the natural world (astrology) as permissible opened up the possibility that others, such as augury (predicting the future from the flight of birds) might also be lawful. The use of brontology (divination by thunder) in pre-Conquest England was an example of divination from a fixed feature

[149] Carey, *Courting Disaster*, p. 19.
[150] Thomas, *Religion and the Decline of Magic*, p. 407.
[151] Young, *Magic as a Political Crime*, pp. 140–1.

of the natural world. Similarly, in the twelfth century, Geoffrey of Monmouth portrayed Merlin's divination from the flight of birds (augury) as legitimate knowledge gained from a readily observable feature of the natural world.[152] Divination of this kind was generally considered lawful, because it was assumed that God disposed everything for a reason and hid his intentions within natural events. However, from the fourteenth century onwards a more active form of divination became popular. This was geomancy, a form of soil divination originating in the Islamic world.

Geomancy was a form of lot-casting for decision-making, based on the interpretation of dots made by ink from a stylus or marks made by a stick in the ground held while the eyes were closed. The dots represented a microcosm reflecting the macrocosm, so the geomancer would make four lines of dots, with each dot standing for a star, each line for one of the four elements, and each figure for the four corners of the world. The geomancer then deployed a numerological formula to link the dots to create a geomantic sign or 'house'. Geomancy depended heavily on astrology (as well as drawing some of its imagery from alchemy), but allowed judicial divination at any time – astrologers, by contrast, had to wait for a clear night to observe the stars.[153]

The question that churchmen invariably posed regarding divination was whether there was any possibility that it might involve the explicit or implicit invocation of supernatural powers other than God. In theory, if

---

[152] Lawrence-Mathers, *True History*, pp. 129–30.
[153] Hughes, *Rise of Alchemy*, p. 72.

divination involved nothing more than 'reading' signs left in nature by God, it was a permissible practice. However, theologians were also conscious that demons had some knowledge of the future owing to their superior intelligence and greater knowledge of the causes of things, and therefore there was always a temptation for those who became addicted to divination to make contact with demons. From a political point of view, the danger of divination was that it would begin to influence events, especially if monarchs came to rely on it to guide their decision-making.

Prophecy, on one level, had little in common with either divination or magic. It was a practice rooted in the Bible, whose prophets claimed to receive direct illumination from God. In a British context, however, prophecy was intimately associated from the twelfth century onwards with Merlin the magician and the prophecies invented for him by Geoffrey of Monmouth. British prophecy was therefore largely a textual tradition focussed on interpreting supposedly ancient prophecies rather than generating many new ones. Henry I patronised the production of both Geoffrey's *History of the Kings of Britain* and *Prophecies of Merlin*, which were politically highly charged works from the beginning.[154] No fewer than 285 medieval manuscripts survive containing the prophecies of Merlin, an enormous number for any medieval text, making it one of the most prolifically reproduced of all medieval works.[155] Few people seem to have been troubled by the magical origin of these prophecies, given

[154] Lawrence-Mathers, *True History*, p. 29.
[155] Lawrence-Mathers, *True History*, pp. 35, 80.

that Merlin's prophetic powers were ascribed to his conception by a demon, although William of Newburgh (a keen critic of Geoffrey of Monmouth) observed that demons did not have unlimited knowledge of the future.[156] Most medieval theologians held that demons had some predictive powers owing to their superhuman intelligence and understanding of causes hidden to humans, but only God could reveal the far future.

Nevertheless, Merlin was rarely seen as a divinely inspired prophet, and no claims of piety were made on behalf of 'Mother Shipton' and 'Old Nixon', the other standard alleged authors of prophecies that circulated in early modern England. The popularity of Merlin's prophecies meant that interpreting them became an essential part of the work of medieval English historians.[157] Furthermore, the use of animal imagery in the *Prophecies of Merlin* represented a uniquely British prophetic tradition that would acquire still greater meaning with the advent of heraldry, since it allowed individuals to be identified by their badges as well as the characteristics they shared with the various animals mentioned in the prophecies.[158] Throughout the Middle Ages, prophecies involving animals based on badges were a highly popular genre, to such an extent that Henry VIII even passed a law against them in 1542 (discussed in Chapter 3). Of all occult traditions that became entangled with politics, prophecy was surely the most popular of them all and the most accessible to ordinary people.

---

[156] Lawrence-Mathers, *True History*, p. 38.
[157] Lawrence-Mathers, *True History*, pp. 40–69.
[158] Lawrence-Mathers, *True History*, p. 72.

The Problem of Witchcraft As an Occult Tradition

In the last century, witchcraft has received a great deal more attention from historians than magic, an asymmetry the historical study of magic has only begun to correct since the 1980s.[159] Witchcraft is, of course, a form of magic, since it involves some sort of application of supernatural power. However, classing witchcraft as a variety of magic is not without problems, since witchcraft was often defined not by the nature of the activity done by the witch but by the witch's malign intention, or even by the social status or gender of the witch. The historical study of witchcraft and the historical study of magic have diverged, to some extent, with anthropologists and social historians tending to concentrate on witchcraft, while magic is seen as the preserve of intellectual historians (and sometimes historians of science).[160]

The frustration of defining witchcraft is such that one historian has resorted to the circular formula, 'A witch is someone who practises witchcraft, and ... witchcraft is what witches do'.[161] One possible definition of a witch is a practitioner of harmful magic,[162] but this approach is not altogether satisfactory. What counts as 'harmful' is clearly open to interpretation. Furthermore, it is clear that many individuals who performed harmful acts of magic in British history – especially elite, learned males – were not considered witches.[163] The tendency of an earlier

---

[159] Fanger, 'Introduction: Theurgy, Magic and Mysticism', p. 2.
[160] Otto and Stausberg, 'General Introduction', pp. 3–4.
[161] Maxwell-Stuart, *Satan's Conspiracy*, p. 3.
[162] Hutton, *The Witch*, p. xi.
[163] Young, *Magic as a Political Crime*, pp. 15–16.

generation of historians to subsume all accusations of magic under the category of 'witchcraft' was clearly misguided when witchcraft is a subset of magic. This mistaken perspective often resulted from reading the early modern preoccupation with witchcraft back onto the Middle Ages, where (in Britain at least) witchcraft was a minor issue and learned traditions of magic were far more significant.[164]

Part of the problem is that 'witch' and 'witchcraft' were terms whose meaning changed over time. In medieval England 'witch' was often a synonym for any practitioner of magic. The earliest English–Latin dictionary translated *wycch* as *magus* ('magician') or *sortilegus/sortilega* ('sorcerer').[165] By the second half of the sixteenth century, however, the English word 'witch' had come to refer to a malicious person capable of causing supernatural harm (the malefic witch). Between the early fourteenth and early fifteenth centuries the Latin word *maleficium* (literally 'evil-doing') underwent a transformation in meaning throughout Europe. Although the word always had supernatural connotations, *malefici* went from being sorcerers who harmed people by magic to being a sect of apostates who made a pact with and worshipped the devil.[166]

The theological transformation of malefic into diabolic witchcraft occurred partly as a result of a conflation of the 'common tradition' of popular magic with the learned magic of clerical demon-conjurers. The church condemned the

---

[164] For an example of this earlier approach see Kittredge, *Witchcraft*.
[165] Maxwell-Stuart, *British Witch*, p. 65.
[166] Bailey, 'From Sorcery to Witchcraft', 961–2.

demon-conjurers, so it also needed to explain the operation of popular magic in terms of demons. This intellectual process laid the foundations for the concept of witchcraft as prosecuted by inquisitors in several European countries.[167] The idea of diabolic witchcraft never really caught on in England. But by the 1640s, even though malefic/diabolic witchcraft and learned ritual magic were punished under the same statute, legal experts clearly distinguished between magicians and witches on the basis that magicians attempted to compel the devil while witches allied themselves with him.[168]

The dominant idea of witchcraft in England and Scotland was the malefic witch, and the idea of witches as a demon-worshipping cult never took hold in England, although there are occasional references to such ideas. In Scotland, from the late sixteenth century onwards, witches were regularly considered to be both a secret society and a threat to the life of the monarch and the stability of the commonwealth, and Scottish witchcraft prosecutions often had an overtly political element. In England, by contrast, no tradition of 'political witchcraft' developed; witches continued to be regarded as solitary nuisances to society, and scarcely any prosecutions of witches can be linked to political accusations.

Witchcraft in England was not political in the direct sense that ritual magic, astrology and alchemy were, insofar as the activities of witches were not perceived as a threat to the government. However, English witchcraft was a political issue in the more general sense that the proliferation of witchcraft was taken as a sign of political decay. Witchcraft was evidence of 'diabolical incursions into the body politic'

---

[167] Bailey, 'From Sorcery to Witchcraft', 965–6.
[168] Young, *Magic as a Political Crime*, pp. 14–15.

and the prosecution of witches was a form of collective exorcism of the nation. It is unsurprising that witchcraft trials sometimes accompanied attempts at political reform (such as the creation of an English republic in the 1640s) because renewal was accompanied by 'a bout of moral cleansing' in which witches and other blots on the godly commonwealth were removed.[169] In contrast to Scotland, where witchcraft was a magical threat to the nation, the relationship between witchcraft and politics in England was complex. The extent and tenor of witchcraft accusations at any given time was certainly determined by political considerations; for example, after the Restoration of the Monarchy in 1660, judges began to refrain from convictions in witchcraft cases because witchcraft accusations had come to be associated with Puritanism. However, the evidence for people being accused of witchcraft for overtly political reasons is slim; it would be more accurate to say that *acquittals* for witchcraft were often politically motivated from 1660 onwards.

Conclusion

The occult traditions described in this chapter cannot always be treated as entirely distinct from one another; for example, ritual and natural magicians often made use of astrology, alchemists were heavily reliant on traditions of natural magic, and accusations of ritual magic sometimes bled into suspicions of witchcraft. However, all of these strands of practical occultism enjoyed some political significance from the twelfth century onwards. This was sometimes because people actually chose to practise the

---

[169] Elmer, *Witchcraft, Witch-Hunting and Politics*, p. 3.

occult arts for political ends; more often, however, the occult arts lent a vocabulary and symbolism that proved useful in the arena of politics. The mystical power with which natural magic promised to imbue earthly symbols was key to the projection of the image of majesty, while alchemy was consistently tempting to rulers as a means of filling the treasury by occult means. Astrology and prophecy promised a means of predicting the future for rulers and – for rebels and traitors – a means of predicting the date of a ruler's demise and spreading anti-royal propaganda. Ritual magic offered the opportunity to enlist the help of disembodied spirits to achieve political aims, from accessing the monarch's counsels to harming and killing the monarch – as well as a convenient smear against opponents.

It is often impossible to establish with certainty whether anyone really did try to influence events by the occult arts, and what stands out in the surviving sources is the power of rumour, suspicion and fear when it came to occult traditions. Not all of the traditions described in this chapter were of equal significance, politically speaking, and some occult arts assumed a political function almost by their very nature; astrology, for example, has been entwined with politics and monarchy from the very beginning of the historical record. Alchemy was of more sporadic importance, while ritual magic largely played a negative role as a damaging accusation at court. Other occult traditions, such as Kabbalism, influenced politics in Britain only briefly. However, in every age evidence can be found that the occult arts became entangled with the dark arts of politics.

2

The Secrets of the King
Occult and Royal Power in Medieval Britain

In the eleventh century, the Isle of Ely was one of the few spots of high land rising above the impassable fens, a huge area of wetland that then covered much of Cambridgeshire and Lincolnshire. Taking advantage of its isolated position, an English rebel against Norman rule, Hereward 'the Wake', took control of Ely in 1070. The Normans, ignorant of the safe paths through the fens, were unable to reach the island and dislodge Hereward, who stood between William of Normandy and the complete conquest of England. Having apparently exhausted all other options, the Normans decided to try magic. The suggestion came from the notoriously brutal knight Ivo Taillebois, who informed William at a council of the Norman forces that he knew an old woman 'who by her art alone could shatter the strength and stronghold [of the English] in the isle'. William hesitated, mindful no doubt of the church's attitude to the woman's 'art', as well as his own reputation for ignoring supernatural beliefs,[1] but in the end he instructed his soldiers to fetch the woman in secret.

---

[1] William was supposed to have declared he put no faith in sorcery after his armour was put on back-to-front (a bad omen) before the Battle of Hastings (Kittredge, *Witchcraft*, p. 41).

A rumour reached the English that William was in possession of some new weapon, but they were not sure what it was. Shaving his hair and beard and disguising himself as a peasant, Hereward set out for the Norman headquarters at Brandon, where he pretended to have no understanding of Norman French and became a guest in the same house where 'that old woman poisoner' (*anus illa venefica*) was staying. Hereward kept a close watch on the woman's movements and saw her creep out in the night to a nearby spring. Hereward watched her supplicate 'the guardian of the springs', of whom she asked questions and received answers.[2] A few days later the Normans, confident of victory, mobilised their forces and gathered them around their secret weapon, the old woman, who was set in a high place and began to yell incantations at the isle. However, just as the woman was about to launch her third attempt at a magical attack against the defenders, they crept out of the reeds and set fire to the trees at the edge of the fen. The old woman was so terrified that she fell from her place and was killed.[3]

The story of William I's engagement of a female magical practitioner ('witch' is perhaps too loaded and anachronistic a term) against English rebels is the first recorded instance of magic playing a key role in an important historical event in medieval Britain. It is no coincidence that this sudden appearance of magic as a weapon of war occurred after the Norman Conquest. For it was the Norman kings who promoted the figure of Merlin, concocted by Geoffrey of Monmouth in the

---

[2] Blake (ed.), *Liber Eliensis*, pp. 182–3.
[3] Blake (ed.), *Liber Eliensis*, p. 186.

1130s, as an archetypal master of occult knowledge at the heart of politics who prophesied – and thereby legitimated – the coming of the Normans. Merlin's prophecies made it possible for the Normans to portray the rule of the English as just one phase in the much longer history of Britain.[4] Yet the Normans' reliance on Merlin and his prophecies meant that their own self-representation effectively depended on an occult tradition. In reality, it was not the imagined secret knowledge of King Arthur's court but the new forms of knowledge from the Islamic world (including astrology, alchemy, geomancy and the ritual invocation of demons) that slowly seeped into Britain after the Conquest. It was at this time that the occult arts and representations of them became, for the first time, part of the business of the powerful and therefore an integral part of politics.

Occult Power and the Royal Court in the Twelfth Century

Geoffrey's Merlin was, first and foremost, a prophet; indeed, there is evidence to suggest that Geoffrey's *Prophecies of Merlin* circulated even before his detailed portrayal of Merlin as a magician in *The History of the Kings of Britain*.[5] Geoffrey was responding to a demand for certainty about the future, since in the 1130s the succession to the throne was far from clear.[6] The death of Henry I's only son William in the sinking of the White

---

[4] Lawrence-Mathers, *True History*, pp. 71–2.
[5] Lawrence-Mathers, *True History*, p. 29.
[6] Lawrence-Mathers, *True History*, p. 23.

Ship in 1120 meant that his daughter, Matilda became Henry's heir – but her claim to rule, as a woman, was unacceptable to many of the Anglo-Norman nobility. Once civil war broke out between the Empress Matilda and Stephen of Blois (a period often called 'the Anarchy'), the nobility began to demand not just prophecies supposedly made centuries ago by Merlin but also a means of predicting specific future events. In around 1140, the astrologer Raymond of Marseilles dedicated a treatise on the astrolabe to Robert, earl of Leicester (1104–68), a key ally of King Stephen. Raymond argued that astrologers were now able not only to study the stars but also to use them to know the past, present and future.[7]

The contending barons of twelfth-century England were attracted by the political potential of astrology even if they did not understand the technicalities of how it worked. Up to that point, astrology had been the concern of a small number of learned clerks, but the political uncertainties of the civil war apparently caused the secular nobility to develop an interest in the art's predictive potential. The twelfth century saw the earliest stirrings of English interest in astrology, but darker rumours of harmful magic never followed far behind the glamour of new knowledge. In 1152 Henry, duke of Normandy, the eldest son of Empress Matilda and Geoffrey of Anjou, married Eleanor, duchess of Aquitaine, a former queen of France. Two years later, Henry succeeded to the throne of England as Henry II. But rumours circulated that Henry was not all he seemed; according to Gerald of Wales in his *De principis instructione* ('On the instruction

---

[7] Watkins, *History and the Supernatural*, p. 154.

of a prince'), Henry's father Geoffrey, count of Anjou, married a mysterious beautiful woman who declined to attend church or receive the sacraments. When Geoffrey finally challenged her, she put two of her children under her arm and flew out of the window, leaving behind the future Henry II and his brother. The idea that Henry II was a fairy changeling, the son of a succubus, served to explain to some why Henry disgraced himself by causing the martyrdom of Thomas Becket – because the House of Plantagenet 'had come of the devil, and to the devil they would go'.[8]

Henry and Eleanor made a formidable partnership – until, that is, the king met Rosamund Clifford, daughter of the Herefordshire Marcher lord, Walter Clifford in 1166. By the time Henry's son and heir, Henry the Young King, rebelled against Henry II in 1173 – with his mother Eleanor's support and assistance – Henry II had begun an affair with Rosamund, perhaps hoping that Eleanor would petition the pope for an annulment that would allow him to marry his new mistress. After the defeat of Eleanor and Henry the Young King in the Barons' War, Henry II held Eleanor under house arrest in various royal residences – while at Everswell, a royal residence next to Woodstock Palace, Henry constructed an orchard, spring and bower that became associated in later tradition with his secret trysts with Rosamund.

Near-contemporary chroniclers were scathing of Rosamund, with Gerald of Wales punningly describing her as *rosa immundi* ('rose of the unclean') in the late 1190s. Rosamund was dead by the beginning of

---

[8] Wade, *Fairies in Medieval Romance*, pp. 120–1.

1176 and was buried at the nunnery of Godstow in the Thames Valley, which Henry richly endowed in her memory. In 1191, the ascetic bishop of Lincoln, Hugh of Avalon, was outraged to find Rosamund's tomb being treated like the shrine of a saint, set in front of the church's high altar and adorned with hangings, lamps and candles.[9] This treatment strongly suggests that Rosamund was regarded as someone who suffered an unjust death, since there are similar cases of people venerated as 'martyrs' in medieval England who were renowned for the unfairness of their deaths rather than for their saintly lives.[10]

We do not find an account of exactly how Rosamund died until the mid-fourteenth century; when it does appear, it is a dramatic story of dark sorcery and sadism. Eleanor managed to enter Rosamund's chamber at Woodstock, where she locked the doors, stripped Rosamund naked and made her sit between two fires. The queen then forced Rosamund into a hot bath while a 'wicked old woman' pierced Rosamund with a lance under both arms until her blood spattered a consecrated host. Another 'sorceress' then appeared with two toads, which she put to suck at Rosamund's breasts, while two other women held Rosamund's arms outstretched to prevent her from escaping and to ensure she bled to death from her wounds, 'and while the filthy toads suckled at the breasts of the beautiful young woman, the queen

---

[9] Archer, 'Clifford, Rosamund', pp. 111–12.
[10] See Wertheimer, 'Clerical Dissent', 3–25 (on the cult of Laurence of Oxford at Peterborough); Gransden, *History of the Abbey of Bury St Edmunds*, pp. 26–7 (on the cult of Simon de Montfort at Bury St Edmunds).

laughed so as to mock her, and had great joy that she was thus avenged against Rosamund'.[11]

Later elaborations of the story emphasised Eleanor's discovery of Rosamund in a complex labyrinth and had Eleanor simply hand Rosamund a cup of poison, forcing her to choose between death by poison or by stabbing. However, toads were invariably associated with poison in medieval medicine and folklore, with many poisons being based on toad venom. The elimination of Rosamund did not free Eleanor from captivity, but it did head off the possibility that Henry might marry a rival. Eventually, in response to his son's dying wish, Henry set her free in 1183 and she resumed her duties as queen. The tale of 'Fair Rosamund' served to stereotype Queen Eleanor as a ruthless, unnatural woman, if not as a witch herself. The same stereotype of the power-hungry queen prepared to use any means to gain her will, including magic, would be deployed against successive English queens, including Isabella of France (the queen of Edward II) and Elizabeth Woodville (the queen of Edward IV). Between them, the earliest stirrings of political interest in astrology during the Anarchy and the rumours of sorcery associated with the death of Rosamund Clifford embody the two very different ways in which occult traditions became entwined with politics. On the one hand, a genuine fascination with occult arts existed at court, but on the other it was always possible to portray a person's interest in occult traditions in the worst possible light – or indeed to destroy a reputation by entirely fictitious allegations.

[11] Aungier (ed.), *Croniques de London*, p. 3.

One such allegation was the old canard that Henry II was the son of a succubus, which resurfaced in 1216 in the aftermath of King John's decision to renege on Magna Carta. The barons determined to install the French dauphin, Louis as an alternative king called the legitimacy of the House of Plantagenet into question through its demonic descent. However, this accusation was not as effective as it might seem; Merlin, after all, was fathered by an incubus, and the author of the romance *Richard Coer de Lion* put his own spin on the Plantagenet succubus libel by making a fairy woman named Cassodorien the mother of Richard I.[12] This served to explain Richard I's legendary prowess as a crusader, placing him alongside Alexander the Great and Merlin as a figure of superhuman abilities with an extraordinary conception. When Caesarius of Heisterbach declared that the kings of England descended from a 'fantastic mother' (*matre phantastica*), meaning a fairy woman, it was no longer intended as libel.[13]

New Merlins: The Rise of the Occult Royal Advisor

In the 1200s, the embryonic knowledge of astrology and alchemy seen in Britain in the previous century began to come to fruition. Even if Merlin was fictitious, genuine royal advisers in the occult arts began to appear during this period. They included one of the most brilliant Christian scholars of medieval Islamic wisdom of the first half of the thirteenth century, the celebrated Michael Scot

---

[12] Wade, *Fairies in Medieval Romance*, pp. 120–1.
[13] Green, *Elf Queens and Holy Friars*, p. 85.

(d. after 1235). Scot was certainly Scottish, but beyond this his exact origins remain obscure, although he may have been born at Balwearie near Kirkcaldy.[14] In around 1210, Scot travelled to Toledo, the city associated more than any other with the forbidden knowledge of the Arab world, and trained as a translator of Arabic and Greek. Scot moved to Bologna in 1220 and eventually entered the service of the Holy Roman emperor, Frederick II, at Palermo as his personal astrologer. In spite of his Continental travels, Scot continued to hold two clerical benefices in Scotland and one in England, and in 1224, Pope Honorius III asked Archbishop Langton of Canterbury to prefer Scot to an English see. Scot was offered the archbishopric of Cashel in Ireland, then under English control, but turned it down on the grounds that he did not speak Irish.[15]

In 1235, Scot played a role in English politics, travelling to England with Piero della Vigna to arrange Frederick II's marriage to Isabella, the sister of Henry III. The Norman French poet Henry of Avranches described Scot on this occasion as 'a watcher of the stars ... an augur, ... a soothsayer, and ... a second Apollo'.[16] Scot was to become the best-known British magician after Merlin himself, featuring in both Dante's *Divine Comedy* and Boccaccio's *Decameron*, not to mention his ubiquitous presence in Scottish folklore. A late medieval 'Compendium of Unnatural Black Magic' (*Compendium magiae innaturalis nigrae*) that circulated widely in

---

[14] Thorndike, *Michael Scot*, p. 11.
[15] Morpurgo, 'Scot [Scott], Michael', pp. 328–32.
[16] Thorndike, *Michael Scot*, p. 38.

medieval Franconia and Bohemia was ascribed to Scot.[17] These later literary and folkloric depictions bore little or no relation to the historical man, although there is no doubt from his writings that Scot at least contemplated the legitimate application of magic, and he displayed a very detailed knowledge of magical texts, as well as a tendency to dwell on the details of magical rites in spite of his professed condemnation of magicians.[18] Scot boasted of his skill in astrology, claiming that the emperor had consulted him on the outcome of military campaigns against rebels.[19] In his *Liber quattuor distinctionum* ('Book of the four distinctions'), Scot condemned necromancers, but argued that magic could also be used for good, so long as the magician took care to avoid contact with evil demons. Elsewhere in the treatise he argued that it was acceptable for a patient to turn to magic when all the resources of medicine had been tried, as long as it was only to seek relief from suffering.[20]

The English scholar, Roger Bacon (1220–92), was as famous as a magician in the later Middle Ages as Michael Scot, and once again with some limited justification. Henry III may have been the patron to whom Bacon dedicated his alchemical treatise *Secreta secretorum* ('Secret of secrets') in 1247, and Bacon understood the political significance of alchemy as a source of wealth to the crown. He also speculated on the numerological

---

[17] Gordon, 'Necromancy and the Magical Reputation of Michael Scot', 73–103.
[18] Gordon, 'Necromancy and the Magical Reputation of Michael Scot', 76.
[19] Lawrence-Mathers, *True History*, p. 108.
[20] Lawrence-Mathers, *True History*, pp. 116–21.

importance of the number five to the defence of the realm in the form of the Cinque Ports (Sandwich, Dover, Hythe, New Romney and Hastings).[21] Bacon's introduction to the *Secreta* distinguished legitimate from false astrology, claiming that the Church Fathers had attacked only a false kind of astrology, just as they inveighed against debased forms of the true sciences of geomancy (divination by earth), hydromancy (divination by water), aeromancy (divination by air) and pyromancy (divination by fire). Bacon went so far as to advise Henry III to do nothing without the advice of learned astrologers.[22] During his lifetime, Henry was credited with using sorcerers to work magic against his enemies,[23] while his justiciar Hubert de Burgh was accused of controlling the king by magic and poisoning key members of the court.[24]

It is difficult to substantiate court gossip of this kind, and the fact that a scholar sought royal attention is never evidence that he actually received it. Nevertheless, an eloquent testimony to Henry III's occult interests survives in the form of an exquisite inlaid marble 'Cosmati' pavement in front of the high altar of Westminster Abbey. Restoration of this pavement was completed in 2010, revealing a pattern laid down in 1268. Modelled ultimately on the marble pavement marking the 'centre of the world' on which the Eastern Roman emperors were crowned in Hagia Sophia, at the centre of the Westminster pavement is a disc of Egyptian onyx on the

---

[21] Hughes, *Rise of Alchemy*, p. 29.
[22] Carey, *Courting Disaster*, pp. 35–6.
[23] Jones, 'Political Uses of Sorcery', 686.
[24] Jones, 'Political Uses of Sorcery', 675.

spot where the throne is placed for a coronation. An inscription around this sphere of marble by the monk John Flete (c. 1398–1466) identifies it as a representation of the 'macrocosm', the spherical medieval universe and its elements.[25] The placement of the coronation chair above a representation of the macrocosm is highly suggestive, and could mean that Henry intended the pavement's mimicry of the pattern of the universe to channel astrological forces from the stars into the person of the king. The Hermetic principle 'as above, so below' on which so much of the theory of natural magic was based meant that a representation of the cosmos on earth was not just a work of art; it was a figure imbued with occult power.

Taken together with the medieval practice of scheduling coronations based on astrological calculations of propitious days, the Westminster Cosmati pavement begins to look like a mystical device for the empowerment of monarchs. It is possible that 'the circle formed from the four corners of the earth' on the pavement represented a version of the seal of Solomon, and it is certainly true that the coronation thrones of Henry III and Edward I both consciously mimicked the throne of Solomon by including two bronze leopards on either side.[26] Edward I's inclusion of a compartment for the Scottish 'Stone of Destiny', captured from Scone Abbey in 1296, and supposed to be the stone on which Jacob fell asleep and dreamt of angels ascending and descending to heaven,

---

[25] Hughes, *Rise of Alchemy*, pp. 30, 87–8, 106–7.
[26] Hughes, *Rise of Alchemy*, p. 107.

enhanced the occult and biblical significance of the coronation chair.

In spite of the growth of political interest in occult traditions in the thirteenth century, the English church showed little interest in demarcating acceptable from unacceptable areas of knowledge and enquiry. On 18 March 1277, Archbishop Robert Kilwardby banned the teaching of thirty propositions at the University of Oxford, apparently in concert with Archbishop Etienne Tempier's 219 condemnations at the University of Paris (which were issued just eleven days earlier). However, whereas Archbishop Tempier condemned works of geomancy, necromancy and divination, Kilwardby's focus was solidly on the condemnation of Aristotelianism as taught by Thomas Aquinas, and he made no mention of occult arts.[27] Nevertheless, the influence of the University of Paris on Oxford meant that the Paris condemnations were still significant in England – they may, for instance, have led to censorship of the more enthusiastic pro-magical statements in Roger Bacon's introduction to the *Secreta secretorum*.[28] The fourteenth century would see the end of this fairly relaxed approach to occult learning, as fear of the political implications of practical occultism turned to panic.

Magical Panic in Fourteenth-Century England and Ireland

In 1301, Sir John Lovetot accused the treasurer, Walter Langton (who was also bishop of Coventry and Lichfield)

---

[27] On Kilwardby's condemnations see Larsen, *School of Heretics*, pp. 25–41.
[28] Carey, *Courting Disaster*, p. 36.

of worshipping the devil and kissing his backside,[29] an early appearance in England of the *osculum infame* ('infamous kiss'), the belief that people were initiated into devil worship by kissing the backside of the devil in the form of a goat. The allegation was so serious that it even caught the attention of Pope Boniface VIII, although he and the archbishop of Canterbury cleared Langton of misconduct. However, the allegation anticipated the panic that was to come. Edward I's son, Edward of Caernarvon, who succeeded to the throne in 1307, had at least some interest in astrology; his horoscope is the earliest to survive for any English monarch.[30] However, Edward II was also the first English king to be the target of treasonous sorcery. In 1314 or 1315, a man named John Tanner (alias Canne), who pretended to be the son of Edward I, was hanged for seeking the devil's aid in attempting to seize the crown. Tanner was accused of having worshipped the devil for three years.[31]

The theme of devil worship continued in the accusations of deadly sorcery levelled against Alice Kyteler and her accomplices in 1324 at Kilkenny in English-controlled Ireland. These were among the earliest charges in Europe to equate sorcery with apostasy and devil worship.[32] Kyteler was accused of performing animal sacrifices to demons at the crossroads, as well as having sexual intercourse with a demon. Although Kyteler managed to escape to England before being sentenced, this

---

[29] Maxwell-Stuart, *British Witch*, p. 39.
[30] Carey, *Courting Disaster*, p. 119.
[31] Carey, *Courting Disaster*, p. 41.
[32] Carey, *Courting Disaster*, pp. 43–57.

notorious case struck to the heart of the English administration of the Pale, and had a significant 'political air about it'.[33] Kyteler's son William Outlaw was a kinsman of Roger Outlaw, chancellor and acting justicar of Ireland, and a friend of the treasurer of Ireland, Walter de Istlip, as well as the seneschal of Kilkenny and Carlow, Arnold le Poer. Le Poer, in particular, aggressively resisted the inquisition against Kyteler by the bishop of Ossory, the English-born Richard de Ledrede (Leatherhead). The case exposed the political gulf that existed between Irish-born people who identified as English and English-born migrants to Ireland, with Le Poer denouncing Ledrede as an 'alien'.[34] Ultimately, Ledrede's belief that his diocese was infested with demon-worshipping heretics incurred the displeasure of Edward II and he was forced to leave Ireland altogether.[35]

The emergence of the idea of diabolic sorcery (Satan-worshipping sorcerers) profoundly transformed the terms of debate about the occult arts in fourteenth-century Europe. In 1326 or 1327, Pope John XXII (reigned 1316–34) issued the decree *Super illius specula* ('Upon his watchtower'), which accused sorcerers of entering into a satanic pact and worshipping devils.[36] The decree reflected John's concerns about sorcery at the papal court, but it may also have been influenced by events in England and Ireland. In 1323–24, twenty-eight citizens of Coventry engaged the magician John of Nottingham to

---

[33] Peters, *The Magician, the Witch, and the Law*, p. 120.
[34] Neary, 'Origins and Character of the Kilkenny Witchcraft Case', 345–6.
[35] Neary, 'Origins and Character of the Kilkenny Witchcraft Case', 349.
[36] Bailey, 'From Sorcery to Witchcraft', 966–7.

kill Edward II and his favourite Hugh Despenser, earl of Winchester, by a combination of effigies and astral magic.[37] Despenser, terrified, wrote to John XXII begging for some protection against sorcerers. However, there is no hint of demon worship in the accusations against John of Nottingham, and the brief panic about devil worshipping sorcerers in England and English-controlled Ireland seems to have subsided by the end of the 1320s. Ledrede failed to impose his theological agenda in Ireland and the idea of sorcerers as a devil-worshipping sect did not take root in England as it did in Continental Europe. Indeed, the idea that witches made a pact with the devil would only gain widespread currency in England in the seventeenth century.[38]

In 1326, Edward II's queen, Isabella, invaded England with her lover Roger Mortimer, seizing power for her son and probably arranging the assassination of Edward II at Berkeley Castle in 1327. Isabella owned books of alchemical medicine in later life, suggesting she had some occult interests. According to her physician, John Argentine, Isabella took an alchemical elixir of youth at the age of seventy that allowed her to have sex with forty young men at a time; such malicious accusations of a rapacious sexual appetite were often levelled at powerful women, from the Empress Theodora onwards. The Augustinian friar and alchemist John Erghome (or Ergum) implied that Isabella secured her son Edward III's accession by occult means, and the imagery surrounding the young king's accession

---

[37] On this plot see Young, *Magic as a Political Crime*, pp. 27–30.
[38] On the handful of isolated examples of idolatry in medieval Britain see Hutton, *Pagan Religions of the Ancient British Isles*, pp. 299–300.

was suffused with alchemical symbolism.[39] The gossip surrounding Isabella ought to be seen in the same light as the stories associated with Eleanor of Aquitaine, which often sprang from misogyny and resentment directed towards powerful women.

In the aftermath of Edward's death, his opponents circulated propaganda claiming that the king was a changeling who had been swapped at birth – implying that the fairies were involved. The rumours were given credibility by the fact that, in 1318, a man named John of Powderham claimed to be the true king who had been replaced with the changeling Edward. Powderham spoke of encountering a spirit in his dreams (and once in waking life) who promised him wealth and informed him he was the true king.[40] Although the king did not treat his claims seriously, Powderham's story was investigated, since it raised the disturbing possibility that the fairies, as well as human magicians, had the capacity to harm the commonwealth and cause political chaos. However, the fact that the concern about diabolic sorcery in Edward II's reign did not take root in English culture more broadly is a reminder that cultural perceptions of occult traditions were largely stable. While ideas imported from abroad might cause a brief disturbance, when they failed to fit with the way magic and magical practitioners were broadly received in English society, they were quickly discarded.

[39] Hughes, *Rise of Alchemy*, pp. 103–5.
[40] Green, *Elf Queens and Holy Friars*, pp. 121–2.

Militarising the Occult Arts: The Hundred Years' War

The fourteenth century saw the rise of royal interest in alchemy across Europe. In his dialogue *De lapide philosophorum et de auro potabile* ('Of the Philosophers' Stone and of potable gold') the fifteenth-century Italian alchemist, Fabri de Dya Fabri praised Edward III for having patronised Ramon Llull, Arnold of Villanova and John Dastin. Fabri claimed that Edward divided his kingdom into three between these alchemists, an allusion to Llull that may have given rise to the well-known legend that Edward imprisoned the Catalan philosopher in the Tower of London until he managed to transmute gold. In reality, Llull never visited England and was not an alchemist.[41] Yet there is a historical core to the myth. During Edward's reign, between 1329 and 1332, an anonymous alchemical work in Majorcan Catalan known as the *Testamentum* was composed at St Katherine's Hospital in London. Llull was a Majorcan and the *Testamentum* was ascribed to an author named Raymund.[42] Furthermore, Edward was sufficiently interested in alchemy to order the capture of two escaped alchemists, John Rous and William Dalby, in 1327. In 1350, Edward funded research into alchemy and committed John de Walden to the Tower with 5,000 gold crowns and 20 pounds of silver with the expectation that he would be able to increase them.[43] Edward's interest may also have gone beyond the financial, since the religious life of his court

---

[41] Hughes, *Rise of Alchemy*, p. 32.
[42] Hughes, *Rise of Alchemy*, pp. 33, 91–5.
[43] Hughes, *Rise of Alchemy*, p. 109; Maxwell-Stuart, *Chemical Choir*, p. 69.

was intimately bound up with a spirituality focused on the possibilities of alchemical medicine.[44]

The Majorcan author of the *Testamentum* may have been the alchemist Raymund of Tallega, who also dabbled in ritual magic; he wrote a now lost *Book of Solomon* and *Invocation of Demons*, both burnt by the church in 1372. Edward III was an educated king who may have acquired an interest in esoteric and secret wisdom from his early tutor, Richard Bury (1287–1345), later bishop of Durham.[45] It was certainly via Bury that the astrologer, Thomas Bradwardine became one of Edward's chaplains in 1339, although it is unlikely that Bradwardine acted as a court astrologer.[46] Preaching to Edward III at Nevilles Cross in 1346, shortly after the Battle of Crécy, Bradwardine denied that it was possible for astrologers to predict military victories, since this deprived God of the freedom to back the victor and deprived the victor of the glory of having received God's favour.[47] However, this did not amount to a complete denunciation of astrology, and Bradwardine may have intended his remarks to clarify the limitations and true nature of astrology.

Another royal astrologer, John Ashenden, was less circumspect than Bradwardine. In 1348, Ashenden composed the *Summa judicialis* ('Compendium of judicial astrology'), which attempted to predict the outcome of Edward's wars with France. Ashenden noted that a conjunction of Saturn and Jupiter was about to occur in the

---

[44] Hughes, *Rise of Alchemy*, pp. 61–3.
[45] Hughes, *Rise of Alchemy*, p. 95.
[46] Carey, *Courting Disaster*, p. 82.
[47] Carey, *Courting Disaster*, pp. 82–5.

tenth celestial house, governed by the watery sign Aquarius. He interpreted this as meaning that a king ruling over waters (England) would have victory – a prediction apparently confirmed by Edward's defeat of the French at Crécy.[48] Similarly, Ashenden predicted that a conjunction of Saturn and Jupiter in 1365 signified the defeat of the Scots by the English.[49] However, Ashenden's *Summa judicialis* may have been calculated to curry favour with Edward III, rather than actually commissioned by the king, and on the whole Edward showed little or no interest in astrology.[50]

An Augustinian canon and alchemist of Bridlington Priory, John Erghome, attributed the failure of Edward II's reign to his neglect of studying the hidden forces of nature. The comment was meant as a rebuke to Edward, implying that the king followed his father in failing to seek after such knowledge.[51] Alchemists viewed the good king as an embodiment of the Philosophers' Stone itself, able to unite warring opposites in harmony.[52] Within the context of medieval thought this was far more than mere symbolism and analogy; it meant that the king stood to gain from astrological observation, geomancy and alchemical medicine.[53]

One English alchemist who may have been patronised by Edward III was John Dastin, who was later reported to have experienced a mystical vision at Northampton in

---

[48] Carey, *Courting Disaster*, pp. 85–6.
[49] Carey, *Courting Disaster*, pp. 88–9.
[50] Carey, *Courting Disaster*, pp. 89–91.
[51] Hughes, *Rise of Alchemy*, p. 96.
[52] Hughes, *Rise of Alchemy*, p. 99.
[53] Hughes, *Rise of Alchemy*, p. 100.

1328, at the start of Edward's reign, which prophesied the redemption and purification of the kingdom under the guise of alchemical imagery.[54] A very practical way in which Edward may have drawn on alchemists' knowledge of sulphur was in the mixing of gunpowder and the construction of cannons to be used in his campaigns in France. Edward deployed the new weapon against both Scotland and France, and his 1346 order that all sulphur and saltpetre should be brought to the Tower of London would have directly affected alchemists, for whom these were key ingredients.[55] The development of military technology was still closely entangled with the occult arts at this time.[56] However, the Scottish King Robert the Bruce's interest in alchemy may have been practically motivated in a different way. In 1341, rumours began to circulate that Robert was suffering from leprosy (which in the Middle Ages was frequently confused with syphilis and other diseases). Dedications of works on alchemical medicine to the Scottish king suggest that he may have been seeking a remedy for his disease in the form of the quintessence, the elixir underlying all the other four elements that was supposed to cure all illnesses and prolong life.[57]

Wars are often an opportunity for opposing nations to influence one another, and it is possible that the Hundred Years' War provided the means for the French preoccupation with political sorcery to influence England. In

---

[54] Hughes, *Rise of Alchemy*, p. 102. On the career of John Dastin see Guerrero, 'Un Repaso a la Alquimia', 92–101.
[55] Hughes, *Rise of Alchemy*, p. 114.
[56] See Eamon, 'Technology as Magic', 185–97.
[57] Hughes, *Rise of Alchemy*, p. 102.

1337, Robert III of Artois, the brother-in-law of the French king Philippe VI, fled to England – allegedly after his confessor exposed to the French king that Robert intended to kill the royal family by sorcery. Robert encouraged Edward III to invade France, an invasion that became the fulfillment of Robert's treasonous intent.[58] However, the French king Charles V (reigned 1364–80) was not averse to using occult arts against the English. He employed the Venetian astrologer, Thomas de Pizan, to make five hollow lead human figures in the hour of Saturn, which were filled with soil taken from the centre and the four quarters of the kingdom of France. Thomas then inscribed the names of Edward III and his principal commanders on the figures, together with features of their horoscopes. The astrologer tied the figures' hands behind their backs, and at the most auspicious time they were buried, one in the centre and the others at the four quarters.[59] Although this kind of astral magic could be justified in learned terms, the manufacture and burial of effigies strongly resembled malicious sorcery.

Writing at the end of the fifteenth century, the French astrologer Symon de Phares claimed that a French knight named Yves de Saint Branchier once deployed his astrological skill against an English army of 30,000 men led by Henry de Grosmont and John de Montfort. The French knight had calculated the English leaders' horoscopes and identified the unfortunate days in their nativities.[60] While there is no corroboration of this particular story, a

[58] Hughes, *Rise of Alchemy*, pp. 114–15.
[59] Campion, *History of Western Astrology*, p. 75.
[60] Carey, *Courting Disaster*, p. 113.

surviving collection of horoscopes cast by a French astrologer before 1437 for the key leaders of the English occupation of France (the duke of Bedford, the earl of Salisbury and Sir John Fastolf) suggests that the French were indeed weaponising astrology in the Hundred Years' War 'to gain tactical advantage in battle, and identify the weaknesses of their opponents'.[61]

The most powerful use of natural magic in England's wars against France was positive rather than negative, however. The practice of English monarchs touching people afflicted with the 'king's evil' (the skin disease scrofula) may have begun as early as the reign of Henry III, in imitation of the practice of the French kings (although legend traced the practice back to Edward the Confessor). The 'royal touch' resembled natural magic because it was considered intrinsic to the royal person rather than dependent on the king's moral merit or any rite of the church. The touch could also be transferred to objects (traditionally the gold coin known as an angel) which were then worn as protective amulets against skin disease. However, with the outbreak of the Hundred Years' War, Edward III's performance of healings by the royal touch took on an additional significance, as the English king attempted to usurp the unique mystique of French royalty.[62] Edward I was the most prolific toucher of medieval English kings, touching 9,896 people between 1276 and 1306 on ten separate occasions. Edward II touched 386 people on three occasions between 1316 and

---

[61] Carey, *Courting Disaster*, pp. 127–8.
[62] McKenna, 'How God Became an Englishman', pp. 26–7.

1321, while Edward III touched 1,389 people on three occasions between 1336 and 1344.[63]

In spite of the fact that it was first struck in 1465, during the reign of Edward IV, folklore associated the gold angel (which had a face value of six shillings and eight pence) with the story of Edward III's imprisonment of Ramon Llull in the Tower of London. Angels had a reputation for purity and 'angel gold' became a by-word for purity in both metals and intentions, owing to the belief that angels were still being struck at the Tower mint from the gold alchemically projected by Llull in the fourteenth century. Indeed, in Elizabeth's reign one cure for the plague advised the sufferer to hold an angel made of 'good old philosopher's gold' in his or her mouth.[64] The belief that the actual material of the angel was magically significant may explain why gold touchpieces continued to follow the angel design long after the royal mint had ceased to strike angels as actual currency.

In the king's twilight years, the threat of harmful sorcery returned to Edward III's court. In 1376, Edward's mistress Alice Perrers was accused of collaborating with a Dominican friar to control the king by means of two wax images, herbs and 'rings of forgetfulness' designed to make the king forget his dead queen, Philippa of Hainault (1314–69).[65] John Erghome attributed Edward's dissolute behaviour in old age to the work of the devil on behalf of his enemies,[66] which might suggest

---

[63] Brogan, *Royal Touch*, p. 36.   [64] Baker, 'The "Angel"', 91.
[65] Maxwell-Stuart, *British Witch*, p. 60; Young, *Magic as a Political Crime*, pp. 33–4.
[66] Hughes, *Rise of Alchemy*, p. 126.

that Erghome and others suspected that Alice Perrers's actions were part of a broader treasonous conspiracy against the king. One chronicler compared the friar to Nectanebus, the enchanter identified in the fourteenth century as the real father of Alexander the Great, who transformed himself into a dragon to have intercourse with Alexander's mother Olympia. Nectanebus then served as Alexander's first tutor, a dark counterpart to Alexander's later wise tutor Aristotle.[67] Nectanebus was a powerful symbol of the undesirable entanglement of magic and political power, an antitype to the more positive figure of Merlin.

The Monarch As Magus: Richard II

No medieval English monarch has been associated with the occult arts more than Richard II. The untimely death of Edward, the Black Prince in 1376 made the prince's nine year-old son, Richard of Bordeaux, the heir to his grandfather Edward III. Some attributed the Black Prince's death to sorcery; John Gilbert, bishop of Bangor, sprinkled holy water in the four corners of the room where the prince was dying, in the belief that evil spirits were preventing the prince from speaking.[68] Shortly thereafter, someone commissioned a questionary horoscope to receive an answer about Richard's succession to the English throne.[69] From the very day of his birth on 6 January 1367, Richard had been overtly and

---

[67] Hughes, *Rise of Alchemy*, p. 114.
[68] Hughes, *Rise of Alchemy*, p. 124.
[69] Carey, *Courting Disaster*, p. 126.

explicitly associated with the most famous magicians of all – the three Magi-kings of Matthew's Gospel. Because it was the king's birthday, the Feast of the Epiphany (or Twelfth Night) would become the principal celebration of Richard's court. The Wilton Diptych, the most famous work of art originating from that court, can be interpreted as a representation of Richard, along with St Edward the Confessor and St Edmund, as one of the three kings in adoration of the Christ Child and the Virgin.[70] Edward the Confessor is depicted holding the ring returned to him by St John the Evangelist, which according to legend imparted to Edward the gift of prophetic vision, while St Edmund was a saint who traditionally appeared to people in dream visions.[71]

During Richard's reign, a vernacular literature in Middle English about alchemy emerged for the first time.[72] Whereas alchemists had previously dedicated Latin works to English kings and received royal support, the transition to English made it possible for Richard's courtiers to speculate for themselves on alchemical matters. The sole surviving book commissioned by Richard was a treatise on geomancy (Bodleian Library MS Bodley 581), although Richard never marked this book so it is difficult to judge the extent to which he used it.[73] The king was also interested in astronomy, owning at least two horary quadrants, although these were fairly unsophisticated instruments.[74] Richard also owned a

[70] Carey, *Courting Disaster*, pp. 129–30.
[71] Young, *Edmund*, p. 122.
[72] Hughes, *Rise of Alchemy*, p. 34.
[73] Carey, *Courting Disaster*, pp. 98–9.
[74] Carey, *Courting Disaster*, p. 97.

treatise on the interpretation of dreams, and Geoffrey Chaucer may have composed his English treatise on the astrolabe for the king.[75] The geomantic work *De quadripartita regis specie* ('Of the king's four-fold splendour') was user-friendly, easily accessible to Richard, and gave him the opportunity to make great decisions of state without the need for human advisers. Richard's interest in divination may therefore have intensified his tendencies towards absolutism, although there is no direct evidence that Richard relied upon oracles for decision-making, and this must remain speculation.[76]

Richard consciously modelled himself on King Solomon, and on Charles V of France, as a royal 'sage' with a vast library who patronised scholars, lawyers and theologians.[77] Richard's desire to be seen as Solomon was not necessarily an indication of occult interests, since Solomon was also proverbial for his wealth, splendour, wisdom and building achievements. Richard aspired to all of these. However, Richard's patronage of scholars at his court extended to astrologers, geomancers and alchemists, suggesting that he embraced the esoteric aspects of Solomon's reputation as well. Richard was determined to make peace with Charles VI of France in 1395, when Richard and Charles met at Calais and Richard married Charles's six year-old daughter Isabella.[78] The childless Richard's attempt to put forward his candidacy as the next Holy Roman Emperor in 1396–7 was inspired by an

---

[75] Hughes, *Rise of Alchemy*, pp. 135–6.
[76] Hughes, *Rise of Alchemy*, pp. 190–1.
[77] Saul, *Richard II*, pp. 356–7.
[78] Hughes, *Rise of Alchemy*, p. 158.

active interest in apocalyptic prophecies about a final world emperor without descendants.[79] However, many of the surviving chronicles of Richard's reign are negative propaganda against him, consisting of gossip that stereotypes Richard as an effeminate tyrant addicted to the advice of soothsayers and sorcerers.[80] The implication in such accusations was that Richard was guilty of a kind of 'magical quietism'; convinced by oracles of the destiny that lay in store for him, he was incapable of responding to the challenges of actual events because he was focussed on the glories prophesied by occult practitioners. Aspiring to be a second Solomon, Richard became a second Rehoboam (Solomon's tyrannical and heterodox successor). Richard never managed to pass himself off as a sage, appearing instead to be a credulous recipient of occult advice.[81]

If Richard had occult interests, so did his opponents. Radical agitators for ecclesiastical and theological reform in Richard's reign, known as Lollards, gravitated towards the alchemical prophecies of John de Rupescissa, who prophesied that the Antichrist would appear in China between 1365 and 1370 and could be defeated only by the formulation of alchemical-astrological medicines that would prolong the lives of the elect. Oxford University and Salisbury Cathedral removed Rupescissa's prophecies from their libraries, concerned about their popularity among the Lollards. Another alchemist, Arnold of Villanova, was arrested for predicting the appearance of

---

[79] Hughes, *Rise of Alchemy*, pp. 168–71.
[80] Carey, *Courting Disaster*, pp. 93–5.
[81] Saul, *Richard II*, p. 465.

Antichrist in 1378,[82] and the Peasants' Revolt of 1381 was stirred up and sustained by popular prophecies. However, alchemy proved to be an ally of the church against the Lollards, who opposed the church's official teaching on transubstantiation (the actual transformation of bread and wine into the body and blood of Christ in the mass). Alchemical theories provided experiential support for the possibility of transubstantiation that was independent of theology, giving the church at least one good reason to leave alchemists unmolested.[83]

In his suppression of the Peasants' Revolt, Richard II took upon himself the role of protector and defender of orthodox religion (including its 'magical' aspects) against the Lollard heresy that motivated the rebels. In one historian's view, 'Richard was becoming increasingly dependent on jewels, relics and rituals that he believed were a manifestation of divine power'.[84] Certainly, Richard's exalted conception of monarchy contributed to a growing authoritarian streak, and he removed the requirement of the 1352 Statute of Treason that an 'overt act' was required for a treason conviction. When a Carmelite friar, John Latimer, accused John of Gaunt of plotting Richard's death in 1384 the friar was tortured over a fire and shackled by a group of knights, fearful that the friar would use sorcery against them – an indication of the level of anxiety surrounding accusations of magical treason at the time.[85]

---

[82] Carey, *Courting Disaster*, p. 52.
[83] Carey, *Courting Disaster*, pp. 66–7.
[84] Carey, *Courting Disaster*, pp. 161–2.
[85] Carey, *Courting Disaster*, p. 203.

The principal legal architect of Richard's authoritarianism was Chief Justice of the King's Bench, Sir Robert Tresilian. In December 1387, the opponents of Richard's diplomatic rapprochement with France, known as the Lords Appellant, defeated Richard's army and entered London, forcing Richard to summon Parliament. The 'Merciless Parliament' then proceeded to convict Richard's advisors of treason, including Tresilian, who was discovered wearing a false beard and disguised as a beggar. On his way to the scaffold, Tresilian boasted that 'he could not die, so long as he had some thing about him'. Tresilian was searched, and was found to be wearing 'certain experiments and certain painted signs in the same, after the manner of the characters of heaven'. These included the painted head of a devil and demonic names. 'Experiment' was a term regularly used by ritual magicians to describe their spells.

In the end, Tresilian was hanged naked and his throat slit after his death to make sure he was dead and annul his sorcery.[86] There was an established tradition of convicted felons attempting to preserve themselves from the scaffold or ease their passing with charms,[87] so Tresilian's behaviour on the scaffold need not necessarily be seen as a political statement,[88] but the report that someone used magic to make an enchanted speaking waxen head in February or March 1388 may have been linked to the charms found on Tresilian's person.[89] However, the story

---

[86] Favent, *Historia*, p. 18.
[87] Young, *Magic as a Political Crime*, p. 196.
[88] Hughes, *Rise of Alchemy*, p. 175.
[89] Hughes, *Rise of Alchemy*, pp. 205–6.

could also have been inspired by a well-known legend that portrayed Pope Sylvester II (d. 1003) as the creator of a magical talking head; this in turn gave rise to English legends of talking bronze heads created by Robert Grosseteste and Roger Bacon,[90] to the extent that the magical talking head became a staple of imagined necromancy.

Tresilian's resort to demonic 'experiments' may have suggested to contemporaries that Richard's supporters would stop at nothing, including necromancy, to secure the king's power. Queen Isabella's secretary, Pierre Salmon, reported that Richard himself asked if Salmon could make a potion to prevent the duke of Orleans harming Charles VI of France by necromancy.[91] After Richard's deposition by Henry Bolingbroke, in the autumn of 1399, a discovery was made which pointed to Richard's personal interest in magic. According to a chronicler:

The king [Henry IV] handed over to the soldiers of Parliament a certain scroll found in a chest of [John] Magdalene, lately a clerk and priest of King Richard, containing magical arts. Enjoining them that they should look over and read the same scroll with the greatest diligence, and that the contents of the same should be seen, they should be referred to the king and to Parliament. However the same [John] Magdalene was not then arrested, since he was an ecclesiastical person. But the next day in convocation, the clerks of St Paul's met concerning this writing. He replied that he did not know what the writing portended; however he said that he had the custody of this

---

[90] On the Gerbert legend see Truitt, 'Celestial Divination', pp. 201–22.
[91] Hughes, *Rise of Alchemy*, p. 186.

scroll, which the king had given him, along with many other things of the king, which had nothing to do with him.[92]

It is impossible to judge, from the chronicler's description, what the 'magical arts' contained in Richard's scroll were; the scroll could have been anything from rituals for summoning demons to a simple astrological chart. Less significant than the possibility that Richard had a personal interest in magic was Henry IV's determination to show that Richard had been under malign magical influence – a claim by which Henry Bolingbroke further legitimated his usurpation.[93] The chronicler, Adam Usk, claimed that one of the reasons Richard was deposed was sacrilege, which could be an allusion to Richard's belief that he was a messianic figure, but this is far from certain.[94] Although there is no sense in which the overthrow of Richard by Henry Bolingbroke, the son of Richard's uncle John of Gaunt, was a religious as well as a political revolution, it remains the case that a number of Bolingbroke's inner circle had Lollard sympathies.[95] Some of these men may have resented Richard's reliance on the sacramental mystique of monarchy, if not his alleged occult interests.

There is no evidence that Richard explicitly commissioned judicial astrologers to direct his decision-making,[96] although an astrologer employed by Richard, the Benedictine monk William Derby, exposed a plot to

---

[92] De Trokelowe and De Blaneforde, *Chronica et annales*, vol. 3, p. 301.
[93] Young, *Magic as a Political Crime*, p. 33.
[94] Hughes, *Rise of Alchemy*, pp. 172–3.
[95] Bevan, *Henry IV*, p. 39. Bolingbroke himself, however, was impeccably orthodox and was responsible for notorious legislation against Lollards allowing them to be burned alive.
[96] Hughes, *Rise of Alchemy*, p. 112.

replace Richard with his uncle Thomas of Woodstock, duke of Gloucester.[97] Yet a letter to Richard from the French nobleman, Philippe de Mezières condemned astrology as undermining free will, suggesting that Richard was also open to less favourable interpretations of the astrologer's art.[98] Nevertheless, Richard was preoccupied with prophecies and portents.[99] In 1397, he was warned by 'certain friars and bishops' that they had discovered by astrological calculation and necromancy that the king would be deposed unless he put to death some of the most powerful lords, and Richard hired a Parisian astrologer to investigate the claims.[100] Later, chroniclers would portray Richard as a second King Saul, who forfeited his kingdom to David (Henry Bolingbroke) because he sought the advice of sorcerers and false prophets.[101] Richard's chaplain John Magdalene was not the only one of the king's inner circle to be accused of involvement in magic. Adam Usk accused the bishop of Worcester, Robert Tideman, of having been expelled from Hailes Abbey 'for the evil arts of brewing charms and weaving spells',[102] and Thomas Walsingham alleged that Richard was enchanted by a friar in the service of Robert de Vere to prevent the king objecting to De Vere's unsuitable marriage in 1387.[103]

Richard took prophecies seriously and feared omens. According to one story, an astrologer told Richard that he

---

[97] Hughes, *Rise of Alchemy*, p. 114.
[98] Hughes, *Rise of Alchemy*, p. 110.
[99] Hughes, *Rise of Alchemy*, p. 195.
[100] Hughes, *Rise of Alchemy*, p. 197.
[101] Hughes, *Rise of Alchemy*, p. 198.
[102] Hughes, *Rise of Alchemy*, p. 200.
[103] Young, *Magic as a Political Crime*, pp. 32–3.

would be 'destroyed by a toad'. Since toad venom was a standard component of poisons, this sounded like a warning about *veneficium*; but when Richard saw Henry Bolingbroke wearing clothes embroidered with toads he remembered the prophecy and exiled Bolingbroke for a decade.[104] A fear of the supernatural may also be suggested by the discovery of bundles of twigs inside Richard II's tomb in Westminster Abbey when it was opened in July 1871. This echoed a later Irish practice, and the twigs were interpreted as charms against witchcraft.[105] Perhaps they were placed there by Richard's supporters as a final protection for the king's body. Overall, the evidence for Richard's personal reliance on occult knowledge is equivocal; clearly, a great deal of the narrative woven around the king was created by his opponents. The notion that Richard was misled by occult prophecies also served the king's defenders, to the extent that it exculpated Richard for his worst decisions. The case of Richard II demonstrates the difficulty of recovering the truth about the extent of a medieval monarch's occult interests – but it also serves as a reminder that knowing that truth can be less important than understanding how a monarch was portrayed in relation to occult wisdom, and why.

Paranoia, Prophecy and Sorcery: The Occult Arts under the Lancastrian Kings

In November 1400, a magical plot by supporters of Richard II to assassinate Henry IV by smearing his saddle

---

[104] Gransden, *Historical Writing in England*, p. 223.
[105] Carey, *Courting Disaster*, p. 98.

with poison was exposed. According to the indictment brought against the conspirators:

John Inglewood, Robert [Marner] and the friar confessor were plotting the death of our lord the king in such manner ... that they would arrange by necromancy and spell to make an ointment with which to anoint the saddle of our said lord the king secretly and cunningly so that no one would know about it, and before he had ridden ten miles he would be quite swelled up and die suddenly, sitting upright in his saddle.[106]

Henry IV was the first king to make a determined effort to apply the Statute of Treason against magicians,[107] and in 1404 his Parliament passed a statute against alchemy as well. Although royal prohibitions of alchemy as potential fraud and counterfeiting were not new, in 1399 the Aragonese inquisitor Nicholas Eymerich had suggested that alchemy was tainted by its association with magic, thus creating the possibility of more hostile evaluations of the claims of alchemists.[108]

Henry's equal condemnation of the anti-magical Lollards, treasonous necromancers and fraudulent alchemists sent a clear message that his reign would be dominated by a sober middle ground of orthodoxy when it came to all heterodox or occult beliefs. However, even Henry IV's court may not have been free from astrology, since Symon de Phares reported that Henry employed the French astrologer Geffroy de Lestainx to detect plots against him.[109] Henry's government attempted to

[106] Sayles (ed.), *Select Cases in the Court of King's Bench*, p. 113.
[107] Young, *Magic as a Political Crime*, pp. 33–4.
[108] Hughes, *Rise of Alchemy*, p. 208.
[109] Carey, *Courting Disaster*, p. 115.

discredit the Welsh leader Owain Glyndŵr, who was crowned prince of Wales in 1404, by accusing him of sorcery, although Henry's critics made the same accusation against the king and accused him of being advised by a demon.[110] The British origins of the figure of Merlin posed a problem for the English government at this point, since the prophecies of Merlin were widely used to support Welsh rebellion against government from London; the prophecies were an invaluable resource for 'political agitators'.[111] Furthermore, Henry IV was especially vulnerable to prophecy because, as the sixth king since John, he was a prime candidate for being 'the accursed Moldwarp' (mole) of Geoffrey of Monmouth's *Prophecies of Merlin*.[112] According to this prophecy, the Moldwarp would be drowned at sea before England was divided into three parts.[113]

During the reign of Henry IV's son, the warrior king Henry V, England continued to be a hostile environment for alchemists, and those practising without a licence were prosecuted.[114] However, Henry V was sufficiently interested in astrology to commission not just a horoscope but also an entire treatise on his nativity, *Nativitas nocturna* ('The birth at night'), which was composed at some point between Henry's accession in 1413 and his death at Vincennes in 1422.[115] In 1415, the bishop of Norwich,

---

[110] Walker, 'Rumour, Sedition and Popular Protest', 55.
[111] Thomas, *Religion and the Decline of Magic*, p. 471; Lawrence-Mathers, *True History*, p. 91.
[112] Lawrence-Mathers, *True History*, p. 89.
[113] Lawrence-Mathers, *True History*, p. 88.
[114] Carey, *Courting Disaster*, p. 136.
[115] Carey, *Courting Disaster*, pp. 129–32.

John Courtenay, summoned the French astrologer Jean Fusoris and asked him to interpret Henry V's horoscope, asking him specifically whether the king was likely to suffer a serious illness. Fusoris, realising the peril of making a firm statement on such a controversial issue, excused himself by claiming it would take him at least a year to interpret the king's horoscope properly.[116] Although Bishop Courtenay was a close friend of Henry's, in other circumstances this scrutiny of a royal horoscope might have been construed as treason. On another occasion Fusoris was shown a book containing Henry's nativity by the dean of the Chapel Royal, Edmund Lacy, and declined to examine it for the same reason.[117]

Accusations of treasonous sorcery returned in Henry V's reign. In 1419, a friar named John Randolph, who was chaplain to the king's mother-in-law, Joan of Navarre, was arrested and, under questioning, accused Joan of plotting Henry V's death. Randolph, whose reputation as a skilled astrologer rendered him liable to the suspicion of sorcery, was incarcerated in the Tower, where he was later murdered by another prisoner.[118] Randolph may have continued his work from prison for a time, however, and it is possible he could have been the *frater Randulphus* who compiled astrological data on the coronation of Henry VI in 1422.[119] The episode represented a low point in the relationship between Henry V and his

---

[116] Carey, *Courting Disaster*, p. 133.
[117] Carey, *Courting Disaster*, pp. 135–6.
[118] Maxwell-Stuart, *British Witch*, pp. 68–9.
[119] Carey, *Courting Disaster*, pp. 120–1.

mother-in-law and, once again, should probably be seen as an attempt to demonise a potentially very powerful woman by smearing her with accusations of sorcery.[120]

Magic As Political Character Assassination: The Trial of Joan of Arc

As we have seen, the political use of accusations of sorcery began in England as early as the 1320s, but nowhere were such allegations used for political character assassination more effectively than at the heresy trial of Joan of Arc, staged by the English government of occupation at Rouen in 1431. The church's case against Joan hinged on allegations that she was a sorceress and had used magic against the English in war. Joan was captured by the Burgundian allies of the English in May 1430 and traded to the English, whose fear of Joan as a sorceress was so great that a locksmith was ordered to make an iron cage in which 'the prisoner would have been held upright, pinioned by neck, feet, and hands, unable to move a muscle'. However, there is no evidence that this contraption was actually used on Joan.[121]

Although the English authorities ostensibly tried Joan for heresy, they were more interested in the allegations of sorcery that allowed them to blame Joan directly for English reverses in battle. This exculpated the English leaders from accusations of incompetence that they were unable to defeat a French army led by a teenage girl. The duke of Bedford described Joan as 'a limb of the fiend'.[122]

---

[120] Hollman, *Royal Witches*, pp. 23–85.
[121] Lucie-Smith, *Joan of Arc*, p. 228.
[122] Lucie-Smith, *Joan of Arc*, p. 213.

To the English, Joan's rapid recovery from an arrow wound at the siege of Orléans proved her supernatural invulnerability and involvement in sorcery. Much later, Shakespeare represented Joan as a witch offering to feed her familiars with blood,[123] which demonstrates the extent to which the idea of Joan as a witch took root in English culture. At her trial, Joan was suspected of having worn a charm inside her helmet so that it shielded her from injury at the Battle of Jargeau.[124] She was also rumoured to have survived a leap from a tower at Beaurevoir Castle on account of her daily reception of holy communion, which was so unusual at the time that it was linked to sorcery, since sorcerers were renowned for their misuse of the consecrated host.[125]

Belief in Joan's magical powers was not confined to the English. Brother Richard, the friar who acted as Joan's 'John the Baptist' at the French court by making the case for Joan and supporting her revelations, had an established reputation as a sorcerer.[126] At the coronation feast of Charles VII on 17 July 1429, one of the nobles who received a pair of the king's gloves lost them and asked Joan for help, believing her to have magical powers. At her trial, this claim became conflated into a story that Joan had obtained one of the French king's gloves, which 'bore traces of the holy unction, in order to use them for some devilish purpose'.[127] Other accusations reflected more

---

[123] Warner, *Joan of Arc*, pp. 94–5.
[124] Warner, *Joan of Arc*, pp. 97–8.
[125] Warner, *Joan of Arc*, pp. 98–101.
[126] Carey, *Courting Disaster*, pp. 153–4.
[127] Carey, *Courting Disaster*, p. 163.

conventional beliefs about magic, such as the claim that Joan had used sorcery to discover a lost cup.[128]

The duke of Bedford, who wanted proof of Joan's sorcery, was at odds with Pierre Cauchon, bishop of Beauvais, who presided over Joan's trial and wanted her to admit to fraud and deception. Cauchon was more interested, in other words, in discrediting Joan (and thereby the claims of Charles VII) than in attributing her victories over the English to sorcery.[129] The trial of Joan of Arc tapped into prevailing demonological debates about the manifestation of the supernatural, in which Joan made herself vulnerable to the accusation of witchcraft by emphasising the physicality of her encounters with the saints.[130] It was not difficult for the judges to twist Joan's words so that her relationships with the saints were made to appear like a witch's relationships with deceptive demons. Joan's trial may have been one of the vehicles by which a fear of sorcery, long widespread among French royalty and nobility, and hitherto primarily a phenomenon of the court in England, entered the mainstream of English culture.[131] As such, although the trial happened in France, it holds an important place in the history of English perceptions of what would later come to be known as witchcraft.

Occult Traditions and the Wars of the Roses

The death of Henry V in 1422 placed his infant son on the throne as Henry VI, resulting in government by Henry VI's uncles. One of Henry VI's uncles was

---

[128] Warner, *Joan of Arc*, p. 76.   [129] Warner, *Joan of Arc*, p. 128.
[130] Warner, *Joan of Arc*, pp. 113–15.
[131] Warner, *Joan of Arc*, p. 83; Maxwell-Stuart, *British Witch*, pp. 69–70.

Humphrey, duke of Gloucester, whose miniature court at Greenwich became a centre of interest in the study of astrology. Gloucester was a figure of immense political significance, since he was both the heir presumptive to the throne and acting regent in England whenever the official regent, the duke of Bedford, was campaigning in France. Two astrologers closely linked to Gloucester's household were Thomas Southwell, who may have been the personal physician of Gloucester's second wife, Eleanor Cobham, and Roger Bolingbroke, an Oxford academic who was the head of St Andrew's Hall at the university. Bolingbroke composed a treatise on geomancy for 'my esteemed and most reverend lady', who was probably Eleanor. Bolingbroke also provided his 'lady' with astrological advice on subjects close to Eleanor's heart, notably conception and death.[132]

Eleanor was anxious to bear a child who could potentially become king; she was also interested in whether the young Henry VI would die. Eleanor may have put this latter question to Bolingbroke and Southwell, who by providing her with an answer fell foul of the Statute of Treason. They had 'compassed and imagined' the king's death, although they were accused (probably for legal and dramatic effect) of having plotted the king's death by necromancy. Learned clerks, especially those skilled in astrology, were always liable to be accused of sorcery at times of crisis.[133] What followed was a major royal scandal in 1441, in which the astrologers were tried and arrested while Eleanor saved herself, first seeking

[132] Carey, *Courting Disaster*, pp. 140–3.
[133] Carey, *Courting Disaster*, p. 140.

sanctuary in Westminster Abbey and then insisting on an ecclesiastical trial, which exempted her from the death penalty.[134]

The response of the king's council to Eleanor Cobham's hostile astrology was not to condemn astrologers in general but to commission a rival horoscope, which was delivered to the king at Sheen on 14 August 1441.[135] The unknown author of the official horoscope argued that Southwell and Bolingbroke had miscalculated the latitude of Windsor, where Henry VI was born, and the tone of the treatise suggests that it was intended to persuade a fearful Henry that he was not in imminent danger of death.[136] The incrimination of Eleanor and her astrologers was primarily a means for the Beaufort family, the retrospectively legitimated descendants of John of Gaunt and Katherine Swynford, to wrest control of government from the duke of Gloucester. Cardinal Henry Beaufort, the bishop of Winchester, noted that Gloucester had exceeded his authority by taking the imprisoned astrologer John Randolph under his protection, and insinuated that Gloucester would have gone further and released Randolph from the Tower if he could have done so.[137]

---

[134] For detailed accounts of the trial of Eleanor Cobham see Griffiths, 'Trial of Eleanor Cobham', pp. 233–52; Freeman, 'Sorcery at Court and Manor', 343–57; Young, *Magic as a Political Crime*, pp. 35–46; Hollman, *Royal Witches*, pp. 89–155.

[135] Carey, *Courting Disaster*, p. 144. For a discussion of the possible authorship of this horoscope see Carey, *Courting Disaster*, pp. 145–6.

[136] Carey, *Courting Disaster*, pp. 147–9.

[137] Maxwell-Stuart, *British Witch*, pp. 71–2.

The proceedings against Eleanor Cobham and her co-conspirators Thomas Southwell, Roger Bolingbroke and Margery Jourdemayne produced the closest thing to a widespread political sorcery panic in medieval England, to the extent that the rebel Jack Cade was even accused of possessing magical books and raising the devil in 1450.[138] However, as well as being painted as sorcerers by propaganda, rebels might also play up to the idea that they were in league with supernatural forces. In 1451, a hundred men 'in riotous manner and arrayed for war' broke into the duke of Buckingham's deer park at Penshurst, 'covered with long beards and painted on their faces with black charcoal, calling themselves servants of the queen of the fairies'.[139] Allegations also circulated that Henry VI's son, Prince Edward, was a fairy changeling.[140] There was also some effort by both church and crown to forge an association between the crimes of sorcery and heresy. Jourdemayne was burnt to death at the stake, and it is possible that she was put to death for heresy (sorcery was not then a capital crime).[141] Similarly, in 1466, a man was tried before a church court at Ely for both heresy and necromancy, but found guilty only of the latter crime.[142] Yet since a developed demonological theory of devil-worshipping sorcerers was not accepted in England, it was difficult for churchmen to make the accusation of heresy stick against sorcerers, since so many magicians

---

[138] Maxwell-Stuart, *British Witch*, p. 76.
[139] Purkiss, *Troublesome Things*, p. 67.
[140] Green, *Elf Queens and Holy Friars*, p. 122.
[141] Young, *Magic as a Political Crime*, pp. 44–5.
[142] Young, *Magic as a Political Crime*, pp. 25–6.

were clearly clerics misusing the rites of the church rather than heretics questioning their efficacy.

The internal feud within the Lancastrian dynasty between Gloucester and the Beauforts weakened the rule of Henry VI, who proved an incompetent king afflicted by what have been interpreted as regular mental breakdowns. By 1456 Henry VI's health was a matter of such concern that a royal commission was established, headed by John Kirkeby, the head of St Frideswide's Hall at Oxford and formerly a friend of the duke of Gloucester (who died in 1449), to discover an alchemical cure for the king.[143] The commissions convened to cure Henry VI catapulted alchemists to national significance, and the monk-poet of Bury St Edmunds, John Lydgate, was working on an English translation of the *Secreta secretorum* for Henry at the time of Lydgate's death.[144] In June 1456, Halley's Comet appeared in the night sky, evoking the comet that Merlin was supposed to have interpreted to Uther Pendragon at Stonehenge as portending a change of dynasty. The comet's arrival came at a time when Henry's Yorkist rival Richard, earl of March, expected to succeed Henry as king.[145]

There is some evidence that, during the 1450s, the alchemist George Ripley (d. 1490), an Augustinian canon of Bridlington, acted as 'a Merlin-like sage' whose prophecies ensured he was perceived as 'the overseer of the destiny of the nation'.[146] Ripley travelled to Italy at

---

[143] Hughes, *Arthurian Myths*, p. 52.
[144] Hughes, 'Politics and the Occult', p. 103.
[145] Hughes, *Arthurian Myths*, p. 169.
[146] Hughes, *Arthurian Myths*, p. 66.

around the time Marsilio Ficino was engaged in translating the *Hermetic Corpus* from Greek into Latin, and he may have been the first person in England to popularise the figure of Hermes Trismegistus and Hermetic learning.[147] In 1471, Ripley dedicated his book *The Compound of Alchemy* to Edward IV, the son of Richard of York who overthrew Henry VI and became king in 1461. Ripley claimed to have passed alchemical secrets to Edward, and the fact that the Yorkist king forgave Bridlington Priory its debts in 1468 is certainly suggestive of a special relationship between Ripley and Edward IV.[148] Ripley, whose name became associated with a celebrated and much copied scroll of alchemical symbolism (the so-called Ripley Scroll) corresponded with Edward from the University of Louvain and offered to reveal to the king alchemical secrets that he would share with no one else.[149] A sixteenth-century writer, Ralph Rabbard, would later describe Ripley as 'our nation's philosopher'. Other alchemists in this period were also close to the centre of power: Gilbert Kymer, astrological physician to the duke of Gloucester and Henry VI; Edward IV's lord chancellor, Archbishop George Neville; and the royal alchemist, Thomas Norton.[150]

In the mid-fifteenth century, a second magical rite associated with the English monarchy came to prominence in addition to touching for the 'king's evil'. This was the royal rite of touching 'cramp rings' on Good Friday.

---

[147] Hughes, 'Politics and the Occult', pp. 102–3.
[148] Gross, 'Ripley, George', pp. 1000–2.
[149] Hughes, 'Politics and the Occult', p. 124. On the Ripley Scroll see Kitch, 'The "Ingendred" Stone', 87–125.
[150] Hughes, 'Politics and the Occult', p. 108.

These were rings presented to the monarch for touching which were then worn as a protection against epilepsy (a disease often associated with demonic attack).[151] Like touching for the 'king's evil', this rite was traced in legend back to Edward the Confessor, but there was clearly some anxiety that the touching of cramp rings might be perceived as superstitious magic, since the rite preserved in Mary I's personal missal (which probably derived from a fifteenth-century original) contained a prayer 'that all superstition may be far removed, and all diabolical deception'.[152]

During the Wars of the Roses, the story of Merlin's discovery of a red and white dragon under Vortigern's tower was given additional political significance. The red dragon represented the Britons while the white represented the Saxons, and Merlin prophesied that the red dragon would eventually overcome the white. Late medieval alchemists interpreted the dragons as red sulphur and white mercury, while Merlin's prophecy was applied to Edward IV, who claimed descent from Welsh princes through his grandmother, Anne Mortimer.[153] However, the prophecy could also clearly be applied at a later date to the Welsh claimant to the English throne, Margaret Beaufort's son Henry Tudor, earl of Richmond, who would unite the warring factions and bring peace in a new Arthurian age.[154]

---

[151] Bloch, *Royal Touch*, p. 103.
[152] Bloch, *Royal Touch*, p. 106.
[153] Hughes, *Rise of Alchemy*, p. 18.
[154] Hughes, 'Politics and the Occult', p. 126.

Edward IV's interest in alchemy was so intense that, in 1468, he ordered two squires of the royal household to kidnap the monk-alchemist Thomas Dalton from Gloucester Abbey. Dalton threw his elixir in a ditch rather than satisfy the king's greed, and after he was brought before Edward the squires held him prisoner for four years.[155] A prophecy attributed to the alchemist, Thomas Norton, blamed Edward's failure to profit from alchemy on his sinfulness:

> Truly King Edward was nigh thereto
> If sin had not kept him therefro'
> But surly sin jointly with grace
> Will not be together in one place.[156]

In July 1469, the earl of Warwick, discontented with Edward IV's marriage to Elizabeth Woodville in 1464, rebelled against the king and imprisoned the defeated Edward in Warwick Castle. In August, Thomas Wake and the duke of Clarence accused Edward IV's mother-in-law, Jacquette of Luxembourg, of making a lead effigy of a man-at-arms, broken in the middle, as a form of love magic to bewitch the king into marrying her daughter.[157] In January 1470, Wake accused Jacquette in front of the bishop of Carlisle, but the testimony of Wake's main witness proved inconsistent.[158] It is possible that Wake was aware of the legendary supernatural ancestry of Jacquette's family, and hoped that it might make his accusations more plausible. The House of Luxembourg

---

[155] Hughes, 'Politics and the Occult', pp. 120–1.
[156] Quoted in Hughes, 'Politics and the Occult', p. 122.
[157] Hughes, *Arthurian Myths*, p. 196.
[158] Young, *Magic as a Political Crime*, pp. 47–8.

traced its origins to the marriage of the snake-woman, Melusine to Raimondin, count of Poitou. The earliest compilation of the legend of Melusine, by Jean d'Arras in 1392–94, tells the story of how Raimondin met and married the half-fairy Melusine, who was condemned to transform the lower half of her body into a serpent every Saturday, when Raimondin was sworn not to enter her chamber.[159]

Another magical scandal erupted at the court in 1477. Isabelle Neville, the wife of Edward IV's brother George, duke of Clarence had died in childbirth in December 1476. The following April, Clarence had Isabelle's attendant Ankarette Twynho arrested without a warrant on a charge of *veneficium*, accusing her of giving Isabelle poisoned ale. Twynho was executed at Warwick without trial, followed by John Thoresby, whom Clarence accused of poisoning his infant son.[160] Edward, offended by this affront to his authority, arranged the arrest of the astrologer John Stacy, who confessed under torture that he and another astrologer, Thomas Blake, had been hired by Clarence's friend Thomas Burdett, 'to calculate the nativities of the King, and of Edward, prince of Wales, his eldest son, and also to know when the king would die'. Stacy and Blake were accused of necromancy for good measure, and Stacy (who was an alchemist as well) was executed for high treason at Tyburn on 20 May 1477;

---

[159] On the Melusine legend's significance for the Luxembourg family see Péporté, *Constructing the Middle Ages*, pp. 75–108. On the accusations against Jacquette and her daughter, Elizabeth see Hollman, *Royal Witches*, pp. 159–275.
[160] Hughes, *Arthurian Myths*, p. 289.

Blake escaped owing to a pardon secured by the bishop of Norwich.[161] This case was especially significant because it led directly to the execution of Edward IV's brother George, duke of Clarence for treason, by the unusual method of being drowned in a butt of wine. Clarence attempted to defend Burdett to the king and, when he failed, Clarence began spreading rumours that the king himself was working sorcery against Clarence and his subjects.[162]

The rumour that Edward IV was himself a sorcerer (or at least a patron of sorcerers) took root, since in later years Edward IV's court became associated with sorcery (whatever the reality). Several sixteenth-century manuscripts of ritual magic contained 'An Experiment of the Spirit Birto as hath often been proved at the Instant Request of Edward the fourth, King of England', a magical operation that later found its way into a grimoire compiled by the eighteenth-century occultist Ebenezer Sibly.[163] It is ironic that the numerous accusations of sorcery made at Edward's court coalesced, in subsequent cultural references, into the belief that Edward himself was the sorcerer. This example serves as a reminder that accusations of an occult nature had a strange tendency to rebound on those who made them, perhaps because *any* interest in magic (even fear or condemnation of it) might come to be represented at a later date as magical skill (Michael Scot is surely the foremost example of this phenomenon).

---

[161] Carey, *Courting Disaster*, pp. 155–6.
[162] Hughes, *Arthurian Myths*, pp. 291–2; Young, *Magic as a Political Crime*, pp. 48–9.
[163] Skinner and Rankine (eds.), *Cunning Man's Grimoire*, p. 20.

Richard III's interest in magic arose primarily from its utility as an accusation against his enemies, but his fear of sorcery may also have been genuine. Richard had a prayer in the form of an adjuration copied into his personal book of hours, calling on Christ to free him from the plots of his enemies. A rubric that was often added to the prayer ascribed it magical efficacy, promising that 'all his trouble will turn to joy and comfort' if a person said the prayer on thirty successive days.[164] Richard revived the old suspicions against Jacquette of Luxembourg as one of his pretexts for declaring Edward IV's marriage to Elizabeth Woodville null and void (and Edward V thereby illegitimate, clearing his own way to the throne), as well as making new accusations that Elizabeth Woodville was trying to waste his body by sorcery.[165] After Richard became king in 1483, Lewis of Caerleon became the favoured astrologer of the queen dowager Elizabeth, along with Lady Margaret Beaufort and her son Henry, earl of Richmond (later Henry VII).[166] Lewis narrowly escaped execution for treason, when Henry Tudor's defeat of Richard III at the Battle of Bosworth led to his release from the Tower.[167] In contrast to the Hundred Years' War, however, the competing factions in the Wars of the Roses do not seem to have deployed astrology to predict the outcomes of battles or intimidate enemies.

---

[164] Duffy, *Stripping of the Altars*, pp. 267–9.
[165] Hughes, *Arthurian Myths*, p. 196; Steible, 'Jane Shore and the Politics of Cursing', 1–17; Maxwell-Stuart, *British Witch*, pp. 80–1; Young, *Magic as a Political Crime*, pp. 49–50.
[166] Carey, *Courting Disaster*, pp. 156–7.
[167] Young, *Magic as a Political Crime*, pp. 50–1.

Conclusion

Occult traditions interacted with politics in medieval Britain in three main ways. Firstly, political sorcery directed against the monarch and his advisers emerged as a source of anxiety in the 1320s, and remained a matter of concern (to some monarchs more than others). However, the idea of political sorcery proved extremely versatile, and the accusation was even directed against kings and queens themselves (Eleanor of Aquitaine, Henry III, Isabella of France, Richard II, Henry IV, Joan of Navarre, Edward IV and Elizabeth Woodville were all portrayed as sorcerers at one time). The idea that occult explanations might exculpate the monarch or his advisers, whether for setbacks in war or other shortcomings, was a second way in which occult traditions might serve political ends. Thirdly, the presentation of the monarch as a 'Solomonic' sage imbued with natural magic was a feature of medieval kingship in England, reaching a high point in the reign of Richard II. In each case, these manifestations of occult belief were linked with political change. While accusations of political sorcery were usually used to uphold the established order, such as when deployed against innovators like Sir Robert Tresilian or rebels like Owain Glyndŵr, sometimes (as in the case of Eleanor Cobham) they masked the attempt of a faction (in this case the Beauforts) to gain control of government. The process of occult exculpation allowed governments to manage radical political changes such as the deposition and murder of Richard II; rumours of occult practices at Richard's court were skillfully deployed by partisans of Henry Bolingbroke to simultaneously smear Richard and portray him as a victim of sorcerers and diviners, incapable of proper government. Finally, the projection of Solomonic imagery onto the king was a tool of royal absolutism, investing the king's will with a mystique that enabled the execution of change by royal prerogative alone.

Although the practice of magic, in and of itself, was never a crime punishable in the secular courts in medieval England, the 1352 Statute of Treason was drafted in such a way that allegations of sorcery were one of the easiest ways to discredit a political opponent. Little was required to demonstrate that a magician or astrologer was guilty of 'compassing and imagining' the death of the king, and the spiritual nature of magic meant that no clear distinction existed between the preparation and commission of the crime. Sorcery was a perennially plausible accusation when levelled against courtiers and clerics, and a number of learned pursuits could be twisted or construed as dabbling in magic. Yet we must also consider the possibility that accusations of political sorcery were sometimes more than just smears. Magic lent power to the powerless, especially to those who felt powerless at the centre of power – such as 'spare part' members of the royal family. The church's condemnation of sorcery meant that, once the allegation was made, an individual was tainted with a suspicion of 'spiritual uncleanness' that was far harder to expunge than conventional allegations of political opposition.

Overall, the positive political potential of occult knowledge exceeded the utility of discrediting opponents for dabbling in the dark arts and blaming others for misfortunes. The institution of monarchy, by its very nature, was a magical one, insofar as the king's physical body was a microcosm embodying and reflecting the macrocosm of the kingdom. At a time when the king's real power depended on the loyalty and good will of powerful barons, the monarch exercised his authority as much through quasi-magical ritual performance as through actual force. Every medieval British monarch consciously modelled himself on King Solomon, the biblical archetype of royal wisdom and splendour, and in medieval culture Solomon's achievements as a ruler and builder were inseparable from his wisdom, including magical skill. No king could escape the fact that Solomon's wisdom and magnificence came with the obligation to control occult forces. It was in the interests of every medieval king to portray himself, to some extent, as a 'benevolent magus' with mastery of hidden forces, and the significance of the Merlin myth to the self-understanding of post-Conquest English monarchs only enhanced the association between monarchy and occult knowledge. Ultimately, whether it was condemned or openly exploited, occult knowledge was too important a potential source of power to be ignored by Britain's most powerful elites.

3
Arthurian Dynasty
The Tudors and Occult Power

In 1516, the young Henry VIII ordered the re-painting of a medieval round table in Winchester Castle that was then believed to be the table made by Merlin for King Arthur and his knights. The double red and white Tudor rose was placed at the centre of the table while Henry VIII was depicted enthroned as Arthur himself.[1] The Winchester round table is perhaps the most striking surviving testimony to the Tudor dynasty's obsession with Arthurian myth, which began with the first Tudor king, Henry VII. Henry Tudor's dynastic claim to the throne of England was shaky at best: his mother, Margaret Beaufort, was descended from the retrospectively legitimated son of John of Gaunt and Katherine Swynford, a line recognised as royal but excluded from the succession to the throne by Henry IV. Henry Tudor's marriage to Edward IV's daughter, Elizabeth (symbolised by the red and white Tudor rose), did something to lend his reign legitimacy, and having defeated Richard III in battle, Henry could also claim to rule by right of conquest.

However, Henry also chose to make use of his father's Welsh lineage and claimed to be descended from Welsh kings and princes, even King Arthur himself, naming his

[1] Biddle, 'Painting of the Round Table', p. 433.

eldest son Arthur and encouraging all forms of 'Tudor Arthurianism'.[2] In 1486, Henry Tudor was welcomed to Worcester as King Arthur himself;[3] his personal standard bore a red dragon, a direct heraldic reference to the young Merlin's vision of fighting dragons, which would be a heraldic supporter of the royal arms of England until 1603 (and even made a brief return during the Interregnum). After Prince Arthur's premature death in 1502, his brother Henry took up the Arthurian mantle. Although Arthurianism was primarily a cult of chivalry, it was also a cult of occult wisdom, for it was Merlin who ensured Arthur's birth and made the round table for Camelot. When the historian Polydore Vergil had the temerity to question the real existence of Merlin in 1534, the royal librarian John Leland hit back with works designed to prove the reality of both Merlin and Arthur in 1536 and 1544.[4] No self-consciously Arthurian royal court could be complete without its Merlin, a role that was finally performed (at least in part) by John Dee for Queen Elizabeth. The Tudors were a dynasty obsessed with royal image, a cult of the visual whose dark side was the potential magical misuse of pictures of the monarch. Elizabethan culture was preoccupied with double meanings, so that symbols (like the Tudor rose, itself a symbol of secrecy as well as a dynastic badge) were frequently suffused with occult power and magical significance.

While Tudor monarchs embraced their supposed Arthurian ancestry and the legacy of Merlin, Henry VIII

---

[2] Fleming, 'The Round Table', pp. 28–9.
[3] Schwyzer, 'King Arthur and the Tudor Dynasty', p. 24.
[4] Lawrence-Mathers, *True History*, p. 12.

also presided over the criminalisation of magical acts and the beginnings of a Reformation rhetoric that systematically stigmatised occult practices. Before the enactment of a statute against magicians in January 1542, no magical activity (except treasonous magic intended to kill the monarch) had been against the law, and the detection and punishment of magic was reserved to the church courts. From 1542 certain kinds of magic (magical treasure-hunting, harmful magic, love magic, and magical thief detection) were defined as felonies punishable by death.[5] This remarkable change, in which magic was transformed from a fairly minor misdemeanour dealt with by the church into a capital offence, is explicable only in the context of the convulsive religious changes of the Reformation. Henry VIII's break with Rome subordinated the church to the state, and the state's wariness of entrusting serious matters to the church led to the statute of 1542 and its successors, the Witchcraft Acts of 1563 and 1604. A parallel Scottish Witchcraft Act of 1563 was similarly linked with Scotland's rejection of Catholicism. However, while the era of the Reformation gave rise to new concepts of harmful magic and an intensified fear of the misuse of occult arts, it would be a mistake to see the religious transformations of the sixteenth century as a wholesale rejection of occult traditions. On the contrary, just as in the Middle Ages, those seeking to facilitate political change continued to appeal to occult ideas both to misrepresent opponents and to strengthen their own agenda.

[5] For the text of the 1542 act see Maxwell-Stuart, *British Witch*, pp. 112–13.

If Henry VIII's reformation was about institutional change, the reformations in England under Edward VI (1547–53) and Elizabeth I (1558–1603), and in Scotland from 1560 onwards, focussed on the adoption of a reformed Protestant faith. Protestants routinely sought to discredit Catholicism as a superstitious faith that was soft on magic and witchcraft and, indeed, no better than magic in its own right. In reality, growing concern about magic was a Europe-wide phenomenon in the fifteenth and sixteenth centuries. Catholics and Protestants were equally worried about the problem; magic was one issue on which both sides of the Reformation controversy, ironically, were more or less on the same page.[6] However, this did not prevent a determined rhetoric in Britain against Catholicism as sorcery, although some Protestants were not immune from similar allegations. The Reformation weaponised the accusation of magic, turning it from a scandalous smear against individuals into a potentially deadly allegation against entire communities of belief, at a time of heightened tension and confessionalised slaughter. Reformation rhetoric has left an indelible mark on British attitudes towards Catholicism to the present day, where lingering suspicions of Catholicism as 'superstitious' still occasionally surface.

Political Sorcery and the Early Tudor Court, 1485–1558

In contrast to his Yorkist predecessors, Henry VII was largely untroubled by magic. The Welsh astrologer Lewis

---

[6] Young, *English Catholics and the Supernatural*, pp. 30–1.

of Caerleon, who very nearly suffered execution under Richard III, was a supporter of Henry Tudor and may have served him as an astrologer; he was certainly rewarded by Henry with a knighthood in 1486.[7] Another figure rehabilitated by Henry VII was John Morton, bishop of Ely, whom Richard III had suspected of trying to poison him. During the duke of Buckingham's rebellion against Richard in 1483, Morton was accused of employing a necromancer named Thomas Nandyke.[8] In contrast to Richard's apparent fear of sorcery, Henry VII adopted a phlegmatic approach to magical plots against him; he even pardoned the grand prior of the knights of St John of Jerusalem, John Kendal, for his part in a magical conspiracy to poison the king in 1496.[9]

Later in his reign, under the influence of European Renaissance fashions, Henry VII employed the Italian astrologer, John Baptista Boerio (c. 1494–1514), as a personal physician, as well as another Italian astrologer, William Parron, between 1490 and 1503. Parron was responsible for the earliest surviving popular astrological almanac from the London press of Wynkyn de Woorde, dating from 1500 (although Parron probably produced earlier almanacs). Almanacs were one of the earliest successes of printing in England and were hugely popular, beginning with single-sheet almanacs in 1498 and then evolving into multipurpose annual calendars.[10] Almanacs contained much more information than just astrological

---

[7] Carey, *Courting Disaster*, pp. 156–7.
[8] Young, *Magic as a Political Crime*, p. 50.
[9] Young, *Magic as a Political Crime*, p. 52.
[10] Erler, 'The Laity', pp. 138–9.

prognostications for the coming year, and came to be relied upon as guides to the agricultural year. It is therefore difficult to establish how seriously people took the astrological element of almanacs, but the popularisation of astrology meant that astrological predictions gradually came to rival traditional heraldic political prophecies.

The early involvement of royal astrologer William Parron at the forefront of this radical new information technology was crucial to ensuring that astrology became part of the royal propaganda machine, although the first almanac by an Englishman (the ex-Carthusian monk Andrew Boorde) did not appear until 1545.[11] In theory, government censorship of printing meant that all public astrological prognostications were under royal control until the English Civil War. However, royal astrologers always ran the risk of losing their positions with an ill-judged prophecy or a prediction that failed to materialise. Parron appears to have offended Henry VII with a hastily prepared horoscope for Henry, prince of Wales (the future Henry VIII); Henry VII may also have been disappointed that Parron's prediction that Queen Elizabeth of York would live to the age of eighty was proved wrong by her death in 1503. Parron left the court shortly afterwards.[12]

The glamorous Henry, prince of Wales succeeded his prosaic father in April 1509. Like his father, Henry patronised astrologers including the German Nicholas Kratzer and the native practitioner John Robins.[13] The

---

[11] Thomas, *Religion and the Decline of Magic*, p. 348.
[12] Carey, *Courting Disaster*, pp. 161–2.
[13] Thomas, *Religion and the Decline of Magic*, p. 342.

beginning of Henry VIII's reign saw the earliest contact between England and the new strand of learned Renaissance magic that emerged in Italy in the aftermath of Marsilio Ficino's translation of the *Hermetic Corpus* and the works of Plato into Latin in the 1460s. Ficino made strenuous efforts to distinguish the theurgy (wonder-working) of the legitimate magus from evil magic done with the aid of demons, an effort in which he was followed by Giovanni Pico della Mirandola (1463–94) and Heinrich Cornelius Agrippa (1486–1535). In 1510 Agrippa, who would later become notorious as the author of the *Three Books of Occult Philosophy*, paid a short visit to London. He stayed with the leading English humanist John Colet (1467–1519), dean of St Paul's Cathedral, with whom he was studying the letters of St Paul.

Agrippa later confessed that 'I was then conducting quite other and most secret business among the Britons'.[14] Although the nature of Agrippa's secret English mission remains a mystery, Agrippa was at a crucial stage in his career. Jean Catilinet, provincial superior of the Franciscans in Burgundy, had recently accused him of being a 'judaizing heretic' for his use of the Hebrew Kabbalah.[15] Agrippa wrote a reply to Catilinet from London, defending his use of the Kabbalah and arguing that the five-letter Hebrew name of Jesus, the pentagrammaton, could be used to demonstrate the true identity of the Messiah to the Jews.[16] Agrippa's future success depended on his ability to show the legitimacy of

---

[14] Quoted in Van der Poel, *Cornelius Agrippa*, p. 20.
[15] Van der Poel, *Cornelius Agrippa*, pp. 18–21.
[16] Agrippa, *Opera*, vol. 2, pp. 508–12.

the Kabbalah within Christianity. Renaissance magic made little impact in England, however. English humanists were curious about the Kabbalah but largely rejected it as a 'blind alley'.[17] They certainly did not explore the Kabbalah's magical potential, as Agrippa did. Surviving English books of magic show comparatively little influence from Renaissance magic and remained largely grounded in medieval traditions of ritual magic throughout the sixteenth century.[18]

Cardinal Thomas Wolsey, lord chancellor from 1515, effectively controlled most aspects of government on behalf of Henry VIII until his dramatic fall from grace in 1529, maintaining a court of his own at his palace of Hampton Court. The enormous influence Wolsey wielded over the king, combined with the fact that Wolsey was a cleric, led many to suspect that he was using magic to retain power. It was rumoured that, at the very least, Wolsey had commissioned a detailed horoscope of the king in order to better control him.[19] One magician claimed to have made a magical ring for the cardinal.[20] The Norfolk magician William Stapleton claimed in a 1528 letter to Wolsey that when he had been a monk of St Benedict's abbey at Holme in the Norfolk Broads, he and several others obtained books of ritual magic in order to hunt for treasure. Stapleton was in need of money to pay for a dispensation from his monastic vows. Hearing that the parish priest of Surlingham, Norfolk, had raised

---

[17] Jones, *Discovery of Hebrew*, p. 168
[18] Klaassen, *Transformations of Magic*, pp. 187–8.
[19] Thomas, *Religion and the Decline of Magic*, p. 342.
[20] Young, *Magic as a Political Crime*, pp. 65–6.

and bound three spirits called Andrew Malchus, Oberion and Incubus, the group visited the priest and persuaded him to raise his spirits. However, Oberion refused to speak; the spirit Andrew Malchus explained that this was because Oberion 'was bound unto the Lord Cardinal'.[21]

Later, in London, Stapleton was told by a servant of the duke of Norfolk that Wolsey had sent a spirit to 'vex' the duke. Stapleton advised the servant to stay out of such affairs of state, but the servant spoke of Stapleton to the duke, who sent for the ex-monk. In spite of the fact that Stapleton was only familiar with magic designed to find treasure, the duke's servant persuaded Stapleton to claim that he could help drive away the spirit Wolsey had sent. Stapleton told the duke he had made a wax effigy, perhaps intended to be an alternative target for the malice of Wolsey's spirit Oberion. The duke interrogated Stapleton about Wolsey's supposed magical operations against him, but then had the entire exchange transcribed and sent to Wolsey himself. As a result, Stapleton was forced to write to the cardinal to beg forgiveness.[22]

After Wolsey's fall from grace in 1529, on account of the cardinal's failure to secure a papal annulment of Henry's marriage to Katharine of Aragon, Thomas Cromwell became the king's principal adviser. The 1530s saw accusations of magic at the very heart of the English court. On the annulment of his marriage to Katharine of Aragon, Henry married Anne Boleyn, who was crowned queen in 1533. However, Anne's failure to

---

[21] Maxwell-Stuart, *British Witch*, pp. 97–9.
[22] Maxwell-Stuart, *British Witch*, pp. 99–100.

produce the male heir Henry so much desired led him to begin seeking grounds to end the second marriage. The imperial ambassador Eustace Chapuys claimed that Henry confessed secretly to a courtier that he had married Anne 'seduced and constrained by *sortilegia*', and that the king considered the marriage void.[23] These rumours, if true, resembled Richard III's allegations against the marriage of Edward IV and Elizabeth Woodville, and may even have been based on them. However, although witchcraft was mentioned as an allegation against Anne when she finally fell in April 1536, the accusation was an afterthought; the foremost charge against her was incest. Anne's subsequent reputation as a witch seems to have been a much later invention by Catholics opposed to the reign of her daughter, Elizabeth.[24]

The major political scandal involving sorcery in Henry's reign occurred in 1540, and was linked to the fall of Thomas Cromwell. Cromwell's close associate Walter Hungerford was accused of working with witches and necromancers to predict and hasten the king's death. Hungerford was executed for treason and 'buggery' on the same scaffold as Cromwell in June 1540.[25] The crime of 'buggery' had been closely associated with illicit magic since the Middle Ages, and 'accusations of sodomy were used to stigmatize a broad spectrum of perceived transgressiveness', including sorcery.[26] Sorcery and homosexuality were both seen as unnatural crimes in this

---

[23] Maxwell-Stuart, *British Witch*, p. 104.
[24] Young, *Magic as a Political Crime*, pp. 71–3.
[25] Young, *Magic as a Political Crime*, pp. 74–6.
[26] Perry, 'Politics of Access', 1059.

era, linked by their perpetrators' disregard for the law of God.

In addition to the earliest English statute against magic and witchcraft, in 1542 Henry's Parliament passed a law against 'false prophecies upon declarations of names, arms and badges'. This new statute was arguably of greater political significance than the act against witchcraft. It outlawed the longstanding English tradition of allegorical prophecies involving animals drawn from the heraldic badges of major political figures.[27] This form of prophecy was not only as popular as astrology (if not more so); it also led some people to regard heraldry as something imbued with occult power and a potential key to decoding the future.[28] The distinctively English preoccupation with political prophecies based on badges and heraldic devices was democratic, requiring none of the learning needed to understand astrology,[29] but it was also dangerous. Such prophecies formed part of the allegations of treason brought against the duke of Buckingham in 1521 and Sir Rhys ap Gruffydd (who attempted to make himself prince of Wales) in 1531.[30] However, prophecies of this kind were still a problem for the government of Elizabeth I.[31]

A further legislative addition of Henry's reign was the remarkable provision that 'the wilful murder of any person ... by means or way of poisoning' was to be considered high treason. This was justified on the grounds of the heinousness of the crime, as a result of which no one

---

[27] Evans, *Collection of Statutes*, vol. 6, p. 229; Thomas, *Religion and the Decline of Magic*, p. 471.
[28] Hughes, *Rise of Alchemy*, pp. 70, 180.
[29] Carey, *Courting Disaster*, p. 96.   [30] Elton, *Policy and Police*, pp. 53-4.
[31] Thomas, *Religion and the Decline of Magic*, pp. 479-84.

could 'live in surety or out of danger'.[32] This act followed the attempted murder of John Fisher, bishop of Rochester by a cook named Roose. The cook mixed poison into the bishop's porridge in 1531. Since high treason was traditionally defined as an attempt to kill or overthrow the king, to define the poisoning of *any* person as high treason sent a strong message about the crown's abhorrence of the crime of *veneficium*, which was then considered an occult offence. Roose was boiled alive in the hope of deterring others from the same crime.[33]

Henry VIII's laws against various forms of treason went further than those of any other English monarch, to the point where the first Parliament of Edward VI, under Lord Protector Somerset, repealed a number of Henry's statutes as 'very strait, sore, extreme and terrible'.[34] These included the 1542 act against witchcraft, meaning that the punishment of witchcraft was effectively returned to the church courts in the reigns of Edward VI and Mary I. Although cases of magical treason did not entirely disappear in these reigns, they were not a significant feature. Edward VI's Protestant bishops regularly thundered against the superstition rife in the country at large, but his court adopted a positive attitude towards astrologers. William Cecil, whose career began at Edward's court, was deeply interested in astrology and invited a young John Dee to become 'an occasional intellectual consultant' to the regime.[35] Dee, who had studied at the University of

---

[32] Stacy, 'Richard Roose and the Use of Parliamentary Attainder', 4–5.
[33] Stacy, 'Richard Roose and the Use of Parliamentary Attainder', 5.
[34] Cressy, *Dangerous Talk*, pp. 54–5.
[35] Parry, *Arch-Conjurer of England*, pp. 22–3.

Louvain in the Netherlands, brought a new astrological theory that it was possible to measure the power of stellar influences. Dee believed that those stars at a perpendicular angle of incidence to the earth at any given time would have the most powerful influence on earthly events.[36] This new 'precision' astrology, based on the latest developments in mathematics, was of great interest to the court.

Payments to 'astronomers' (who in this case were probably astrological physicians) regularly featured in the accounts of Edward VI's royal household, alongside payments to surgeons, physicians and apothecaries. The institution of the royal astrologer-physician was essentially imported from Renaissance Italy. Already, at the end of the fifteenth century, astrologers such as Lewis of Caerleon and John Argentine were aware that the tradition of English astrology was passing away, and made conscious efforts to collect surviving manuscripts.[37] However, although astrology was democratised by printing, there was still a significant role to be played by the court astrologer in Tudor England, especially by individuals such as Dee who were in possession of the most up-to-date knowledge. Dee, like other astrologers, was expected to apply his knowledge to medical matters; this was one reason why he claimed the title 'doctor', in spite of the fact that he never formally proceeded to a doctoral degree.[38]

---

[36] Parry, *Arch-Conjurer of England*, pp. 17–18.
[37] Carey, *Courting Disaster*, p. 162.
[38] Parry, *Arch-Conjurer of England*, pp. 18–19.

Massmongers and Witchmongers: Discrediting Catholicism

In the epistle to the reader prefacing his celebrated denunciation of magical belief, *The Discoverie of Witchcraft* (1584), Reginald Scot explained that his polemic was directed equally against 'massmongers' (Catholics) and 'witchmongers' (advocates of belief in magic and witchcraft):

> I will prove all Popish Charms, Conjurations, Exorcisms, Benedictions and Curses, not only to be ridiculous, and of none effect, but also to be impious and contrary to God's Word ... I doubt not, but to use the matter so, that as well the Massemonger for his part, as the Witchmonger for his, shall both be ashamed of their Professions.[39]

Although Scot himself was at the more radical end of the spectrum of English Protestantism, his attempt to link Catholicism with magic, credulity and superstition had long been official policy. Indeed, attacks on the rites of the Catholic church as 'superstitious' and magical were not a new phenomenon in England in the sixteenth century. As early as the fourteenth century, Lollards had aimed this criticism against the rites of the church. Furthermore, even pre-Reformation Catholic clergy themselves were sometimes anxious about unapproved 'custom of folk' that had no authority in official liturgical manuals.[40] Church courts regularly dealt with individuals accused of using 'superstitious arts'.[41]

---

[39] Scot, *Discovery of Witchcraft*, 'To the Readers'.
[40] Duffy, *Stripping of the Altars*, p. 18.
[41] Parish (ed.), *Superstition and Magic*, p. 16.

The effort to discredit the church and its clergy by accusations of magic first assumed real political importance in the 1530s as Henry VIII, Thomas Cromwell and Thomas Cranmer laid the legal and canonical foundations of England's break with the papacy. If Henry failed to suppress conservative Catholic opposition to his project to establish the Church of England as an independent jurisdiction, there was a real risk that the emperor Charles V or a coalition of 'crusading' powers put together by the pope might see an opportunity to launch an invasion of England. The stakes were high, and the task of discrediting virtually the entire framework of parish religion in which everyone in England and their ancestors had been immersed from their earliest childhoods was a daunting one indeed. Throughout the 1530s Henry's Lord Privy Seal, Thomas Cromwell, adopted a policy of gathering information about monks and clergy accused of all kinds of occult practice, whether or not it directly concerned the fate of the king and his religious reforms.[42] In many cases, Cromwell's information led to accusations of treason,[43] most notably in the case of Elizabeth Barton, the 'Holy Maid of Kent'. Barton was a poor visionary who became a Benedictine nun at Canterbury under the patronage of Archbishop William Wareham. She drew the ire of Henry VIII by denouncing the king's efforts to obtain the annulment of his marriage to Katharine of Aragon. Even Henry's devout Lord

---

[42] On Cromwell's campaign against prophecy see Thomas, *Religion and the Decline of Magic*, pp. 475–7.
[43] Elton, *Policy and Police*, pp. 46–82; Young, *Magic as a Political Crime*, pp. 57–70.

Chancellor, Thomas More, was sceptical of Barton. More implied that Barton was a witch by reporting that the devil was seen in her chamber in the form of a bird (an incident easily interpreted as the visitation of a demonic familiar), and her later reputation was as a ventriloquist (someone possessed by a spirit which spoke from the person's stomach).[44] However, Barton was put to death for treason rather than witchcraft, since no such capital crime as witchcraft existed in 1534.

Prophecy, perhaps even more than belief in the magical powers of the clergy, was a threat to the Henrician Reformation. On the outbreak of the northern rebellion known as the Pilgrimage of Grace, which developed in response to the dissolution of the monasteries in 1536, there was a resurgence of the old Moldwarp prophecy, this time directed against Henry VIII.[45] There were numerous arrests of clergy claiming that Henry was the Moldwarp, while prophecies attributed to Bede, Merlin, Thomas the Rhymer and John of Bridlington circulated in large numbers.[46] At Syon Abbey, a house of Bridgettine monks and nuns that was a key centre of resistance to Henry VIII's ecclesiastical supremacy, the monks carefully studied prophecies attributed to Merlin for signs of the times.[47] After the dissolution, prophecies were often attributed to the monks and said to have been printed from mysterious prophetic manuscripts discovered among

---

[44] Maxwell-Stuart, *British Witch*, p. 102.
[45] Thomas, *Religion and the Decline of Magic*, p. 473.
[46] Thomas, *Religion and the Decline of Magic*, p. 472.
[47] Thomas, *Religion and the Decline of Magic*, p. 474.

monastic ruins,[48] suggesting that the occult reputation of the monks survived their suppression.

In the reign of Henry's son Edward VI, under the two successive Lord Protectors (the dukes of Somerset and Northumberland) who ruled on behalf of the boy king, the English reformation moved from merely suppressing the independent power of the church to a thoroughgoing effort to stamp out all remaining vestiges of Catholic belief and worship. As early as 1549, Edward's bishops denounced the 'conjured bread and water' of Catholics.[49] At the forefront of the campaign to discredit the mass, the central act of Catholic worship, was John Bale (1495–1563), a former Carmelite friar from Suffolk who was appointed bishop of Ossory in Ireland in 1552. Bale portrayed the mass as 'a form of ecclesiastically sanctioned magic', rehabilitating old Lollard criticisms of the doctrine of transubstantiation as sorcery.[50] Official Catholic doctrine held that when the priest pronounced the words of consecration over the bread and wine, their substance was really and actually changed into the body and blood of Christ by virtue of the sacramental authority given to the priest at his ordination, while the 'accidents' (the physical appearance and taste) of the consecrated elements miraculously remained those of bread and wine.

Bale denounced priests as 'chattering charmers' and called the consecration 'a new found toy of ... sorcery'.[51] The mass, according to Bale:

---

[48] Thomas, *Religion and the Decline of Magic*, pp. 463–4.
[49] Parish, 'Magic and Priestcraft', p. 394.
[50] Parish, 'Magic and Priestcraft', pp. 396–7.
[51] Parish, 'Magic and Priestcraft', p. 398.

… serveth all witches in their witchery, all sorcerers, charmers, enchanters, dreamers, soothsayers, necromancers, conjurers, cross diggers, [and] devil-raisers … For without a mass, they cannot well work their feats … Where are the names of God, of his angels, and of his saints more rife than among witches, charmers, enchanters and sorcerers?[52]

Bale had a point. The use of the consecrated host and holy names was well-established in medieval popular and ritual magic, and pre-Reformation devotional literature appeared to ascribe magical efficacy both to the mass and the host.[53] The complex ritual actions required of the priest at mass (and especially the practice of blowing on the host) made it easy to see the priest as a magician.[54]

Bale's assault on the Catholic clergy as conjurers was so effective because it contained a kernel of truth. A 'clerical underworld' of learned necromancy did indeed exist among the clergy, just as some clergy were guilty of promoting or fabricating fraudulent miracles.[55] Furthermore, priests were quite literally 'conjurers', since they received the minor order of exorcist on the way to the priesthood, and 'conjurer' was just a synonym for 'exorcist'.[56] A priest exorcised or 'conjured' every time he baptised, and traditional exorcisms of salt and water preceding the mass were considered an integral part of the rite. Even if transubstantiation was not magic, it was undeniable that 'conjuration' was part of the mass and part of the work of a Catholic priest. Bale's accusation

[52] Quoted in Parish, 'Magic and Priestcraft', p. 400.
[53] Parish, 'Magic and Priestcraft', p. 395.
[54] Parish, 'Magic and Priestcraft', pp. 400–1.
[55] Parish, 'Magic and Priestcraft', pp. 408–9.
[56] Young, *History of Exorcism*, p. 18.

was not just that *some* priests were sorcerers, but that all priests were engaged in sorcery by virtue of their office. Priests were 'those two-horned whoremongers, those conjurors of Egypt, and lecherous locusts leaping out of the smoke of the pit bottomless, which daily deceive the ignorant multitude with their sorceries and charms'.[57]

Many reformers believed that the age of miracles had ended with the death of the last apostle (a theological position known as cessationism). This meant that, by definition, any 'miracles' claimed by Catholics were either cleverly faked or worked by magic that invoked demonic power.[58] The doctrine of transubstantiation claimed that any priest was able to perform a miracle daily. The mass, in Protestant eyes, constituted public deception on a massive scale, and reformers mingled accusations of demonic magic with allegations of sleight-of-hand and legerdemain. Similarly, the text of the Scottish Witchcraft Act of 1563 seemed to suggest that witchcraft was not real, yet it was also portrayed as an abominable crime whose practitioners deserved death.[59] From a modern point of view, the combination of these two apparently contradictory allegations might seem odd: priests were either faking miracles or they were sorcerers in league with the devil – they could hardly be both. However, the double accusation of fraud and demonic entanglement against magicians was deeply embedded in Christian anti-magical rhetoric, and magicians themselves made little distinction between magical operations and illusions we might

[57] Bale, *Select Works*, p. 259.
[58] Parish, 'Magic and Priestcraft', p. 405.
[59] Goodare, 'Scottish Witchcraft Act', 52.

consider to be party tricks. No distinction between 'stage magic' and occult magic had yet developed.

However, the 'linguistic ambiguity' inherent in the reformers' condemnations revealed a tension between two very different interpretations of magic: on the one hand, fear of magic as a genuine threat, and on the other hand, ridicule of magic as an illusion perpetrated in the age of superstition.[60] As time went on, the elision of accusations of fraud and magic became increasingly unsatisfactory, and the conviction that magic could not simply be dismissed as fraud contributed to the criminalisation of magic beyond the church courts. Although the Continental belief that magicians belonged to demon-worshipping sects did not take off in England, magistrates became increasingly convinced that magic had real effects because the devil was involved. An older reformation discourse, in which magic was portrayed as fraud and deception, was marginalized in favour of a more alarmist discourse on witchcraft.

John Bale went further, however, than just portraying contemporary priests as sorcerers. While some reformers attempted to argue that the church in England had never truly been subject to Rome, Bale sought to discredit the entire history of the medieval church in England by portraying Augustine of Canterbury, the apostle of the English, as a master of 'cunning sciences' whose 'incantations' deceived King Ethelbert of Kent into adopting the Roman faith. St Oswald, the martyred king of Northumbria, learnt necromancy at the French abbey of Fleury, while St Dunstan was a demonic sorcerer who

[60] Parish, 'Magic and Priestcraft', p. 401.

used necromancy to kill proponents of clerical marriage when a floor collapsed at the Council of Calne.[61] Bale may have taken his inspiration from late medieval traditions associating Archbishop Dunstan with alchemy, as well as from the famous curse supposedly laid by Augustine on the men of Dorchester whose children were thereafter born with tails.[62] Bale made an unprecedented effort to read his own ideas of harmful magic back onto earlier history, even writing a play in which King John was killed by *veneficium* at the hands of monks.[63] Other Protestants also rejected the medieval accommodation of natural magic. In 1550, William Harrison condemned Roger Bacon as a demonic sorcerer, brushing aside John Dee's attempts to defend Bacon,[64] and Robert Greene's play *Friar Bacon and Friar Bungay* (first performed in around 1589) portrayed Bacon as a 'Nigromancer'.[65]

The Reformation's denigration of the great figures of medieval England as mere sorcerers was balanced by Protestant veneration for British antiquity. Henry VIII's break with Rome was grounded in the notion that, at some time in the past, Britain had been an 'empire' separate from the authority of the pope. That time, according to most scholars of the era, had been the reign of King Arthur. According to Bale, Merlin had predicted the Reformation,[66] and reformers re-cast the ancient British

---

[61] Parish, 'Magic and Priestcraft', p. 412.
[62] Lloyd, 'West Country Adventures', 413–34.
[63] Young, *Magic as a Political Crime*, pp. 70–1.
[64] Parry, *Arch-Conjurer of England*, p. 11.
[65] Kavey, *Books of Secrets*, p. 42.
[66] Thomas, *Religion and the Decline of Magic*, p. 484.

church as the possessor of a pure 'ancient theology'.[67] The Reformation was therefore an opportunity to recapture an ancient 'good' magic as well as dispelling the bad magic of the Catholic past.

The reign of Edward VI was the high tide of the Protestant reformation in England, when the most thoroughgoing effort was made to stamp out all relics of Catholicism as 'superstition'. In 1549 John Hooper, bishop of Gloucester, condemned belief in magic and witchcraft ('such as fear the menaces and threatenings of ... devilish people'), but also inveighed against astrology as superstition and a violation of the first commandment ('You shall have no other gods but me').[68] This was a controversial position to take at the time, when astrology (or most of astrology) was widely accepted as a permissible form of knowledge, and Hooper recognised that even some of 'them that hath a right knowledge of God' (Protestants) believed in astrology. Hooper equated 'priests that bless water, wax, bone, bread, ashes, candles' with 'witches or soothsayers' as 'superstitious persons'.[69]

The restoration of Catholicism under Mary I between 1553 and 1558 was portrayed by later Protestant authors as a dark time of superstition and magic,[70] although Mary's bishops, as well as Catholic bishops in mid-sixteenth-century Scotland, preached against witchcraft as forcefully as their Protestant counterparts.[71] With the

---

[67] Hart, *Art and Magic*, p. 31.
[68] Parry, *Arch-Conjurer of England*, p. 25.
[69] Maxwell-Stuart, *British Witch*, p. 119.
[70] Young, *Magic as a Political Crime*, pp. 90–1.
[71] Young, *English Catholics and the Supernatural*, pp. 125–6. On Scotland see Maxwell-Stuart, *British Witch*, p. 123.

accession of Elizabeth I in 1558, polemic against Catholicism as superstition resumed. In 1565, James Calfhill denounced the Catholic sign of the cross as a sign used in 'witchcraft and conjuration', and argued that any alleged miracles done after the age of the apostles were accomplished through sorcery.[72] In 1561, the bishop of London, Edmund Grindal, was horrified to discover that no law existed to punish two conjuring priests and made strenuous efforts to arrange their prosecution.[73] Later, as archbishop of Canterbury from 1576, Grindal's visitation articles (instructions for local parishes) singled out practitioners of 'charms, sorceries, enchantments, witchcraft, soothsaying, or any such like devilish device'.[74] For a committed Protestant such as Grindal, Catholicism was bad enough, but the practice of magic added insult to injury and merited special punishment.[75]

One reason why the representation of Catholicism as magic, or at least the representation of Catholics as credulous about magic, became a central plank of the Reformation in England and Scotland was because it obviated the need to designate Catholicism as heresy. Henry VIII had no desire to smear his royal predecessors as heretics, especially since the Henrician Reformation was not primarily a doctrinal realignment. Instead, the centrality of accusations of superstition to Reformation polemic highlighted the notion that the medieval church was decayed and corrupt, and presented reforming efforts

---

[72] Cameron, *Enchanted Europe*, pp. 207–10.
[73] Young, *Magic as a Political Crime*, p. 102.
[74] Quoted in Parry, *Arch-Conjurer of England*, p. 157.
[75] For similar cases linking 'superstitious' Catholic practices with magic see Maxwell-Stuart, *British Witch*, pp. 158–9.

as a process of purification. Furthermore, by presenting the Reformation as the purification of the land from superstitious practices, monarchs of the Reformation era portrayed themselves as Old Testament monarchs clearing the kingdom of soothsayers and tearing down the shrines of strange gods. While reformers accused the Catholic church of moral and financial crimes, it was essential for the success of reform that the church was also spiritually tainted with idolatry and sorcery. It is therefore hard to overstate the importance of accusations of magical corruption to the Reformation project.

Elizabeth's Merlin: John Dee

John Dee is undoubtedly the best known of England's historical 'court magicians'. Yet it is clear from an examination of the evidence that Dee did not fulfil this stereotyped role in reality in the same way as he is so often imagined doing in historical fiction. Dee's personal meetings and communications with Elizabeth herself were fairly few and far between, and most of his more overtly magical activities were private and revealed only after his death. However, Dee's relationship with the queen was well established, and went back to the period before her accession. In April 1555, during Mary's reign, Dee had cast horoscopes for Elizabeth, Mary and Philip of Spain (Mary's husband) at Woodstock Palace – an unwise action for which he was imprisoned and perhaps tortured.[76] However, Dee tainted his later reputation by subsequently entering the service of Bishop Edmund Bonner

---

[76] Parry, *Arch-Conjuror of England*, pp. 31–4.

of London, possibly to save himself. Bonner was notorious for his persecution of Protestants and the association between Bonner and Dee, immortalised in John Foxe's *Actes and Monuments*, cast a cloud over Dee throughout Elizabeth's reign.[77]

Dee formally entered Elizabeth's service in December 1558, providing an electionary horoscope for the date of her coronation, but Elizabeth failed to double the stipend he had received from Edward VI, as she had promised.[78] The early years of Elizabeth's reign were bedevilled by plots against her in favour of her cousin Mary, queen of Scots and Yorkist descendants of Edward IV's brother George, duke of Clarence. These early plots often contained a magical element.[79] Robert Dudley's patronage of 'conjurators' may have led Dudley's political rival William Cecil to try to implicate Dudley in the plots.[80] Dudley was Dee's patron as well, and the association did Dee few favours at this time.

In 1563, Dee discovered a work called *Steganographia* by Johannes Trithemius (1462–1516), abbot of the German abbey of Spanheim, which proposed a system of instantaneous communication using spirits summoned by ritual magic (not unlike the role fulfilled by Ariel for Prospero in Shakespeare's *The Tempest*). Dee wrote to Cecil, describing *Steganographia*'s magical telegraphy as 'The most precious jewel that I have yet of other men's travails recovered'. The promise of instantaneous magical

---

[77] Parry, *Arch-Conjuror of England*, pp. 38–9, 64–6.
[78] Parry, *Arch-Conjuror of England*, pp. 48–9.
[79] Young, *Magic as a Political Crime*, pp. 87–118.
[80] Parry, *Arch-Conjurer of England*, p. 61.

communication was something that would certainly have appealed to a political operator like Cecil, but it is also possible that Dee had understood the hidden message of *Steganographia*, which is actually a treatise on cryptography disguised as a grimoire.[81] Either way, Cecil would have been interested.

However, Elizabeth was most intrigued not by Dee's discovery of *Steganographia* but by Dee's Kabbalistic work *Monas Hieroglyphica* ('The Hieroglyphic Monad'), published in 1564, which attempted to produce a universal symbol based on Dee's study of alchemy and oriental languages.[82] More interestingly, from Elizabeth's point of view, the *Monas* claimed to reveal alchemical secrets.[83] Elizabeth's hunger for learning extended to the occult sciences, including alchemy and astrology. This was not lost on those who created images of the Virgin Queen, who regularly incorporated the pelican and the phoenix in their portraits.[84] Although these birds had traditional Christian (and non-alchemical) meaning, their alchemical and Hermetic resonances were widely known in an Elizabethan world dominated by complex and polyvalent symbolism. Most notoriously, the poet George Chapman compared Elizabeth's rule to that of an enchantress and spoke of her 'magic authority' in his 1594 poem *The Shadow of Night*.[85]

---

[81] Woolley, *Queen's Conjurer*, pp. 75–81.
[82] Parry, *Arch-Conjuror of England*, p. 69.
[83] Parry, *Arch-Conjuror of England*, p. 75.
[84] Parry, *Arch-Conjuror of England*, pp. 71–3. See also Hart, *Art and Magic*, pp. 67–8.
[85] Hart, *Art and Magic*, p. 5.

Dee was outraged whenever he was called a 'conjurer' (or even 'the Arch-conjurer, of this whole kingdom'), believing that it implied he summoned evil spirits.[86] Publicly, Dee was an astrologer, alchemist and mathematician. Yet in his personal magical practice (which did not come to light until the mid-seventeenth century) summoning spirits was exactly what Dee did. However, Dee was convinced his spirits were angels rather than demons, allowing him to repudiate any suggestions of necromancy. The Elizabethan court, however, was not interested in the angel magic Dee practised in private (and for which he is best known today) but in alchemical transmutation. Tudor court interest in alchemy was less speculative and mystical than that of medieval monarchs; Elizabeth and her courtiers expected results, not just profound philosophical meditations.[87]

Dee was loyal to the Elizabethan religious settlement, yet while the prayers that were part of Dee's magical practice were ostensibly Protestant in content, his determination to communicate with angelic beings as God's representatives was well outside the bounds of Protestant orthodoxy.[88] Dee, along with the explorer Humphrey Gilbert (c. 1539–83), espoused a 'reformed magic' in contrast to the unreformed magic offered by cunning-folk who often catered for those who hankered after the old suppressed Catholic practices. Gilbert, like Dee, dabbled in crystal-gazing, although he left aside 'Catholic' elements from ritual magic such as fasting and

---

[86] Parry, *Arch-Conjuror of England*, pp. 66–7.
[87] Hughes, *Rise of Alchemy*, p. 8.
[88] Martin, *Literature and the Encounter with God*, p. 27.

celibacy.[89] Some Protestants seemed more troubled by the Catholic legacy than by magic itself, such as the sixteenth-century owner of a manuscript of the *Ars Notoria* (a text of ritual magic) who defaced a prayer to the Virgin Mary as 'papist' but continued to treasure the grimoire.[90]

Elizabeth I remains the only English monarch (with the possible exception of Charles II) who is known to have personally practised alchemy.[91] She worked with the female alchemist Millicent Franckwell, who practised alchemical medicine by distilling potions for Elizabeth in the queen's chamber,[92] and ordered the construction of 'manifold still-houses' (distillation was a key part of alchemy) at Hampton Court shortly after her accession.[93] When Sir John Davies praised Elizabeth as refining the nation 'even like an alchemist divine', he may not have realized how apt his words were.[94] Alchemists who corresponded with the queen wrote as if they presumed an advanced understanding of the subject on her part. One alchemist, Thomas Charnock, styled himself 'the Queen's philosopher'. Charnock situated himself in a succession of English alchemical adepts including Roger Bacon and George Ripley, and claimed that Henry VII had been in possession of the Philosophers' Stone in 1504. Charnock promised to purify the nation's currency, tapping into a

---

[89] Klaassen, 'Ritual Invocation', pp. 341–66.
[90] Page, *Magic in Medieval Manuscripts*, p. 91.
[91] Parry, *Arch-Conjuror of England*, p. 77.
[92] Parry, *Arch-Conjuror of England*, p. 72.
[93] Parry, *Arch-Conjuror of England*, p. 215.
[94] Hart, *Art and Magic*, pp. 30–1.

perennial anxiety of early modern monarchs concerning debased coinage.[95]

Although it was Elizabeth who practised alchemy, to a large extent it was Cecil's enthusiasm for the possibility that alchemy might solve the kingdom's financial woes that resulted in government expenditure on alchemical projects. One alchemist, Cornelius de Lannoy, was given a generous pension and the use of Somerset House for his experiments. De Lannoy's failure to produce the gold he promised for the crown was explained not in terms of experimental failure or deception; instead, Cecil and others suspected De Lannoy of keeping the gold he had made for himself.[96] Cecil imprisoned De Lannoy and moved on to another alchemist, John Prestall, who promised to make gold in return for a pardon for his involvement in treasonous magic against the queen.[97] Cecil's willingness to agree to this remarkable demand is an indication of the depth of his interest in alchemy.

In February 1568, Dee finally secured an audience with Elizabeth, but his highly intellectual version of alchemy was uncompetitive in comparison with the practical schemes put forward by De Lannoy and Prestall.[98] Where Dee was a sincere speculative thinker and seeker after knowledge, others were shameless confidence tricksters. John Prestall was chief among these, renewing his treasonous activities in 1569 when the duke of Norfolk launched a new plot to marry Mary, queen of Scots, and

---

[95] Parry, *Arch-Conjuror of England*, p. 74.
[96] Parry, *Arch-Conjuror of England*, pp. 74–8.
[97] Parry, *Arch-Conjuror of England*, pp. 78–9.
[98] Parry, *Arch-Conjuror of England*, p. 80.

seize the throne. According to William Camden, the court organised a tournament in November 1570 in defiance of the anti-Elizabethan prophecies of 'wizards'. These 'accession day tilts' became an annual feature, and increasingly used imagery susceptible to an occult interpretation.[99] Elizabeth was 'worshipped' by her knights as the 'Fairy Queen' at a time when the fairies were still objects of genuine fear. The words of a masque performed before Elizabeth at Hengrave Hall in Suffolk excused the transformation of fairies into benevolent beings for the purposes of royal propaganda: 'The hagges of hell, that hateful are of kind, / to please the time, had learnd a nature new'. But it was still possible for Catholic opponents of Elizabeth to allege that the accession day ceremonies threatened 'to reduce people backe againe to heathenish Paganisme'.[100]

Elizabeth's adoption of a fairy identity was all the more remarkable in light of an established association between fairy lore and subversion. The leaders of Thomas Cheyne's rebellion in 1450 had called themselves the King and Queen of Fairyland (the latter, curiously, being a title assumed by a male leader).[101] Fifteenth-century poachers called themselves servants of the Fairy Queen, and in 1601, a man named John Cradocke conducted an elaborate mock service beneath a maypole at Tattershall, Lincolnshire which included readings and 'prayers' from a 'booke of Mabb' named after the Fairy Queen – all of this

---

[99] Yates, *Giordano Bruno*, p. 318.
[100] Green, *Elf Queens and Holy Friars*, pp. 199–200.
[101] Green, *Elf Queens and Holy Friars*, p. 22.

directed against the earl of Lincoln.[102] Talk of fairyland offered oppressed people 'a shared language that they felt they could use against their oppressors',[103] while the Fairy Queen became an alternative source of political authority.

In 1569, against the background of a rebellion in the north by the earls of Westmoreland and Northumberland, the duke of Norfolk was questioned about his knowledge of prophecies and astrological predictions touching Elizabeth's future. Prestall, caught up in this rebellion, ended up fleeing over the Scottish border, where he became an alchemist for Lord Maxwell.[104] Prestall subsequently fled to the Low Countries where he plotted an attack on the port of Rochester using 'wildfire' manufactured by alchemy, probably a version of the ancient naval weapon known as 'Greek fire'.[105] Dee responded to the vogue for prophecy among Elizabeth's opponents by reviving the prophecies of Joachim of Fiore (the same prophecies once applied to Richard II), applying them first to the Habsburg emperor Maximilian II,[106] and later to Elizabeth. Dee believed Elizabeth would be an apocalyptic 'Last World Empress', uniting and ruling over both Catholics and Protestants.[107] The explorer Humphrey Gilbert, who may have experimented with a scrying stone and was close to Dee, advocated the establishment of an academy that, among other things, would teach alchemy

---

[102] O'Conor, *Godes Peace and the Queenes*, pp. 119–22.
[103] Green, *Elf Queens and Holy Friars*, p. 22.
[104] Parry, *Arch-Conjuror of England*, p. 82–3.
[105] Young, *Magic as a Political Crime*, p. 115.
[106] Parry, *Arch-Conjuror of England*, pp. 58–9.
[107] Parry, *Arch-Conjuror of England*, p. 47.

and encourage its students to attempt transmutation.[108] Gilbert's proposals reflected his pragmatic approach to ritual magic as an experimental, Baconian alternative to the natural magic of discredited Scholasticism.[109] Cecil was not interested in the project, however, and the academy was never established. In April 1571, another alchemist, William Medley, began transmuting iron into copper for the court, using a technique that genuinely worked but proved too expensive.[110] Dee continued to be left out in the cold in favour of bolder alchemists, but he still had a scheme he hoped would catch Elizabeth's attention.

An Occult Empire

One of the earliest statutes to legally establish Henry VIII's break with Rome, the Act in Restraint of Appeals (1533) declared that 'this realm of England is an empire'.[111] In the language of the time, this did not mean that England was a nation with imperial colonies or possessions, but rather that English monarchs were subject to no authority, including that of the pope as the 'father of kings and princes'. The declaration was intended to set Henry on a par with the Holy Roman Emperor, but it also fed into a long-established Tudor mythology that associated the Welsh dynasty with King Arthur and an imagined sixth-century 'British empire' conquered by the legendary king.[112] The ultimate origin of the belief

---

[108] Parry, *Arch-Conjuror of England*, pp. 41, 84–5.
[109] Klaassen, 'Ritual Invocation', pp. 356–7.
[110] Parry, *Arch-Conjuror of England*, p. 88.
[111] Armitage, *Ideological Origins of the British Empire*, p. 35.
[112] Yates, *Occult Philosophy*, pp. 84–5.

that Arthur had ruled the Americas was Geoffrey of Monmouth's allusion to the conquest of 'islands of the Ocean' by the 'Boar of Cornwall' in the *Prophecies of Merlin*.[113]

The fall of Calais to the French in January 1558, the last fragment of the territory captured by England in the Hundred Years' War, meant that from the beginning of Elizabeth I's reign English eyes began to turn elsewhere for territory where the queen might make good her imperial aspirations. Samuel Norton, the grandson of the fifteenth-century alchemist, Thomas Norton, applied his grandfather's prophecy of 'a woman fair of face, whose grace would secure revelation of the philosopher's stone' to Elizabeth. Already, in *The Twelve Gates of Alchemy*, George Ripley had made a connection between alchemy and exploration of the globe. Ripley was interested in the geometry of the globe, writing of 'the ocean sea, which round is without end' – referring to the same geographical reasoning that would lead explorers such as the English-sponsored John Cabot and the Spanish-sponsored Christopher Columbus to seek a way to the Indies by sailing westwards.[114]

John Dee's unsurpassed mathematical knowledge, combined with his enthusiasm for Arthurian myths, made him the leading advocate of global empire in Elizabethan England. Dee's work *On the Limits of the British Empire* (1578) was inspired as much by his interest in occult philosophy as by the practical aim of discovering a north-western passage to the Indies. Dee claimed to unveil an

---

[113] Lawrence-Mathers, *True History*, p. 73.
[114] Hughes, 'Politics and the Occult', pp. 127–8.

'Incredible Political Mystery',[115] arguing that Elizabeth already possessed the New World by right of conquest, since it had been discovered by Madoc ap Owen, prince of Gwynedd (an ancestor of the Tudor dynasty) in 1170.[116] In November 1577, Dee obtained an audience with the queen in order to reassure her about the significance of a recent comet, but he took the opportunity to encourage Elizabeth to pursue her title to the Americas, assuring her that the Philosophers' Stone would restore the ancient 'British empire' he imagined.[117] Dee's vision of British empire also extended beyond the Americas to take in the restoration of all the lands supposedly once dominated by King Arthur, for which Dee appealed to the authority of the notorious angel-conjuring Abbot Trithemius.[118] Dee's claim that he had been 'strangely, and vehemently' instructed by God to write about the British empire may imply that he did so as a result of angel conjuring.[119] In December 1581, a 'spirit' told Dee 'Thou beginnest new worlds, new people, new kings, and new knowledge of a new government'.[120]

When it came to the practicalities of navigation, which relied heavily on mathematics, Dee boasted rather more than he really understood. Martin Frobisher, whom Dee tried to advise on advanced navigational techniques, ignored the mathematician's advice and relied on existing

[115] Parry, *Arch-Conjuror of England*, p. 113.
[116] Parry, *Arch-Conjuror of England*, p. 95.
[117] Parry, *Arch-Conjuror of England*, p. 97.
[118] Parry, *Arch-Conjuror of England*, pp. 106–7.
[119] Parry, *Arch-Conjuror of England*, p. 110.
[120] Quoted in Parry, *Arch-Conjuror of England*, p. 112.

practical approaches.[121] Nevertheless, Dee was an investor in a voyage that discovered rocks apparently containing gold and silver ore in March 1577. Dee used his alchemical and astrological knowledge to advise on the smelting of these ores, claiming that their discovery had been foretold by the appearance of a new star in the heavens in 1572,[122] although in the end the rocks proved worthless.[123] Dee, however, remained convinced that his occult knowledge would allow him to discover riches for the crown; one way to see his imperial speculation is as a global version of the magical treasure hunts that were so popular in early modern England,[124] and in which Dee himself enthusiastically engaged.

Frobisher was not the only Elizabethan explorer to accept occult advice. Henry Percy, 9th earl of Northumberland, who was known as the 'Wizard Earl' for his enthusiasm for alchemy, joined the circle of Sir Walter Raleigh in the 1580s and advised him on guns and explosives.[125] The science of gunnery was regarded at this time as an abstruse and almost occult field, requiring knowledge of mathematics and alchemy. Northumberland was the most senior English nobleman in sixteenth-century England to acquire a reputation as a 'wizard', largely on account of his very extensive library and his patronage of alchemists, mathematicians and astrologers including Thomas Hariot, Walter Warner and Robert

---

[121] Parry, *Arch-Conjuror of England*, pp. 98–100.
[122] Parry, *Arch-Conjuror of England*, p. 122. The 'new star' was the supernova observed in the constellation Cassiopeia by Tycho Brahe.
[123] Parry, *Arch-Conjuror of England*, pp. 101–2.
[124] Parry, *Arch-Conjuror of England*, pp. 105–6.
[125] Lawrence, *The Complete Soldier*, p. 113.

Hues, who were known as the earl's 'three magi'.[126] Raleigh himself held controversial views on magic, arguing in his *History of the World* that a magician 'is no other than ... a studious observer and expounder of divine things'. Nevertheless, Raleigh believed that true forms of magical knowledge (such as astrology) had become corrupted by the conjurations of necromancers.[127] Raleigh enjoyed a posthumous reputation as an alchemist, owing to a myth that he set up a still during his imprisonment in the Tower of London and created an alchemical 'Great Cordial' (sometimes called 'balsam of Guiana') which he offered visitors to the Tower. Some of the cordial reached the queen, Anne of Denmark, who was supposedly cured by it, and a controversy subsequently erupted about whether Raleigh should have been released from the Tower for this service to the royal family.[128]

While Frobisher and Raleigh were reputed to have benefitted from magical advice, the explorer and privateer Sir Francis Drake (c. 1540–96) soon gained a reputation as a wizard. The idea of Drake as a magician originated among the Spanish, Drake's implacable foes, who feared his raids on Spanish shipping and settlements and struggled to explain how Drake defeated the overwhelming force of the Spanish Armada in 1588 with his remarkable fire ships. Drake's surname (meaning 'dragon') assisted the growth of his legendary reputation. He was supposed to have been in possession of a magic mirror

---

[126] Nicholl, *The Reckoning*, pp. 231–2.
[127] Kassell, 'All was this land full-fill'd of faerie', 112.
[128] Mendelsohn, 'Alchemy and Politics in England', 59–60.

that allowed him to spy on the movements of the Spanish fleet. Drake's reputation as a magician later spread into English folklore, although it is unclear whether such stories circulated in his lifetime except among his enemies.[129] The historical Drake used accusations of conjuration and witchcraft against Thomas Doughty and his brother John, who accompanied him on one of his voyages in 1577–78. Drake believed the Doughty brothers were working for Cecil, who opposed Drake's privateering against Spanish ships and ports, and might give away his plans to the Spanish. Drake ordered the execution of Thomas Doughty for sorcery on 2 July 1578.[130]

The apocalyptic prophecies revived by Dee, which pictured Elizabeth as the final World Empress, were a tool used by Leicester in an effort to persuade Elizabeth to intervene aggressively in the Protestant Dutch revolt against Spanish rule, even to the extent of encouraging Elizabeth to assume sovereignty over the Protestant Netherlands.[131] For Dee, the restoration of Arthur's supposed ancient empire, which had covered not only some of the New World but most of Europe, also meant restoring the lost wisdom of Arthur's court.[132] He considered the discovery of the Philosophers' Stone essential to advancing Elizabeth's imperial claims, proposing the establishment of an alchemical research institute even more far-reaching than the one proposed by Humphrey Gilbert a few years earlier.[133] Dee also advocated a larger

---

[129] Westwood and Simpson, *Lore of the Land*, pp. 183–5.
[130] Kelsey, *Sir Francis Drake*, pp. 100–9.
[131] Parry, *Arch-Conjurer of England*, pp. 108–9.
[132] Parry, *Arch-Conjurer of England*, p. 107.
[133] Parry, *Arch-Conjurer of England*, p. 111.

PLATE 1. Vortigern hears red and white dragons fighting beneath his fortress, British Library MS Egerton 3028 fol. 25r © The British Library Board

PLATE 2. Merlin Ambrosius interprets a comet for King Uther, British Library MS Egerton 3028 fol. 33r © The British Library Board

PLATE 3. King Nectanebus enchanting ships through sympathetic magic, British Library MS Royal 20 B XX, fol. 4v © The British Library Board

PLATE 4. The coronation of Richard II in 1377, Royal 20 C. VII, fol.192v © The British Library Board

PLATE 5. English artillery at the siege of Orléans in 1429, Bibliothèque Nationale de France MS Français 5054, fol. 54v © Alamy

PLATE 6. Margery Jourdemayne conjures a demon for Eleanor Cobham, duchess of Gloucester in Shakespeare's *Henry VI Part Two* (colour stipple print by C. G. Playter and R. Thew after J. Opie, 1796) © Wellcome Colleetion

PLATE 7. Detail of the Ripley Scroll (watercolour copy) © Wellcome Collection

PLATE 8. Astrolabe made for Edward VI with astrological information in 1552 © Royal Museums Greenwich

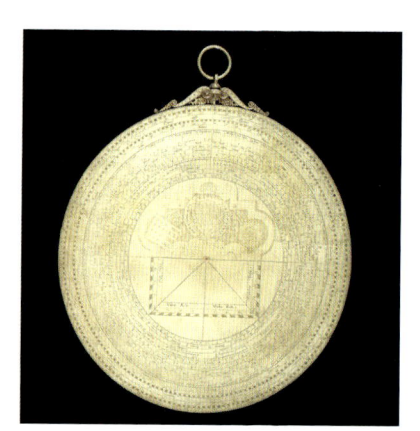

PLATE 9. Astrological sphere graffito in the Salt Tower, Tower of London by Hew Draper, 1561 © the author

Plate 10. John Dee (1527–1608/9), engraved by Franz Cleyn, 1658
© Wellcome Collection

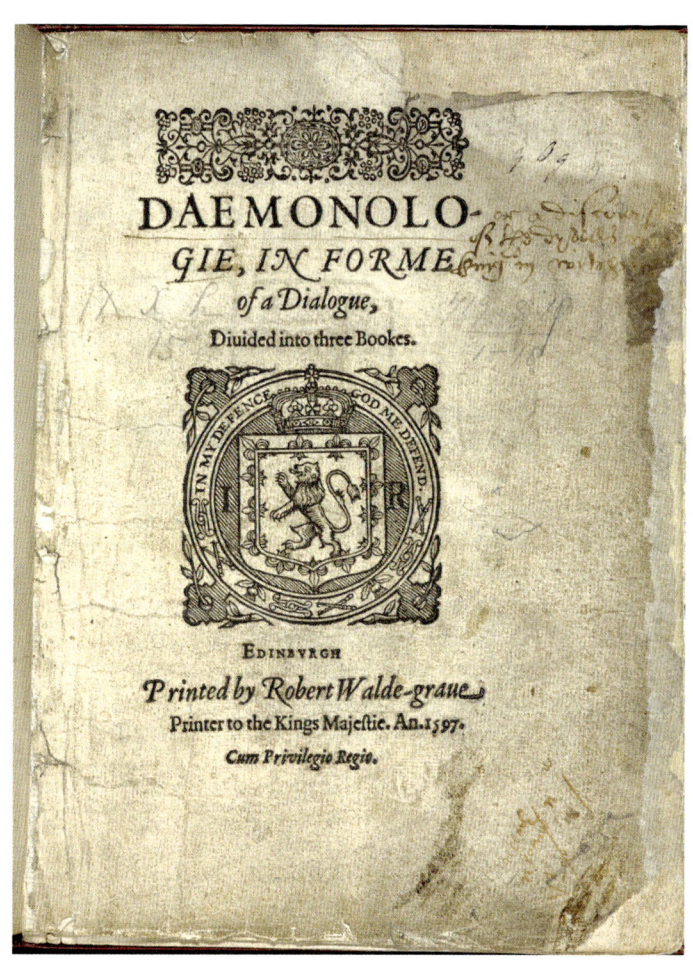

Plate 11. Frontispiece of King James VI's *Daemonologie*, 1597 © The British Library Board

A MOST
Certain, Strange, and true Discovery of a
VVITCH.

Being taken by some of the Parliament Forces, as she was standing on a small planck-board and sayling on it over the River of *Newbury*:

Together with the strange and true manner of her death, with the propheticall words and speeches she used at the same time.

Printed by John Hammond, 1643.

PLATE 12. Frontispiece of a pamphlet depicting the witch of Newbury, 1643 © The British Library Board

PLATE 13. William Lilly (1602–81), astrologer and supposed Parliamentarian 'wizard general', engraving from the frontispiece of *Merlini Anglici Ephemeris*, 1660 © Wellcome Collection

PLATE 14. 'Devills in the Ayre Bewitching M[onmouth]'s Army', from a set of playing cards commemorating the Monmouth Rebellion, 1685
© The British Museum

PLATE 15. Aleister Crowley in a self-designed uniform as 'Baphomet', 1919 © Alamy

navy in order to protect Elizabeth's maritime interests,[134] and opposed Elizabeth's marriage to the duke of Anjou.[135] During the late 1570s and early 1580s, Dee was not so much an adviser to Elizabeth as a client of Leicester, who sought to represent himself in increasingly Arthurian terms, with Dee as his Merlin.[136]

Dee's unique occult skills proved useful to Elizabeth in August 1578 when the Privy Council was thrown into panic over the discovery of what were apparently wax effigies of Elizabeth, Cecil and Leicester in a barn at Islington. The councillors, who were then on progress with Elizabeth in East Anglia, suspected that harmful sorcery was being worked against the queen and asked Dee to do something to counteract it. Dee rode from Mortlake to Norwich where he performed some sort of magical ritual to neutralise the effigies, although Elizabeth herself had already moved on to the next stage of her progress. As it turned out, however, what Leicester was convinced was foul play by Catholics turned out to be love magic unconnected to the queen or affairs of state. However, Elizabeth's ill health (attributed by her courtiers to magical attack) ensured that Dee secured another interview with her in October 1578.[137]

Leicester initially attempted to turn the search for the perpetrators of the effigy magic into a confessional witch-hunt against Catholics, but after torturing John Prestall and others without results, Leicester was forced to

---

[134] Parry, *Arch-Conjurer of England*, pp. 115–17.
[135] Parry, *Arch-Conjurer of England*, pp. 127–8.
[136] Parry, *Arch-Conjurer of England*, p. 125.
[137] On the affair of the Islington effigies see Young, *Magic as a Political Crime*, pp. 119–29.

concede defeat.[138] When the sorcerer who admitted to the original love magic, Thomas Elkes, turned out to have connections with Leicester, the earl was forced to discontinue the investigation for fear it might incriminate his own followers.[139] Nevertheless, the momentum created by Leicester's initial investigation continued in the provinces even after the Islington effigies were exposed as having nothing to do with treason. Magistrates remained in a state of high alertness regarding anything that smacked of treasonous magic. Paranoia ran so high that it even spilled over into the prosecution of people for witchcraft,[140] a crime not normally connected with affairs of political importance.

In October 1580, Dee met with Elizabeth and Cecil over a period of several days, setting out what he believed was Elizabeth's claim to the New World based on her Arthurian ancestry, as well as a claim to rule the kingdoms of Castile and Leon inherited from her Plantagenet ancestors. Cecil was sceptical of the value of Dee's genealogical claims, although in 1585 he did go so far as to assert that Elizabeth possessed 'some good pretence of title by lawful descent' to parts of the Low Countries in a document justifying English aid to the Dutch rebels.[141] However, Philip II's invasion of Portugal (a key English ally) in 1580 and the failure of negotiations with German Protestant princes left Elizabeth diplomatically isolated, while Frobisher's failure to discover any remains of the

---

[138] On Leicester's witch-hunt see Young, *Magic as a Political Crime*, pp. 129–37.
[139] Elmer, *Witchcraft, Witch-Hunting and Politics*, p. 30.
[140] Young, *Magic as a Political Crime*, pp. 137–8.
[141] Parry, *Arch-Conjurer of England*, pp. 141–2.

'Arthurian civilisation' that Dee believed had once existed in North America undermined his claims.[142]

Dee was frozen out of royal counsels but remained an important figure at court. It is an indication of Dee's perceived importance that the anonymous libel *Leicester's Commonwealth* (1584), originating among the English Catholic exiles on the Continent, accused Leicester of being a sorcerer and poisoner,[143] as well as claiming that Leicester retained Dee (described as an 'atheist') for 'figuring and conjuring'.[144] In reality, however, Dee was becoming desperate for patronage. On 17 November 1582, he consulted the angels in his crystal (via his medium Edward Kelley) about gaining the favour of Philip II, to whom Dee had dedicated a treatise on converting the indigenous peoples of the Americas to Christianity.[145] One of the angels warned him, 'Great care is to be had with those that meddle with princes' affairs'.[146] Dee was engaged in a dangerous game, and suffered disturbing dreams in which an angry Cecil came to his house at Mortlake to seize his library.[147] Yet Dee's project to convince Elizabeth to adopt a new calendar, which was also inspired by his confidence in apocalyptic prophecies, was also a failure,[148] precipitating Dee's departure for Bohemia in 1583.[149]

---

[142] Parry, *Arch-Conjurer of England*, pp. 143–4.
[143] Perry, 'Politics of Access', 1058.
[144] Parry, *Arch-Conjurer of England*, p. 128.
[145] Parry, *Arch-Conjurer of England*, p. 148.
[146] Dee, *Diaries*, p. 50.
[147] Parry, *Arch-Conjurer of England*, p. 149.
[148] Parry, *Arch-Conjurer of England*, pp. 147–57.
[149] Parry, *Arch-Conjurer of England*, p. 161.

Occult Missionary or Magical Spy? Giordano Bruno in England

In April 1583, not long before John Dee left for Eastern Europe, another celebrated magus arrived in England. Giordano Bruno (1548–1600) was a fugitive ex-Dominican friar who is famous today for his advocacy of heliocentrism in astronomy. Yet Bruno was just as well known in his own lifetime for his occult 'art of memory', a mnemonic technique with magical applications. Bruno's art of memory, elaborated from rhetorical techniques attributed to Cicero and heavily dependent on the work of the medieval Catalan philosopher Ramon Llull, was a technique for remembering vast amounts of complex information through the creation of imaginary spaces and signs (similar to the contemporary idea of a 'memory palace').

Bruno's technique had obvious political applications for government intelligence gathering, where secrecy and accurate recall of information were of paramount importance – but it was also avowedly a form of magic. Bruno's mnemonic images were not chosen at random; they derived from astrological and Hermetic literature, and he believed that contemplating the images would 'help not only the memory but also all the powers of the soul in a wonderful manner'.[150] In other words, Bruno was building on an established technique of natural magic that involved the creation of bronze talismans imprinted with astrological images in order to draw down astral influences. In a stroke of genius, Bruno 'cut out the middle

---

[150] Quoted in Yates, *Art of Memory*, p. 214.

man' and turned the human mind itself into the astrological talisman, meaning that his art of memory would draw down celestial influences into the mind and give human beings magical powers.

Surprisingly, given their overlapping interests, Dee and Bruno never met during the months both men were in England, and it is even possible that one of the reasons for Dee's departure was to avoid meeting the Neapolitan magus.[151] At the time of his arrival in England, Bruno was under the patronage of King Henri III of France and he was officially a guest of the French ambassador, Michel de Castelnau, at his London house, Salisbury Court.[152] Tudor England had a history of sheltering the pope's enemies, including French, Dutch and Italian religious reformers, but Bruno was a rather different kind of refugee, preaching a novel, mystical religion based on the Kabbalah, the *Hermetic Corpus*, and Heinrich Cornelius Agrippa's *Three Books of Occult Philosophy*.[153] Even in Elizabethan England, therefore, Bruno was a controversial figure. He aroused considerable interest on his arrival in England, engaging in academic disputations at Oxford and revelling in controversy. He had soon recruited the Scottish philosopher, Alexander Dicsone (d. 1604) as a disciple. Dicsone went on to write his own treatise on the art of memory in 1584,[154] as well as following Bruno by becoming a spy in Flanders on behalf of the Catholic

---

[151] Yates, 'Renaissance Philosophers in Elizabethan England', pp. 211–12.
[152] Bossy, *Giordano Bruno and the Embassy Affair*, p. 14.
[153] Yates, *Occult Philosophy*, p. 105.
[154] Beal, 'Dicsone [Dickson], Alexander', pp. 131–2.

nobles of the Scottish court.[155] Dicsone may have been responsible for introducing the art of memory to Scottish Freemasonry.[156]

Bruno was a significantly more radical occult thinker than Dee, rejecting the Christian faith in favour of a Hermetic religion of his own devising. Furthermore, Bruno declared himself to be opposed to mathematics, meaning that he rejected Dee's beloved astrology as part of the proper work of a magus.[157] However, both men were interested in proclaiming a new, unifying occult political theology, even if Dee's focus was on Elizabeth and Bruno's on Henri III of France as the unifying figure of a new Christendom. Both Dee and Bruno saw the Spanish Habsburgs and Counter-Reformation Catholicism as the enemies of occult exploration.[158]

Bruno was genuinely enthusiastic about Elizabeth, praising her as *diva Elizabetta* ('divine Elizabeth'), words that would be brought up many years later when he was on trial for heresy in Rome.[159] In his *Cena de le ceneri* ('Ash Wednesday Supper'), published in 1584, Bruno identified Elizabeth with Amphitrite, the personification of the sea, and declared that she was worthy to rule over the New World as well as the old. However, for Bruno, Amphitrite was more than just a goddess; she was the personification of 'the ocean of the fountain of ideas' and the ultimate unity of all things. Elsewhere Bruno identified Elizabeth

---

[155] Schuchard, *Restoring the Temple of Vision*, p. 222.
[156] Schuchard, *Restoring the Temple of Vision*, p. 234.
[157] Yates, 'Renaissance Philosophers in Elizabethan England', pp. 216–17.
[158] Yates, 'Renaissance Philosophers in Elizabethan England', p. 220.
[159] Yates, *Giordano Bruno*, p. 316.

with the virgin goddess Diana and portrayed her as the chief of the nine 'nymphs of Father Thames' who brings about the esoteric illumination of Britain.[160]

Bruno's devotion to Elizabeth may have extended to practical action. The historian John Bossy suggested that Bruno worked for Elizabeth's spymaster Sir Francis Walsingham under the cover name 'Henry Fagot', passing on information about Castelnau's contacts with the Spanish ambassador, English Catholics and Elizabeth's Catholic rival Mary, queen of Scots.[161] Although the identification of Bruno as a spy remains unproven, Bruno certainly had the motive (hatred of Spain), the means (his expanded 'artificial memory') and the opportunity (his residence with the French ambassador) for espionage. In the sixteenth century, magicians and spies had much in common; both were risk-takers, living dangerous lives, and both were obsessed with secrecy and cryptography – not to mention the regular involvement of magicians in plots against the state. The idea that Walsingham recruited individuals like Dee and Bruno to work for him is by no means implausible; magicians made excellent spies.

In the summer of 1584, Lord Henry Howard, a younger brother of the 4th duke of Norfolk and a well-known crypto-Catholic, published a book attacking prophecies, 'star divinity' (astrology) and magic, including 'rifling in the mysteries of Egypt', as dangerous to the state. Bruno condemned Howard's *Defensative against the*

---

[160] Yates, *Giordano Bruno*, pp. 317–18.
[161] Bossy, *Giordano Bruno and the Embassy Affair*, pp. 15–16.

Poyson of supposed Prophecies as heretical and treasonous. The book seemed to allude to Dee, describing someone who communicated with angels in dreams and cast horoscopes trying to ensnare 'Diana' (Elizabeth). Howard also echoed the accusations of *Leicester's Commonwealth*, alleging that Leicester and his allies used diabolic arts to frustrate Elizabeth's marriage to the duke of Anjou and the rightful succession of Elizabeth's heir apparent, the queen of Scots.[162]

It is possible that Bruno's opposition to Howard's book emerged from a belief that 'the mantle of Dee' as Elizabeth's occult adviser and protector had fallen to him when Dee departed for Bohemia.[163] The veiled attack on Dee clearly touched a sore nerve in a magician who was later perfectly prepared to use magic for his own political ends. Bruno seems to have believed that he could use magic against Pope Clement VIII to escape execution for heresy,[164] but the magus was unable to obtain a personal audience with the pope before he was burned as a heretic in Rome's Campo de' Fiori on 17 February 1600. Nevertheless, in spite of his brief stay, Bruno left a legacy in Britain, most notably in his Scottish follower Alexander Dicsone, who kept alive the flame of Bruno's philosophy. As late as 1630 Thomas Carew composed a masque for the court of King Charles I heavily influenced by Bruno's writings.[165]

---

[162] Bossy, *Giordano Bruno and the Embassy Affair*, pp. 99–101; Elmer, *Witchcraft, Witch-Hunting and Politics*, p. 26.
[163] Bossy, *Giordano Bruno and the Embassy Affair*, p. 101.
[164] Bossy, *Giordano Bruno and the Embassy Affair*, p. 154.
[165] Hart, *Art and Magic*, pp. 40–2.

The Turn against Occultism

On 3 December 1589, John Dee finally returned to England after his wanderings in Europe,[166] only to find his extensive library at Mortlake despoiled. Dee's stay at the court of Rudolf II in Prague had ended ignominiously; suspected of being a spy, Dee was banished by the emperor.[167] Elizabeth was initially generous to Dee, but primarily because she hoped that his scryer, Edward Kelley, who had stayed behind in Bohemia and convinced the Emperor Rudolf II that he possessed the secret of the Philosophers' Stone, would be lured back to England.[168] In Prague, Kelley seems to have infiltrated the expatriate English Catholic community to spy for Burghley.[169] However, Dee's patron Leicester had died in 1588 and Sir Francis Walsingham, another friend to Dee, died shortly after Dee's return. The magus was left isolated in a changed England where a new political establishment was hostile to reform of all kinds. The hostility was directed primarily towards Puritan calls for further reform of the Church of England, led by Archbishop John Whitgift and the bishop of London, John Aylmer.[170] However, the new hostility to Puritanism also impacted on attitudes to occult traditions because Puritans were often open to prophecies and visions.

Although radical Protestants were ostensibly opposed to magic as a popish practice, the line between political

---

[166] Parry, *Arch-Conjurer of England*, p. 204.
[167] Woolley, *Queen's Conjurer*, pp. 270–1.
[168] Parry, *Arch-Conjurer of England*, p. 205.
[169] Honan, *Christopher Marlowe*, p. 267.
[170] Parry, *Arch-Conjurer of England*, p. 207.

iconoclasm and malign effigy magic was sometimes blurred. In 1583, John Copping and Elias Thacker, two Puritans, defaced the royal arms in St Mary's church, Bury St Edmunds with texts from the Book of Revelation alluding to the Whore of Babylon.[171] This was more than just an act of vandalism and political sedition, because defacing the image of the queen, and even her heraldic representation, always had overtones of sorcery. In 1585, an itinerant confidence trickster, William Awder, who sometimes claimed to be a schoolmaster or a minister, claimed to be able to kill anyone whose image he made in wax,[172] and in July 1591, a maltmaker named William Hacket, who claimed to be the messiah, was hanged for stabbing an image of the queen (probably a cheap mass-produced print) in the heart.[173] Incidents of this kind convinced Elizabeth's government that radical Protestants were as dangerous as the Catholics who continued to menace the queen's life with ongoing plots.

Emboldened by the new atmosphere of hostility to occult practices, the Kentish magistrate Reginald Scot published his avowedly sceptical *Discoverie of Witchcraft* in 1584, which took aim at Leicester and, without naming him, at Dee as well.[174] However, the change in atmosphere meant that not only the overt practice of magic but also the 'prophetic politics' beloved of Dee and sustained

---

[171] Collinson, *From Cranmer to Sancroft*, p. 35.
[172] Young, *Magic as a Political Crime*, pp. 142–3.
[173] On the Hacket case see Walsham, 'Frantick Hacket', 27–66; William, 'Exorcising Madness in Late Elizabethan England', 30–52; Young, *Magic as a Political Crime*, pp. 143–4.
[174] Parry, *Arch-Conjuror of England*, p. 208; Elmer, *Witchcraft, Witch-Hunting and Politics*, pp. 27–8.

by astrology came under attack.[175] Even the use of occult imagery in Elizabeth's cult of personality met with a frosty reception. In 1590, Edmund Spenser's *The Faerie Queene*, a wide-ranging mythological epic poem directed at Elizabeth and suffused with alchemical, Neoplatonic and Hermetic symbolism, gained the poet little favour. It has been suggested that the poem's heady mix of patriotic imagery and prophetic enthusiasm may have been linked to Dee's Arthurian theories about the 'British empire',[176] but publication came at the wrong time. In England in the 1590s 'the spirit of reaction' prevailed against 'the daring spiritual adventures of the Renaissance'.[177]

Nevertheless, in spite of official hostility to magic, Elizabeth remained fascinated by alchemy and continued to hope for the Philosophers' Stone, employing Dee in alchemical experiments from July 1590. Elizabeth also began her own personal correspondence with Edward Kelley, promising him incentives to return to England as her personal alchemist.[178] However, by May 1591 Burghley had lost patience with Kelley's claims. Meanwhile, the alchemist was imprisoned in Bohemia by Rudolf II for killing another man in a duel.[179] Dee may have temporarily won his way back into Elizabeth's favour in June by claiming occult knowledge of a Spanish invasion,[180] but the subsequent discovery of threats to the queen's life that summer by William Hacket and other

---

[175] Parry, *Arch-Conjuror of England*, p. 209.
[176] Yates, *Occult Philosophy*, pp. 105–7.
[177] Yates, 'Renaissance Philosophers in Elizabethan England', pp. 212–13.
[178] Parry, *Arch-Conjuror of England*, pp. 213–14.
[179] Parry, *Arch-Conjuror of England*, pp. 215–16.
[180] Parry, *Arch-Conjuror of England*, p. 218.

messianic Protestant sectaries did not shed a very flattering light on Dee's style of political prophecy.[181]

In January 1592, the exiled English Catholic leader Cardinal William Allen, an implacable enemy of Elizabeth, claimed that the 'conjurer' Dee 'told the Council by his calculation, that the Realm indeed shall be conquered',[182] and Dee's visit to Nonsuch Palace on 7 August 1592 may have been connected to a further warning to the Privy Council about imminent invasion, since it was followed by the widespread arrests of prominent Catholics thought to favour the Spanish.[183] Historians are divided on the identity of the 'necromancer' whom Robert Parsons accused of being the 'master' of 'Sir Walter Raleigh's school of Atheism' (also called the 'School of Night'), where students were allegedly taught to spell the name of God backwards. The astronomer, Thomas Harriot, who accompanied Raleigh to North America in 1585–86, has usually been identified as the conjurer of Parsons's libel,[184] but Dee is also a possibility.[185] The opposition directed against Dee by the Catholic exiles indicates the importance he appeared to have within the Elizabethan regime, at least to the eyes of the outside world.

Incidents of magical treason continued into Elizabeth's last years. In November 1594, a woman held prisoner in the Fleet, Jane Shelley, was accused of employing 'sorcerers, witches, and charmers' to find out the date of

[181] Parry, *Arch-Conjuror of England*, pp. 219–21.
[182] Quoted in Parry, *Arch-Conjuror of England*, p. 226.
[183] Parry, *Arch-Conjuror of England*, p. 229.
[184] See Strathmann, 'John Dee as Ralegh's "Conjurer"', 365–72.
[185] Parry, *Arch-Conjuror of England*, p. 231.

Elizabeth's death and the truth about the succession to the crown.[186] This was testament to the anxiety created by Elizabeth's lack of an heir and her refusal to give her own view on the royal succession. In the 1590s, 'an increase of general underlying fearfulness' led to a spike in witchcraft prosecutions that would never be exceeded, even during the witch-hunts of the 1640s.[187] These were years of crop failure, disease, poverty and general hardship, which led in turn to suspicion and witchcraft allegations. If not political, this rise in witchcraft prosecutions was certainly connected to the mood of the nation. Catholics continued to conspire against the queen, too, and a group of them attempted to poison Elizabeth in 1598.[188]

Yet the final treason of Elizabeth's reign would be the betrayal of the queen by Robert Devereux, earl of Essex. The notorious cunning-man and astrological physician, Simon Forman (1552–1611), who was regularly asked by his clients about political events,[189] performed astrological calculations to assess the success of Essex's expedition to Ireland in March 1599.[190] After Essex's failed rebellion and arrest, in February 1601 Frances Seymour, countess of Hertford asked Forman to calculate whether or not Essex would be executed for high treason. The result was that Essex would 'not die but live in prison'. Forman's calculation was proved wrong when Elizabeth decided that she would indeed execute Essex, in one of the last major political acts of her reign.[191]

---

[186] Maxwell-Stuart, *British Witch*, p. 159.
[187] Maxwell-Stuart, *British Witch*, pp. 160–1.
[188] Young, *Magic as a Political Crime*, p. 146.
[189] Thomas, *Religion and the Decline of Magic*, pp. 370–1.
[190] Cook, *Dr Simon Forman*, p. 123.
[191] Cook, *Dr Simon Forman*, p. 150.

Conclusion

It is difficult to overstate the importance of representations of occult knowledge as a way of facilitating political change in sixteenth-century England. Government fear of hostile harmful sorcery provided an element of continuity between early modern and medieval perceptions of occult power, but the addition of the new crime of witchcraft from the 1540s onwards complicates the issue of political sorcery because the criminalisation of witchcraft effectively made it a political act. However, the government's concerted efforts to stigmatise Catholicism as magic and superstition from the 1530s represented a completely new way of using occult accusations and representations to effect change. Thomas Cromwell's portrayal of the Catholic church as corrupted by occult practices enabled the unthinkable – the replacement of traditional allegiances to Rome with a new allegiance to Henry VIII's Church of England.

Perhaps more than any English monarch since Richard II, Elizabeth I constructed herself in magical terms and relied on occult philosophy to bolster her reign. Elizabeth was forced to turn what would otherwise have been perceived as fatal weaknesses – being an unmarried woman without heirs – into strengths, and for this she had to rely on all the power of ideas, imagery and pageant, as well as an established Tudor tradition of Arthurianism. The 'cult of Gloriana', regarded by Catholics as a blasphemous parody of the cult of the Virgin Mary,[192] became a sort of 'secular religion' during her reign that drew on

---

[192] Young, *Magic as a Political Crime*, p. 153.

alchemical and Hermetic imagery. Elizabeth's reliance on Arthurian myth made it inevitable, perhaps, that she would require a Merlin. John Dee obligingly fulfilled the role, although Dee's period of true influence over Elizabeth and government policy was brief. For the most part, Dee viewed himself as more important to Elizabeth than she ever considered him to be. Even the greatest magical service Dee performed for Elizabeth – using counter-magic against the wax effigies discovered in 1578 – turned out to be unnecessary. Elizabeth was always interested primarily in the potential financial returns of alchemy rather than the prophetic destiny of the nation. Years after her death, Elizabeth's old adversary Robert Parsons went so far as to accuse the queen herself of being a witch just like her mother Anne Boleyn.[193] Yet occult imagery, and the search for occult knowledge, underpinned Elizabeth's reign to an unprecedented degree – and perhaps facilitated acceptance of a monarch who subverted both preconceived ideas of masculine kingship and dynastic marriage.

[193] Young, *Magic as a Political Crime*, pp. 153–4.

4

House of the Unicorn

Stuart Monarchy and the Contest for Occult Authority

~

In the late 1440s, a group of Scottish envoys in Flanders encountered an astrological physician (known only as 'Andrew'). Andrew's skills so impressed the envoys that they reported back to King James III, and the king invited the astrologer to Edinburgh. Once in the Scottish capital, Andrew told James that he was in danger of death 'from his own' (*a suis*). For a king, this could mean either that James was threatened by his own people or by his family. James chose to adopt the latter interpretation, and in 1479 the king arranged for his brother John's throat to be slit in prison. The king then tried to blame twelve *foeminis veneficis* ('women poisoners/witches') who were tortured and burned alive.[1]

This incident inaugurated a long and troubled relationship between the House of Stewart (the gallicised form 'Stuart' was not adopted until the late sixteenth century) and the occult arts. The Stewarts ruled Scotland from 1371 and then England as well between 1603 and 1714, making them one of the most enduring royal dynasties in British history. Yet in spite of their longevity the reigns of

---

[1] Maxwell-Stuart, *British Witch*, pp. 77–8.

Stewart monarchs were often troubled. In Scotland, Stewart monarchs contended with the nobility for control of the nation and proved reluctant to embrace the Protestant Reformation that was received enthusiastically by many Scots. The first two Stewart monarchs of Great Britain, James VI and I and Charles I, tended towards absolutism at a time when Parliament was itching to assert its authority – a combination that, in Charles's case, would have fatal consequences. Throughout all of this, the Stewarts regularly used accusations of sorcery to discredit their enemies and even to keep control of the nation, but they were also fascinated by the positive contribution of occult traditions to strengthening the authority, power and prestige of the monarchy. According to the sixteenth-century Scottish historian George Buchanan, James III was fond of consulting witches (*maleficarum mulierum*) as well as burning them, and the king employed the archbishop of St Andrews, William Scheves, as his personal physician and astrologer between 1471 and 1480. Scheves had studied under the great astrologer Spiricus at the University of Louvain.[2]

Occult Traditions in Scotland

The kingdom of Scotland emerged in the ninth and tenth centuries, uniting a collection of Gaelic, Pictish and British kingdoms (as well as the northernmost portion of the Old English-speaking kingdom of Northumbria). Medieval Scotland was significantly more culturally and linguistically diverse than England, and the range of

---

[2] Maxwell-Stuart, *British Witch*, pp. 77–8; Carey, *Courting Disaster*, p. 160.

occult beliefs was correspondingly more complex. For example, although the fairies are occasionally mentioned in English accounts of magic, the activities of the Gaelic *sìthean* were an integral part of Scottish belief in magic and witchcraft.[3] Arthur's Seat (the hill that towers over the old town of Edinburgh in the grounds of Holyrood Palace) was strongly associated with the summoning of the fairies, perhaps because the Neolithic arrowheads found there were interpreted as 'fairy shot'.[4] Furthermore, Scotland had a strong tradition of charming and magical curing, especially in the Highlands and Western Isles.[5] Another distinctively Gaelic belief that filtered into the rest of Scottish society was the idea of a spiritual 'second sight' that allowed certain gifted individuals to foretell the future and see spiritual beings such as the fairies.[6] This contrasted with the usual belief in England that divination was a technique requiring skill rather than an intrinsic capability of some individuals.

Perhaps the best-known story of occult knowledge in early Scottish history is that of the 'three witches' who promise the throne to Macbeth, who was king of Scots between 1040 and 1057. William Shakespeare borrowed the story from the *Chronicles* of Raphael Holinshed (published in 1577), but neither Holinshed nor Shakespeare actually describes the women whom Macbeth encounters as witches. For Holinshed, they are 'Weird Sisters ... the goddesses of destiny, or else some nymphs or fairies

[3] Maxwell-Stuart, *British Witch*, pp. 10–17.
[4] Maxwell-Stuart, *British Witch*, p. 179.
[5] Maxwell-Stuart, *Satan's Conspiracy*, pp. 17 23.
[6] Maxwell-Stuart, *Satan's Conspiracy*, pp. 23–6.

endued with knowledge of prophecy by their necromantical science'. The notorious London magician Simon Forman, who was also an aficionado of Shakespeare's plays, described the characters as '3 women fairies or nymphs' at a 1611 performance of the Scottish Play.[7] The earliest version of the story can be found in a Scots verse chronicle written in around 1440 by Andrew of Wyntoun, where Macbeth encounters the three women in a dream rather than in reality; once again, there is no mention of witches:

> He saw three women by going,
> And those three women then thought he
> Three weird sisters like to be.
> The first he heard say going by:
> 'Lo, yonder the thane of Cromarty!'
> The other sister said again:
> 'Of Moray yonder I see the thane.'
> The third said: 'Yonder I see the King'.[8]

The term 'weird sisters' derives from Old English *wyrd*, meaning 'fate'. Wyntoun's and Holinshed's sisters correspond to the personified Fates of Greece and Rome, or the Norns of Norse mythology.[9] The weird sisters in the tale of Macbeth should be seen as part of Scottish fairy belief (the word 'fairy' comes ultimately from *fatae*, 'the Fates'), or even a classicising tendency in late medieval Scots poetry; their connection with witchcraft came much later. People in Gaelic areas of Scotland (the Highlands and Western Isles), as in Gaelic Ireland, did not share the

---

[7] Shamas, *'We Three'*, p. 11.
[8] Quoted in Shamas, *'We Three'*, p. 10 (spelling modernised).
[9] Shamas, *'We Three'*, p. 17.

Lowland Scottish and English belief in malefic witches who could kill or harm by supernatural means, believing only that witches had very restricted powers to steal butter on May Eve. Individuals could protect themselves against these 'butter-stealing witches' with relative ease,[10] and although people in Gaelic areas also believed in the 'evil eye' (an unintentional and inherited ability to cause people misfortune by looking at them),[11] the primary focus of supernatural fear was not witches but the fairies.[12] Consequently, Gaelic Ireland and Scotland were relatively free from epidemic witch-hunting, since fear was directed elsewhere.[13]

Even in the Lowlands, medieval Scots do not seem to have been any more afraid of harmful magic than anyone else in the British Isles. From 1510 onwards, there was a slow but steady stream of ecclesiastical trials of people accused of witchcraft in pre-Reformation Scotland,[14] but there was no criminal offence of witchcraft in the country until 1563.[15] Apart from the single incident involving James III in 1479, there is no certain case of someone being accused of magical treason in pre-Reformation Scotland. In 1537, Janet Douglas, Lady Glamis was burned to death at Edinburgh Castle for conspiring to kill James V 'by the worst poison' (*per pessimum venenum*), and a priest was arrested and tortured. Apart from the fact that poisoning was almost always associated with occult

---

[10] Sneddon, *Witchcraft and Magic in Ireland*, pp. 11–13.
[11] Sneddon, *Witchcraft and Magic in Ireland*, pp. 13–14.
[12] Sneddon, *Witchcraft and Magic in Ireland*, pp. 14–15.
[13] See Hutton, 'Witch-Hunting in Celtic Societies', 43–71.
[14] Maxwell-Stuart, *British Witch*, pp. 30–3.
[15] Goodare, 'Witch-Hunting and the Scottish State', p. 125.

knowledge, however, no contemporary allegations of magic are associated with Janet Douglas (who was burned for treason rather than witchcraft). A later sixteenth-century historian asserted that Lady Glamis was suspected of witchcraft,[16] but it is possible that this was a result of confusion based on the double meaning of *veneficium* as both 'poisoning' and 'witchcraft'.

Scottish monarchs were content to draw on the power and imagery of magic when they needed to do so. During the reign of James I (1406–37), a chained and crowned unicorn first appeared as the emblem of the Scottish monarchy,[17] with unicorns later becoming the supporters of the royal arms. The unicorn was a staple of alchemical and, later, Rosicrucian imagery, with the unicorn's purity standing for mercury and its savagery for sulphur.[18] This does not mean that the Scottish royal family adopted the unicorn with this meaning in mind; it is more likely that the unicorn's combined purity and savagery, and its Christian symbolism, made it appealing as a heraldic supporter. However, by making use of a mythical beast the Stewarts enabled occult interpretations, which were fully exploited in the seventeenth century.[19]

In 1494, Pope Alexander VI sent King James IV a sceptre that was later topped with a ball of transparent rock crystal believed to have healing powers.[20] Crystals of clear quartz ascribed occult powers belonged to several Scottish clans, including the *Clach-na-Bratach* or 'Stone of

---

[16] Maxwell-Stuart, *British Witch*, p. 104.
[17] Stevenson and Durie, *Heraldry in Scotland*, p. 397.
[18] Hughes, *Rise of Alchemy*, pp. 63–4.
[19] Hart, *Art and Magic*, pp. 63–6.
[20] Thomas, 'Crown Imperial', p. 55.

the Standard' which belonged to Clan Donnachaidh from 1315. Water in which the *Clach-na-Bratach* was dipped by the chief (but only by him) was believed to have healing powers for people and cattle. The stone also acted as a shewstone, revealing the future, but only for the chief on the eve of battle. Other stones were believed to have healing properties alone, and were set in silver or gold.[21] The Stewart dynasty's decision to set such a stone in the sceptre of Scotland was an indication of their willingness to draw on a traditional Gaelic source of occult power as well as the more conventional divine power of kingship. Of all the articles of Scottish royal regalia, the sceptre remained in use the longest, since it was used to touch all acts of the Scottish Parliament to symbolise royal assent between 1603 and 1707, when Scotland's Parliament was abolished after the Act of Union that created the United Kingdom of Great Britain.

Supernatural Paranoia and Reformation in Sixteenth-Century Scotland

The death of King James V in 1542 unleashed decades of political and religious instability in Scotland. James's only child, Mary, was just days old when her father died, so Scotland was governed by regents until 1561. Although the first regent, the earl of Arran, was sympathetic to the Protestant Reformation, he was succeeded in 1554 by James V's widow, Mary of Guise. Like Mary I of England, Mary of Guise attempted to reverse the

---

[21] Mackinlay, *Folklore of Scottish Lochs*, p. 258. See also Simpson, 'Notes on Some Scottish Magical Charm-Stones', 211–24.

Reformation. When Queen Mary returned to Scotland in 1561 the country was simply too unruly for her to govern effectively. Scotland had not experienced the reign of a centralising, bureaucratic monarch like Henry VII of England, and the crown was therefore subject to the competing interests of the nobility. Matters were further complicated by the religious divide between Catholic and Protestant nobles, while the fiery Calvinist preacher John Knox agitated for the most thoroughgoing of reformations. In October 1562, Knox became deeply concerned that one of the leading Catholic magnates, the countess of Huntly, was consulting her own 'personal witches', which may have been the reason why the 1563 Scottish Witchcraft Act criminalised the 'seeker of the response or consultation'.[22]

The Scottish Witchcraft Act implicitly associated 'witchcrafts, sorcery, and necromancy' with Catholicism by describing them as 'such vain superstition'.[23] Since Catholicism was routinely equated with superstition by Scottish Protestants, the use of the word in the Witchcraft Act has strongly anti-Catholic connotations,[24] and it is possible that a clause explicitly linking Catholicism to witchcraft existed in the draft bill and was struck from the final text.[25] Unlike its English counterpart, which criminalised the act of harming someone by magic or witchcraft, the Scottish act criminalised anyone who

---

[22] Goodare, 'Scottish Witchcraft Act', 56.
[23] Maxwell-Stuart, *Satan's Conspiracy*, pp. 35–6.
[24] Maxwell-Stuart, *Satan's Conspiracy*, p. 40.
[25] Goodare, 'Scottish Witchcraft Act', 49–50. Goodare also argues (62–3) that the act's explicit mention of 'necromancy' was intended as an attack on Catholicism because necromancers made use of Catholic rites.

consulted a witch or sorcerer and allowed for a very broad interpretation of 'witchcraft', which might include local healers, cunning-folk and charmers.[26]

From the very beginning, the prosecution of witchcraft in Scotland was a highly politicised business because the monarch's council decided whether the courts should prosecute. In practice, this meant that the council decided the outcome of the case and the court hearing was a formality, since the council would not authorise a trial unless the evidence convinced them that the suspect was guilty.[27] This also gave the council the opportunity to promote and direct witch-hunting centrally, which occurred during the witch panic of 1628–30.[28] The council thus dealt with witchcraft much as it dealt with treason, conducting an extensive pre-trial inquisition that determined the outcome of any future proceedings. Furthermore, the Scottish Parliament also issued commissions for the trials of individual witches.[29] The involvement of organs of central government (the monarch's council and Parliament) in dealing with witchcraft was something that did not happen in England, and this may have contributed to the extensive politicisation of witchcraft in Scotland. In contrast to most other European countries, witch-hunting in Scotland was a national, government-sponsored affair rather than something enacted solely on the local level.[30] Scotland was especially vulnerable to witchcraft panics because, in

[26] Goodare, 'Scottish Witchcraft Act', 54–5.
[27] Goodare, 'Witch-Hunting and the Scottish State', p. 131.
[28] Goodare, 'Witch-Hunting and the Scottish State', p. 133.
[29] Goodare, 'Witch-Hunting and the Scottish State', p. 135.
[30] Goodare, 'Witch-Hunting and the Scottish State', p. 136.

post-Reformation Lowland Scottish culture, witchcraft was not perceived as a malicious activity of solitary individuals (as it was in England) but as something perpetrated by sects or 'covens' of witches conspiring together.[31]

In the context of this 'conspiratorial' model of witchcraft, if one case of witchcraft was discovered then the discovery was accompanied by the expectation that other witches were probably involved, and that there was likely to be a broader conspiracy. The Scottish royal council saw witches as a national problem to be dealt with on a national scale,[32] and only the prosecution of treason was more tightly managed by central government. This meant that witch-hunting was one of the ways in which central government could impose its authority on local magnates, allowing Scotland to emerge as a modern nation state.[33] Witch-hunting served to legitimise the Scottish state and may have been one of the ways in which the state sought stability at times of anxiety and turmoil.[34] In other words, the one thing the state could be relied upon to do was hunt witches. Witch-hunting lay at the foundation of the 'theocratic government' of early modern Scotland, legitimating the Stewarts' 'godly' rule as divinely ordained kings.[35]

Furthermore, the propaganda of Scottish reformers managed to create the impression of a much closer connection between witchcraft and Catholicism than English

---

[31] Goodare, 'Witch-Hunting and the Scottish State', p. 137.
[32] Goodare, 'Witch-Hunting and the Scottish State', pp. 137–8.
[33] Goodare, 'Witch-Hunting and the Scottish State', p. 139.
[34] Goodare, 'Witch-Hunting and the Scottish State', pp. 140–1.
[35] Goodare, 'Witch-Hunting and the Scottish State', p. 145. On witch-hunting as state-building see Clark, *Thinking with Demons*, p. 554.

Protestants ever managed. Even Queen Mary herself was not immune from suspicion. The clergyman William Harrison was convinced that Mary practised sorcery and that she married Henry Stewart, Lord Darnley in 1566 on the advice of witches, who promised Queen Elizabeth's death and Mary's succession to the English throne.[36] When Mary gave birth to the future James VI in June 1566, it was widely reported that the countess of Atholl attempted to use sympathetic magic to transfer Mary's labour pains to another person, perhaps with Mary's connivance.[37]

In 1567, Mary was deposed and fled to England, leaving the government once more in the hands of regents. In the succeeding years, treasonous attempts by witches against the lives of Scotland's rulers became commonplace. Violat Mar was convicted of attempting to kill the earl of Morton by magic in 1577,[38] and in 1590 a far-reaching conspiracy by witches was discovered at North Berwick to kill James VI.[39] The North Berwick witches were accused of having tried to sink James's ship on his return from Denmark in 1589, as well as handing a picture of James to the devil in person and planning to murder the king with poison from a toad.[40] The plot was traced back to James Hepburn, earl of Bothwell. Bothwell was banished and died in exile in Italy.[41] However, there are signs that the connection between the accused witches and Bothwell

---

[36] Parry, *Arch-Conjurer of England*, p. 70.
[37] Maxwell-Stuart, *Satan's Conspiracy*, pp. 48–9.
[38] Maxwell-Stuart, *Satan's Conspiracy*, pp. 90–1.
[39] Maxwell-Stuart, *Satan's Conspiracy*, pp. 144–7.
[40] Maxwell-Stuart, *Satan's Conspiracy*, p. 154.
[41] Maxwell-Stuart, *Satan's Conspiracy*, pp. 171–80.

may have been fabricated, and it is not certain that the North Berwick witches were originally engaged in political magic.[42] Bothwell was not the only Scottish nobleman whom James VI succeeded in discrediting by accusations of treasonous magic. In August 1600, John Ruthven, earl of Gowrie was killed by James's retainers after Gowrie apparently attacked James in a house in Perth. The discovery of a supposed book of magic on Gowrie's body allowed his treasonous intentions to be interpreted within the tradition of malignant magic against the monarch.[43]

James VI's engagement with the occult arts was much more extensive, however, than merely being the victim of a number of magical plots. In 1597, a year of intense witch-hunting and political paranoia in Scotland,[44] James published his own treatise on witchcraft, entitled *Daemonologie*, as a riposte to Reginald Scot's sceptical book *The Discoverie of Witchcraft* (1584). James's *Daemonologie* would go on to become one of the most influential books about witchcraft in British history. This was partly because its author was the king of Scots and the heir apparent to the English throne (ensuring that the book was reprinted and eagerly devoured in England), but James also introduced new demonological ideas from his wide reading of European authors. In post-Enlightenment history books, James was routinely stereotyped as 'the wisest fool in Christendom' for his misdirected learning,[45] but this was not how

---

[42] Maxwell-Stuart, *British Witch*, p. 195.
[43] Booth, 'Standing within the Prospect of Belief', p. 51.
[44] Maxwell-Stuart, *British Witch*, p. 196.
[45] A phrase supposedly coined by Sir Anthony Weldon (1583–1648). See Smith, 'Politics in Early Stuart Britain', p. 238.

contemporaries viewed the king's occult interests. *Daemonologie* established James as 'a godly magistrate against whom the gates of Hell had not prevailed and would not prevail in future, and an authoritative arbiter of disputes regarding Satan, his minions, and the other world'.[46] In other words, James's experience as a target of magical attacks lent him authority on the subject.

Nevertheless, it is clear that James's interest in the occult extended beyond the demonological analysis and theological denunciation we find in the pages of *Daemonologie*. In 1607, in a private conversation with Sir John Harington, James asked Harington's views on witchcraft and said that some people gifted with the second sight in Scotland had foreseen his mother's execution in 1587, in the form of 'a bloody head dancing in the air'. James 'did remark much on this gift [of second sight], and said he had sought out of certain books a sure way to attain knowledge of future chances',[47] suggesting that the king's fascination with the occult was practical as well as theoretical. Perhaps James even believed that he himself was gifted with a form of second sight.

In addition to James's fascination with the second sight, which was clearly tied to the traumatic story of his mother's execution, James's interest in the occult may have had another outlet in the form of engagement with Freemasonry. Freemasonry developed in late medieval Scotland as a 'craft mystery' among practising stonemasons. Medieval craft guilds were drawn to biblical

---

[46] Maxwell-Stuart, *British Witch*, p. 198.
[47] Maxwell-Stuart, *British Witch*, p. 208; Schuchard, *Restoring the Temple of Vision*, p. 223.

stories that related to their own professions, sometimes staging mystery plays on the subject, and stonemasons were naturally drawn to the Old Testament's detailed specifications for the building of Solomon's Temple. However, the building of the Temple soon acquired layers of esoteric meaning as learned gentlemen who were not practising stonemasons began to be admitted to the craft mystery as 'accepted masons'. By the late sixteenth century, Scottish Freemasons were already deeply versed in Hermetic lore, and James VI may have been one of them. In 1589, when his council attempted to oppose the king's marriage with Anne of Denmark, James:

> ... caused one of his most familiar servants to deal secretly with some of the deacons of the craftsmen of Edinburgh, to make a mutiny against the Chancellor and Council, threatening to slay him in case the marriage with the King of Denmark's daughter were hindered, or longer delayed.[48]

Although the 'deacons' (apprentices) might have belonged to any craft guild, the Freemasons' superior organisation makes them likely suspects, especially as James's 'familiar servant' was probably his Master of Works, the stonemason William Schaw. On his visit to Denmark, James showed great interest in the 'occult architecture' of the great astronomer Tycho Brahe's 'Temple of Urania' on the island of Hven, and even patronised the local Danish stonemasons.[49] On his return to Scotland, James was approached by John Napier of Merchistoun (whose cousin Richard Napier was an English astrological

---

[48] Schuchard, *Restoring the Temple of Vision*, p. 216.
[49] Schuchard, *Restoring the Temple of Vision*, p. 217.

physician who preserved many of John Dee's manuscripts) about royal patronage for a revival of mathematical learning, perhaps inspired in part by Dee's unsuccessful approach to Queen Elizabeth for the establishment of an academy in 1570.[50] Napier had a number of Masonic interests, even speculating that James would be the king who would restore Solomon's Temple in Jerusalem.[51] It may be too simplistic to think of James as a Freemason in the modern sense (a member of a secret or semi-secret society); rather, the king may have thought of himself as the patron of Freemasonry as a distinctively Scottish institution.

The Demonologist King: James VI and I's English Reign

On 24 March 1603, according to legend, the River Tweed burst its banks and its waters joined with the River Pausyl at a site known as 'Merlin's grave', fulfilling a prophecy attributed to Thomas the Rhymer:

When Tweed and Pausyl meet at Merlin's grave,
 Scotland and England shall one monarch have.[52]

That day James VI of Scotland succeeded as James I of England, although he did not arrive in London until 7 May. James's interest in witchcraft was widely known, and his appearance in the English capital, heralded as the

---

[50] Schuchard, *Restoring the Temple of Vision*, p. 220.
[51] Schuchard, *Restoring the Temple of Vision*, p. 221.
[52] Pennecuik, *Works*, p. 253

fulfillment of ancient prophecies,[53] coincided with the publication of new editions of his *Daemonologie* and plays with witchcraft-related themes. Furthermore, between March and July 1604 the English Parliament brought forward a new Witchcraft Act to replace the old act of 1563. This flurry of activity suggests that James's English subjects may have been trying to curry favour with the new monarch by showing an interest in one of James's known preoccupations.[54] However, there is no evidence that James himself asked for or encouraged the 1604 act,[55] whose moving spirit was probably Chief Justice of the Court of Common Pleas, Edmund Anderson.[56]

James VI and I's preoccupation with witchcraft was far too complex to be characterised as a fear of witches. Indeed, there is no convincing evidence that James actually *was* afraid of witches; quite the opposite seems to have been true. It is unlikely that James's decision to examine the North Berwick witches in person meant that he did not believe in the power of witchcraft; rather, following the celebrated witch-hunting manual *Malleus maleficarum* ('Hammer of Witches'), James may have believed that it was impossible for witches to harm those who proceeded judicially against them – especially a divinely ordained king.[57] When the North Berwick witches asked the devil why they could not harm James, they received the reply

---

[53] Thomas, *Religion and the Decline of Magic*, pp. 494–6; Hart, *Art and Magic*, pp. 33–4.
[54] Maxwell-Stuart, 'King James's Experience of Witches', pp. 38–41; Maxwell-Stuart, *British Witch*, p. 199.
[55] Maxwell-Stuart, *British Witch*, pp. 42–4.
[56] Maxwell-Stuart, *British Witch*, pp. 200–1.
[57] Young, *Magic as a Political Crime*, p. 17.

(in French), 'He is a man of God'.[58] James's subjects did not always share the king's own confidence in his divine protection, however. In 2014, a bedroom built by Thomas Sackville, earl of Dorset for the king's visit to Knole House, Kent in 1606 was found to be covered in elaborate 'ritual protection marks' designed to trap any evil spirit that came down the chimney and into the fireplace.[59] Even if James did not fear witches, his subjects feared on his behalf.

James was anxious to be perceived not only as an expert on witchcraft but also as a wary and circumspect judge of witchcraft cases, and on his arrival in England he intervened personally in a case of bewitchment by examining Anne Gunter at Oxford in August 1605, a young woman who claimed to have become possessed as a result of witchcraft. Gunter confessed her fraud to the king.[60] James's behaviour, from a modern point of view, seemed to oscillate between credulity and scepticism when it came to the issue of witchcraft. During his English reign, James repeatedly sought to expose alleged witchcraft as fraud in individual cases. However, when Archbishop George Abbot suggested that there might not be such a thing as witchcraft on the grounds that the Bible did not specify what witchcraft was, the king openly rebuked the archbishop for his naivety in relying solely on Scripture. This incident took place during the course of the enquiry into the alleged bewitchment of Robert Devereux, 3rd earl of

---

[58] Clark, *Thinking with Demons*, p. 552.
[59] Patel, 'Treason, Plot, and Witchcraft', 23.
[60] Sharpe, *Bewitching of Anne Gunter*, p. xii; Elmer, *Witchcraft, Witch-Hunting and Politics*, p. 51.

Essex.[61] James allowed himself to be represented in court masques as a 'philosopher king'[62] – or even a benign magus, if Shakespeare's Prospero is to be understood as a representation of James.[63] Similarly, these masques presented Queen Anne of Denmark as an 'oppositional figure' to caricatures of witches as personifications of chaos.[64] Only legitimacy separated the dark magic of witches from the ritually projected magic of monarchy.[65]

All of this suggests that James upheld the reality of witchcraft and was content for his divine right to be understood and presented in occult terms. On the other hand, James removed the controversial word *mirabile* from the inscription on royal touchpieces, *a Domino factum est istud et est mirabile in oculis nostris* ('The Lord has done this and it is marvellous in our eyes'), suggesting he wanted to expunge any suggestion he was imbued with magical power in the ceremony of the royal touch.[66] These gold coins were touched by the king, given to sufferers from skin diseases and usually treasured as talismans. James may have seen himself as someone who possessed the biblical gift of 'discerning spirits' (cf. 1 John 4:1) – at least this is one way to make sense of his decision to pardon a number of convicted witches in the early years of his reign,[67] as well as his willingness to expose a man who claimed to preach sermons in his sleep as an

---

[61] Elmer, *Witchcraft, Witch-Hunting and Politics*, pp. 64–5.
[62] Maxwell-Stuart, *British Witch*, p. 209.   [63] Hart, *Art and Magic*, p. 10.
[64] See Dunn-Hensley, *Anna of Denmark*, pp. 45–74.
[65] Clark, *Thinking with Demons*, p. 552.
[66] Baker, 'The "Angel" of English Renaissance Literature', 88.
[67] Maxwell-Stuart, *British Witch*, p. 209; Schuchard, *Restoring the Temple of Vision*, p. 280.

imposter.[68] A self-proclaimed *expert* on the supernatural, by definition, could not accept every accusation of witchcraft at face value; universal credulity suggested ignorance, and James claimed to be in possession of specialist knowledge that could determine a witch's guilt. James aspired to be a wise and critical commentator on witchcraft, neither accepting all accusations as real nor exonerating everyone accused.

It is even possible that, if James did indeed identify himself as a Freemason, he saw himself as a magus using good magic against the witches who threatened him and his kingdoms.[69] In his *Daemonologie*, James used Masonic language to describe magic, writing of 'craft', 'entrances', apprenticeship and initiation. Uniquely among all writers on witchcraft and magic, James described trainee magicians as 'deacons', a term used by Freemasons.[70] It is clear from this that James saw witches and magicians as an organised 'order' antithetical to the Freemasons whose vocabulary he used – which in turn suggests that James may have seen himself as a Freemason. James extended his patronage to the astrological physician and self-proclaimed Rosicrucian, Robert Fludd (1574–1637),[71] and, in common with his medieval predecessors, the king saw himself as a latter-day Solomon, seeking after wisdom and prioritising grand building projects over the waging of wars.[72]

---

[68] Elmer, *Witchcraft, Witch-Hunting and Politics*, p. 51.
[69] Schuchard, *Restoring the Temple of Vision*, pp. 222–3.
[70] Schuchard, *Restoring the Temple of Vision*, pp. 227–8.
[71] Schuchard, *Restoring the Temple of Vision*, p. 307.
[72] Schuchard, *Restoring the Temple of Vision*, p. 401; Hart, *Art and Magic*, p. 26.

The Demonologist King: James VI and I's English Reign

On one interpretation, James and his successor, Charles I, saw themselves as 'Mercurian monarchs' after the pattern established by Edmund Spenser, who symbolically identified Elizabeth I with the element of mercury in his poetry as a way of proclaiming her power over nature.[73] A Mercurian monarch was, by definition, a Hermetic monarch. This was because 'Thrice-Great Hermes' (Hermes Trismegistus), the supposed author of the *Hermetica*, was identified with the Greek god Hermes and therefore with his Roman analogue Mercury, who in turn lent his name to the element so dear to the alchemists. Sir Francis Bacon proclaimed in 1605 that the king was 'invested of that triplicity which in great veneration was ascribed to ancient Hermes: the power and fortune of a King, the knowledge and illumination of a Priest, and the learning and universality of a Philosopher'. Fludd, no doubt remembering Bacon's praise, even addressed James in 1617 as *Ter Maximus* ('thrice-great') – the Latin equivalent of the Greek title *Trismegistus*;[74] although at a more prosaic level, James's association with triplicity simply derived from his rule of the three kingdoms of England, Scotland and Ireland.

Even if James did not see himself as a Hermetic monarch, his eldest son Henry, prince of Wales (1594–1612) certainly did. Henry was 'the prince *par excellence* of Renaissance hermetic science' and collected an extensive library of works by Trithemius, the Christian Kabbalist Johann Reuchlin and other Renaissance advocates of

---

[73] Hart, *Art and Magic*, pp. 25–9.
[74] Hart, *Art and Magic*, p. 26.

magical theurgy.[75] Henry commissioned the architect and garden-designer Salomon de Caus, who had worked for Dee and Kelley's patron Emperor Rudolf II in Prague, to design mechanical wonders for his garden at Richmond.[76] However, Henry's untimely death at the age of eighteen put an end to what might have been a Stuart court very open to learned Renaissance magic.

The Rosicrucian movement, which was centred on the claim that there existed a secret society of illuminated occult adepts, was central to the bid for the crown of Bohemia launched by the Elector Palatine Frederick and his wife Elizabeth Stuart, the eldest daughter of James VI and I. Frederick and Elizabeth portrayed themselves, in contrast to their devoutly Catholic competitor Archduke Ferdinand, as proponents of a mystical form of religious tolerance, and filled their court with alchemical and Hermetic imagery.[77] It is possible that some of the ideas of Hermetic and alchemical political transformation circulating in Bohemia in 1619, when Frederick and Elizabeth briefly became king and queen, represented the fruition of Dee's work in the 1580s.[78] If it was indeed true that Dee intellectually prepared the ground for an anti-Habsburg monarchy in Bohemia, then Dee had a significant posthumous effect on English influence in Europe – albeit briefly, since the Elector Palatine's regime was quickly overthrown, precipitating the Thirty Years' War.

[75] Strong, *Henry, Prince of Wales*, pp. 213–15.
[76] Hart, *Art and Magic*, pp. 92–100.
[77] Hart, *Art and Magic*, pp. 3–4.
[78] Yates, *Giordano Bruno*, p. 56.

Another respect in which Dee's legacy was posthumously honoured was in the promotion of Vitruvian architecture by James and Charles, something that Dee had advocated as early as 1570 as a path to transcendent wisdom.[79] In 1613, Inigo Jones, the first British Vitruvian architect, was appointed Surveyor of the King's Works, having previously worked on the stage designs of royal masques. Jones believed, following Dee, that architecture was an opportunity to realise a Platonic ideal of beauty and enable the mind to comprehend supreme truth.[80] The royal masques designed by Jones went beyond mere entertainment and became something like talismanic rituals designed to draw down benign astral influences on the court, with Jones acting as the presiding magus who understood the correspondences between earthly and heavenly things.[81] As much as masques and architecture, the temporary architecture and elaborate decorations that accompanied Stuart royal processions in London constituted 'a form of ceremonial magic centred on the image of the monarch as the sun'.[82]

Although Jones's architecture is conventionally described as classical, both Jones and the court he served believed that it embodied the architecture of King Arthur's supposed British empire, which James was reviving by uniting the island under one king.[83] Stonehenge, which according to Geoffrey of Monmouth had been transported from Ireland by Merlin and rebuilt on

---

[79] Hart, *Art and Magic*, p. 15.
[80] Hart, *Art and Magic*, p. 16.
[81] Hart, *Art and Magic*, pp. 17–20.
[82] Hart, *Art and Magic*, p. 162.
[83] Hart, *Art and Magic*, p. 36.

Salisbury Plain, provided the supreme evidence of Arthurian architecture.[84] The propagandists of Stuart monarchy also drew on the Kabbalah. James displayed a personal interest in the Kabbalah,[85] because it appeared to be consistent with Protestant enthusiasm for the Bible in its emphasis on the intrinsic power of the Word of God in the original Hebrew, then widely considered to be God's original language of creation. John Gordon, dean of Salisbury, informed James in 1605 that it could be proved from the Kabbalah that Britain was the land of God's chosen people, since the Hebrew words *brit*, *an* and *iah* (making *britaniah*) meant 'covenant', 'there' and 'God'.[86] The French author George Marcelline in his *Les trophées du roi Iacques I. de la Grande Bretaigne* (translated in 1610 as *The Triumphs of King James the First*) drew on Kabbalistic numerology to argue that James's position as the 107th king of Scotland meant that he would found the New Jerusalem.[87] Furthermore, in 1613 Michael Drayton argued that the learning of the ancient British druids exactly mirrored Kabbalistic wisdom.[88]

Sorcery and Corruption at the Jacobean Court

Between 1613 and 1628 the Stuart court was the scene of a number of scandals involving allegations of illicit magic.

---

[84] Hart, *Art and Magic*, pp. 52–9.
[85] On English Protestant interest in the Kabbalah see Jones, *Discovery of Hebrew*, pp. 168–74; Harkness, *John Dee's Conversations with Angels*, pp. 157–94. On King James's interest in the Kabbalah see Schuchard, *Restoring the Temple of Vision*, pp. 177–371.
[86] Hart, *Art and Magic*, p. 48.   [87] Hart, *Art and Magic*, p. 148.
[88] Hart, *Art and Magic*, p. 55.

Although no scandal directly involved the monarch himself, the cumulative reputational damage done to the monarchy by these revelations of sorcery was ultimately devastating. For Puritans and other opponents of the absolutist monarchical styles of James I and Charles I, the practice of magic at court was a sign of the decadence at the heart of the nation. Magical corruption would go on to be one of the motifs exploited by anti-royal propagandists in the years leading up to the English Civil War, and throughout that conflict. The practice of illicit magic close to the person of the monarch graphically demonstrated his inability to banish ungodliness from the realm.

In 1610, Simon Forman, the London astrological physician who had wrongly predicted that the earl of Essex's life would be spared in 1601, was drawn into a major court scandal. Frances Howard, countess of Essex despised her husband Robert Devereux, 3rd earl of Essex, whom she believed to be impotent. She was in love with James's favourite Robert Carr, viscount Rochester. Forman supplied Howard with love philtres, magical sigils and 'jellies', although whether these were designed to maintain Essex's impotence or to induce Carr to love Frances Howard is unclear.[89] Howard confided in Forman, but his death on 8 September 1611 left her without guidance and she turned to Mary Woods, a cunning-woman expert in fortune-telling and love magic. Meanwhile, Carr confided his affair with Frances Howard to his friend Sir Thomas Overbury.

---

[89] Cook, *Dr Simon Forman*, pp. 193–4.

Although initially sympathetic, Overbury began to encourage Carr to break off his relationship with Frances Howard, whose husband refused to countenance an annulment. Carr and Overbury were soon embroiled in a public row over the proposed annulment and other matters.[90] The annulment was finally obtained in September 1613 on the grounds of 'relative impotence', meaning that Essex was unable to have sexual intercourse with his wife, but was capable of doing so with other women.[91] The use of relative impotence as grounds for an annulment was strongly associated with the belief that a man could be rendered impotent by magic or witchcraft;[92] by admitting to these grounds for annulment, Essex inevitably cast suspicion on his wife for resorting to sorcery.

In 1613, James offered Overbury the chance to become a foreign ambassador. For his rude refusal Overbury was imprisoned in the Tower, where he died in September. Rumours soon spread that Overbury had been poisoned with white arsenic. When it emerged that one of the gaolers, Richard Weston, had acted as a go-between for Frances Howard in her communications with Mary Woods, Weston was arrested along with Anne Turner, the wife of the physician George Turner who had been Frances Howard's initial go-between with Simon Forman in 1610. James had only just conferred the title of earl of Somerset on Carr, and the newly married earl and count-

---

[90] Cook, *Dr Simon Forman*, pp. 198–9.
[91] Luthman, *Love, Madness, and Scandal*, p. 67.
[92] See Rider, *Magic and Impotence in the Middle Ages*, pp. 113–34.

ess of Somerset were also confined to the Tower.[93] The poisoning of Sir Thomas Overbury was of direct concern to James, since it involved a favourite whom the king had trusted to deal with sensitive foreign dispatches.[94]

The trial of Anne Turner, which began on 7 November 1615, brought to light sensational details of Simon Forman's magical dealings with Frances Howard and other ladies of the court. The indictment against Turner charged that she had introduced Howard to Simon Forman, 'that by force of magic, he should procure the now Earl of Somerset, then Viscount Rochester, to love her'.[95] Obscene lead effigies and other outlandish objects, including a piece of a dead child's skin and a wax effigy were displayed as exhibits in court, exciting such curiosity that the crowd in the public gallery moved forward to view them. Hearing a loud crack (presumably in the timbers of the flimsy gallery), the spectators feared that 'the Devil had been present and grown angry to have his own workmanship showed by such as were not his own scholars'. Of greater political import, however, was a list discovered by Forman's wife after his death which contained details of 'which ladies loved which gentleman at Court'.[96] Forman was alleged to have required those who wanted to make use of his services as a love magician to write their names in a book, an act that had strong resonances of a diabolic pact.[97]

---

[93] Cook, *Dr Simon Forman*, pp. 200–1.
[94] Cook, *Dr Simon Forman*, p. 198.
[95] Quoted in Bellany, 'Mistress Turner's Deadly Sins', 186.
[96] Cook, *Dr Simon Forman*, pp. 202–3.
[97] Kassell, *Medicine and Magic*, p. 170.

Although Coke called Turner a 'witch' and 'sorcerer' in passing sentence, she was executed not for witchcraft but for her complicity in the poisoning of Overbury.[98] The earl and countess of Somerset were also put on trial and found guilty, but not executed. The pair were confined to the Tower and not released until 1622. The 'Overbury Plot', especially the testimony of Anne Turner, threatened to expose a dark web of love magic at the Jacobean court, but it would not be the last intrusion of allegations of magic into the court. In 1619, James's Latin Secretary, Sir Thomas Lake (1561–1630), found his family in trouble after his wife and daughter were placed on trial for slandering Robert Cecil's wife, the countess of Exeter. The pair were accused of forging a letter in which the countess confessed that she tried to poison Lake's daughter, Lady Ros. Lake employed a schoolmaster named Peacock 'to infatuate the King's judgement by sorcery', in a clear case of magical treason. Unusually, James adjudicated the case personally in Star Chamber and imposed large fines on the Lake family.[99] The king's personal involvement is an indication that he took court scandals of this kind very seriously and believed they impinged on his royal reputation.

In 1621, Frances Coke, the wife of John Villiers, viscount Purbeck, separated from her husband. John Villiers was the brother of James's foremost favourite at the time, George Villiers, duke of Buckingham (1592–1628), who was the most influential man in the kingdom. Buckingham was alarmed when his brother began

---

[98] Cook, *Dr Simon Forman*, pp. 203–4.
[99] Young, *Magic as a Political Crime*, pp. 167–9.

suffering bouts of insanity, and when Frances became pregnant by Sir Robert Howard, Buckingham became convinced that she was attempting to work sorcery against him and his brother John with the help of a notorious magician, John Lambe (1546–1628).[100] Lambe was a convicted witch and rapist of very unsavoury reputation, who had obtained a royal pardon for rape, partly because he claimed to know the location of lost royal jewels, as well as claiming to have new intelligence about the Gunpowder Plot.[101] Early in 1625, Frances Coke was put on trial for adultery in an ecclesiastical court, with some witnesses stating that Lambe had made 'pictures of wax' for Coke as well as facilitating trysts between her and Howard.[102] Buckingham pressured Lambe and another magician, Humphrey Frodsham, to admit to harmful magic but they refused to do so, meaning that the accusations of sorcery against Frances Coke were eventually dropped from her trial.[103]

Buckingham's anxiety about his brother led him to ask his personal chaplain, William Laud (the future archbishop of Canterbury), whether resorting to 'not natural medicine' to cure his brother was lawful.[104] Buckingham's concern about magic in the case of the countess of Somerset was ironic, given that rumours of both sodomy and witchcraft swirled around Buckingham throughout

---

[100] Luthman, *Love, Madness, and Scandal*, p. 86.
[101] Bellany, 'Murder of John Lambe', 58; McConnell, 'Lambe, John', pp. 296–7.
[102] Bellany, 'Murder of John Lambe', 59; Luthman, *Love, Madness, and Scandal*, p. 86.
[103] Luthman, *Love, Madness, and Scandal*, p. 87.
[104] Gaskill, 'Witchcraft, Politics, and Memory', 302.

his period as a royal favourite of both James I and Charles I.[105] Beyond the court, Buckingham was 'infamous for his frequent consultations with the ring-leaders of witches',[106] and a servant of the duke was said to have remarked that 'the duke need never fear Parliament or doubt the king's favour, while he wore that he had on himself'.[107] An amulet given to Buckingham by an Irish magician named Pierce Butler was rumoured to give Buckingham control over the king.[108]

One libel went even further, alleging that Lambe conjured a demon to serve as a spectral double of Buckingham to go into battle against the Spanish on the Île de Ré while the real duke hid in the hold of his ship among coils of rope.[109] However, the most damaging accusation of magic against Buckingham was that, in 1625, he and his mother Mary Villiers, countess of Buckingham, had murdered King James by poison.[110] These accusations were not enough, however, to prevent Buckingham becoming as influential a figure at the court of Charles I as he had been with Charles's father.

Towards an Occult Revolution

In spite of Buckingham's belief that John Lambe had been working magic against him on behalf of Viscountess Purbeck, by 1626 Lambe was rumoured to be in

---

[105] Perry, 'Politics of Access', p. 1059.
[106] Bellany, 'Murder of John Lambe', 60.
[107] Perry, 'Politics of Access', p. 1059n.
[108] Bellany, 'Murder of John Lambe', 62.
[109] Bellany, 'Murder of John Lambe', 60.
[110] Bellany and Cogswell, *Murder of King James I*, p. 185.

Buckingham's employ. On one occasion, Lambe supposedly raised a supernatural mist on the Thames in front of Buckingham House.[111] Amid rising tensions, Lambe was killed by a London mob on 14 June 1628 and the hated Buckingham was assassinated not long after, on 23 August. The two events were later connected by prophecy and omen; a woman named Eleanor Davies predicted that Buckingham would die in August, and on the day of Lambe's death Buckingham was supposedly struck in the face and a portrait of him fell off a wall.[112] The assassinations of both men took place at a time of constitutional crisis, when Charles I was attempting to use his royal authority to extract forced loans to fund a war against Spain instead of levying taxation via Parliament.[113] The king, although he observed that John Lambe was a 'vicious fellow', was disturbed by the sorcerer's assassination and ordered an inquiry into the disorder that led to Lambe's murder, eventually fining the City of London.[114]

The accusations of magic levelled against Buckingham and his acolyte John Lambe reflected public disquiet with the Stuart regime, but they also served the important purpose of exculpating the king himself from wrongdoing. If the king was bewitched or under magical influence, he could not be held responsible for his actions or those of his government.[115] This was the 'face saving'

---

[111] Young, *Magic as a Political Crime*, p. 174.
[112] Bellany, 'Murder of John Lambe', 67–8.
[113] Bellany, 'Murder of John Lambe', 45.
[114] Bellany, 'Murder of John Lambe', 40–1.
[115] Bellany, 'Murder of John Lambe', 62.

function of magic and witchcraft, which excused bad behaviour and maintained the illusion of the stable hierarchy that mattered so much to early modern people.[116] Allegations of sorcery were thus a political device for those who wanted to oppose the government without appearing disloyal to the king. Buckingham's assassination, in the words of one libel, delivered the kingdom from 'magic thraldom',[117] since the wizard Lambe had controlled the duke, while the duke controlled the king.

If people believed that the deaths of Buckingham and his 'wizard' John Lambe would end Charles's abuse of power they were mistaken. Charles dissolved Parliament in March 1629 and ruled without it for the next eleven years. During Charles's personal reign the 'quasi-sacerdotal' rite of royal touching for scrofula began to appear in some editions of the Prayer Book, as Charles sought to preside like a sort of 'universal bishop' over the church.[118] However, until the 1640s Charles was reluctant to actually exercise the royal touch, perhaps because he feared public disorder, and this resulted in the appearance of some rival healers who claimed to cure disease in a similar fashion.[119] Charles finally revived royal touching in the 1640s, fearful that his power was slipping away, but it proved too late to reinvigorate the magic of monarchy.[120] For Puritans, the flourishing of witchcraft throughout the land vindicated their belief in the decay of church and state and the growth of ungodliness; by the same token,

---

[116] Thomas, *Religion and the Decline of Magic*, p. 643.
[117] Bellany, 'Murder of John Lambe', 70.
[118] Turrell, 'Ritual of Royal Healing', 30–1.
[119] Elmer, *Witchcraft, Witch-Hunting and Politics*, p. 78.
[120] See Richards, 'His Nowe Majestie', 86–94.

Charles's administration was unwilling to countenance witch trials because they undermined the idea that England was an ordered and godly nation under Charles's rule.[121]

Charles was perhaps more concerned with his image than any other English king,[122] and like his father he used masques and court ceremonial to present himself as a benevolent magus.[123] In one masque performed in January 1640 Charles's 'secret wisdom' magically repelled the personifications of Discord,[124] at a time when rebellion in Scotland was making it impossible for Charles to maintain his personal rule. Charles may even have believed that carefully constructed masques served, like talismans, to draw down forces of order and protect the realm.[125] Yet this attempt to solve problems by magic 'gave the Caroline Court an insularity and air of blind invincibility' which increasingly made open conflict look inevitable.[126] This mood spread throughout the country, with one man reporting in February 1639 that even the fairies were training with pikes and muskets near Knaresborough in Yorkshire.[127] In February, Charles was finally forced to summon Parliament in an effort to raise money for a campaign against the Scottish rebels. Ultimately, Parliament proved too strong for Charles, who fled the capital and raised his standard against

---

[121] Elmer, *Witchcraft, Witch-Hunting and Politics*, pp. 84–5.
[122] Hart, *Art and Magic*, p. 4.
[123] Turrell, 'Ritual of Royal Healing', 75–6.
[124] Schuchard, *Restoring the Temple of Vision*, p. 443.
[125] Hart, *Art and Magic*, p. 12.
[126] Hart, *Art and Magic*, p. 190.
[127] Elmer, *Witchcraft, Witch-Hunting and Politics*, p. 88.

Parliament in August 1642. England's Civil War had begun.

The outbreak of war intensified attempts by the supporters of Parliament to associate Royalism with popery, witchcraft and magic. He had already been dead for well over a decade, but the memory of John Lambe and his relationship with Buckingham was recycled as 'one of the blackest stains' on England's recent history. A 1641 pamphlet portrayed the Church of England as a ship manned by Archbishop Laud and the bishop of Ely, Matthew Wren, with 'Dr Lamb' between them,[128] and Laud was openly accused of conjuration by Puritans in the years leading up to the Civil War.[129] Puritans wielded the old sixteenth-century Protestant 'Catholicism as magic' polemic against Archbishop Laud and other 'Laudian' bishops who were attempting to enhance the liturgical worship of the Church of England. John Cosin, the future bishop of Durham, was accused of imitating 'necromancers and sorcerers' by insisting on facing east to celebrate holy communion, while a Puritan minister condemned the 1559 *Book of Common Prayer* as 'nothing but a piece of conjuration'. Another man at Earls Colne in Essex even 'swam' the Prayer Book like a suspected witch and destroyed it after he discovered it floated.[130] In East Anglia, during the great witch-hunt of 1645–47, the most intense activity focussed on areas politically dominated by

---

[128] Gaskill, 'Witchcraft, Politics, and Memory', p. 303.
[129] Elmer, *Witchcraft, Witch-Hunting and Politics*, p. 104.
[130] Elmer, *Witchcraft, Witch-Hunting and Politics*, pp. 102–3.

Catholics or 'high church' followers of Archbishop Laud.[131]

One of the more substantial accusations against Laud was his use of 'Solomonic ceremonies' at the reconsecration of St Paul's Cathedral in 1633.[132] However, it was the fact that Laud had been Buckingham's chaplain at the time Buckingham was supposedly patronising Lambe that rendered the connection between Laud and sorcery plausible in the popular imagination. Yet the details scarcely mattered; by the 1640s Lambe was a symbolic figure who embodied the conjunction of witchcraft, popery and corrupt court politics. In Puritan eyes, 'Magic . . . became the corollary of absolutism, the ultimate sign of absolute power'.[133]

In this propaganda battle Laudians gave as good as they got. Matthew Wren, the Laudian bishop of Ely, was reported to have condemned the Puritan practice of extempore prayer as being 'as bad to him as a Spell or a Charm [and] must not be used upon any Occasion', while one Essex clergyman denounced his Puritan congregation as 'no better than Witches or Devils' for refusing to kneel at the altar rails for holy communion.[134] Allegations of witchcraft and magic were 'weaponised' as never before in the 1640s by both sides in the English Civil War. In April 1644, Edmund Staunton preached before Parliament that Royalists could be expected to hire magicians to curse the supporters of Parliament:

---

[131] Elmer, *Witchcraft, Witch-Hunting and Politics*, pp. 123–4.
[132] Hart, *Art and Magic*, pp. 106–7.
[133] Hart, *Art and Magic*, p. 191.
[134] Elmer, *Witchcraft, Witch-Hunting and Politics*, p. 91.

The enemy relies much upon this art .... [T]here is yet one sin more they much lean upon, Magic and Witchcraft; Balaam must be hired to curse Israel: and if Witches and Wizards have any power in their black art, now is a time for them to drive a full trade.[135]

Confirmation that Royalists were indeed employing witches as a weapon of war was apparently received in 1645 when a pamphlet reported that witches convicted at Bury St Edmunds as part of Matthew Hopkins's East Anglian witch-hunt had been serving in the royal army.[136] James More of Halesworth, Suffolk, confessed that he had 'returned his imp Nan to his sister Everard to send with others to P[rince] R[upert]', presumably to aid the Royalist war effort.[137] Mary Skipper of Copdock, Suffolk, confessed to giving one imp to her son, which 'he had in the army, being resolved to go to the King's party with it'.[138] However, the most politically charged witchcraft accusation was that made against the vicar of Brandeston in Suffolk, John Lowes. Lowes was hated locally for being a 'non-preaching' parson sympathetic to Laudian ritualism.[139]

Lowes was accused of sending out an imp to sink a newly built ship that he spotted while preaching at Landguard Fort.[140] The allegation echoed the charges against the North Berwick witches in 1589 as well as the well-known story that the Egyptian king and sorcerer

---

[135] Quoted in Elmer, *Witchcraft, Witch-Hunting and Politics*, p. 106.
[136] Gaskill, *Witchfinders*, p. 166.
[137] Ewen, *Witchcraft and Demonianism*, p. 294.
[138] Ewen, *Witchcraft and Demonianism*, p. 297.
[139] Gaskill, *Witchfinders*, pp. 138–44.
[140] Ewen, *Witchcraft and Demonianism*, pp. 291–2.

Nectanebus used to sink ships by creating models of them in wax and submerging them (although Lowes was accused of sending out his imps to sink ships, without the need for such sympathetic magic).[141] Similar stories had circulated around the time of Prince Charles's return from Spain in October 1623, where the prince had been attempting to secure a marriage to the Spanish Infanta. Charles had faced 'a most tempestuous and cruel storm ... the like having not been seen in them parts before, in so much as it is thought the Witches or devils of Spain were in action'.[142]

In 1643, a woman believed to be a witch, who was supposed to have walked on water and prophesied against the Parliamentarian army, was summarily shot by Parliamentarian soldiers after the battle of Newbury. Then, in June 1644, the Royalist besiegers of Lyme Regis were reported to have 'procured a witch, who had undertaken to fire the ... houses; and ... to sink the Lord Admiral's squadron of ships, by devilish art and practice'.[143] In 1644, Royalists attributed the lengthy siege of Wardour Castle to the witchcraft of the Puritan minister Robert Balsom, who was inside the besieged garrison.[144] Yet the most extreme 'weaponisation' of accusations of witchcraft occurred in June 1645 after the Parliamentarian victory at Naseby. Around a hundred female camp followers of the Royalist army were mas-

---

[141] Page, *Magic in Medieval Manuscripts*, p. 21.
[142] Elmer, *Miraculous Conformist*, p. 134, n. 60.
[143] Elmer, *Witchcraft, Witch-Hunting and Politics*, p. 112.
[144] Thomas, *Religion and the Decline of Magic*, p. 645; Elmer, *Witchcraft, Witch-Hunting and Politics*, p. 113.

sacred after the battle and others had their faces mutilated, ostensibly on the grounds that they were Irish witches who had been seen flying through the air from one side of the Royalist army to the other.[145] Irish Catholics were widely suspected of witchcraft by English Parliamentarians.[146] However, this may have been a retrospective excuse for a massacre that was perpetrated as revenge for Catholic attacks on Protestant settlers in Ireland.

Accusations of witchcraft were most often an expression of local rather than national political concerns, but the largest witch-hunt in English history, conducted in East Anglia by Matthew Hopkins and John Stearne between 1645 and 1647, can only be adequately explained by the politicisation of witchcraft in the period.[147] In East Anglia, the dominant view among the clergy and gentry was in favour of the central imposition of presbyterian church government; many of those accused of witchcraft opposed this orthodoxy, either on account of their continued adherence to episcopacy or their association with Puritan independents. In Kent the situation was reversed, and radical sectaries in the 1650s levelled witchcraft accusations against those in favour of religious uniformity.[148] The trial of Anne Bodenham at Salisbury in 1653, a cunning-woman who admitted to having been an apprentice of John Lambe in the 1620s, was especially politically charged because it revealed sensational details about the

---

[145] Stoyle, *Soldiers and Strangers*, pp. 139–40.
[146] Elmer, *Witchcraft, Witch-Hunting and Politics*, p. 107.
[147] Elmer, *Witchcraft, Witch-Hunting and Politics*, p. 115.
[148] Elmer, *Witchcraft, Witch-Hunting and Politics*, p. 144.

supposed 'murder' of James I.[149] Furthermore, England's annexation of Scotland in 1652 was justified by some English commentators on account of the barbarism of the Scots, shown by their fear of witchcraft. However, there is little sign that witch-hunting declined in Scotland during the period of occupation, and the English administrators of the country continued to be concerned about it.[150]

Motifs of witchcraft and magic were deployed as war propaganda,[151] such as the Parliamentarian claim that the Royalist commander, Prince Rupert of the Rhine, was a witch assisted by a familiar in the form of his dog, Boy.[152] Naturally, when Boy was shot at the battle of Marston Moor in 1644 it was widely rumoured that the Parliamentarian soldier who did it had been skilled in necromancy.[153] According to one Royalist in 1657, Cromwell 'came by hearing of all things contrived against him ... by witchcraft or familiarity with the Devil',[154] and it was widely rumoured among Royalists that Cromwell made a pact with a devil before the battle of Worcester in 1651.[155] Cromwell began the siege of Drogheda and won the battles of Dunbar and Worcester on the same date, 3 September – the same date on which, in 1658, Cromwell died in the midst of a storm. All this was clear

[149] Elmer, *Witchcraft, Witch-Hunting and Politics*, pp. 154–5.
[150] Elmer, *Witchcraft, Witch-Hunting and Politics*, pp. 156–8.
[151] Elmer, *Witchcraft, Witch-Hunting and Politics*, p. 70.
[152] Stoyle, *Black Legend of Prince Rupert's Dog*, pp. 1–4.
[153] Gaskill, *Witchfinders*, p. 149.
[154] Elmer, *Witchcraft, Witch-Hunting and Politics*, p. 154.
[155] Elmer, *Witchcraft, Witch-Hunting and Politics*, p. 643.

evidence, to some Royalists, that the Lord Protector had sold his soul to the devil.[156] Furthermore, Royalists blamed an anonymous witch for advising Cromwell to put Charles I on trial for treason,[157] and Royalist propaganda even personified Parliament as a witch who was unable to recite the Lord's Prayer and the Creed.[158] Royalists did not hesitate to blame the epidemic of witchcraft apparently exposed by Matthew Hopkins in Suffolk and Essex on those counties' allegiance to the Parliamentarian cause.[159]

Astrological almanacs claiming to predict the course of the war were a crucial component of the propaganda war for both Parliamentarians and Royalists.[160] William Lilly (1602–81) had set up practice in London in 1633 at a time when there was very little knowledge of practical astrology in the capital. Like many astrologers, including Dee and Forman, Lilly was also a practitioner of ritual magic. Indeed, Lilly's interest in magic was initially sparked by a talisman made by Forman. Although Lilly always denied he was a magician, 'He used magic as an intellectual tool to further his political and medical interests'.[161] Lilly consciously identified himself with Merlin, and obtained from his friend and fellow magician Elias Ashmole a translation of the prophecies of Merlin, which he would use in the 1660s to justify his change of heart in deciding to support Charles II.[162]

[156] Quaife, *Godly Zeal and Furious Rage*, p. 151.
[157] Young, *Magic as a Political Crime*, pp. 185–6.
[158] Elmer, *Witchcraft, Witch-Hunting and Politics*, pp. 95–6.
[159] Clark, *Thinking with Demons*, p. 557.
[160] Capp, *England's Culture Wars*, p. 66.
[161] Timbers, *Magic and Masculinity*, p. 52.
[162] Lawrence-Mathers, *True History*, pp. 93–4.

Lilly's astrological medicine treated the important Parliamentarian leader Bulstrode Whitelocke (1605–75), who would later serve briefly as Lord President of the English Council of State, gaining Lilly an important and influential ally in government. In 1644, Lilly published the almanac *Merlinus Anglicus Junior* ('The Younger English Merlin'), which was initially censored but later reissued in unabridged form. In 1645, Lilly's second almanac successfully predicted the Parliamentarian victory at Naseby and discredited the rival Royalist astrologer Sir George Wharton.[163] Wharton was later arrested in November 1649 for attacking Parliament in an astrological almanac and only narrowly escaped being executed for treason.[164]

As the title of his almanac suggests, Lilly revived the time-honoured English tradition of ascribing prophecies to Merlin and other prophetic figures from the past. Thomas Heywood argued in his *Life of Merlin* (1641) that Merlin had been a Christian, and repeated the claim made by John Bale a century earlier that Merlin predicted the Reformation.[165] Lilly made skilful use of astrological signs to prophesy the end of the Stuart monarchy. On 19 November 1644, the birthday of Charles I, an atmospheric halo visible in London made it appear that there were three suns in the sky (a phenomenon known as parhelia or 'sundogs'). The phenomenon occurred at the same location in the constellation Sagittarius where a 'great conjunction' had occurred in 1603, signifying the

---

[163] Curry, 'Lilly, William', p. 796.
[164] Capp, *England's Culture Wars*, p. 60.
[165] Thomas, *Religion and the Decline of Magic*, p. 486.

beginning of the House of Stewart's English rule. Using this phenomenon and a forthcoming solar eclipse on 11 August 1645, Lilly argued that Charles's days were numbered and implied that the king would die a violent death.

Lilly did not hesitate to make use of more traditional forms of political prophecy as well as technical astrological prognostications.[166] He was so successful as an occult propagandist that Royalists even attempted to kidnap him in a bid to silence the astrologer.[167] On one occasion, at the siege of Colchester in 1648, Lilly was even summoned to encourage Parliamentarian troops. Meanwhile, the Royalist astrologer John Humphrey, who was inside Colchester, confidently predicted a Royalist victory.[168] However, the radicalism of Lilly and other astrologers extended beyond just criticising monarchy; it included calls for the overthrow of all forms of hierarchy and even the abolition of religion itself – an agenda just as abhorrent to the Parliamentarian government as it was to the Royalists.[169]

Although the Royalist astrologer George Wharton attempted to counter Lilly's predictions with his own,[170] other Royalist pamphleteers ridiculed judicial astrology altogether and published spoof almanacs, calling Lilly Parliament's 'wizard-general'.[171] In this respect there was a difference between Parliamentarian and Royalist

---

[166] Thomas, *Religion and the Decline of Magic*, pp. 488–90.
[167] Curry, 'Lilly, William', p. 796.
[168] Thomas, *Religion and the Decline of Magic*, p. 406.
[169] Capp, *England's Culture Wars*, p. 81.
[170] Capp, *England's Culture Wars*, p. 75.
[171] Capp, *England's Culture Wars*, p. 77.

occult propaganda. Parliamentarians were more likely to be afraid of witchcraft, while Royalists accused their opponents of witchcraft while also ridiculing excessive belief in the supernatural. Furthermore, the more conservative Parliamentarians (especially those who supported a presbyterian religious settlement) increasingly came to see witch-hunting as an encouragement to the sectaries, who presented a greater danger than witches themselves. These Parliamentarian conservatives accordingly expressed their scepticism about witchcraft.[172] Other conservative Parliamentarians accused Baptist sectaries of being no better than witches because, like the witches of Continental demonology, Baptists required their adherents to renounce their original baptism.[173]

Lilly was not an uncritical supporter of the Commonwealth, and his 'astral republicanism' was tempered by the conviction that Charles I could live if he submitted to Parliament's demands. Lilly continued to take clients of all political hues throughout the conflict,[174] and became friends with the Royalist alchemist and natural magician Elias Ashmole. In 1647, Lady Jane Whorewood even approached him for advice on a hiding place for Charles I if the king could be freed from Carisbrooke Castle on the Isle of Wight. In 1653, Lilly's almanacs were censored after he criticised Parliament, and he was the target of attacks from Puritans who disapproved of astrology.[175] However, Lilly's closeness to the

---

[172] Elmer, *Witchcraft, Witch-Hunting and Politics*, pp. 158–74.
[173] Elmer, *Witchcraft, Witch-Hunting and Politics*, pp. 128–9.
[174] Thomas, *Religion and the Decline of Magic*, pp. 371–4.
[175] Curry, 'Lilly, William', p. 796.

Parliamentarian regime meant that there were also sustained attacks against his reputation after the Restoration. Lilly was denounced in pamphlets as a fraud, a cunning-man, a sorcerer, a wizard and a worshipper of the devil.[176]

Conclusion

In the first half of the seventeenth century, Britain experienced the greatest political upheavals it had seen for two centuries. New ways of thinking challenged established hierarchies, and individuals found themselves (whether they wanted to or not) being forced to justify behaviour that would previously have been considered treason or rebellion. Occult traditions such as alchemy, astrology and magic gave many people the intellectual framework in which the politically unthinkable became possible. Astrological prophecies vindicated change by portraying it as immutably written in the stars, or in the prophetic books of ancient sages such as Merlin. What was apparently new and radical could be portrayed as timeless. Old magical scandals were revived in order to discredit the existing order as corrupt and ungodly, while rumours of the military deployment of witches tapped into people's darkest fears.

The Stewart dynasty's long relationship with the occult arts, which began when Stewart monarchs were ruling Scotland alone, came to a crisis in the reign of Charles I. The murder of John Lambe, allegedly the personal wizard of the king's favourite, represented an extreme politicisation of magic as an instrument of an evil and corrupt court

---

[176] Timbers, *Magic and Masculinity*, p. 54.

against the godly population. On the outbreak of Civil War in 1642, politicisation became weaponisation: accusations of witchcraft aimed against the forces of both crown and Parliament became part of the political armoury of both sides, with deadly consequences for individuals such as John Lowes and the female camp followers of the Royalist army at Naseby. The Civil War represented the failure of attempts by James I and Charles I to use occult propaganda to their own advantage. James's Masonic-Solomonic pretensions and Charles's Hermetic masques proved powerless against the force of rumour and the misuse of sorcery (real or rumoured) by members of the court, which produced a series of damaging scandals. However, it is impossible to associate accusations of magic exclusively with one side in the Civil War; the situation was far more complex than godly Puritans deploying anti-magical rhetoric against Royalists. The role of William Lilly demonstrates that Parliamentarians were willing to deploy occult knowledge against their adversaries too, rendering themselves vulnerable to the charge that Lilly was Parliament's 'wizard general'. Yet as subsequent events would show, it proved to be just as easy to represent the Restoration of the monarchy in occult terms as its downfall.

5
Politics and the Decline of Magic, 1649–1714

In 1684 William Boreman, a physician who also practised as an exorcist and had a strong interest in magic and witchcraft, received a fine for saying that Charles II's brother, the duke of York, was 'a great wizard ... and that he rides about at night in fiery chariots to torment souls, and [is] preparing for a field of blood [with] his witchcraft [and that he] will lay the nation in blood and Popish slavery'.[1] Boreman's mixture of prophetic denunciation and traditional witchcraft libel is a reminder of the extent to which suspicions of witchcraft were entangled with religious belief at the end of the seventeenth century. Both were entangled with politics – in this case, the struggle between the Tory supporters of royal prerogative and the Whig supporters of parliamentary sovereignty. The conflict between Tories and Whigs was, in turn, rooted in the older clash between Royalists and Parliamentarians in the Civil War. The Whigs were the eventual victors, installing a constitutional monarchy definitively beholden to Parliament on the death of Queen Anne in 1714. In hindsight, many later historians tended to view the proponents of constitutional reform as representatives of the Enlightenment, replacing the irrationality of absolutism with the rational idea of an

[1] Elmer, *Witchcraft, Witch-Hunting and Politics*, p. 199.

accountable ruler. Yet the wild allegations levelled against the future James II by the Whig Boreman show that belief in magic cannot be linked simplistically with any one political tendency. There was no straightforward dichotomy between 'superstitious' conservatives and 'rational' political reformers in the second half of the seventeenth century. The reality was more complex.

The execution of Charles I in 1649 was a watershed in British (and arguably European) history. It was an unprecedented event. Kings had been killed before, sometimes in the most sordid of circumstances – but always in palace coups, in political assassinations or on the field of battle. A public, judicial execution of the king as a traitor was calculated to evacuate the sacredness and magic of monarchy, although for Royalists the set-piece death of Charles also gave him the perfect martyrdom. Thenceforth the country was divided between those anxious to restore the magic of monarchy and those keen to pursue a post-monarchical future. The 1650s saw unprecedented freedom of speech, religion and ideas. Occult traditions were an important part of the mix, inspiring the radical sectaries of the period and even influencing the course of political events.

The restoration of Charles II in 1660 resulted in the overthrow of many of the freedoms of the 1650s, but Charles was also compelled to accommodate some of the social changes of the Interregnum, making the 1660s 'the beginnings of a genuinely plural society'.[2] The restored Church of England, divided within itself, was unable to suppress entirely the 'speculative religion' that had

[2] Elmer, *Witchcraft, Witch-Hunting and Politics*, p. 174.

received so much encouragement from the freedoms of the Interregnum.[3] Furthermore, Charles himself was interested in the occult, patronising alchemists, rewarding magicians and taking control once more of astrological publications. Ever shadowed by his father's ignominious fate, Charles II was anxious to project an image of his quasi-magical power, and he touched more frequently for the king's evil than any other monarch in English history.

Charles II's failure to produce a legitimate child meant that the succession devolved upon his brother James, duke of York, an unpopular figure whose conversion to Catholicism did his reputation no favours with the majority of the country. At the end of the 1670s, a strand of radical Protestantism violently opposed to the accession of the duke of York produced a massive conspiracy theory, the so-called Popish Plot, which spawned in turn a parliamentary attempt to exclude the duke from the throne on the grounds of his faith (the Exclusion Crisis). When James II finally became king, his failure to convince the population at large of the benefits of religious toleration for Catholics and dissenters precipitated an invasion of England by the stadtholder of the Netherlands, James's nephew and son-in-law William of Orange, resulting in James's flight to France and the installation of William III and his wife Mary II (James's eldest daughter) as joint monarchs.

Throughout all of this political turmoil, occult traditions continued to play a role in the political life of the nation. Belief in occult ideas cannot be associated with one particular faction in the tumultuous events of

---

[3] Monod, *Solomon's Secret Arts*, p. 29.

seventeenth-century Britain, despite the attempts of some earlier historians to link it with radicalism.[4] Political conservatives such as Royalists and, later, Jacobites had their own reasons for engaging in occult practices, which were not necessarily the same as those of Interregnum radicals and Restoration Whigs. For political radicals, the potential of occult traditions to reconcile paradox rendered them a means of coming to terms with a dramatically changed political reality, while the emphasis on direct experience rather than received wisdom in some occult traditions chimed with the preoccupations of radical forms of Protestantism. For conservatives, by contrast, astrology, alchemy, prophecy and natural magic provided a reassuring connection with an ancient past and served to validate the institution of monarchy, encoding private political meanings that could not always be openly expressed.

However, the period between the execution of Charles I and the death of Queen Anne also witnessed the decline of official support for the persecution of accused witches and the dwindling of accusations of magical treason. A longing for stability after the chaos of the Civil War, and a lingering association between fear of witchcraft and religious and political fanaticism, may explain the reluctance of post-Restoration politicians and legislators to get involved with the issue of witchcraft (at least in England). Just as medieval Chinese emperors' persecution of sorcerers undermined their desired self-image as benevolent Confucian monarchs,[5] the presence of witchcraft in

---

[4] Mendelsohn, 'Alchemy and Politics in England', 31.
[5] Zhao, 'Political Uses of Wugu Sorcery', 144.

Restoration England undermined the legitimacy and credibility of the regime, so it was better to ignore witches than to persecute them. The decline of government involvement in the punishment of occult crimes did not necessarily reflect a decline of belief in magic and witchcraft; rather, what took place was a dissociation of supernatural crimes from politics. The practice of magic lost none of its stigma, but witchcraft was relegated to being a crime exclusively against individuals rather than an offence against the state.[6]

An Occult Republic, 1649–1660

Following the execution of Charles I on 30 January 1649, England was formally a republic for eleven years until 1660. The whole period is sometimes referred to as the Commonwealth, although the period between 1653 and 1660 is often called the Protectorate; another term for the entire period is the Interregnum. The religious views of supporters of the new English republic were diverse, ranging from orthodox Calvinist presbyterianism and theologically conservative independent congregationalism to a variety of radical sects who adopted non-traditional interpretations of the Bible and even accepted the validity of personal illumination alongside or even ahead of Scripture. In one sense, the collapse of Stuart monarchy meant the end of a court politics sustained by Neoplatonic and Hermetic ideas and an occult national myth woven

---

[6] On the similar process of disassociation of magic and political crime that occurred in ancient China, see Zhao, 'Political Uses of Wugu Sorcery', 159–60.

around the figures of Merlin and King Arthur.[7] In another sense, however, the Civil War and the triumph of Parliament opened a Pandora's Box as far as popular knowledge of occult traditions was concerned. The breakdown of old orthodoxies meant that some were prepared to experiment with dangerous ideas hitherto forbidden, considered socially unacceptable, or confined to a learned elite.

The tight control the government had traditionally maintained on printing broke down in the 1650s, resulting in the virtual end of censorship. This enabled, among other things, the publication of books about magic, although their authors numbered both Royalists and Parliamentarians.[8] They included defences of 'good' magic such as Thomas Vaughan's *Magia Adamica* (1650),[9] as well as translations of previously illicit books such as Agrippa's *Three Books of Occult Philosophy* (translated by Robert Turner in 1651) and even the notorious pseudo-Agrippan *Fourth Book of Occult Philosophy* (translated by Turner in 1655).[10] By contrast, between 1621 and 1643 even pamphlet accounts of witchcraft had not appeared, probably because James's and Charles's bishops wanted to discourage witch-hunting as a Puritan preoccupation.[11] Witchcraft was always perceived as a sign of disorder, and its existence in the nation was therefore a potential rebuke to Charles's personal rule.[12]

---

[7] Hart, *Art and Magic*, p. 192.
[8] Mendelsohn, 'Alchemy and Politics', 33.
[9] Kassell, 'All was this land full-fill'd of faerie', 114–17.
[10] Young, *Magic as a Political Crime*, p. 183.
[11] Elmer, *Witchcraft, Witch-Hunting and Politics*, pp. 71–8.
[12] Elmer, *Witchcraft, Witch-Hunting and Politics*, p. 79.

In 1650, Parliament repealed the Act of Uniformity of 1559, which had required everyone to attend services of the Church of England, inaugurating a period of unprecedented religious liberty. The idea of religious toleration was strongly associated at this time with mystical beliefs, since it was generally only those who believed in truths transcending the dogmas of individual Christian denominations who were prepared to countenance the co-existence of a variety of beliefs. For the presbyterians and congregationalist independents who dominated the higher echelons of the Puritan Parliamentarian state, toleration was an opportunity to make the case for their brand of religion as the new official religion of England, and not a good in and of itself. Yet alchemists had long advocated a radical form of religious tolerance, believing that the division of Christendom brought about by the Reformation was an unnatural state of affairs that would be resolved only by an alchemical illumination transcending doctrinal divisions.[13] During the Interregnum, the learned Polish émigré, Samuel Hartlib (1600–62), advocated the establishment of a 'Solomon's House' for the sharing of all wisdom, after the model proposed in Francis Bacon's *New Atlantis* (1627). Hartlib received the support of many future fellows of the Royal Society,[14] and in 1649 his follower John Hall addressed Parliament on the need to advance learning in 'chymistry'.[15] Similarly,

---

[13] Janacek, *Alchemical Belief*, p. 163.
[14] Elmer, *Miraculous Conformist*, p. 143.
[15] Mendelsohn, 'Alchemy and Politics', 49.

the radical occultism of Paracelsus flourished for the first time in England during this period.[16]

Gerard Winstanley (1609–76), a leader of the 'True Levellers' or Diggers, who argued for political and social equality and began to occupy common land in 1649, was one of the radicals inspired by alchemical thought. He may have been influenced to think along alchemical lines by another Digger, William Everard, who had a reputation as a conjurer and was influenced in turn by the Behmenist minister John Pordage.[17] The natural magician Elias Ashmole was the patron of Pordage's living, and admired Pordage's knowledge of astronomy in spite of his political differences (Ashmole was a committed Royalist). However, Pordage was deprived from the ministry in 1654 for blasphemy and necromancy.[18] Pordage's 'communism' rejected the state, private property and even the family (his followers were expected to renounce sexual relations) on the basis of Jacob Boehme's theory of hermaphroditic genesis, in which God originally created a single sex.[19] Another Interregnum radical with an interest in alchemy, although he kept it concealed from all but his close friends, was the 'chronic conspirator' and Leveller John Wildman (c. 1621–93), who ended up as Postmaster General under Charles II.[20]

Winstanley considered the interaction of original sin, the four elements and the Holy Spirit to be an alchemical

---

[16] Rattansi, 'Paracelsus and the Puritan Revolution', 24–32.
[17] Timbers, *Magic and Masculinity*, p. 98; Mulder, *Alchemy of Revolution*, p. 65.
[18] Monod, *Solomon's Secret Arts*, p. 85.
[19] Mendelsohn, 'Alchemy and Politics', 39.
[20] Clark, *Goodwin Wharton*, pp. 71–4.

process, identifying human rebelliousness with 'masculine' sulphur and the elements with 'feminine' mercury.[21] Winstanley believed that the curse of death brought by Adam's disobedience caused human bodies to decay in the earth, thereby corrupting the entirety of material creation. The Holy Spirit was, for Winstanley, a purging alchemical fire that would purify mercury (the elements) from original sin (sulphur).[22] Winstanley believed that this purifying spirit had been released in 1649 and would soon bring an end to all conflict, resulting in the abolition of private property:[23]

[T]hese masculine powers of the poisoned flesh stand it out against the King of glory, till he cast them into the lake of fire, into his own spirit, by which they are tried, and being but chaff, and not able to endure, are burned, and consumed to nothing in the flame.[24]

Winstanley's belief in alchemy allowed him to come to terms with the Diggers' overthrow of the established hierarchy, because the political disruption of the 1640s could be interpreted in terms of God's alchemical purification of human nature.[25] That purification would result in a mystical union of spirit and matter that would end storms, earthquakes and other portents of divine displeasure.[26] Winstanley was neither a learned man nor (so far as we know) a practising alchemist; his use of alchemical

---

[21] Mulder, *Alchemy of Revolution*, pp. 54–6.
[22] Mulder, *Alchemy of Revolution*, p. 56.
[23] Mulder, *Alchemy of Revolution*, p. 57.
[24] Quoted in Mulder, *Alchemy of Revolution*, p. 59.
[25] Mulder, *Alchemy of Revolution*, p. 61.
[26] Mulder, *Alchemy of Revolution*, p. 62.

ideas and vocabulary is an indication of the extent to which this language had entered the common intellectual vernacular by the mid-seventeenth century, which can be attributed in large part to the spread of the mystical philosophy of Jacob Boehme (1575–1624). Although Boehme's writings were initially popularised in England by the mainstream Puritan lawyer John Sparrow – who wanted Charles I to read them – they were soon picked up by religious radicals including Henry Pinnell, William Erbery, Morgan Llwyd, John Webster, Lodowick Muggleton and the Quakers.[27]

The emphasis of alchemy – or more specifically its medical branch, iatrochymistry – on the possibility of universal panaceas and the indwelling of a divine principle in the human body meant that those who were steeped in this doctrine were open to radical notions of personal illumination.[28] Extreme theological and philosophical speculations did not always translate into revolutionary politics in practice, but it did not take long for opponents of the sectaries such as the Puritan theologian Richard Baxter to see occultism of any kind, which he traced back to 'Paracelsus a drunken Conjurer', as an existential threat to the Commonwealth.[29] Similarly, the presbyterian minister, Thomas Hall railed against the 'Familistical-Levelling-Magical' temper of the times.[30] In the 1650s, the prophecy of Mary Clary that the secret of the Philosophers' Stone would be generally known by

---

[27] Mendelsohn, 'Alchemy and Politics', 34–5.
[28] Mendelsohn, 'Alchemy and Politics', 37.
[29] Mendelsohn, 'Alchemy and Politics', 38.
[30] Quoted in Mendelsohn, 'Alchemy and Politics', 78.

1661 even led some radicals to plan a utopian colony in which the search for alchemical enlightenment could finally be realised.[31]

England's republic may have been a short-lived experiment, but it had one very important result that depended to a large extent on the influence of radical mystical thought. In 1656, the first Jews openly settled in England since Edward I's expulsion of all Jews from the country in 1290. Although the re-admission of the Jews to England was partly motivated by financial and mercantile considerations, there was also a strong religious element to the argument for re-admission, which drew on apocalyptic and occult beliefs. Although anti-Semitism had been rife in the Christian church since its early centuries, the Renaissance discovery of Hebrew studies gave rise to a great deal of enthusiasm for the Jewish Kabbalah, which was widely believed to be as old as Moses himself. As early as 1641, the Parliamentarian mathematician and natural philosopher John Wilkins reported that some said the Jewish Kabbalah encoded 'every secret that belongs to any art of science', although Wilkins himself remained sceptical of this claim.[32] If the Jews were the custodians of this secret source of knowledge, this strengthened the case for admitting them to England.

The first stirrings of interest in a Christian form of Kabbalah occurred in pre-Reformation England among a small group of Renaissance humanists. Interest in Kabbalah continued in Elizabeth's reign, albeit on a small scale. Alongside John Dee, the leading Catholic Sir

[31] Mendelsohn, 'Alchemy and Politics', 52.
[32] Schuchard, *Restoring the Temple of Vision*, p. 597.

Thomas Tresham explored the possibilities of Kabbalistic numerology for concealing his profession of the Catholic faith,[33] while a small community of exiled 'New Christians' (converted Jews) from Spain and Portugal in London may have explored Kabbalism.[34] It is possible that Jewish exiles from Iberia in the 1590s considered settling in England before they decided on Amsterdam as their destination.[35] At the Stuart court in the 1630s, apocalyptic Kabbalism was one of the influences that the regime's propagandists drew upon to proclaim the dawning of a 'Golden Age'.[36]

The English Revolution of the 1640s, with its strong religious emphasis on the Old Testament, was accompanied by apocalyptic expectations of the imminent end of the world, which some believed could occur only when the Jews were scattered to the ends of the earth. Furthermore, the Book of Revelation seemed to stipulate that the end of the world would come only after the salvation of 144,000 Jews, which led some Puritans to believe the conversion of Jews was an urgent priority. Some Puritans even went so far as to move to Amsterdam and convert to Judaism themselves, while John Tany, a religious radical whose writings drew on Agrippa and Jacob Boehme, claimed to be 'high priest of the Jews', sent to gather up the remnant of Israel in England. Tany attacked a doorkeeper in the House of

---

[33] Young, 'Sir Thomas Tresham', 155–68.
[34] Yates, *Occult Philosophy in the Elizabethan Age*, p. 111.
[35] Yates, *Occult Philosophy in the Elizabethan Age*, p. 113.
[36] Hart, *Art and Magic*, pp. 194–5.

Commons in 1655 after hearing that Oliver Cromwell was to be offered the crown.[37]

Menasseh ben Israel (1604–57), the Amsterdam rabbi who interceded with Cromwell for the return of the Jews to England, shared these apocalyptic expectations in a slightly different form. A follower of the influential Kabbalist Isaac Luria (1534–72), Menasseh ben Israel believed that the coming of the Messiah was imminent and might be hastened by meditation on the mysteries of the Hebrew alphabet.[38] Lurianic Kabbalism was concerned not so much with using mystical means to change history, but with hastening the end of history by achieving an occult understanding of the process by which creation came into being in the first place.[39] Luria believed that God required Jews to co-operate with him to achieve the restoration (*tikkun*) of all things to their primordial state, hastening the appearance of the Messiah and thereby the end of history.[40] The act of restoration was, in a sense, a magical process because it was dependent on the exercise of 'mystical intention' (*kawannah*) by individuals who directed the power of their wills towards the achievement of *tikkun*.[41] For a Lurianic Kabbalist such as Menasseh ben Israel, therefore, the return of the Jews to England would be achieved not just by negotiation but also by a form of directed magical intent. Indeed, the Lurianic Kabbalists' view of prayer was always in danger of

---

[37] Timbers, *Magic and Masculinity*, p. 98; Monod, *Solomon's Secret Arts*, pp. 84–5.
[38] Yates, *Occult Philosophy in the Elizabethan Age*, pp. 184–6.
[39] Scholem, *Major Trends in Jewish Mysticism*, pp. 245–6.
[40] Scholem, *Major Trends in Jewish Mysticism*, p. 274.
[41] Scholem, *Major Trends in Jewish Mysticism*, p. 275.

'degeneration into mechanical magic and theurgy'.[42] It is unlikely that Ben Israel regarded the return of the Jews to England as the result of magic; but it was, for Kabbalists, the outcome of *kawannah*, a special kind of directed prayer with the power to achieve real-world results.

The early Jewish settlers of 1656, although they were technically still without a legal basis to practice their religion, established a crucial foothold for non-Christian religion in England. The contemporary Sephardic Jewish community in Britain traces its origins directly to this seventeenth-century settlement. The integration of Jews into English society would lead, ultimately, to the political and social emancipation of Jews and other non-Christians, as well as weakening the case for restricting civil rights to Trinitarian Christians. The mystical speculations of Menasseh ben Israel and his supporters, therefore, produced results of profound significance for Britain's future as an open, tolerant society.

Restoring the Magic of Monarchy, 1660–1685

The proliferation of sects interested in occultism during the Interregnum produced something of a reaction against magic at the Restoration, and belief in magic was satirised at the time by poets and dramatists.[43] Yet Charles II's own approach to natural magic was positive. Desperate to revive the mystique of monarchy that had been fatally undermined by the public execution of his father in 1649, Charles made strenuous efforts to

---

[42] Scholem, *Major Trends in Jewish Mysticism*, p. 277.
[43] Monod, *Solomon's Secret Arts*, pp. 82–3.

reinvigorate the ceremony of royal touching for the king's evil. Charles was by far the most prolific of royal touchers, regularly touching 600 people in one ceremony,[44] and touching as many as 100,000 people during the course of his reign.[45] Furthermore, where Elizabeth, James and Charles I had discouraged a view of the ceremony as 'magical', Charles allowed this perception to creep back. One author of a pamphlet on the royal touch published in 1665, *The Excellency or Handy Work of the Royal Hand*, declared that 'when a man [i.e. the king] does that which another cannot do, we usually say *He conjures* ... that Magic is laudable, and lawful, where there is not *Potentia in nocendo sed restituendo* [not power to do harm, but to restore or cure]'.[46] Since this pamphlet got past the royal censors, its content is an indication that Charles's government was prepared to tolerate (if not endorse) the view that the king was performing natural magic.

Individuals who went to receive the royal touch sometimes sold the gold coin touched by the king as a magical charm,[47] and touchpieces were also swapped without monetary exchange. This was especially true of angels touched by Charles I, which were considered relics of the martyred king during and after the Interregnum and were eagerly shared by Royalists, adding an extra layer of supernatural power to an already magical object.[48] The transformation of touchpieces into exchangeable amulets

---

[44] Brogan, *Royal Touch*, p. 101.
[45] Elmer, *Miraculous Conformist*, p. 117.
[46] Quoted in Brogan, *Royal Touch*, p. 162.
[47] Turrell, 'Ritual of Royal Healing', 33.
[48] Baker, 'The "Angel"', 89. See also Toynbee, 'Charles I and the King's Evil', 1–14.

clearly implied the magical nature of the royal touch and undermined official statements that the royal touch was nothing more than a special form of prayer. However, like his father, Charles II was forced to contend with a rival practitioner of miraculous healing by touch. In 1666, an Irish Protestant landowner, Valentine Greatrakes (1629–83) arrived in London and began 'stroking' people suffering from various illnesses, including scrofula. Although Greatrakes had been involved with the Cromwellian regime in Ireland, his patrons were largely drawn from the scrupulously loyal Royalist establishment in both Ireland and England. Nevertheless, Greatrakes's claim to be able to cure the king's evil by touch was politically sensitive, and in February 1666 he was summoned to demonstrate his abilities to the king himself, who was less than impressed.[49]

Nevertheless, Greatrakes's supporters seized on his loyalism as evidence 'that all revelations were not fanatical'.[50] Maintaining the authenticity of Greatrakes was crucial for conformists who wanted to refute both materialists like Thomas Hobbes and the accusation that wonder-working was confined to the sectaries. Greatrakes was a hero for the 'anti-Sadducists', a movement of churchmen who were concerned that Interregnum sects such as Muggletonianism had undermined traditional belief in the afterlife and in disembodied spirits. For the anti-Sadducists, it was necessary to tread a fine line between the religious fanaticism associated with Puritanism and the 'atheism' of Hobbes and the

---

[49] Monod, *Solomon's Secret Arts*, p. 102.
[50] Elmer, *Miraculous Conformist*, p. 151.

libertines of the Restoration court. Court preachers did not pull their punches against the Puritans, portraying the Restoration as the literal exorcism of the nation from bewitchment by the 'state-witches' and 'state-wizards' of the Commonwealth, with Thomas Reeve declaring from the pulpit of Waltham Abbey in 1661 that 'The whole Land hath been possessed with evil spirits, and Westminster hall hath been a Demoniac'.[51] The rhetoric was even ceremonially enacted during Charles's coronation procession, when the king passed under a triumphal arch in which the personifications of Rebellion and Confusion appeared as hideous witches.[52]

Charles II took back control of astrological almanacs, requiring each one to be licensed by the astrologer George Wharton, who had suffered during the Interregnum for his Royalist prognostications.[53] Charles relied on Elias Ashmole for astrological advice on his dealings with Parliament, asking Ashmole to calculate the most propitious time to ask Parliament in person for money for the war against the Dutch, which he did on 27 October 1673.[54] The palmist Richard Saunders recommended in 1663 that the king should have no fewer than three permanent astrological advisers.[55] In 1669, Louis XIV, hearing from Charles's illegitimate son the duke of Monmouth that the English king was fond of astrologers, appointed a well-known French astrologer and alchemist, the Abbé Pregnani, as a diplomatic envoy

---

[51] Elmer, *Miraculous Conformist*, 120.
[52] Elmer, *Miraculous Conformist*, pp. 121–2.
[53] Capp, *England's Culture Wars*, p. 66.
[54] Thomas, *Religion and the Decline of Magic*, p. 371.
[55] Thomas, *Religion and the Decline of Magic*, p. 393.

to the English court. However, Charles was unimpressed when Pregnani failed to predict any winning horses on a visit to Newmarket with the king.[56] Pregnani was also supposed to be assisting the alchemists in Charles's personal laboratory, while in reality he was conducting secret diplomacy on behalf of Louis.[57]

The Exclusion Crisis of 1679–81, when Parliament attempted to exclude Charles's Catholic brother James from the succession to the throne, produced rival astrological prognostications from the pro- and anti-exclusionist parties.[58] The idea of astrological calculation as a treasonous act also persisted after the Restoration. In 1667, George Villiers, 2nd duke of Buckingham was accused of engaging the astrologer John Heydon to calculate the date of the king's death. Heydon was imprisoned in the Tower and used the opportunity to write tomes of Rosicrucian philosophy.[59] The astrologer John Gadbury was forced to deny that he had offered his services when, during the so-called Popish Plot of 1678, he was confronted with evidence that a woman had asked him to calculate Charles's horoscope.[60] The Royal Navy apparently continued to take the threat of witchcraft seriously: in 1667 two women were arrested in Ipswich after a ship's captain reported that a ship was lost in storms after two witches perched on the maintop.[61] Yet the Popish Plot of 1678–81, in spite of the fact that it

---

[56] Thomas, *Religion and the Decline of Magic*, p. 345.
[57] Mendelsohn, 'Alchemy and Politics', 62.
[58] Thomas, *Religion and the Decline of Magic*, p. 407.
[59] Monod, *Solomon's Secret Arts*, p. 70.
[60] Thomas, *Religion and the Decline of Magic*, p. 408.
[61] Ewen, *Witchcraft and Demonianism*, p. 458.

coincided almost exactly with a huge panic about treasonous sorcery at the French court (the 'Affair of the Poisons'), was remarkably free from accusations of magic.[62] Sir Edmund Berry Godfrey, whose murder prompted the supposed 'disclosure' of the plot, was a close friend and supporter of the healer Valentine Greatrakes, while Israel Tonge, who helped Titus Oates fabricate allegations against Catholics, was interested in alchemy,[63] but the absence of an obvious occult element from the Popish Plot (in spite of the wild accusations of Oates and others) is surely an indication that interest in the occult arts was no longer associated (as it had been a century earlier) with Catholics.

Charles II patronised alchemists as well as astronomers, bringing with him back to England the French alchemist Nicolas le Fèvre, who established a laboratory in St James's Palace.[64] Charles's personal physicians Edmund Dickinson and Albert Otto Faber were also dedicated alchemists,[65] and it has even been suggested that Charles died of kidney failure in 1685 as a result of mercury poisoning from alchemical experiments conducted beneath his chamber in a laboratory built in 1672.[66] Charles may have maintained alchemical laboratories not only in the hope of filling the treasury like earlier monarchs, but also to underscore the point that the Restoration was an event of alchemical significance, 'the resurrection of the dead king' and the restoration of

---

[62] Young, *Magic as a Political Crime*, pp. 193–5.
[63] Monod, *Solomon's Secret Arts*, pp. 105–6.
[64] Mendelsohn, 'Alchemy and Politics', 30.
[65] Monod, *Solomon's Secret Arts*, p. 26.
[66] Monod, *Solomon's Secret Arts*, p. 29.

the body politic to the purity of gold.[67] The language of alchemy was intrinsically monarchical, perhaps reflecting the fact that it originated with medieval alchemists who served in royal courts.[68] However, Le Fèvre hinted in a letter of 1660 that Charles was personally interested in occultism and was a 'Teutonicus' (follower of Jacob Boehme). Instead of ordering Le Fèvre to multiply gold for the treasury, following the pattern of medieval monarchs, Charles commanded the French alchemist to begin work on the 'Great Cordial' proposed by Sir Walter Raleigh, an alchemical elixir that was supposed to cure all ills by harnessing the 'inner light'.[69] Nevertheless, the officials of Charles's court seem to have regarded Le Fèvre as little more than an apothecary and neglected to pay him until 1663.[70] Le Fèvre's 'sovereign remedy', promising 'restoration' of health, was surely a political double-entendre that directly symbolised Charles's rule. The recipe called for gold, pearls, ambergris, spices, rare roots and the flesh, heart and liver of a viper.[71]

Alchemical talent was a commodity in demand at the Restoration court. The gifted London cunning-woman, Mary Parish, was repeatedly harassed by Prince Rupert for her alchemical secrets and finally recruited by Thomas Williams, Charles II's 'chemical physician', to assist him in distilling alchemical medicines for the king. Parish soon realised that Williams not only wanted to seduce

---

[67] Hughes, *Rise of Alchemy*, p. 5.
[68] Mendelsohn, 'Alchemy and Politics', 53–4.
[69] Mendelsohn, 'Alchemy and Politics', 63.
[70] Mendelsohn, 'Alchemy and Politics', 59.
[71] Mendelsohn, 'Alchemy and Politics', 60–1.

her sexually but was also after her trade secrets.[72] Parish also told her lover Goodwin Wharton that she had received a personal audience with the future James II (then the duke of York) not long before Charles II's death in which James had asked her for 'a certain plaster she was known to make that prevented miscarriages' (James's wife Mary of Modena had suffered a series of them).[73] Mary Parish was not entirely without connections to the royal court. Her uncle John Tomson was a learned physician and magician who was informed by a spirit guide – a Spanish lady who had been his mistress during life and helped him find buried treasure. Tomson was knighted by Charles II after the king witnessed him walk successfully 'perfectly on foot without any device or trick over the Thames straight from Whitehall without being any otherwise wet than his feet a little'.[74] There were limits, however, to Charles's encouragement of the occult sciences, and he did not grant a petition to create a 'Society of Chymical Physicians' as a rival to the Royal College of Physicians.[75]

The End of Witchcraft?

Witchcraft was still very much accepted as a reality during the Restoration years by both high and low alike, but the scepticism expressed by some during the Interregnum was sowing the seeds of the eventual demise of witchcraft as a

---

[72] Clark, *Goodwin Wharton*, p. 24; Timbers, *Magical Adventures of Mary Parish*, pp. 153–4.
[73] Timbers, *Magical Adventures of Mary Parish*, p. 172.
[74] Clark, *Goodwin Wharton*, pp. 25–6.
[75] Monod, *Solomon's Secret Arts*, p. 27.

felony.[76] During the 1650s, when Puritans were finally in charge and had the opportunity to prosecute witches as they had long wished, no consensus had emerged on a religious settlement for England, and therefore the witch-hunting project failed.[77] In the aftermath of the Civil War and Interregnum, witchcraft allegations were so closely tied to political agendas that judges invariably treated the motives of accusers with suspicion.[78] Many supporters of the established church, especially those who had suffered persecution or exile for their loyalty to Charles II, saw the Restoration as a 'dispossession' of the nation from the diabolical influence of Puritanism. The proliferation of witchcraft in the Interregnum was a sign of the spiritual corruption of republicanism; Royalists were consequently reluctant to accept the continuing existence of such beliefs in the post-Restoration world. Furthermore, they associated a preoccupation with witches with the Puritanism they aimed to stamp out.[79] The banishment of witchcraft from the kingdom was a sign of the success of the Restoration.[80]

The ritual burning of effigies of Cromwell that followed the Restoration carried with it heavy overtones of counter-magic; in Dorset and Northamptonshire the effigies were even dressed as witches.[81] Nevertheless, there was no upsurge of prosecutions of witches in the 1660s. Generally speaking, the association of witchcraft

---

[76] Elmer, *Witchcraft, Witch-Hunting and Politics*, p. 174.
[77] Elmer, *Witchcraft, Witch-Hunting and Politics*, p. 131.
[78] Elmer, *Witchcraft, Witch-Hunting and Politics*, pp. 137–8.
[79] Elmer, *Witchcraft, Witch-Hunting and Politics*, p. 177.
[80] Elmer, *Miraculous Conformist*, pp. 122–3.
[81] Elmer, *Witchcraft, Witch-Hunting and Politics*, p. 178.

with the Cromwellian regime was understood in metaphorical terms and related to the warning of 1 Samuel 15:23, 'For rebellion is as the sin of witchcraft'. The Protestant dissenters who refused to conform to Charles II's restored religious settlement became the most vocal advocates of prosecuting actual witches.[82] Furthermore, witchcraft trials spiked at moments of political tension, such as in the immediate aftermath of the Second Conventicle Act (1670), which outlawed the assembly of dissenting congregations.[83] It is tempting to interpret the proliferation of witchcraft accusations among dissenters as a reaction to the political powerlessness of a community that could only lash out against its own members and its local community as insufficiently godly, since it no longer had an influence over national events.

In the late 1670s, attitudes to witches 'developed a serious political aura', as sceptical repudiation of the invisible world became associated with the proponents of the exclusion of the duke of York from the throne, while defences of the reality of witchcraft and magic became associated with the duke's supporters.[84] It is to the exclusionists and anti-exclusionists that we can trace the factions later known as Whigs and Tories that would come to dominate English politics until the 1730s and, in different forms, even beyond. Any defence of belief in magic could easily be stigmatised as a sign of ultra-conservative Toryism or, worse still, Catholicism. Furthermore, it was at this period that belief in witchcraft was associated

[82] Elmer, *Witchcraft, Witch-Hunting and Politics*, pp. 178–9.
[83] Elmer, *Witchcraft, Witch-Hunting and Politics*, p. 191.
[84] Maxwell-Stuart, *British Witch*, p. 335.

specifically, for the first time, with the lower classes and with ignorance, allowing belief in witchcraft to be ridiculed as a rustic superstition.[85] In reality, however, the proponents of exclusion were as keen to look to prophecies and portents as anyone else, and pro-exclusion pamphlets were full of such material.[86]

The last accused witches to be executed in England were Temperance Lloyd, Mary Trembles and Susanna Edwards at Exeter on 25 August 1682, although witchcraft trials would continue for many years after that.[87] However, in subsequent English trials the suspects either died before coming to trial, were pardoned after conviction, or were acquitted owing to insufficient evidence. In the 1680s the authorities in Scotland were too busy dealing with Covenanters to worry much about witchcraft, and there was likewise a lull in convictions in England in the 1690s.[88] This was partly a deliberate decision on the part of the judicial authorities: Sir John Holt, Lord Chief Justice 1689–1710, was a Whig who made clear his unbelief in witchcraft and always secured an acquittal from the jury.[89] By 1718 the judge Whitlocke Bulstrode could confidently assure a jury that there was 'no such practice [as witchcraft] now, blessed be God, within this kingdom' – a rather ambiguous statement which did not amount to a denial of the existence of witchcraft, but simply asserted (contrary to all evidence) that it no longer

---

[85] Maxwell-Stuart, *British Witch*, pp. 339–40.
[86] Elmer, *Witchcraft, Witch-Hunting and Politics*, p. 181.
[87] Maxwell-Stuart, *British Witch*, p. 329.
[88] Maxwell-Stuart, *British Witch*, p. 349.
[89] Maxwell-Stuart, *British Witch*, p. 361.

existed.[90] Thereafter, commentators and journalists from the early eighteenth century to the twentieth century managed to sound surprised whenever it became clear that ordinary people in Britain still believed in witchcraft and magic, in spite of the abundant and continuing evidence that such belief remained very much alive. Witchcraft beliefs failed to conform to the narrative of 'civilisation' and education that befitted the heart of the British Empire, but they nevertheless persisted with or without judicial and legislative sanction.

The notion that the dominance of Newtonian philosophy in and of itself made it impossible for people to believe in witchcraft and magic is unsustainable, since elite belief in witchcraft persisted long after Newton's mechanical philosophy began to be taught at Oxford and Cambridge. On closer examination, it has become clear that the eighteenth century was far from the 'age of reason' that certain vocal writers of the period pretended it to be; one historian has described the eighteenth century as 'the age of credulousness tempered in places by a combination of curiosity and doubt'.[91] Nevertheless, it is fair to say that, after 1688, belief in magic 'never again attained the intellectual impact or coherence' of earlier times.[92] The decline of magic as a political force can be attributed partly to political factors that mitigated the impact of belief in magic even where it remained. For example, the Treaty of Union between England and Scotland in 1707 led to the abolition of the Scottish privy

[90] Maxwell-Stuart, *British Witch*, p. 376.
[91] Maxwell-Stuart, *British Witch*, p. 397.
[92] Monod, *Solomon's Secret Arts*, p. 8.

The End of Witchcraft?

council, which had previously played a key role in witch-hunting in Scotland by deciding to prosecute and seek out witches. This did not stop witch trials in Scotland altogether (the last execution of an accused witch in Scotland occurred as late as 1727), but it removed any political impetus to target witches, and discontinued the direct involvement of the government in the process.[93] Nevertheless, Archbishop Thomas Tenison of Canterbury was aware that Scottish attitudes were significantly different from those in England, and in 1706 he dissuaded Francis Hutchinson from publishing his polemic against witchcraft, *An Historical Essay concerning Witchcraft*, in case it harmed the chances of political union with Scotland.[94]

The Scottish government's increasing reluctance to prosecute witches in the late seventeenth century can also be linked to the political state of the nation. In 1689, the Scottish Parliament had deposed King James VII and II, offering the throne to William of Orange and his wife Mary (the so-called Claim of Right). William could not claim to rule Scotland by divine right like his Stuart predecessors, and the new king's close advisor on Scottish affairs, James Johnstone, was sceptical of witch-hunting. When the consent of the Scottish Parliament alone legitimated William's rule, the new king was without any of the Stuarts' aura of divine kingship. That divine kingship had been reinforced by righteous witch-hunting, which was no longer needed to serve a legitimating

---

[93] Goodare, 'Witch-Hunting and the Scottish State', p. 142.
[94] Monod, *Solomon's Secret Arts*, p. 155.

function for the monarchy after 1689.[95] The new Scottish monarchy of the Claim of Right rested on parliamentary rather than legitimist foundations.

Occult Revolutions, 1685–1688

The accession of Charles II's Catholic brother James II in 1685 alarmed many Protestants who believed the new king was intent on restoring the kingdom to Catholicism. In the months before Charles II's death on 6 February 1685, the Whig politician Goodwin Wharton (1653–1704) received angelic messages via his lover and medium Mary Parish, warning of the king's impending death. The angels even instructed Wharton and Mary Parish at one point that they should visit the king in order to encourage him to repent his sins. Wharton believed he had magically acquired healing powers, and was anxious to use them on the king, but the angels cautioned him that Charles was beyond his help.[96]

Wharton had been receiving magical advice from Mary Parish since he first met her in 1683. Parish convinced Wharton that she was in contact with a fairy realm under Hounslow Heath known as the 'Kingdom of the Lowlanders', and told Wharton that he had been made king of the fairies but could not yet personally rule his realm.[97] Over the years, she produced numerous excuses to explain why Wharton was unable to see or visit the Lowlanders, but he seems never to have lost faith in their

---

[95] Goodare, 'Witch-Hunting and the Scottish State', p. 144.
[96] Clark, *Goodwin Wharton*, pp. 114–16.
[97] Clark, *Goodwin Wharton*, p. 106.

existence. Wharton was a serial fantasist whose willingness to believe in the supernatural was as intense as his political ambition. Wharton's combination of credulity and ambition was not altogether unusual for the period, but there were several moments when Wharton wielded genuine political influence. He constructed an altar in his lodgings where he and Parish performed rituals to summon angels and receive advice from them (although Wharton remained troubled that the voices of the angels always proceeded from the direction of Mary Parish).[98] Wharton's detailed journals suggest that he was not without intelligence or critical faculties; however, Wharton had invested so much in his beliefs that the 'will to believe' usually triumphed over any suspicions he may have had. Reassuringly, by 1686 Wharton found that he was receiving his own visions, and therefore did not have to rely on Parish entirely.[99]

Wharton was also an alchemist, and one of his collaborators in this and other occult activities was the old Leveller, John Wildman, who became involved in 1685 with the plot by Charles II's illegitimate son the duke of Monmouth to invade England and overthrow James II. Wildman, like Wharton, relied on Mary Parish for angelic messages to guide his actions, although he was careful how much he revealed of his treasonous intent. He received his first, vague angelic message on 8 March 1685,[100] and hoped Mary Parish's magic might yet help him find buried treasure that would fund the rebellion.

[98] Clark, *Goodwin Wharton*, pp. 108–12.
[99] Clark, *Goodwin Wharton*, p. 145.
[100] Clark, *Goodwin Wharton*, p. 124.

Wildman continued to receive evasive written messages from the angels, but he was not always allowed to open them.[101] The angels were unwilling to give any definite answer when Wildman asked them about Monmouth's fate, and as a result Wildman kept his distance from the plot.[102]

Wildman was not the only occult practitioner interested in Monmouth's cause. A government agent in Amsterdam reported that the duke of Monmouth's sisters were boasting that they were in possession of 'a Magical Sword which in the Pommel contains such a Potent Talismanic Spell, that when it is once drawn [Monmouth's] Enemies must have fled before the Bearer'. The maker of the sword was William Boreman, who had once slandered King James by calling him a wizard.[103] An order was issued for Wildman's arrest even before Monmouth landed in England, but Wildman managed to slip away.[104] Monmouth's rebellion was a failure; after landing at Lyme Regis, the duke's army was decisively beaten by government forces at Sedgemoor in Somerset on 6 July 1685. One card in a set of playing cards printed at the time portrayed 'Devils in the air bewitching M[onmouth]'s army'.[105] This implied both that Monmouth himself had a belief in magic and that James II might have used magic against the duke – an accusation against James that would return a few years later. Judging by the discovery of paper covered in

[101] Clark, *Goodwin Wharton*, p. 127.
[102] Clark, *Goodwin Wharton*, pp. 128–9.
[103] Elmer, *Witchcraft, Witch-Hunting and Politics*, p. 199.
[104] Clark, *Goodwin Wharton*, p. 130.
[105] Humphreys, *Some Sources of History for the Monmouth Rebellion*, p. 20.

magical characters found on the duke's person after his execution, Monmouth did indeed put his faith in the occult.[106] Wildman remained in hiding while James II's government rounded up Monmouth's supporters, until on 9 August the angels summoned by Parish and Wharton advised Wildman to surrender to the king. On this occasion Wildman ignored the angels' advice and wisely went into exile in the Netherlands;[107] James's lack of clemency in dealing with the rebels would become notorious.

At least one Tory supporter of James II attempted to offer him occult advice, although there is no evidence that James ever took it. Robert Plot (d. 1696), an alchemical physician and former secretary of the Royal Society, drafted a petition to James for the foundation of a college of alchemical physicians or 'iatrochymists'. The iatrochymists' struggle against the Royal College of Physicians (which represented traditional Galenic medicine) was a longstanding one; in the 1660s a 'Poor Man's Society of Chymical Physitians' had received an audience with Charles II and received an impressive level of support from the Restoration court, but no letters patent.[108] However, Plot's new petition for a college of iatrochymists was supported by the bizarre claim that an unnamed physician of Plot's acquaintance had discovered an island called Bensalia while searching for a northeast passage to China. Bensalia was ruled by a philosopher king together with the 'Sophi', a society of alchemical physicians.

---

[106] Young, *Magic as a Political Crime*, pp. 213–14.
[107] Clark, *Goodwin Wharton*, pp. 137–8.
[108] Mendelsohn, 'Alchemy and Politics', 65–7.

According to Plot, the Sophi showed the unnamed physician 'a strange sort of Menstruum which was one of the noblest liquors (for the solution of bodies) in the world, being the same or equivalent to that highly valued the grand liquor Alkahest'. This alchemical medicine was the same discovered by Paracelsus and Van Helmont.[109]

Plot's political intent becomes clear when he claims that the king of Bensalia had written a letter to James in which he explained the governance of the island:

> they have no parliaments and ... because they have no taxes, or impositions for raising monies upon the people (the great work of parliaments) inasmuch, as what money upon any public account they at any time want, the King is upon all such occasions plentifully furnished by the Sophi, whose treasure is inexhaustible.[110]

Since Plot described the Sophi as 'adepts', the implication was clear; the wealth of the Sophi, and therefore the wealth of Bensalia, derived from alchemy. Plot was offering James an occult solution to the dilemma that had been the undoing of his father Charles I; how was absolute monarchy possible when funds could be raised only by calling parliaments? Plot may have been right in detecting absolutist tendencies in James, but there is no evidence that James ever took Plot's petition seriously or believed alchemy could solve the Stuart political conundrum.

Meanwhile, in 1687 Goodwin Wharton convinced himself that James II's queen, Mary of Modena, was in

---

[109] Gunther (ed.), *Early Science in Oxford*, p. 411.
[110] Gunther (ed.), *Early Science in Oxford*, p. 412.

love with him.¹¹¹ Wharton believed he was destined to rule England, and that James II would give way to him when the king realised that Wharton was able to father the child that James could not.¹¹² He arrived in Bath with the intention of seducing the queen, and came to understand by interior revelation that the queen was being advised of Wharton's movements by a spirit called Phocas, raised by a conjurer for the king and queen.¹¹³ On his return to London, Wharton believed that he was in magical communication with King James via the spirit Phocas, through whom he challenged James to a duel.¹¹⁴ Later, Wharton believed he could punish James by sending him headaches, as well as instructing Phocas and the ghost of Charles II to pull the king's nose.¹¹⁵ At the same time, Mary Parish began to believe (likewise by interior revelation) that James II wanted her to run the royal alchemical laboratory, but that James just kept putting off meeting her about it.¹¹⁶

Wharton remained convinced, as late as October 1688, that he was 'a divinely-guided minister' who could bring peace to England by persuading James II to revert to Protestantism, and still believed that James would raise him to power.¹¹⁷ Yet in late 1688 James II fled to France, having failed in his project to implement religious toleration of Catholics and dissenters in England.

---

¹¹¹ Clark, *Goodwin Wharton*, pp. 192–4.
¹¹² Clark, *Goodwin Wharton*, pp. 184–5.
¹¹³ Clark, *Goodwin Wharton*, pp. 188–9.
¹¹⁴ Clark, *Goodwin Wharton*, pp. 202–5.
¹¹⁵ Clark, *Goodwin Wharton*, p. 211.
¹¹⁶ Clark, *Goodwin Wharton*, p. 213.
¹¹⁷ Clark, *Goodwin Wharton*, p. 242.

James's nephew and son-in-law William of Orange, whose invasion had precipitated James's flight, was installed as king along with James's daughter Mary in 1689 at the behest of Parliament. Ironically, Wharton's supernatural revelations and his indefatigable belief that the king would turn to him for support meant that he took no active part in the Revolution of 1688. Others who shared his politics had long since abandoned hope that James would change his ways and were backing an invasion by the Prince of Orange.

The revolution in government and in the constitution in 1688, which set Parliament above the monarchy, has often been seen as the beginning of modern Britain, nearly coinciding with the publication of Isaac Newton's *Principia* in 1687, the defining book of the 'Age of Reason'. Later propaganda smeared the supporters of James II and his successors, the Jacobites, as hopelessly superstitious, while the Whig supporters of William and Mary stood for enlightenment and rationality. Nevertheless, James's opponents seem to have entertained supernatural beliefs about him prior to William's invasion, especially the large hat James wore whenever he visited his army's camp on Hounslow Heath. Some suspected that the hat:

was a Conjuring Hat, and that it would prevent any sort of Witchcraft, or any manner of Attempts of that nature, that might by some envious or spiteful Persons be attempted to be inflicted on the King. – And others said, they were well assured that this choice Hat was at last sent him by some great Popish Necromancer, who when he wore it in the Camp, by virtue of the Necromancy couch'd in it,'twould discover to his Majesty any wicked Thought, Plot, Contrivance or Rebellion formed or carried on, were they never so private in their Contrivance against him; nay, such a great Virtue there was in it, that it would at once discover even the Name or Names, let them be never so many, that were carrying on such Designs; and further, with a Wish the King, without any more to do, by virtue thereof, could inflict any Punishment privately or publicly which he pleased on them, all without their Knowledge how they fell into such Misfortunes.[118]

Some went even further, claiming that James's mysterious popish necromancer had control of the winds and, like John Lowes, had the power to sink William's fleet.[119] Similarly, Goodwin Wharton believed that James employed six priests who conjured an adverse wind to keep William of Orange in the Netherlands; it was the priests' failure to perform their rituals one day that finally allowed William to slip through.[120] Traditional prophecies, often attributed to Nostradamus, were also revived on the Williamite side during the Revolution of 1688, just as they would be in the eighteenth century for the American War of Independence and the French Revolution.[121]

Goodwin Wharton: The Last Merlin

It seems likely that William III and Mary II were the last reigning British monarchs to be advised by a practising

---

[118] *Revolution Politicks*, vol. 2, pp. 44–5.
[119] Thomas, *Religion and the Decline of Magic*, p. 645.
[120] Clark, *Goodwin Wharton*, p. 243.
[121] Thomas, *Religion and the Decline of Magic*, p. 492.

magician. Queen Mary seems even to have been aware of Goodwin Wharton's esoteric interests. Wharton enjoyed a relationship with William and Mary similar to John Dee's relationship with Elizabeth I. Both Dee and Wharton considered themselves men of destiny with a great deal to offer the monarchy, yet their opportunities to offer direct advice were sporadic. Both men's perception of their relationship with the monarch did not always correspond with reality, and both had a tendency to inflate the significance of their counsels. Wharton resembled Dee in other ways, too, receiving communications from angels, experimenting with alchemy, and repeatedly searching for buried treasure that never materialised. Furthermore, although Wharton's relationship with his medium Mary Parish was sexual, in other ways it resembled the association of John Dee with Edward Kelley, and both Dee and Wharton might be seen as the victims of elaborate and extended confidence tricks. Wharton, however, lived at what was perhaps the last historical moment when someone could simultaneously inhabit the world of high politics and the world of magic and fairy belief without being considered insane.

Wharton's relationship with the future monarchs began in December 1688, when he was invited to advise the prince of Orange on establishing a new government. Wharton repeatedly asked Mary Parish to channel messages from God and the fairies in order to guide him.[122] After William proved largely indifferent to Wharton's advice, Wharton turned to Queen Mary and, as with Mary of Modena, became convinced that the queen was

[122] Clark, *Goodwin Wharton*, p. 249.

in love with him. The angels who communicated with Mary Parish reported that William would soon die and Mary would raise Wharton 'to eminence'.[123] Wharton had the opportunity to advise Mary directly in the summer of 1690, and agonised over whether he should tell her about a Jacobite plot revealed to him by the angels. Then, after the defeat of the English navy at the battle of Beachy Head on 1 July 1690, Wharton drew on his alchemical skills to begin assembling a device 'for launching great stars and darts of fire' with the help of the angels and an assistant named Milford. Wharton also hoped for help from the fairies, asking them to make him a magical diving suit so he could disable the rudders of French ships and a mortar that could hurl fireballs at the enemy. Wharton even hoped that the fairies might sneak aboard French vessels and pour water on their gunpowder.[124]

On 25 July, Wharton obtained another audience with Queen Mary and spoke to her about the magical forces that had opposed the revolution, including James II's dabbling in black magic and the priests who conjured a contrary wind against William's fleet. The queen, according to Wharton, received these revelations positively.[125] Wharton was unable to secure another private interview with the queen but managed to give her a written account of his revelations, noting in his diary that he thought the queen was 'really touched and convinced

---

[123] Clark, *Goodwin Wharton*, p. 255.
[124] Clark, *Goodwin Wharton*, pp. 265–6.
[125] Clark, *Goodwin Wharton*, p. 267.

by them'.[126] Although we cannot be certain that Mary ever read Wharton's document, the fact that she did not banish him from court on discovering his bizarre beliefs suggests that she was at least prepared to tolerate them.

Although it seems to have had nothing to do with Wharton's influence, William's new government was responsible for repealing Henry IV's act against alchemists, which was replaced in August 1689 by a new act that encouraged the extraction of metal from ores (a key aim of the alchemists). The pioneering chemist Robert Boyle enthusiastically welcomed the repeal as an endorsement of alchemy.[127] The new climate of openness to alchemy was reflected in the appointment of Isaac Newton as Warden of the Royal Mint in the Tower of London in 1696, not long after he claimed to have discovered an alchemical process which would 'multiply to infinity'.[128] No medieval monarch had ever gone so far as to put an alchemist in charge of the mint. Nevertheless, it was undeniable that alchemy was in decline. This was not because it had been refuted by scientific discoveries, but because the secrecy of alchemy was out of step with a Whig political culture that discouraged 'cunning' and secrecy as traits of the Jacobite enemy.[129] Furthermore, the spread of print made it possible for anyone who could read to learn what were formerly secrets revealed only to acolytes in various arts and crafts.[130]

[126] Clark, *Goodwin Wharton*, p. 269.
[127] Monod, *Solomon's Secret Arts*, p. 123.
[128] Monod, *Solomon's Secret Arts*, p. 124.
[129] Monod, *Solomon's Secret Arts*, p. 133.
[130] Monod, *Solomon's Secret Arts*, pp. 106–7.

The post-revolutionary period also witnessed the final flowering of English astrology. Astrological almanacs had been a key source of propaganda during the Exclusion Crisis of 1679–83. *Poor Robin's Almanac* abused the Protestant dissenters who supported exclusion, and the Tory astrologer John Gadbury was so hated he was burnt in effigy by Whig protestors.[131] In 1680, the bishop of Norwich remarked that astrology 'lies in the midway between magic and imposture',[132] suggesting that critics of astrology were now as likely to regard it as fraudulent as morally impermissible. Publication of learned speculations on the nature of astrology declined after 1688, although almanacs remained popular. The astrologer John Partridge, an ardent Whig who returned from exile after the revolution, maintained traditional astrological methods – to the point where he stubbornly rejected Copernican heliocentrism, by then virtually universally accepted. Partridge's rival, the pro-Jacobite John Gadbury, embraced a heliocentric universe with equal fervour.[133]

Partridge accused Gadbury, a convert to Catholicism, of having changed his coat many times, saying that Gadbury had been a Ranter, a supporter of Cromwell, and then a Tory. Gadbury accused Partridge of being a secret republican who disparaged the memories of Charles I and Archbishop Laud.[134] Similarly, Partridge attacked the almanac writer George Parker as 'a broken

---

[131] Monod, *Solomon's Secret Arts*, p. 60.
[132] Maxwell-Stuart, *British Witch*, p. 341.
[133] Monod, *Solomon's Secret Arts*, p. 120.
[134] Monod, *Solomon's Secret Arts*, p. 134.

Jacobite cutler' and a conjurer.[135] Partridge's relentless politicisation of astrology, combined with his dominance of the market and his outdated views of the solar system, inevitably damaged the reputation of what had once been esteemed a noble art.[136] Nevertheless, Partridge's clients included the leading Tory politicians Robert Harley and Henry St John, presumably because, in spite of his political views, Partridge still had the reputation of London's leading astrologer.[137]

The political term 'cabal', which derived from the Hebrew Kabbalah and referred to a secret group seeking to hold onto power, originally retained some of its mystical significance in Charles II's reign. In 1676, the Royalist newspaper *Poor Robin's Intelligencer* satirically reported that the 'Green ribbon'd cabal' (the Green Ribbon Club, whose members would go on to form the core of the Whig party) was meeting with Rosicrucians, alchemists and Freemasons.[138] However, this is unlikely to have been intended as an accusation that the members of the Green Ribbon Club were actually interested in the occult – rather, it was mockery of political clubs and their pretensions to secrecy and exclusivity. The so-called Cabal ministry governed between 1668 and 1674, a group characterised by its close-knit secrecy (as well as by the fact that the initial letters of the leading ministers spelled the word 'cabal').

[135] Monod, *Solomon's Secret Arts*, p. 137.
[136] Monod, *Solomon's Secret Arts*, pp. 138–9.
[137] Monod, *Solomon's Secret Arts*, p. 140.
[138] Monod, *Solomon's Secret Arts*, p. 113.

In addition to the turn away from political secrecy that followed the 1688 revolution, there was also pressure on magicians to demonstrate the claims of occult philosophy by empirical experimentation. The materialism of Thomas Hobbes and the eagerness of orthodox establishment authors such as Joseph Glanvill to uphold the reality of the spiritual world by means of evidence created a climate that pushed occultists like Boyle and Newton towards something resembling the methods of modern science.[139] It helped that occultists had always been willing to draw their conclusions from 'experiments' rather than from the authority of ancient authors such as Aristotle and Galen, so defying the ancients came more easily to natural philosophers schooled in magic than to anyone else. As early as the sixteenth century, individuals like Dee and Humphrey Gilbert who rejected Scholastic philosophy's authoritarian approach to knowledge had opted for the direct revelation promised by ritual magic. Although the Royal Society (founded in 1660) distanced itself from 'speculative' subjects such as alchemy, it did so because the occult smacked of the 'enthusiasm' associated with the sectaries of the Interregnum rather than because the occult was 'unscientific'. Many early fellows of the Royal Society were private practitioners of magic.[140]

Throughout 1693 Mary Parish repeatedly prophesied that William would soon die and Wharton would be offered preferment by Queen Mary.[141] In February 1694, Wharton received a commission as a lieutenant

---

[139] Monod, *Solomon's Secret Arts*, p. 95.
[140] Monod, *Solomon's Secret Arts*, pp. 100–1.
[141] Clark, *Goodwin Wharton*, p. 285.

colonel and was promised by Parish that he would be a full colonel and general within nine months. Parish insisted that Wharton would 'overcome the enemy' in the English assault on Brest on 7 June 1694.[142] When the attack failed, Wharton rationalised the prophecy as having been conditional on his courage, which he failed to show by not joining the landing troops. However, when Wharton returned to England, Mary Parish explained that it was the commanders' change of plan that had altered Wharton's destiny.[143]

Queen Mary contracted smallpox towards the end of 1694, and Wharton attempted to save her by invoking the angels with whom Mary Parish claimed to communicate. They gave evasive answers, with the archangel Gabriel announcing that he retained 'great hopes' for the queen's recovery just three hours before she died.[144] After Mary's death, William showed some favour to Wharton, which Wharton believed was due to 'secret papers' about fairies and angels, given to her by Wharton, that William found among Mary's papers.[145] For whatever reason, by August 1697 William had appointed Wharton a Lord of the Admiralty. Wharton made use of Parish's magical advice in an attempt to predict the outcome of a proposed attack on the fleet of the French privateer, Jean Bart in the port of Dunkirk. Parish had a vision of burning ships, which corroborated Wharton's plan to attack the French with

---

[142] Clark, *Goodwin Wharton*, pp. 288–90.
[143] Clark, *Goodwin Wharton*, pp. 292–3.
[144] Clark, *Goodwin Wharton*, p. 294.
[145] Clark, *Goodwin Wharton*, p. 296.

fire ships. However, in the event an electrical storm prevented Wharton from even reaching the English fleet.[146]

King William's death on 8 March 1702 placed the youngest daughter of James II, Anne, on the thrones of England, Scotland and Ireland. Wharton was convinced that he had a magical hold over Anne, as he had had over her sister Queen Mary, and instructed Mary Parish to prepare 'a paper inscribed with a magic love formula' for him to carry on his person when in the presence of the new queen. Finally, in October 1702, Wharton received a vision to the effect that Prince George of Denmark, Queen Anne's husband, would shortly die, leaving Anne free to marry Wharton.[147] Although Mary Parish died not long after this, Wharton remained convinced that the queen was in love with him, and even contemplated declaring his love in January 1704.[148] Wharton died on 25 October 1704, apparently committed to his political fantasies to the last.[149]

Queen Anne continued to touch for the king's evil, partly in order to emphasise her right to rule instead of her half-brother James Edward, the son of James II and Mary of Modena. However, as concerns grew that the rite might be seen as magical, the liturgy that accompanied the ceremony was drastically revised. The cutting of Belinda's hair in Alexander Pope's poem *The Rape of the Lock* has been interpreted as a comment on the loss of the magical power of monarchy in Anne's reign.[150] The

---

[146] Clark, *Goodwin Wharton*, pp. 308–9.
[147] Clark, *Goodwin Wharton*, p. 319.
[148] Clark, *Goodwin Wharton*, p. 323.
[149] Clark, *Goodwin Wharton*, p. 326.
[150] Hart, *Art and Magic*, p. 192.

queen favoured the Tories throughout much of her reign, yet many Tories tolerated Anne's rule in the hope that the legitimate monarch, James Edward Stuart, would be restored on her death. Instead, Parliament installed George, elector of Hanover as king in 1714, an act that definitively established Britain as a constitutional monarchy under parliamentary sovereignty. George discontinued the practice of royal touching, but discussion of the royal touch continued, with doctors concluding in the 1720s that any healings that took place should be ascribed to suggestion.[151] The liturgy for royal touching even continued to appear in some prayer books into the reign of George II, in spite of the fact that no Hanoverian monarch ever performed the ceremony, as a last lingering vestige of the English monarchy's belief in its magical power.[152]

Conclusion

Although it is undoubtedly the case that occult traditions declined in political significance between 1649 and 1714, the nature and causes of this decline have frequently been misunderstood. Public and elite adoption of 'scientific' scepticism during the period played a meagre role, although a strand of scepticism regarding occult claims had existed in Britain since the work of Reginald Scot in the 1580s. Religious and political radicals and Whigs who might have been expected to oppose occult beliefs were often just as preoccupied with the occult as their

---

[151] Brogan, *Royal Touch*, pp. 211–12.
[152] Turrell, 'Ritual of Royal Healing', 34–5.

conservative opponents. The committed Whig Goodwin Wharton, as an advisor to William and Mary who in turn took his advice from conjured angels, stood at the end of a long line of royal supernatural counsellors that, in legend at least, stretched back to Merlin.

In reality, it was not the triumph of a 'scientific' worldview but the relentless politicisation of occult claims that diminished their influence during the period. The overuse of witchcraft as a political metaphor during and after the Civil War meant that accusations of witchcraft came to be associated with political instability and religious 'enthusiasm'. As witchcraft and witchcraft-belief became politically toxic, an uncomfortable reminder of a sectarian past best forgotten, legislators and jurists were unwilling to engage with them. Since many supernatural beliefs were lumped together with witchcraft as 'superstition', the demise of witchcraft had an impact on learned magical practices as well. In spite of the Williamite regime's support for alchemy, interest in the subject dried up, and political infighting brought discredit to astrology. Like belief in witchcraft, astrological prognostications remained popular among ordinary people. Yet elite interest in astrology – and therefore its political importance – largely disappeared. With the discontinuation of royal touching on the death of the last reigning Stuart monarch, the monarchy's last vestige of magic vanished as well. Yet, as the next chapter will show, occult traditions would remain entwined with politics into the eighteenth, nineteenth and even twentieth centuries.

6

Emanations of Albion
Politics and the Occult in Modern Britain

~

On 3 May 1926, a general strike began throughout Britain, led by miners determined to resist plans by mine owners to cut their wages. It was a tense period, when the government feared that suppressed revolutionary elements within British socialism, sympathetic to Bolshevism, might gain control of the Labour movement. However, a priest in Lincolnshire, Gilbert Shaw (1886–1967), had a rather more specific fear. Deep in mystical prayer, Shaw sensed that dark magicians in Moscow were projecting 'psychic pressures' against Britain, calculated to produce political instability, and were using ley lines to do so. Shaw believed that one of these ley lines ran from Russia to Snowdonia, passing through the Lincolnshire village where he happened to be vice-principal of a theological college. Shaw believed he could block the 'psychic pressures' by performing a ritual of exorcism on an ancient tumulus next to the church, which would sanctify the ground and cut off the ley line.[1] By 12 May, the general strike was over.

Gilbert Shaw acted with no official sanction on this occasion, but within a few years Shaw was the Church of England's leading expert on combatting black magic. He

---

[1] Hacking, *Such a Long Journey*, pp. 17–18.

was consulted by the archbishop of Canterbury and, so he claimed, the domestic intelligence service MI5.[2] Shaw was one of many occult practitioners who claimed to have provided supernatural assistance to his country in the Second World War. Although it is often difficult to sift fact from fiction in such claims, the sheer proliferation of them might suggest that, at a time of great crisis, elements in Britain's government did turn to the supernatural in search of aid. There is evidence of the entanglement of occult traditions with politics in the life of the nation in the eighteenth, nineteenth and twentieth centuries. Such traditions were frequently despised, derided and denied, but they were nonetheless present.

Politics and the Occult in Enlightenment Britain

The repeal of England's 1604 Witchcraft Act in 1735 was a watershed in official and elite attitudes to magic. The new 1735 Witchcraft Act (which remained in force until 1951) made it a criminal offence to pretend to have supernatural powers, including claiming to be a witch. In reality, however, the new law marked a shift in legislative and judicial attention away from supposed witches and towards violations of public order committed by witch-hunting vigilantes. After 1735, prosecutions of people for slandering others as witches, and for anti-witchcraft vigilante violence, greatly outnumbered prosecutions of people pretending to be witches under the new Witchcraft Act. This was largely because Georgian

[2] Young, *History of Anglican Exorcism*, pp. 112–14.

courts saw themselves as eradicating harmful superstition among the lower orders.[3]

Not every politician approved of the new, fashionable attitude to witchcraft as nothing more than a deception of the ignorant. There was a short-lived campaign against the new Witchcraft Act,[4] which one Scottish MP, James Erskine, opposed. Erskine was a Tory and a brother of the Jacobite earl of Mar, as well as the possessor of a large library of books on demonology at his home near Prestonpans. Erskine's opposition to the act may have been greeted with derision in London, but he represented a significant strain of Scottish opinion.[5] For Tories like Erskine (especially Scottish ones with Jacobite sympathies), the Witchcraft Act was yet another way in which the Whigs were riding roughshod over Britain's ancient laws and constitution.

Although Enlightenment legislators were determined to stamp out traditional belief in witchcraft and magic as socially unacceptable 'superstition' in Britain, the government was also faced with the challenge of ruling colonial territories where belief in witchcraft was even stronger than it was at home. In 1760 Jamaica's House of Assembly passed an act against 'Obeah or Witchcraft'. Unlike the English act of 1735, the Jamaican act did not make it an offence to accuse someone of 'obeah',[6] and by adopting the name for witchcraft used by Afro-Caribbean people themselves, the authorities somewhat distanced the new

[3] See Davies, *Witchcraft, Magic and Culture*, pp. 79–119.
[4] Porter, 'Witchcraft and Magic', p. 210.
[5] Monod, *Solomon's Secret Arts*, p. 201.
[6] Paton, 'Witchcraft, Poison, Law, and Atlantic Slavery', 258–9.

law from European Enlightenment legislation against belief in witchcraft.[7] The English Witchcraft Act of 1735 had little appeal in territories where belief in witchcraft was strong enough to stimulate and sustain rebellion; obeah was a political threat to British authority because rebel leaders sometimes claimed to draw their power from it.

It was in the interests of the British government to exploit the power of 'superstition' as well as undertaking attempts at education. While the public justification for empire was to bring 'civilisation' and British rationality to 'primitive' societies, in reality there were advantages to the apparent credulity of subject peoples. The very process of colonisation involved a kind of 'political magic', in which Britain attempted to awe less sophisticated nations by the mysterious power of its superior military technology.[8] Stuart court masques repeatedly emphasized 'the magical powers of the British monarchy' in its supposedly complete control of the seas after 1588.[9] Furthermore, it sometimes served Britain's colonial interests to accuse subject peoples of witchcraft. Alexander Whittaker, a clergyman who visited Jamestown, Virginia in 1611 interpreted the religious behaviour of the Native Americans as witchcraft,[10] and in 1637, a massacre of Native Americans in the Massachusetts Colony was partly justified by stories about the Pequot warriors receiving assistance from the devil.[11] The idea that Africans were too superstitious and

---

[7] Paton, 'Witchcraft, Poison, Law, and Atlantic Slavery', 237.
[8] Loar, *Political Magic*, p. 3.
[9] Hart, *Art and Magic*, p. 7.
[10] Gaskill, *Between Two Worlds*, pp. 29–30.
[11] Gaskill, *Between Two Worlds*, p. 142.

addicted to witchcraft to govern themselves was routinely deployed as a justification of empire in the 1950s.[12] By the nineteenth century British imperial policy was generally to combat 'superstition' through such measures as preventing violence against alleged witches in the colonies,[13] although political expediency sometimes resulted in colonial administrations turning a blind eye to the execution of accused witches (as occurred in New Zealand in the 1870s).[14]

Although more general royal charitable benevolence replaced the magical ceremony of the royal touch after 1714, the physical presence and touch of the monarch retained their mystique. As late as February 1896, the future Queen Mary gave her son Albert (the future King George VI) a pierced gold touchpiece of Queen Anne,[15] although it is unclear if she intended the child to wear it as an amulet. Throughout the eighteenth century, the Jacobite pretenders in exile continued both to touch and to issue angel touchpieces in order to emphasise their legitimacy. The youngest son of the 'Old Pretender', Cardinal Henry Benedict Stuart ('King Henry IX' to Jacobites) was still issuing silver touchpieces up to his death in 1807.[16]

Occult beliefs also continued to play a role in popular politics in the eighteenth century. Ruth Osborne, who drowned in a witch-swimming in 1751, was accused by

---

[12] Waters, *Cursed Britain*, pp. 179–80.
[13] Waters, *Cursed Britain*, pp. 161–2.
[14] Waters, *Cursed Britain*, p. 161.
[15] Wheeler-Bennett, *King George VI*, p. 7.
[16] Baker, 'The Angel', p. 90.

the mob of speaking in favour of the Young Pretender.[17] In 1755, it was confidently asserted that Merlin had prophesied in favour of the rights of the common people in a dispute over public access to Richmond Park.[18] Similarly, the Cheshire prophet Robert Nixon, who was supposed to have lived in the fifteenth century but was invented in the eighteenth, supported the Hanoverian dynasty in his prophecies.[19] The Philadelphian minister Richard Roach, inspired by the French Prophets, announced in 1727 that the foundation of the 'Solomonitical kingdom' that would precede the Second Coming was close. He warned that 'Divine *Magi*' would first have to fight a Satanic army 'instructed in Witchcraft and in the dark *Magia*'.[20] It was increasingly individuals on the political margins of eighteenth-century England, such as Tories, Jacobites, Nonjurers and religious dissenters, who were attracted to occult ideas as a form of resistance against the Whig orthodoxy of scientific progress.[21] The Jacobites' Whig opponents routinely mocked them for their credulity and dependence on magic and prophecies.[22] A Scottish follower of Jacob Boehme, James Cunningham, was almost drowned by a mob after he was prompted by spirits to call out 'Repent! Repent!' during evensong in St Paul's Cathedral in 1712. The spirits later prompted Cunningham to join the

---

[17] Monod, *Jacobitism and the English People*, p. 233.
[18] Thomas, *Religion and the Decline of Magic*, pp. 492–3; Harris, *Politics and the Nation*, p. 86.
[19] Monod, *Solomon's Secret Arts*, p. 197.
[20] Monod, *Solomon's Secret Arts*, p. 209.
[21] Monod, *Solomon's Secret Arts*, p. 189.
[22] Maxwell-Stuart, *British Witch*, p. 395.

Jacobite rising of 1715 and he died a prisoner after being captured by Hanoverian forces at the battle of Preston.[23]

The Scottish Jacobite Andrew Michael Ramsay (1686–1743), who briefly tutored the Old Pretender (James II's son James Francis Edward Stuart), identified the Jacobite cause with universal religious toleration and gave it an esoteric interpretation. James II's moves towards religious toleration in 1687–88 had been the king's undoing, but the Jacobite pretenders continued to promise toleration in the event that they ever successfully regained their thrones. For Ramsay, the practice of 'mental prayer' advocated by François Fénelon revealed the existence of a *prisca theologia* underlying all faiths and spiritual practices, hidden 'under Symbols, Hieroglyphics and Allegories'.[24] Like many Jacobite exiles Ramsay was a Freemason, and in 1734 he was elected Grand Chancellor of the Freemasons of France. He viewed prayer as 'an experimental science', advocating unity of purpose between religion and science but also portraying contemplative prayer as an instrument in the quest for knowledge that blurred the boundary between religious devotion and natural magic.[25]

Several Masonic lodges in and around London continued to regard the Stuart pretenders as the 'hereditary grand masters' of Scottish and English Freemasonry, and there was some overlap between Masonic lodges and Jacobite clubs. Furthermore, Ramsay's election as leader of the French Masons meant that Jacobite Freemasonry

---

[23] Monod, *Solomon's Secret Arts*, pp. 206–7.
[24] Glickman, *English Catholic Community*, p. 231.
[25] Glickman, *English Catholic Community*, p. 234.

became the point of contact between the British and Continental Masonic traditions. In 1736, Ramsay wrote a pseudo-history of Freemasonry that provided the basic building-blocks of the mythology of modern esoteric Freemasonry, such as ancient Egyptian origins and a link between the Freemasons and the medieval Knights Templar. However, Ramsay also had political ambitions for Freemasonry, describing Masons as 'a spiritual nation' within the 'great Republic' of the world with a specific mission to revive the *prisca theologia*.[26]

Government interest in occultism re-emerged suddenly in the 1790s in response to concerns that occult societies were a breeding ground for radical and revolutionary ideas. For instance, in 1795 a committee of the Privy Council questioned the esoteric prophet Richard Brothers, who claimed God would take away the power of King George III and give it to Brothers as a messianic king. The Privy Council committed Brothers to a madhouse.[27] However, Brothers's prophecies were not isolated. At around the same time, the mystical prophet Mary Pratt (who claimed to have studied ritual magic) apparently attacked George III as 'Pharaoh' and announced that 'The times wear a most favorable aspect viz. the French Republic',[28] although she had earlier urged people to pray for the king's recovery from madness.[29] As late as 1838, newspapers reported that 'superstitious madness' provoked by the circulation of popular curses and

---

[26] Monod, *Solomon's Secret Arts*, pp. 256–7.
[27] Monod, *Solomon's Secret Arts*, p. 316.
[28] Monod, *Solomon's Secret Arts*, p. 330.
[29] Monod, *Solomon's Secret Arts*, pp. 328–9.

prophetic verses inspired a rising against the Poor Law in Kent.[30] The suppression of belief in witchcraft in the population was, for many Liberals, not just a matter of moral improvement but also a matter of pacification.[31]

The Vagrancy Act of 1824 overlapped with the 1735 Witchcraft Act because it made it possible to prosecute 'every person pretending or professing to tell fortunes, or using any subtle craft, means, or device, by palmistry or otherwise, to deceive and impose on any of his Majesty's subjects' (a clause repealed only in 1989). The 1824 Act led to increased prosecutions of cunning-folk and fortune-tellers because magistrates had hitherto been reluctant to use the 1735 Act, which used the embarrassing word 'witchcraft'.[32] Although the 1735 Act referred only to 'pretended' witchcraft, for a magistrate to convict someone under the act still implied that witchcraft was a meaningful concept.

Occultism and Politics in the Romantic Era

In the early nineteenth century, the mystical poet William Blake (1757–1827) drew on earlier traditions to inaugurate a 'mystical nationalism' focused on the myth of Glastonbury as the New Jerusalem. Blake's 1804 preface to *Milton: A Poem in Two Books* was adapted into the hymn *Jerusalem* and set to music by Hubert Parry in 1916, quickly acquiring the status of an unofficial English national anthem. The hymn references a legend that the

[30] Waters, 'Magic and the British Middle Classes', 648.
[31] Waters, *Cursed Britain*, p. 52.
[32] Sneddon, *Witchcraft and Magic in Ireland*, p. 130.

boy Jesus travelled with Joseph of Arimathea on a trading mission to Britain, and, implicitly, the story of Joseph's later return to Britain with the vials of Jesus' blood and sweat that gave rise to the national alchemical Grail legend so popular in the Middle Ages. In his prophetic book *Jerusalem: The Emanation of the Giant Albion* (unrelated to the poem 'Jerusalem' itself) Blake offered a new and elaborate esoteric interpretation of themes drawn ultimately from Geoffrey of Monmouth.[33] Blake's mystical nationalism gave birth in turn to 'British Israelism', popularised from 1840 by John Wilson, which claimed that the British were direct descendants of a lost tribe of Israel. The theory tapped into earlier strands of apocalyptic providentialism going back to the Interregnum and earlier. Furthermore, the emphasis on the British as God's chosen people offered a theological explanation for the success of the British Empire and set it within an imagined divine plan.[34]

In 1852, the first Spiritualist séance took place in England, after the practice of 'table-rapping' arrived from America via France. As many contemporary commentators pointed out, the Spiritualists' deliberate attempts to contact the dead made them necromancers, but the absence of occult symbolism and ritual from Spiritualist séances, as well as the Spiritualists' insistence that they were engaged in scientific enquiry regarding the afterlife, meant that most people did not regard Spiritualism as a form of magic. Nevertheless, the Spiritualists developed their own idiosyncratic forms of ritual in order to invoke

[33] Blake, *Jerusalem*.
[34] Hale, 'John Michell', 89–90.

and banish spirits, reinventing necromancy for the 'scientific' nineteenth century.[35]

Although Spiritualism was of no obvious political importance in and of itself, the widespread and growing acceptance of the plausibility of Spiritualist claims had the effect, in the late nineteenth and early twentieth centuries, of normalising discourse about the supernatural to a greater extent than at any time since the seventeenth century. A new vocabulary developed for discussing supernatural harm, rehabilitating belief in witchcraft among an elite minority in a way that might have seemed inconceivable a century earlier.[36] A new discipline, parapsychology, even evolved to test the claims being made by Spiritualist mediums. The senior Conservative politician Lord Halifax (Edward Wood, Viscount Halifax), condemned Spiritualism but was fascinated by ghosts and the possibility of communication with the dead, publishing a book on the subject.[37] By the early twentieth century, widespread public acceptance of Spiritualism made it possible for a senior political figure to express such beliefs in public without ridicule.

Although Spiritualism revived the occult tradition in a new form, knowledge of medieval and early modern traditions of ritual magic was very rare indeed in Britain until the late nineteenth century. Freemasonry was one of the few mainstream institutions that kept interest in esoteric

---

[35] On the spread of Spiritualism in British society see Oppenheim, *The Other World*; Byrne, *Modern Spiritualism*; Young, *History of Anglican Exorcism*, pp. 82–93.
[36] Waters, *Cursed Britain*, p. 155.   [37] Byrne, *Modern Spiritualism*, p. 25.

beliefs alive throughout the eighteenth century,[38] with the result that the magicians of the late nineteenth and early twentieth centuries were preoccupied with issues of initiation and succession and wedded to a Masonic model of 'lodges'. The trend of imagining magical knowledge as something passed on by secret societies can be traced back to the late seventeenth century; it was a reaction to the reality that all forms of occult knowledge were accessible via 'vulgarising' print culture. The fantasy that a purer form of magic had somehow been preserved by secret societies and was only accessible to the initiated salvaged some of the old mystique of the occult arts that was lost in the age of print.[39]

Although they were influenced by other contemporary trends in occultism such as Spiritualism and Theosophy, the principal inspiration for late nineteenth-century ritual magicians was the French author Alphonse-Louis Constant ('Eliphas Levi'), whose *Dogme et rituel de la haute magie* ('Dogma and Ritual of High Magic') was published in 1856. Constant was the 'narrow channel' through which traditions of ritual magic reached the nineteenth century,[40] and his writings inspired the beliefs and practices of the London-based Hermetic Order of the Golden Dawn, founded in 1887.[41] Because the Golden Dawn inspired so much of contemporary occultism, few modern occult and magical traditions can be traced back much further than the nineteenth century.[42]

[38] Harvey, 'Elite Magic in the Nineteenth Century', p. 550.
[39] Monod, *Solomon's Secret Arts*, p. 111.
[40] Harvey, 'Elite Magic in the Nineteenth Century', p. 560.
[41] Harvey, 'Elite Magic in the Nineteenth Century', p. 563.
[42] Monod, *Solomon's Secret Arts*, p. 2.

In contemporary Britain and America, belief in magic is often associated with Neopaganism, and sometimes inaccurately conflated with New Age beliefs. The perceived 'transgressiveness' of magic makes it attractive to some people who are also attracted by radical politics. In America, especially, Neopaganism was associated from the beginning with radical feminism, environmentalism and other preoccupations generally linked to the political left. The British origins of the nineteenth-century revival of ceremonial magic and the twentieth-century creation of Neopaganism, by contrast, were firmly rooted in political conservatism. Samuel Liddell MacGregor Mathers (1854–1918), one of the founders of the Hermetic Order of the Golden Dawn, was fascinated by legitimist monarchism; W. B. Yeats, an early Golden Dawn member, flirted with fascism; Aleister Crowley (1875–1947) was 'a lifelong high Tory', while Gerald Gardner (1884–1964), the founder of Wicca, was 'almost certainly' a supporter of the Conservative Party. Alex Sanders (1926–88), who created a blend of Wicca and ritual magic, also admired monarchy and hierarchy. Magic may be transgressive, but adopting a magical outlook in the twentieth century also implied a radical rejection of modernity accompanied by nostalgia for an occult past, making magicians ideal conservatives – and even ideal fascists.[43]

Of all the members of the Hermetic Order of the Golden Dawn, the most notorious was Aleister Crowley, who would go on to be one of the most influential

---

[43] Hutton, *Triumph of the Moon*, pp. 360–1; Harvey, 'Elite Magic in the Nineteenth Century', pp. 571–2.

occultists of the twentieth century. One biographer has suggested that Crowley joined the Golden Dawn on the instructions of British intelligence, which was concerned about the legitimist monarchist beliefs of its co-founder Samuel Mathers. Mathers supported the Carlist rebellion against the Spanish Queen Isabella II, but the evidence that Crowley was working for the British government at this point is circumstantial.[44] Crowley was heavily influenced by the magic of John Dee, dubbing it 'Enochian' and experimenting with conjurations taken from Meric Casaubon's 1659 edition of some of Dee's 'spirit diaries'.[45] However, in spite of the availability of all of Dee's manuscript writings in the reading room of the British Museum in the late nineteenth and early twentieth centuries, Crowley relied on the limited printed documents and thus operated with a rather skewed view of Dee's magic.[46] Crowley ascribed to Dee his own belief in the libertine philosophy of Thelema ('Do what thou wilt shall be the whole of the law'),[47] which was hardly an accurate reflection of the beliefs of the historical Dee. More importantly, however, Crowley seems to have believed that he, like Dee, was a man of destiny with a historical mission to accomplish.

On the outbreak of war in 1914, Crowley claimed that in 1910 he and others had summoned Bartzabel, a spirit of Mars, who told the conjurers there would be war in Europe within five years.[48] There is abundant evidence

---

[44] Spence, *Secret Agent 666*, pp. 22–8.
[45] Kaczynski, *Perdurabo*, p. 85.
[46] Asprem, '*Logaeth, q consibra a caosg*', pp. 96–7.
[47] Kaczynski, *Perdurabo*, p. 128.
[48] Davies, *Supernatural War*, p. 26.

that supernatural belief was rife during the First World War, both among soldiers and those on the home front, including belief in magic. Soldiers on all sides carried talismans and even circulated magical books in the trenches in the hope of receiving supernatural protection.[49] The war produced a surge of demand for protective magic, as well as interest in Spiritualism and a romantic desire to re-enchant a world scarred by conflict.[50] While at home the anthropologist and writer on witchcraft Margaret Murray made and melted a wax effigy of Kaiser Wilhelm II,[51] Crowley spent the war in America, writing 'absurd' propaganda for the pro-German American periodical *The Fatherland*.[52] Crowley described George V as an 'obscure dwarf' and declared Kaiser Wilhelm II the new Parsifal on a quest for the Holy Grail.[53] Crowley later claimed that he was employed by British intelligence during the First World War to goad the Germans into behaving so badly that America would be drawn into the War,[54] although he admitted that his attempts to obtain an official job with British intelligence met with failure.[55] Many suspected Crowley of pro-German activity during and after the War, but his later involvement with British naval intelligence in the Second World War may be evidence that he was indeed acting on official instructions rather than

---

[49] Davies, *Supernatural War*, pp. 190–2.
[50] Davies, *Supernatural War*, pp. 218–21.
[51] Waters, *Cursed Britain*, p. 217.
[52] Kaczynski, *Perdurabo*, p. 287.
[53] Kaczynski, *Perdurabo*, p. 292.
[54] Kaczynski, *Perdurabo*, p. 285.
[55] Kaczynski, *Perdurabo*, p. 286.

genuinely sympathising with the Germans in the First World War.[56]

Crowley's actions, characteristically, did not help his reputation. On 3 July 1916, at a time and date he determined astrologically, Crowley and others approached the Statue of Liberty by boat and unfurled a green flag bearing a golden harp. Crowley tore up an envelope which he claimed contained his British passport and solemnly proclaimed the Irish Republic.[57] Crowley was told that he would be threatened with arrest as soon as he set foot on British soil,[58] but as with many of Crowley's actions, his proclamation of the Irish Republic seems to have been a quixotic whim inspired by his friendship with the poet W. B. Yeats (a fellow member of the Golden Dawn) rather than an expression of overtly anti-British sentiment.[59]

In May 1917, Crowley's occult order MMM (Mysteria Mystica Maxima) was raided at 93 Regent Street by Detective Inspector John Curry of New Scotland Yard, apparently as a result of official concern about Crowley's political writings advocating his philosophy of Thelema. Crowley had declared his philosophy of Thelema 'A universal law for all nations, classes and races', proclaiming the decadence of the old political and social order.[60] Although Crowley was making a philosophical rather than a political claim, at a time when revolutionary political theories such as Bolshevism were threatening the old

---

[56] Kaczynski, *Perdurabo*, p. 288.
[57] Kaczynski, *Perdurabo*, p. 291.
[58] Kaczynski, *Perdurabo*, p. 293.
[59] Kaczynski, *Perdurabo*, p. 292.
[60] Kaczynski, *Perdurabo*, p. 499.

order of Europe, Crowley's words sounded more than a little dangerous. Curry arrested Crowley's medium Mary Davies, describing Crowley as he did so as 'a man of evil reputation and a traitor to this country'.[61] The arrest was made under the 1824 Vagrancy Act,[62] but it seems to have been motivated primarily by concerns about Crowley's apparent politically seditious activities.

A visit by Crowley to Cambridge in 1908 had a profound effect on one undergraduate, Gilbert Shaw,[63] who was sufficiently troubled by what he saw as Crowley's abuse of spiritual power that he embarked on a spiritual journey of his own that would lead him to ordination. Beginning in the 1920s, Shaw played a key role in the revival of the practice of exorcism in the Church of England. Shaw was convinced that 'black magicians' were reactivating the power of ancient pagan sacred sites and using ley lines to launch 'psychic attacks'.[64] Shaw seems to have been one of the first people to give a spiritual interpretation to ley lines, whose existence was first proposed as trackways linking ancient sites by Alfred Watkins in *The Old Straight Track* (1925).[65] Later, Shaw came to believe in the existence of a global 'Satanist Society' that was using animal sacrifice and the power of ancient sacred sites in the landscape to exert psychic control over people.[66]

[61] Kaczynski, *Perdurabo*, p. 317.
[62] Kaczynski, *Perdurabo*, p. 631, n. 206.
[63] Hacking, *Such a Long Journey*, pp. 14–15.
[64] Hacking, *Such a Long Journey*, p. 17.
[65] Hacking, *Such a Long Journey*, pp. 17–18.
[66] Hacking, *Such a Long Journey*, pp. 75–8, 81–3.

Crowley was initially enthusiastic about Hitler before the Führer's election as German chancellor in 1933, believing that Hitler might be converted to Crowley's magical philosophy of Thelema. He annotated a copy of the book *Hitler Speaks*, which he believed alluded to Thelema. Crowley's German follower Martha Küntzel had even attempted to deliver a copy of Crowley's *Book of the Law* to Hitler in the 1920s. However, the Nazis' crackdown on German occultists in 1933 disillusioned Crowley and he withdrew his support from Hitler and the Nazis.[67] Crowley was personally attacked in *The Fascist* (the newspaper of the Imperial Fascist League, a British fascist organisation) in May 1935, but decided not to pursue libel action against the paper.[68] Meanwhile the clouds of war were gathering over Europe. Some believed that a BBC broadcast in April 1939 reactivated an ancient curse, which was to blame for the eventual outbreak of war. Live on air, a trumpeter from the Royal Hussars blew on one of the 'cursed' silver trumpets discovered in the tomb of Tutankhamen in 1922, releasing 'the dogs of war' and ensuring Britain was drawn into the conflict.[69]

The Occult during the Second World War

The role of stage magicians who worked with British military intelligence to produce illusions to deceive the enemy in the Second World War, most notably Jasper

---

[67] Kaczynski, *Perdurabo*, p. 484.
[68] Kaczynski, *Perdurabo*, p. 229.
[69] Kingsley, *God's Gold*, p. 122.

Maskelyne (1902–73), is fairly well known.[70] However, individuals with pretensions to occult powers also attempted to serve their country. The Spiritualist medium Geraldine Cummins (1890–1969) performed psychic investigations between 1940 and 1944 'for patriotic motives', and the records of these investigations are supposed to remain in the possession of the British government.[71] Colonel Charles Seymour (d. 1943), an MI6 officer who later became head of the Dutch section of the Special Operations Executive (SOE),[72] began developing his own magical practice, which he called 'the Merlin Temple', in 1937. It involved 'tapping the traditional power centres of Britain' in an effort to create a psychic 'shield' around the coast of Britain after the War began.[73] Seymour also sent his scryer Christine Hartley 'into the crystal' in order to 'seek out and fight the Black Magicians ... behind Hitler's regime'.[74] The belief that Hitler was employing his own occultists was widespread within the British esoteric community, and while there is no evidence of official Nazi efforts to use magic against the Allies, SS chief Heinrich Himmler's personal obsession with the occult is well documented.[75]

In October 1939, shortly after the outbreak of war, the founder of the Society of the Inner Light, Dion Fortune (Violet Firth), began sending out a series of letters to her disciples every Wednesday. The letters instructed them to

---

[70] See Fisher, *The War Magician*.
[71] Gaskill, *Hellish Nell*, p. 289.
[72] Howard, *Modern Wicca*, p. 39.
[73] Richardson, *Priestess*, p. 230.
[74] Richardson, *Dancers to the Gods*, p. 98.
[75] On this subject see Goodrick-Clarke, *Black Sun*.

use their magical imaginations to construct an astral 'cave' underneath Glastonbury Tor. The visits to the 'cave', which gradually filled with the figures of 'contacts' such as Arthur, Merlin and the Virgin Mary, psychically strengthened the magicians and were supposed to tap into Britain's national will.[76] After the evacuation of Dunkirk in May 1940, Fortune and her disciples began invoking 'active presences', astral beings who would go out and protect Britain and Europe.[77] France capitulated in June, in spite of the group's visualisation of a protective 'beam of light' shooting out of Glastonbury Tor and falling across France.

Fortune was convinced that Nazi occultists were working directly against her. She concluded that the Nazis had magical help because they did not seem to be winning in Europe by the exercise of overwhelming force. Rather, the national resolve of the countries they invaded simply collapsed before them, which suggested the overpowering influence of a magical will. For twentieth-century magicians, the exercise of the will was at the heart of magic, since magic boiled down to a projection of the individual's will bringing about changes in events. Nevertheless, Fortune refused a request she received from someone in France to launch personal psychic attacks against the Nazi leaders, believing that this would make her just as bad as her enemies.[78] However, the War Office did employ an astrologer, Louis de Wohl, to cast Hitler's

---

[76] Richardson, *Dancers to the Gods*, pp. 228–30
[77] Richardson, *Dancers to the Gods*, p. 231.
[78] Richardson, *Dancers to the Gods*, p. 233.

horoscope in the hope of predicting his actions.[79] In spite of believing that her London house was magically reinforced with psychic power, Fortune was bombed out on 27 October 1940.[80]

While the magical activities of Seymour and Fortune were recorded in their contemporary diaries, other alleged magical operations during the Second World War are difficult to separate from legend. Gerald Gardner, the founder of modern Neopagan Wicca, claimed that the woman who initiated him into witchcraft, 'Old Dorothy', 'called up covens right and left' after the fall of France in June 1940, even though covens were not supposed to know the identities of one another's membership. The witches formed a great circle in the night in the New Forest and danced until 'a cone of magical energy [was] raised and directed against Hitler, as one had according to tradition been sent against the Spanish Armada and Napoleon'. This magical operation, which has become known in subsequent folklore as 'Operation Cone of Power', was supposedly performed four times and resulted in the deaths of some older coven members from exhaustion.[81] Some have interpreted these alleged deaths as a form of voluntary human sacrifice,[82] and there have been claims that other covens performed similar rituals in Kent, Sussex, Cheshire, and the Chiltern Hills.[83]

The founder of the Museum of Witchcraft, Cecil Williamson (1909–99), claimed in 1992 that Gardner

---

[79] Gaskill, *Hellish Nell*, pp. 288–9.
[80] Richardson, *Dancers to the Gods*, p. 234.
[81] Hutton, *Triumph of the Moon*, p. 208.
[82] Richardson, *Dancers to the Gods*, p. 230.
[83] Howard, *Modern Wicca*, p. 38.

had in fact borrowed the story of 'Operation Cone of Power' from him, and that Williamson organised a ritual in the New Forest at the behest of MI5.[84] Williamson had been recruited to MI6 by Colonel Edward Maltby, himself a magical practitioner, in 1938, at whose behest Williamson established a 'Witchcraft Research Centre' to investigate high-ranking Nazis with occult interests.[85] Others have claimed that there was no 'Operation Cone of Power' in the New Forest and that, instead, an occult ritual took place in Ashdown Forest, Sussex called 'Operation Mistletoe'. The ritual was performed not by a coven but by Aleister Crowley at the request of MI5. The ritual 'involved a flaming dummy in Nazi dress launched along a cable from a church tower, within two circles of soldiers wearing robes over their uniforms', and the result of the ritual was the bizarre decision of Hitler's deputy Rudolf Hess to fly to Scotland in May 1941.[86]

Williamson claimed that both 'Operation Cone of Power' and 'Operation Mistletoe' took place, and that the latter was psychological warfare designed to unnerve the Nazi leaders (known to believe in the occult), regardless of whether British intelligence believed in its effectiveness.[87] However, Crowley's detailed diaries for the period make no mention whatsoever of such a ritual, which seems to have been a fabrication of the author Amado Crowley (who claimed to be Crowley's illegitimate son).[88] Similarly, it is impossible to substantiate

[84] Howard, *Modern Wicca*, p. 39.
[85] Gaskill, *Hellish Nell*, p. 289.
[86] Hutton, *Triumph of the Moon*, p. 208.
[87] Gaskill, *Hellish Nell*, p. 289.
[88] Gaskill, *Hellish Nell*, p. 209.

Gardner's claim about the New Forest coven, since there is no firm evidence that any covens existed until Gardner founded his own Bricket Wood coven in around 1946. The legend of 'Operation Mistletoe' may have been inspired by an American anti-Nazi magical ritual that really did take place in a Maryland forest in January 1941, led by William Seabrook, which involved a dummy dressed as Hitler.[89]

Crowley never claimed to have performed an anti-Nazi ritual in Ashdown Forest, but he did claim that early in 1941 he was the inventor of the 'V for Victory' hand signal. According to his own account, Crowley suggested the signal to Naval Intelligence Division, who passed it on to Winston Churchill for acceptance. Crowley subsequently had several meetings with a Major Penny from the Air Ministry, and later claimed that he managed to 'sneak' the idea of the 'V for Victory' sign past the BBC. Crowley viewed the 'V for Victory' sign as a magical sigil that had the power to counteract the Nazi swastika.[90] Furthermore, others envisaged using Crowley as an intelligence asset; Ian Fleming, who later created the character of James Bond, came up with a plan to smuggle Crowley into Germany to make contact with Rudolf Hess, who was known to be fascinated by the occult. In the event, Hess's mysterious flight to Scotland in 1941 made the plan unnecessary.[91]

Those who defend the idea that Crowley had some involvement with British intelligence note that the Nazi

---

[89] '*Life* Goes to a Hex Party', 86–9.
[90] Kaczynski, *Perdurabo*, pp. 511–12.
[91] Lachman, *Politics and the Occult*, p. 166.

propagandist William Joyce ('Lord Haw-Haw') considered Crowley sufficiently important to attack him in one broadcast. Joyce suggested that Britain replace its national days of prayer with a Black Mass performed by Crowley in Westminster Abbey. One interpretation of this attack on Crowley is that Joyce knew Crowley was actively working for the Allies.[92] On the other hand, if Crowley was worried that Joyce was trying to discredit him, his own reputation had done a good job of that already. Crowley had already been a target of fascist newspapers in the 1930s for dropping his earlier support for Hitler. In August 1941, Crowley received the Navy's support to publish a propaganda poem based on the 'V for Victory' sign, and even hoped to meet Churchill personally. Crowley wanted to 'put up to [Churchill] the 2nd half of my V plan'. He suggested that this might be a 'war engine', and referenced 'AL iii.7–8'.[93]

'AL' was Crowley's book *Liber AL vel Legis*,[94] which he claimed had been dictated to him in Egypt in 1904 by a variety of deities including Ra-Hoor-Khuit. Crowley was referring to a section of the book in which Ra-Hoor-Khuit announces himself as a god of war:

3. Now let it first be understood that I am a god of War and of Vengeance. I shall deal hardly with them.
4. Choose ye an island!
5. Fortify it!
6. Dung it about with an enginery of war!
7. I will give you a war-engine.

[92] Kaczynski, *Perdurabo*, p. 516.
[93] Kaczynski, *Perdurabo*, pp. 516–17.
[94] See Crowley, 'Liber AL vel Legis', 11–34.

8. With it ye shall smite the peoples; and none shall stand before you.
9. Lurk! Withdraw! Upon them! This is the Law of the Battle of Conquest ...
11. I forbid argument. Conquer! That is enough ... Worship me with fire & blood; worship me with swords and with spears.

The text of *Liber AL vel Legis* does not make clear what the 'war engine' is, although it is possible that Crowley had clearer ideas about this by 1941. Perhaps, given his preoccupation with John Dee, Crowley envisaged himself as Churchill's occult adviser, but the hoped-for meeting with Churchill never occurred. Furthermore, Crowley's desire to visit (and perhaps move to) California was frustrated, since the FBI picked up on Crowley's old reputation as a traitor. An occult bookseller even informed them that Crowley was 'Hitler's advisor on black magic' and the Bureau concluded that he was 'a notorious moral pervert' and refused him a visa.[95]

Just as Crowley may have imagined himself as a latter-day Merlin dispensing magical advice to Churchill, so Dion Fortune took upon herself the role of a national prophet. Fortune foresaw a final Allied victory and future periods of global dominance by America, Russia and China, although, like Dee before her, she believed the British Empire would eventually triumph as the supreme world power.[96] Gilbert Shaw later claimed to have been

---

[95] Kaczynski, *Perdurabo*, p. 520.
[96] Richardson, *Dancers to the Gods*, pp. 236–7.

called in during the War to assess the Nazis' capabilities in psychic warfare.[97] However, this claim, like Crowley's, needs to be treated with caution. After the War, many people who did not serve in the armed forces felt the need to play up their involvement in the conflict, and occultists were no different in this regard. One man, Ernesto Montgomery, even claimed to have been part of a secret MI5 unit whose members projected their 'astral bodies' behind enemy lines.[98]

Yet perhaps the most notorious British story of the occult and the Second World War does not concern ceremonial magicians but a Spiritualist medium, Helen Duncan (1897–1956). As early as 1940, a British newspaper alleged that German spies were attending Spiritualist séances in order to learn military secrets from the spirits of dead servicemen summoned by mediums. One MI5 officer, Roy Firebrace, was a believer in Spiritualism and attended one of Helen Duncan's séances in May 1941.[99] It is an indication of the extent to which the reality of Spiritualist claims had come to be accepted in mid-twentieth-century Britain that, just before the outbreak of war in 1939, a majority of an official commission convened by the Church of England concluded that it was more probable than not that at least some Spiritualist 'communication' came from 'discarnate spirits'. The report was immediately suppressed by the archbishop of Canterbury.[100]

---

[97] Hacking, *Such a Long Journey*, p. 86.
[98] Gaskill, *Hellish Nell*, p. 289.
[99] Gaskill, *Hellish Nell*, p. 184.
[100] Byrne, *Modern Spiritualism*, p. 180.

In the context of such widespread acceptance of Spiritualism, even at the heart of the British establishment, it is not altogether surprising that MI5 contemplated the possibility that Spiritualists posed a threat to national security. However, all sources of information and disinformation in wartime were a matter of interest to the security services, and MI5's interest in putting a stop to Helen Duncan's séances need not be taken as evidence that its agents actually believed in her powers. The Magic Circle, an association of professional stage magicians founded in 1905, established an 'Occult Committee' as early as 1914 to investigate the claims of mediums and other occult practitioners, and to expose fraud. There is evidence that the Magic Circle's Occult Committee actively assisted the police and security services during the Second World War by identifying mediums such as Helen Duncan.[101] War-time regulations added to the 1824 Vagrancy Act the additional words 'pretending to communicate with the spirits of dead persons', since the Ministry of Information believed that false information provided by mediums harmed public morale. By contrast, the Ministry considered that astrology boosted morale and continued to permit the publication of horoscopes in newspapers.[102]

On 25 November 1941, the British Royal Navy's HMS *Barham* was torpedoed and sunk by a German U-boat.[103] Firebrace was present at a séance at which Duncan, apparently at a time before news of the sinking of HMS *Barham*

[101] Byrne, *Modern Spiritualism*, p. 292.
[102] Gaskill, *Hellish Nell*, pp. 187–8.
[103] Gaskill, *Hellish Nell*, p. 181.

had become public knowledge, supposedly materialised the spirit of a sailor from the ship from the 'ectoplasm' that issued from her body during séances. The dead sailor reported the loss of the vessel.[104] However, it seems likely that this story is an embellishment of real events and it is possible that at the time of the séance (which took place in Portsmouth) Helen Duncan was party to information about the sinking of the *Barham*.[105] Nevertheless, the Spiritualist press represented Helen Duncan's arrest under the Vagrancy Act in January 1944 as due to the government's fear of ghosts.[106]

The fining of mediums under the Vagrancy Act was commonplace, but the trial of Helen Duncan became scandalous because, in March 1944, Duncan was sentenced under the 1735 Witchcraft Act in order to secure a nine-month custodial sentence.[107] Although the 1735 Act concerned only 'pretended' witchcraft, the title of the act led most people to believe (including, apparently, Churchill himself) that Duncan had actually been found guilty of witchcraft.[108] After the War, rumours spread that MI5 had been determined to incarcerate Duncan in order to prevent her revealing the secret preparations for D-Day. Although there is nothing to substantiate these rumours directly, the courts did treat Duncan most unusually. A case which would normally have been heard at the local assize in Portsmouth was relocated to the Old Bailey in London on the spurious grounds that

---

[104] Gaskill, *Hellish Nell*, p. 197.   [105] Gaskill, *Hellish Nell*, pp. 229–30.
[106] Gaskill, *Hellish Nell*, p. 194.   [107] Gaskill, *Hellish Nell*, pp. 4–5.
[108] Gaskill, *Hellish Nell*, p. 297. There is no firm evidence that Churchill was himself interested in Spiritualism, as some have claimed (pp. 295–6).

most of the witnesses lived in London.[109] Furthermore, although no MI5 officer attended the trial itself (by law, all military officers had to wear uniform in court, thereby making the presence of MI5 personnel obvious), an officer was apparently present at a meeting of police chief constables at which the Duncan case was discussed.[110]

The Second World War also saw a revival of ancient prophecies about the fate of the nation. Dion Fortune, as we have seen, drew on the myth of King Arthur sleeping beneath Glastonbury Tor, but in the summer of 1944 a completely new prophetic legend was created. The idea that the ravens in the Tower of London must be kept there by having their wings clipped, 'otherwise Britain will fall', is routinely reported today as ancient.[111] In fact, although ravens have been kept in the Tower since at least the seventeenth century, their association with protecting the Tower came about as a result of a request from a local brewery, Watney's of Pimlico, who asked for one of the ravens from the Tower to warn its workers of air raids. Although it is quite possible that ravens really could give advance warning of an air raid, the idea of its ravens playing a protective function was adopted by the Tower, given a supernatural and national significance and presented as an ancient legend.[112] As recently as January 2021, the disappearance (and presumed death) of one of the Tower ravens – fittingly named Merlina – was a major story in the British media amid the twin crises of Brexit

---

[109] Gaskill, *Hellish Nell*, p. 290.
[110] Gaskill, *Hellish Nell*, p. 294.
[111] Sax, 'Medievalism, Paganism, and the Tower Ravens', 62.
[112] Sax, 'Medievalism, Paganism, and the Tower Ravens', 73–4.

and the COVID-19 pandemic.[113] The prophecy concerning the Tower ravens, even if it only dates from the Second World War, was less a marketing ploy than a response to crisis that sprang from a desire to believe such legends. It helped that the legend was, to some extent, rooted in a genuinely ancient tradition that the head of the British god Bran (a deity closely associated with ravens) was buried on the site of the Tower in order to protect Britain from invasion.[114]

Politics and the Occult in Postwar Britain

The Second World War ended with Europe and the world divided between American and Soviet spheres of influence. The atmosphere of the Cold War exacerbated, if anything, the climate of secrecy that may have made it possible, in 1944, for MI5 to countenance the possibility that Helen Duncan represented a genuine threat to national security. In 1949, Geraldine Cummins once again carried out a 'patriotic' psychic investigation which, like her earlier work, has never been released. Consequently it is difficult to judge whether Cummins really did any of this at the behest of any government official.[115]

The atomic age did not entirely bring to an end fears of magic worked to political ends. In late October or early November 1953, the Revd E. G. Jay, a chaplain to the archbishop of Canterbury at Lambeth Palace (the

---

[113] 'Tower of London's "queen" raven Merlina missing'.
[114] Sax, 'Medievalism, Paganism, and the Tower Ravens', 63–5.
[115] Gaskill, *Hellish Nell*, p. 289.

archbishop's London residence), prepared a briefing paper for Archbishop Geoffrey Fisher on an unusual case that had come his way. A Hungarian woman living in London, Emma Hajdu, had written to the archbishop asking for help against a group of people, also Hungarian émigrés, who she believed were practitioners of black magic trying to put a curse on her. Jay informed the archbishop that 'One or two persons in M.I.5 keep a look out for any news of [magical] activity as in some cases the exponents of black magic aim at getting people within their power with subversive intentions'.

Jay was an official at the heart of the British establishment at a time when the Church of England, with the archbishop of Canterbury at its head, was even more deeply embedded in that establishment than it is today. Although Jay did not specify which 'people' he thought magicians were trying to influence, his mention of MI5 might have led Fisher to believe they were members of the government. Hungary was a country in the Soviet sphere of influence and therefore any Hungarian citizens in Britain were subject to political suspicion. By 1953 the Cold War was at its height, and it is not entirely implausible that MI5 might have been monitoring a group of Hungarian ritual magicians. However, this does not mean that MI5 suspected that the Hungarians were actually in possession of occult powers. British intelligence might simply have suspected that ritual magic was, in this case, a front for politically subversive activity.

E. G. Jay's 'knowledge' of the activities of MI5 in fact derived from an earlier correspondence with Gilbert Shaw, by then the Church of England's acknowledged expert on demonology. Shaw was the first person whom

Jay contacted about the Hungarian woman's claims, writing to him on 23 October 1953. Shaw replied on 26 October with this advice for Jay:

> The seriousness or not of this business depends a good deal on the character of the group, whether it is merely a collection of perverted exhibitionists or whether they have a more sinister purpose of gaining power over others definitely to spread moral breakdown and subversive activity. If we have any suspicion of the latter I think I can get it looked into in ways other than by the ordinary police.

Shaw's oblique reference to 'ways other than by the ordinary police' may have led Jay to extrapolate that Shaw was talking about MI5, although it is not certain that Jay did not have other sources of information. Jay later told the archbishop that Shaw had suggested 'the name of Mr. Gardner might be kept in mind as being connected with some of these groups in the past'. This was probably a reference to Gerald Gardner, who became widely known through media interviews in 1951 after the repeal of the 1735 Witchcraft Act made it legal to proclaim oneself a witch. However, it is also possible that Shaw was referring to the leading Theosophist, Edward Gardner (1869–1969).[116] Whether Jay's comment meant that Shaw thought the police and MI5 were interested in Gardner is unclear, however.

Shaw died in 1967, but his protégé, Max Petitpierre (who became an Anglican Benedictine monk in 1947 and changed his name to Robert), went on to become the Church of England's leading exorcist. Petitpierre edited

---

[116] Young, *History of Anglican Exorcism*, p. 113.

a report on exorcism commissioned by the Bishop of Exeter in 1972 and then chaired the body that emerged from that report, the Christian Exorcism Study Group, which advised the bishops on exorcism and demonology. One striking feature of the Exeter Report, which gained semi-official status in the Church of England after 1975, was its interest in magic. The report claimed that it could be 'in some measure substantiated' that magicians were able 'to instigate and operate "haunts"', and it speculated that 'the influence of magicians' might be behind some poltergeist phenomena. Picking up on earlier claims made by Shaw, Petitpierre claimed that the activity of magicians 'frequently revivifies ancient celtic sites such as tumuli, circles, and snake-path shrines'.[117] Elsewhere in his writings Petitpierre also echoed Shaw's belief that practitioners of magic posed a threat to national security:

The dangers inherent in these covens ... is not widely enough recognised. They constitute a very dangerous element in our social life because of this wish to impose their views and ideas ... [S]uch influences could be directed into social and political fields with incalculable consequences. I have been told that certain groups, indeed, are already carrying out experiments to see if they can influence political life.[118]

Some occultists themselves believed that the authorities were showing an interest in their activities. Ronald 'Chalky' White, a prominent follower of the early pioneer of Neopagan witchcraft Robert Cochrane, claimed he was once visited by MI5 officers in the 1970s and questioned

---

[117] Petitpierre, *Exorcism*, pp. 21–2.
[118] Petitpierre, *Exorcising Devils*, p. 131.

about rituals in which he assumed the identity of Merlin as 'kingmaker'.[119] It is possible that White made up this story in order to inflate his own importance, and it seems somewhat unlikely that British intelligence took seriously magical ritual performances in which members of the covine took on roles such as King Arthur, Merlin, Queen Elizabeth and John Dee.[120]

One political effect of the Cold War on British magic was the influence exerted by American radical feminist witchcraft on British Gardnerian Wicca. From September 1981, the 'peace camp' established at Greenham Common to protest against the installation of US nuclear missiles became a focus of 'Dianic witchcraft' that saw a cross-fertilisation of ideas from feminist witchcraft and 'Goddess spirituality' to established British forms of Neopagan religion. From the 1980s, some individuals in Britain who self-identified as witches were not only making a religious and spiritual choice, but also making a political statement about feminist identity and the rejection of a patriarchal society.[121] A similar transition of occult traditions to radical politics can be discerned in the iconoclastic Chaos Magick movement, which originated in Stoke Newington in 1976. Chaos magicians or 'Chaotes' soon became associated with Punk Rock music and political anarchism.[122]

---

[119] Howard, *Children of Cain*, p. 96.
[120] See Luhrmann, *Persuasions of the Witch's Craft*, pp. 206–19 for descriptions of the kind of rituals the Regency may have been engaged in.
[121] See Feraro, 'Invoking Hecate', 226–48.
[122] Lachman, *Dark Star Rising*, pp. 44–6.

Political exploitation of occult beliefs was part of the British army's strategy for spreading disinformation in Northern Ireland in the 1970s, at the height of the conflict known as the 'Troubles'. According to his own testimony, a small team led by a British military intelligence officer named Colin Wallace began fabricating evidence of 'black magic' rituals in the mid-1970s in order to spread the idea that sectarian paramilitaries were involved in the occult, thereby discrediting them in the eyes of a largely devout population.[123] Wallace, who was brought up in Northern Ireland, was inspired by the 'stories about the wee folk' he heard as a child, along with the 'great belief in the other world' within the Northern Irish community.[124] Whether or not they were deliberately caused by the British army, rumours of black magic swirled around both the Protestant and Catholic communities, with one loyalist newspaper reporting that IRA members were practising necromancy to summon the souls of dead paramilitaries to instruct them on how to continue the struggle for a united Irish republic.[125] However, the black magic rumours in Northern Ireland were not always given an overtly politicised or sectarian interpretation; for many, the reports of black magic and Satanism were simply an outcome of the debasement of morality produced by rampant paramilitary violence. The anthropologist Richard Jenkins, in his definitive study of this cultural episode, associated the proliferation of supernatural experiences in 1970s Northern Ireland with the

---

[123] Jenkins, *Black Magic and Bogeymen*, pp. 75–93.
[124] Jenkins, *Black Magic and Bogeymen*, p. 77.
[125] Jenkins, *Black Magic and Bogeymen*, p. 11.

extreme stress induced by conflict, in much the same way that wartime stress made people believe they saw apparitions in the English Civil War and First World War.[126]

Extreme Politics and the Occult

Occultist and Neopagan movements have been associated with radical politics of both the far right and the far left,[127] and the attraction of occult traditions to people on the far right and far left of politics was a feature of the postwar period in Britain. John Michell (1933–2009), a prolific writer on 'Earth Mysteries' from the 1960s onwards, saw Britain as a sacred land that was 'a site of spiritual redemption in the New Age', via its ancient monuments and ley lines. Michell advocated a form of 'mystic nationalism' and a return to a traditional, hierarchical society.[128] He was sympathetic to the esoteric traditionalist beliefs of the Italian magician Julius Evola (1898–1974), who has frequently been associated with fascism.[129] Michell was a monarchist and advocated the restoration of the doctrine of divine right, including touching for the king's evil. Michell was troubled by the monarch's lack of power in a constitutional monarchy, and advocated empowering the crown:

[O]ur divinely authorised Queen should be encouraged to fulfill what she knows to be her sworn duty, to use the powers invested in her for invoking God's kingdom upon earth and

---

[126] Jenkins, *Black Magic and Bogeymen*, p. 182.
[127] Strmska, 'Pagan Politics', 5–44.
[128] Hale, 'John Michell', 82.
[129] Hale, 'John Michell', 83.

restoring this country to its natural state as a terrestrial paradise.[130]

Michell's political views have been described as 'anarcho-monarchist', in the sense that he advocated the replacement of existing bureaucratic and capitalist structures of authority with sacred monarchy.[131] Michell's view of humans as fundamentally ritual animals led him to the belief that a society based on ritual order was the natural state of human existence.[132] Michell advocated racial segregation and praised eugenics, but considered himself an 'ethno-pluralist' rather than a racist.[133] Under the influence of British Israelism, Michell believed that Glastonbury would be the site of a New Jerusalem from which Britain would lead Europe back to the true path.[134]

'British nativist spirituality' has not been confined to advocates of 'Earth Mysteries' spirituality, and has found expression among druids and Wiccans, inspiring the Neofolk movement, Identitarianism and Radical Green traditionalism.[135] Although the association between Neopagan and occultist groups and the 'alternative right' in contemporary Britain is much weaker than it is in North America or Eastern Europe, the belief that the identity of the nation is invested in sacred sites within the landscape has taken root in popular culture since the 1970s. The extent to which this renewed connection with the land, mediated via esotericism, informs nationalist

[130] Michell, *Confessions of a Radical Traditionalist*, pp. 128–30.
[131] Hale, 'John Michell', 95–6.
[132] Hale, 'John Michell', 83.
[133] Hale, 'John Michell', 84–5.
[134] Hale, 'John Michell', 88–9.
[135] Hale, 'John Michell', 87.

politics in the UK is more difficult to gauge. Figures who combine political action with magical practice, such as Troy Southgate, a far-right activist and Evolan occultist, remain at the political fringe.[136] On the other hand, William Blake's land-based mysticism is at the symbolic heart of English nationalism in the hymn *Jerusalem*.

Doreen Valiente (1922–99), the High Priestess of Gerald Gardner's Bricket Wood Coven in the 1950s and one of the twentieth century's most influential writers on modern witchcraft, became interested in far-right politics in the 1970s. In 1973 Valiente joined the National Front. She had earlier been involved in founding the Pagan Front (now the Pagan Federation), an organisation dedicated to campaigning for civil rights for Neopagans. Valiente designed a banner for a local branch of the National Front but she was disappointed by the organisation's views on several issues and resigned after eighteen months. Valiente also joined an even more extreme neo-Nazi group, the Northern League. Valiente's biographer has suggested that she may have been infiltrating both organisations on the instructions of British intelligence,[137] but apart from the fact that Valiente worked at Bletchley Park during the War, there is no direct evidence that she worked for the security services. All in all, it seems somewhat unlikely that MI5 would have made use of a high-profile individual with as colourful a reputation as Valiente. However, Valiente's burgeoning interest in far-right politics may have been influenced by

---

[136] Hale, 'John Michell', 93.
[137] Heselton, *Doreen Valiente*, pp. 153–8. See also Hutton, 'Valiente [*née* Dominy], Doreen Edith', p. 61.

her encounter with the writings of John Michell at around the same time.[138]

Although the connections between Germanic and Norse reconstructionist Neopaganism and the far right are well-known, 'Celtic' and British nativist mysticism has generally been viewed as less politically significant, except perhaps to nationalists in Scotland, Wales and Cornwall. However, it is clear that 'pagan' and 'Celtic' themes are increasingly being co-opted by the 'New Right'.[139] In Britain's departure from the European Union, at least one of John Michell's aspirations for the nation has been fulfilled; Michell was deeply opposed to the UK's membership of the EU, partly because it diminished British spiritual particularism but primarily because he believed (in error) that the UK had adopted the metric system as a result. The metric system, for Michell, replaced a traditional measuring system linked to the natural world and spiritual kingship.[140] For Michell, Britain was the spiritual centre of the world, and therefore it was wrong for Britain to be subsumed in a larger association of nations.[141]

Political interest in the occult was not confined to the far right. In December 2015, Aravindan Balakrishnan was convicted of false imprisonment, rape and sexual assault for holding several woman captive in a 'Maoist cult' he founded in 1974. Balakrishnan, who originally believed the formation of his 'Workers' Institute of Marxism-Leninism-Mao-Zedong Thought' would bring about an

---

[138] Heselton, *Doreen Valiente*, pp. 172–5.
[139] Hale, 'John Michell', 94–5.
[140] Hale, 'John Michell', 87.
[141] Hale, 'John Michell', 91.

invasion of Britain by the Chinese People's Liberation Army, convinced his followers that he possessed occult powers of mind control and the ability to make events happen at a distance, even claiming during his trial that he was responsible for the *Challenger* Space Shuttle disaster in 1986 and the election of Jeremy Corbyn as leader of the Labour Party.[142]

As late as 1987, a compendium of the work of the Christian Exorcism Study Group stated with confidence that the police would take an interest in the activities of groups of ritual magicians 'Once the matter has been explained to them',[143] although the book made no reference to seditious activity by magicians against the state. The Exorcism Study Group was right, since in 1988 police began to investigate claims of the 'Satanic Ritual Abuse' of children by groups practising ritual magic – claims which psychologists have subsequently shown were produced by leading questioning by social workers and false memories constructed through suggestion.[144] The rituals described in reports of Satanic Ritual Abuse in the United Kingdom in the 1980s and 1990s are spurious and have no basis in the practices of any genuine occult or Neopagan tradition.[145]

The conservative political climate in Britain at the time of the allegations, including campaigns led by evangelical Christians against the celebration of Hallowe'en, contrib-

---

[142] 'Maoist cult leader sexually assaulted followers and kept daughter as slave for 30 years, court hears'.
[143] Perry (ed.), *Deliverance*, p. 93.
[144] La Fontaine, *Speak of the Devil*, p. 1.
[145] La Fontaine, *Speak of the Devil*, p. 44.

uted to the 'moral panic' surrounding the allegations.[146] On 19 December 1988, the Conservative MP David Wilshire raised the issue of Satanic Ritual Abuse in Parliament during a broader debate about child abuse,[147] and the alleged victims of Satanic Ritual Abuse were one of the causes taken up by the Conservative MP Geoffrey Dickens. On 10 May 1990, Dickens asked Deputy Prime Minister Geoffrey Howe if the government would consider 'a [parliamentary] debate on the spread of satanism and devil worship in the United Kingdom and the involvement of children'. Dickens went on, 'Two years ago, I warned of the spread of devil worship, satanism and black witchcraft ... We now know that that is true because of the NSPCC report. Such a debate would help me to identify others in this House who are willing to stand up to those people'. Howe's reply indicated that the government did not take the allegations especially seriously:

In view of my honourable Friend's self-proclamation of his powers of prophecy in respect of these matters, it would not be wise of me to dismiss altogether the warnings that he utters about devilish-sounding things in the form of satanism, devil worship and black witchcraft, but I cannot promise an immediate debate on the matter.[148]

The debate about Satanic Ritual Abuse never happened, although the Labour MP Andrew Bennett again called for one in Parliament on 14 March 1991.[149] Reported satanic

---

[146] La Fontaine, *Speak of the Devil*, p. 21.
[147] Hansard, 19 December 1988.
[148] Hansard, 10 May 1990.
[149] Hansard, 14 March 1991.

rituals added additional horror to stories of child abuse, but it is unclear why the idea of these rituals took hold unless, at some level, people continued to fear the harmful potential of magic in the 1990s. The report of a government enquiry in 1994 concluded that there was no basis to the idea that Satanic Ritual Abuse existed, but this did not stop *The Sunday Express* claiming as late as 2013 that Jimmy Savile had perpetrated Satanic Ritual Abuse.[150] Clearly, the idea of Satanic Abuse still exists in British popular culture even after it has been discredited by experts and the government.

Unlike the confected concept of Satanic Ritual Abuse – and not to be confused with it – the abuse of children and adults linked with African beliefs in witchcraft is a very real phenomenon in some communities in Britain. Incidents such as the murder of Victoria Climbié in 2000 and the discovery of the torso of a young boy in the River Thames in 2001 – apparently the victim of a black magic ritual – increased officials' awareness of the threat posed by magical practices originating in Africa. In 2005, London's Metropolitan Police established a unit specifically to deal with child abuse resulting from belief in witchcraft, and a debate continues concerning whether the UK should follow some African countries by legislating explicitly against accusing children of witchcraft.[151]

Occult Traditions and the Modern Monarchy

In 1880 Albert, the prince of Wales (the future Edward VII) was lying sick at Sandringham in Norfolk. The

[150] Fielding, 'Jimmy Savile was part of satanic ring'.
[151] Waters, *Cursed Britain*, pp. 247–51, 265.

princess of Wales and her sister-in-law, Grand Duchess Olga of Russia, were seeking alternative means to restore the prince to health, so kitchen staff directed the princesses to a cunning-woman living in the nearby village of Flitcham. The woman offered the princess of Wales a bottle of homemade mandrake-root wine. When the prince recovered he gave the old woman a purse of gold and took three more bottles.[152] Although this story is unconfirmed folklore, the notion that elite individuals who publicly repudiated occult beliefs might turn in desperation to the poor for unconventional remedies is plausible. A hundred years later, certain members of the British royal family still displayed a fascination with the occult and a willingness to explore the positive potential of magic. Diana, Princess of Wales (1961–97) engaged a number of astrologers in the 1980s and 1990s including Penny Thornton, Debbie Frank and Felix Lyle, owing to her apparent lack of confidence about making decisions on her own. Some of these advisers were referred to the princess by the duchess of York, a regular client of psychics and astrologers.[153]

On one occasion the astrologer Felix Lyle was brought in to advise the princess, via an astrological reading, whether she should publish a book exposing Prince Charles's affair with Camilla Parker-Bowles.[154] The princess also engaged a psychic medium, Rita Rogers, and an 'energy healer', Simone Simmons,[155] while the

---

[152] Pearson, *The Devil's Plantation*, pp. 86–8.
[153] Smith, *Diana in Search of Herself*, p. 187.
[154] Clayton and Craig, *Diana*, pp. 217–19.
[155] Clayton and Craig, *Diana*, p. 251.

clairvoyant Betty Palko claimed she had helped the princess communicate with the spirit of her father, Earl Spencer.[156] Although these astrologers and psychics primarily advised the princess on her personal life, Penny Thornton (whom the princess first met in 1986) went further and speculated on the future of the royal family, forecasting in 1995 that Prince Charles would never be king and that the UK would become a republic by 2009.[157] However, there is no evidence that Thornton ever shared these predictions – which in earlier centuries would undoubtedly have been treated as treasonous – with the princess. On 12 August 1997, shortly before her death, the princess flew by helicopter to see her psychic Rita Rogers, who had successfully predicted that the princess would 'meet a dark man at sea' (the princess interpreted this as a prophecy of her relationship with Dodi Fayed).[158]

For the commentator Christopher Hitchens, Diana, Princess of Wales's interest in astrology was a deliberate ploy to keep the public interested in the royal family, since 'the sort of people who adore astrology and supermarket trash also adore the dysfunctional House of Windsor'. Furthermore, Hitchens saw Prince Charles's 'conversations with shrubs and frequenting the company of dubious mystics' (perhaps a reference to Charles's friendship with the Jungian mystic Laurens van der Post) as 'his own version of the New Age'.[159] In a

---

[156] Waters, *Cursed Britain*, p. 222.
[157] Thornton, *With Love from Diana*, p. 163.
[158] Clayton and Craig, *Diana*, p. 336.
[159] Hitchens, *For the Sake of Argument*, p. 195.

constitutional monarchy where the monarch is virtually powerless and other members of the royal family largely help to fulfil official functions, royal interest in the occult may have more to do with a search for personal meaning than the traditional royal desire to obtain and secure power. Diana, Princess of Wales's interest in sources of occult knowledge might be compared to the future George IV's willingness to attend high-society demonstrations of 'animal magnetism' in the 1780s.[160] Contemporary royal interest in astrology and mysticism reflects a broader celebrity culture of personal referral to prestigious paid spiritual experts, although even that culture is rooted in older traditions of occult practitioners associated with royal courts.

Conclusion

The political significance of occult traditions in Britain declined drastically from the eighteenth century onwards, but it did not disappear. Accusations of treasonous sorcery of the old kind had already dried up by the end of the seventeenth century; the last person known to have stuck pins in the effigy of a British ruler was Caroline of Brunswick, the jilted queen of George IV, and then only as a form of after dinner entertainment.[161] Although occult beliefs were subjected to systematic ridicule by the press and the vast majority of authors in the eighteenth and nineteenth centuries, this ridicule served a political purpose in its own right. Although press reports

---

[160] Monod, *Solomon's Secret Arts*, p. 307.
[161] Young, *Magic as a Political Crime*, p. 198.

of 'superstition' often expressed outrage that such beliefs existed, the existence of 'superstition' legitimated Britain's colonial policies. A similar situation pertained in 1980s China, where the Communist Party denounced magic as a relic of 'feudalism', but nevertheless used reports of magic as a way of indirectly addressing other social issues. Just as in ancient China, sorcerers had been portrayed as the followers of an imagined 'evil cult',[162] so in modern China magic served a useful political purpose by providing a counter position to the state's avowedly rational, secular approaches to social issues.[163] Yet there is a risk in making magic a 'negatively defined category'; governments risk inadvertently investing magical thinking with the power of a rival political and intellectual system to that of the regime,[164] something that certainly occurred in the resistance to colonial domination in Britain's African colonies.

On the other hand, in the nineteenth century occult traditions reasserted themselves in new forms that quickly became socially acceptable in Britain, most notably the Spiritualist séance. The recrudescence of supernatural belief during the First and Second World Wars, including the British government's willingness to both employ and persecute occultists, suggests that even in a modern technological society occult beliefs can once again become politically significant at times of extreme stress. The tradition of political prophecy was especially long-lived, perhaps because wide-ranging prophecies about the fate of

---

[162] Zhao, 'Political Uses of Wugu Sorcery', 161.
[163] Anagnost, 'Politics and Magic in Contemporary China', 42.
[164] Anagnost, 'Politics and Magic in Contemporary China', 58.

nations are inevitably political, although such apocalyptic speculations have rarely been seen as a threat in modern times.

The noticeable political association of magic with the far right in modern Britain may owe something to a perceived alignment between the transgressiveness of far-right politics within a liberal social democratic society and the transgressiveness of belief in magic within a modern scientific outlook. Both beliefs are a form of contemporary 'heresy'. Just as the era of unlimited information and misinformation emboldens some to adopt contrary intellectual and political positions, so some may flirt with occultism in defiance of modernity. On the other hand, belief in magic is also a deeply rooted trait of human beings and a continuously evolving and adaptable tradition. It would be unfair to place it in the same category as other contrarian political positions such as opposing vaccination or denying the reality of climate change, since many people of all levels of education and all political persuasions continue to believe in magic. Yet, just like religion, occult belief always has the potential to be harnessed and abused to political ends.

Politicians, no less than occult practitioners, often have a love of secrecy and have no desire to disclose the means by which they accomplish what they do. The high expectations of the public, like unrealistic public expectations of doctors and scientists, can have the effect of turning politicians into modern-day magicians, both good and bad, as the language we choose to describe politics makes clear. Successful politicians, supported on a wave of hope, are expected to work miracles, and their failure to do so is soon vilified using the vocabulary of occult belief.

Politicians are practitioners of 'the dark arts' of secrecy and conspiracy, while more than one female politician in Britain has been vilified as a 'witch'. Of course, the use of such language does not mean that many British people really believe in magic – in contrast to some people in Africa, who attribute the economic and political success of the West to 'the superiority of their witches or sorcerers' in harnessing occult powers.[165] Yet the resurgence of a vocal minority in America who advocated magic as an instrument of political change during the presidency of Donald Trump raises intriguing and potentially troubling questions about how the line should be drawn between metaphor and genuine belief in contemporary expressions of occult traditions – including the possibility that no such line between symbol, metaphor and reality truly exists.

---

[165] Harnischfeger, 'State Decline and the Return of Occult Powers', 76.

Conclusion

Occult traditions are almost uniquely capable of subverting and inverting established views of the world, and therefore perfect tools to be deployed in the dark arts of politics. The general observation that politics inherently contains elements of magic – and, conversely, that magic has political aspects – is not a new one, but it has been the aim of this book to explore exactly *how* politics and magic have interacted historically in one country. Understanding that interaction is important, just as it is important to understand the historic interaction of politics and religion, politics and law, or politics and economics. As Stuart Clark argued in the 1990s, unless we acknowledge the magical and mystical dimensions of political history the emergence of the early modern state becomes just as inexplicable as the emergence of modern science, which likewise has magic as an ancestor.[1] Yet political historians have generally been less willing than historians of science to pivot to a greater recognition of the significance of occult traditions. It is a truism that historians always view the past through the lense of the present; perhaps because occult beliefs were perceived as playing no role in the disenchanted mainstream politics of

---

[1] Clark, *Thinking with Demons*, pp. 554–5.

the twentieth century, historians were reluctant to concede any role for them in the past either.

The Re-enchantment of Politics?

The twenty-first century is challenging any notion that politics can be free of magical thinking. We are compelled, once and for all, to set aside Francis Fukuyama's thesis that the establishment of liberal democracies represents 'the end of history',[2] at a time when liberal democracy seems to command diminishing popular consensus. The resurgence of authoritarianism in established democracies in the second decade of the twenty-first century saw the return of occult ideas to politics. For example, in July 2013 an advisor to Turkish prime minister (subsequently president) Recep Tayyip Erdoğan claimed that a 'giant telekinetic attack by dark forces' had been directed against Erdoğan.[3] Support for Brazilian president Jair Bolsonaro is often suffused with mystical intensity,[4] while populist governments like Bolsonaro's often eschew normal sources of scientific and academic authority in favour of conspiracy theories.[5]

In the summer of 2017, European Union officials accused the UK government of 'magical thinking' about the border between the Republic of Ireland and Northern Ireland, using the language of the supernatural in an effort to draw attention to what EU officials considered the

---

[2] Fukuyama, 'The End of History?', 3–18.
[3] Gibbons, 'Erdoğan's chief advisor knows what's behind Turkey's protests'.
[4] Cesarino, 'How Social Media Affords Populist Politics', 417.
[5] Saltman, 'Salvational Super-Agents', 51–63.

failings of a British government ill-prepared for Brexit.[6] Reliance on magical thinking by populist leaders has been matched by the behaviour of their opponents; attempts by 'witches' to 'bind' US president Donald Trump were widely reported in February 2017 and seized upon by some conservative Christian supporters of the US president as evidence of the demonic inspiration of his political enemies.[7] The rapid pace of political change in America and Britain after 2016, which saw the election of President Trump and the unexpected victory of 'Leave' in the Brexit referendum left many people feeling disoriented and unsure of the future, as old certainties were replaced by a much less predictable present where traditional sources of information and education have been replaced by the chaotic information maelstrom of social media. According to Gary Lachman, 'meme magick' with its roots in the work of Chaos magicians inspired by Julius Evola played a role in both the UK's vote for Brexit and the election of Donald Trump.[8] It is tempting to see politics divorced from any pretence to practicality as an occult tradition in and of itself, as Malinowski first suggested in the twentieth century: a magic with its own initiated practitioners, its own talismanic memes, and its own power to summon dark forces.

While it may be too much to expect the return of recognisable occult beliefs and practices from the past to contemporary Britain and America – except among those

---

[6] Rankin, 'Britain accused of "magical thinking"'.
[7] 'Witches cast "mass spell" against Donald Trump', *BBC News*. See also Nash, '#Magicresistance: The Rise of Feminist Witchcraft'.
[8] Lachman, *Dark Star Rising*, pp. 46, 111.

already curious about such practices – the fraught debates surrounding Britain's departure from the European Union and the anxiety engendered by the COVID-19 pandemic have produced a strange political climate. During the process of the UK's exit from the European Union some supporters of Brexit invoked abstractions such as 'sovereignty' in an almost talismanic fashion whenever confronted by practical difficulties associated with Britain's departure. For its most dedicated supporters, Brexit took on the status of a 'prophetic moment' to which British history had been leading, which stands in isolation from any negative consequences or pragmatic considerations (although *The Daily Express* lamented in January 2019 that Nostradamus, the perennially popular prophet, failed to predict the outcome of Brexit).[9]

Brexit arguably introduced patterns of thought into British politics that resemble belief in magic, divorced from practical economic, political and democratic considerations, with the 'Remain' camp hoping for the 'miracle' of a cancellation of Brexit while some 'Leave' supporters believed leaving the European Union without a deal would do no harm to the UK. As one journalist opined in September 2018, commenting on the cultural prominence of occult themes that year, 'when society has reached the stage where some people believe that ... a no-deal Brexit will provide a £1.1 trillion boost to the UK's economy, then perhaps the occult starts to look positively

---

[9] Kettley, 'Nostradamus 2019 prediction: Donald Trump assassination, war and hard Brexit'.

reasonable'.[10] Just as the most entrenched supporters on both sides of the Brexit debate have become vulnerable to magical thinking, so partisans on both sides showed themselves willing to believe conspiracy theories, ready to accuse opponents of 'treason' on a daily basis. The COVID-19 pandemic only intensified the grip of conspiracy theories on the public imagination. In April 2020, government minister Michael Gove was even forced to address a groundless conspiracy theory that linked the pandemic to 5G masts that even produced vigilante attacks on employees of utility companies as enablers of a mysterious invisible force of evil.[11] While the language of the 5G panic was pseudoscientific rather than supernatural, the parallels with vigilante activity against suspected witches in the nineteenth century are striking.

The historian Thomas Waters recently argued that the state can have a significant impact in suppressing harmful belief in witchcraft, noting that belief in witchcraft reached its lowest ebb when the government clamped down on 'alternative healthcare' practitioners.[12] Be that as it may, any effort by the state to suppress supernatural belief is marked by the irony that (as we have seen) governments themselves are drawn to magical thinking. In historical perspective, the strangeness of British and American politics since 2016 is not quite as strange as it first appears. Politics always contains an element of the occult, mystical and magical; the recent breakdown of the

---

[10] Armstrong, 'Coven ready: from Instagram to TV, why are witches so popular?'.
[11] Jolley and Paterson, 'Pylons Ablaze', 628–40.
[12] Waters, *Cursed Britain*, p. 265.

political inhibitions of the 1990s and 2000s simply made these elements more apparent. There is little or nothing to be gained from a reductive or functional explanation of the entanglement of politics with occult ideas, but it is possible to identify broad themes that emerge across British history in the way politics interacts with magic. This conclusion discusses eight of those strands (although these are by no means the only themes that might be drawn from the foregoing discussion): the importance of the royal occult adviser; the ruler's role as a benevolent magus; the ruler as a witch (or victim of bewitchment); sorcery as a form of treason; the use of occult techniques in warfare; the association between occultism and political secrecy; the popularity of occult prophecy and 'magical saviours'; and finally the danger of 'magical quietism', the ultimate cost of political magic.

The Royal Occult Adviser

The mythical Merlin confected by Geoffrey of Monmouth in the twelfth century established a pattern and an imagined standard for royal occult advisers. From at least the thirteenth century onwards, monarchs sporadically sought advice from individuals skilled in astrology, alchemy and other occult arts. The first such adviser in Britain may have been Roger Bacon, who counselled Henry III, although the Scottish-born Michael Scot fulfilled a similar role at the imperial court in Sicily. If later accusations are to be believed, Richard II may have consulted on occult matters with his chaplain John Magdalene, and there is some evidence to suggest that Edward IV was advised by the alchemist George Ripley, who saw himself as a Merlin-like figure. Similarly, the favour shown to the astrologer Lewis of Caerleon by Henry Tudor, together with Lewis's involvement in a rebellion against Richard III, suggests that the Welsh astrologer played a political role in the reign of the first Tudor king.

However, the evidence for these occult advisers is equivocal compared with the rich evidence in John Dee's diary for his relationship with Queen Elizabeth – a relationship that stretched back to a time even before Elizabeth was queen. Dee is the first occult practitioner for whom we have direct evidence of personal audiences with the monarch, and whose occult speculations we know to have influenced government policy – in Dee's case, the short-lived adoption by Elizabeth's government of Dee's suggestion that England lay claim to 'Arthurian' rights in North America. In James I's English reign, the architect Inigo Jones used images drawn from Hermetic magic to project the majesty of Stuart monarchy and to reassure the court through highly ritualised masques. During the Interregnum Royalists accused the astrologer William Lilly of acting as Parliament's 'wizard-general'. Then, after the Restoration, the learned natural magician Elias Ashmole served as an adviser to Charles II, Robert Plot attempted to offer occult advice to James II, and Goodwin Wharton proffered his bizarre mystical counsel to William and Mary. Even in the eighteenth, nineteenth and twentieth centuries, individuals sometimes sought to notify governments of their mystical revelations. As we have seen, the last person to aspire seriously to the status of a magical adviser to a British ruler was Aleister Crowley, who believed Winston Churchill would call on his occult expertise to defeat the Nazis in the Second World War.

It is easy to see the succession of occult advisers in British history as Merlins, assuming the role of the mythical wizard. That role included not only the display of marvellous technical skill and the giving of counsel, but also the darker aspects of Merlin's legend: his madness and eventual ignominious death. Even David Kelly, the UK government scientist who committed suicide in an Oxfordshire wood in July 2003 after questioning the evidential basis for launching a war against Iraq, has been compared to Merlin.[13] However, just as Merlin himself is a legendary figure, so those who have assumed the mantle of Merlin through the centuries have either woven myths around themselves, or have been the subject of mythmaking by others. Judging by the tangled web of unconfirmed anecdotes that circulate concerning the involvement of occult advisers in the Second World War, it is very difficult for the historian to judge the veracity of claims about the provision of such counsel. Just because alchemists, astrologers and astrological physicians dedicated their works to monarchs, this does not mean monarchs actually read their works or took their advice. Even John Dee, who certainly did advise a monarch who was very well aware of his occult pretensions, seems to have had an inflated view of his own significance in Queen Elizabeth's counsels. Being wholly or partly ignored has been the traditional fate of Britain's historic Merlins.

[13] Knight, *Merlin*, p. 222.

Conclusion

The Ruler As Benevolent Magus

It was desirable – and even necessary – for a successful medieval or early modern monarch to identify with King Solomon, proverbial for his splendour but also renowned for wielding occult powers. The notion of monarchy is arguably a magical one in and of itself. The effective functioning of a pre-constitutional monarchy requires faith in one man or one woman's ability to exercise perfect justice and wisdom in the execution of all aspects of government, down to responding to hundreds of petitions from the humblest of subjects. It is difficult to believe in such a person without imagining him or her as imbued with powers beyond the ordinary. In medieval and early modern England the magic of monarchy took a very literal form in the ceremony of touching for the king's evil, a rite that theologians struggled to explain in non-magical terms but which the population at large resolutely regarded as an exercise of natural magic.

Royal touching was of great political significance at any time, but especially so during the Hundred Years' War when the warring kings of England and France both claimed the ability to cure scrofula by touch. The centrality of monarchical authority to the English Reformation meant that the royal touch survived, in spite of its clear associations with magic, and the most prolific royal toucher of all was Charles II – a king desperate to restore the magic and mystique of monarchy in whatever ways he could after the devastating public execution of his father Charles I. However, royal touching was just one way in which the monarch was portrayed as a benevolent magus. Elizabeth I was consistently portrayed as the Fairy Queen, while the masques designed by Inigo Jones at the court of Charles I reiterated time and again the message that the king was in possession of occult powers to heal the country, if he were only allowed to do so.

By the same token, the health of the monarch was linked sympathetically to the political health of the nation – a belief that explains the urgency of attempts to cure Henry VI by alchemical medicine and the concern of Elizabeth's councillors when she became ill in the aftermath of harmful sorcery apparently directed against her. Both Elizabeth and Charles II are known to have personally practised alchemy – primarily of the medical kind, in the search for life-prolonging elixirs. Although Elizabeth's motivations for her alchemical activities remain obscure, Charles's personal alchemist thought that the king was inspired by a personal interest in the mystical philosophy of Jacob Boehme. The monarch, it seems, was sometimes the nation's supreme alchemist not only in rhetoric but also in reality, seeking to restore the health of the nation by accomplishing the 'great work'.

The Ruler As Witch or Bewitched

If the monarch was sometimes perceived – or perceived him or herself – as a benevolent magus, some of their subjects also believed monarchs recruited the assistance of malevolent magicians – or even practised malevolent magic themselves. Accusations of witchcraft against monarchs were sometimes made by rebels, such as Owain Glyndŵr's allegations against Henry IV. Similarly, the duke of Clarence started rumours that his brother, Edward IV, was trying to control his subjects by witchcraft – a move that led to the duke's downfall. Popular folklore portrayed Mary I as a witch who gave birth to a serpent at Framlingham Castle,[14] while the Jesuit Robert Parsons insinuated that Elizabeth I was a witch with the power to pass through walls. The last English monarch to be the subject of allegations of bewitching his own subjects was James II, who was accused of sending devils against the army of the duke of Monmouth and employing Catholic priests to prevent the landing of the prince of Orange by sorcery.

Alongside direct libels against monarchs as witches, a persistent strand of political rhetoric excused the bad behaviour of monarchs by portraying them as 'bewitched' by evil advisers. The ultimate evil advisor was also an evil magician: an inverted Merlin. The rise of 'evil advisor' rhetoric can be traced to the progressive replacement of hereditary noble officials of the court in the early modern period with lowborn bureaucrats, such as Cardinal Wolsey and Thomas Cromwell. Resentful of the disproportionate power wielded by 'new men', the nobility and others sometimes manufactured allegations of sorcery against royal advisors.[15] In recent times, Boris Johnson's special advisor Dominic Cummings was called 'Svengali' or 'Rasputin' in the British press, evoking anxieties about unaccountable power and mysterious influence over the decisions of the powerful.

Such rhetoric was not directed solely against the lowborn, however. The duke of Buckingham's influence on Charles I provided the perfect opportunity for an 'evil

---

[14] Westwood and Simpson, *Lore of the Land*, p. 694.
[15] Zhao, 'Uses of Wugu Sorcery', 149.

advisor' narrative, since Buckingham was widely regarded as a patron of the 'wizard' John Lambe. In the fervid atmosphere of the 1620s and 1630s, Lambe became a symbol of the magical corruption of the court, and Archbishop Laud's metaphorical 'bewitchment' of the court with liturgical ritualism became bound up in Puritan propaganda with the memory of 'Dr Lambe'. Similarly, the Whig politician Goodwin Wharton was convinced for a long time that James II's mistakes could be explained by his alliance with unscrupulous magicians, and believed the king could be led back to the right path by Wharton's own occult counsels.

Sorcery As Treason

The use of allegations of sorcery against individuals accused of high treason is a prominent theme in the political history of British magic. Insinuations and direct accusations of sorcery often played an essential role in cases of constructive treason in the Middle Ages, as a versatile allegation that had considerable power to cling to and besmirch reputations. The importance of such allegations as a tool of government continued undiminished into the sixteenth century, and the idea of occult conspiracies with a treasonous element was especially prominent in early modern Scotland. It was only the breakdown of accepted hierarchies and norms of respect for authority in the 1640s that largely brought an end to the custom of accusing traitors of sorcery.

While there is ample evidence for governments smearing traitors or would-be traitors with allegations of sorcery, the evidence for people actually attempting magical operations as part of a treasonous conspiracy is equivocal at best. Some of the surviving confessions were either extracted under torture or are obviously fanciful, and in the majority of cases no confessions survive at all. It is possible to compare the allegations of the courts to the surviving evidence for magical practice in general, in order to establish the basic plausibility of accusations, but beyond this it is not possible (in most cases) to know with certainty whether traitors really did try to use magic against the monarch. However, the question of whether magical treason was real is perhaps less important than whether monarchs and royal counsellors thought it was real – for it was belief in the threat that changed behaviours. Numerous prominent individuals were imprisoned or put to death wholly or partly as a result of such allegations, sometimes with far-reaching political consequences, including Eleanor Cobham, duchess of Gloucester, Anne Boleyn, and Lord Hungerford.

In addition to the numerous allegations that individuals used magic treasonously to threaten the life, health or judgement of the monarch, there were also times when occult practices were portrayed as inherently rebellious. This was especially true during the English Civil War, when Royalists spoke of Parliament's 'state-wizards' and called William Lilly the 'wizard general' of the Commonwealth. Occult ideas and philosophies were indeed invoked by John Pordage, Gerard Winstanley and others to subvert traditional hierarchies, although the idea that mystical philosophies were generally rejected after the Restoration because they were associated with the radicals of the Interregnum period is no longer tenable. Nevertheless, it is possible that the overt politicisation of magic and witchcraft during the conflict made people more reluctant to engage with such accusations from the 1660s onwards, thereby contributing to a long-term decline in the political significance of magic. On another interpretation, the creation of the state and the establishment of a more reliable rule of law 'removed people's fear of one another'; people and governments were therefore less likely to believe in 'possible conspiracies being set in motion by monstrous means'.[16] Thus, although numerous wild conspiracy theories about political sorcery circulated during the period of the Revolution of 1688, the conspiracy theories seem to have had little impact on the course of events – perhaps because the priority of those in power was to preserve the rule of law.

Occult Weapons of War

The predictive potential of astrology as a form of military intelligence seems to have been accepted in England from as early as the twelfth century. Astrology was deployed by both sides in the Hundred Years War to detect the weaknesses of opponents and determine the outcomes of battles, as well as for generating propaganda. The early development of gunnery relied on the expertise of alchemists, who continued to make claims about their power to develop extraordinary weapons into the early modern period. Accusations that Joan of Arc used witchcraft against English armies were a key component of the charges against Joan at her trial. The idea that witchcraft might be weaponised returned in the Civil War. Both

---

[16] Harnischfeger, 'State Decline and the Return of Occult Powers', 78.

Royalists and Parliamentarians made numerous accusations about witches serving in the enemy's army, sinking ships and offering wicked counsel to political leaders. Such fears seem to have returned at the time of the Glorious Revolution of 1688, especially among Whig supporters of William of Orange. Claims that magic was used against the Nazis with the support of the British government during the Second World War are more doubtful, but the evidence that the government feared the subversive potential of Spiritualism in the infamous 1944 case of Helen Duncan is more convincing. The heightened alertness of wartime, combined with an atmosphere of fear, secrecy and paranoia, is certainly the perfect breeding ground for rumours of malevolent magic, and this remained the case during the Cold War and the 'Troubles' in Northern Ireland. The evidence for actual attempts to use magic in warfare in British history is thin, yet it is plain that the idea of magical warfare was often a fantasy people entertained about their enemies, as well as a valuable source of black propaganda and 'psy ops' against enemies.

Occult and Political Secrecy

Secrecy, whether real or feigned, is surely central to occult traditions – by definition. The proscription and persecution of occult practitioners, or the routine misinterpretation of their beliefs and activities, also fostered secrecy, as did the desire to preserve the aura of mystery surrounding occult knowledge. The supposed secrecy and obscurity of occult traditions sustains perennial interest in them; everyone wants to know what is secret (whether the information is intrinsically valuable or not). Before the eighteenth century, conventions of secrecy ensured that magical practitioners rarely questioned the effectiveness of magic as a whole. The use of ciphers to encode illicit magical texts and politically sensitive documents developed in tandem, and officials such as William Cecil and Francis Walsingham seem to have been well aware that magicians made excellent spies. Magicians, like spies and spymasters, are addicted to secrecy as a way of life; they cultivate a prodigious memory; and they are familiar with both the making and breaking of ciphers. We may never know whether Walsingham really did recruit Giordano Bruno as a spy, or the extent to which Cecil made use of John Dee's expertise as a cryptographer, but the idea that occultists had something to contribute to the secret operations of the state re-emerged during the Second World War. It is difficult to separate what really happened from apocryphal stories and anecdotes unsupported by evidence, but it is clear that some members of the intelligence services MI5 and MI6 had a personal interest in magic – perhaps unsurprising in organisations renowned for recruiting lovers of puzzles and secrets.

Occult Prophecy and Magical Saviours

A strand of occult prophecy runs through British history, pre-dating the emergence of Merlin in the twelfth century but frequently associated thereafter with the celebrated occult advisor to King Arthur's court. British political prophecy was sometimes linked with astrology but often constituted an occult tradition in its own right, with no clear indications as to how individuals such as Merlin,

Mother Shipton and Old Nixon actually knew the future. Importantly, however, the 'future' of traditional political prophecies was actually the present, projected into an imagined past where a prophet had foreseen it. Prophecy was first and foremost a form of political commentary, veiled in occult terms.

One recurring theme in political prophecy was the arrival of a 'magical saviour', a ruler who would restore the 'good old days' and return from the dead to save the nation. Merlin's kingmaking, which ensured that Arthur ruled Britain, set the pattern for this idea, which reached its apogee in the notion that a sleeping Arthur would awake and return to save Britain in its hour of need. Richard II enthusiastically embraced his assumed identity as a prophesied saviour, while others saw Queen Elizabeth as a similar figure – although it was Sir Francis Drake, in the end, who became the focus of a revived Arthurian myth in the story he who would come back to save England when his drum was beaten. In contemporary British politics, the oft-expressed desire for a 'Churchillian' leader who will save the nation in its time of need seems to have taken the place of the traditional mythology of King Arthur; it is not now Arthur or Drake but Sir Winston Churchill who will make a metaphorical return in the person of a politician who shares his attributes.

'Magical Quietism': The Cost of Occult Politics?

Quite apart from theoretical questions about the effectiveness or permissibility of occult practices, the very fact of believing in occult knowledge posed a potential threat to rulers because it might result in poor decision-making, or even a form of political paralysis. Methods of divination such as astrology and geomancy carried with them the danger that a monarch with unlimited access to occult advisors might come to rely on oracles about the future rather than developing practical wisdom based on experience. Concern about the king's excessive reliance on oracles seems to have been a reason (or at least an excuse) for Henry Bolingbroke's coup against Richard II in 1399. Reliance on the occult compounded weakness in an already weak monarch, and Henry VI's search for an alchemical cure for his mental illness only diminished his political credibility. Furthermore, monarchs who placed their faith in the powers of alchemists to multiply gold for the treasury ran the risk of mismanaging the nation's finances.

Occult knowledge offered weak and indecisive monarchs the illusion that they were in control of events when they were not, and the resulting 'magical quietism' – in which a monarch opted for inaction while relying on oracles or occult promises – was a serious threat to the nation's wellbeing. Thus Charles I poured money into elaborate court masques that portrayed the king's magical restoration of a divided nation while ignoring the true causes of division that would undo his reign. In the twentieth century, Diana, Princess of Wales apparently allowed herself to be guided by astrologers and occult advisors, perhaps rendering an already indecisive individual even less capable of making wise decisions. Although her actions were of limited political significance within a modern constitutional monarchy, they nevertheless had a lasting impact on the wider public standing of the royal family.

The danger of a ruler falling into the torpor and complacency of magical quietism when they believe their rule is secured by supernatural forces is perhaps the true cost of the deployment of magic in politics. Far from being ineffective (magic is, after all, as effective as we believe it to be), magic is *too* effective a political instrument, lulling rulers into false security and insulating them from the reality that lies beyond their gilded world. Just as in legend Merlin met his downfall through complacency, allowing himself to be held captive forever in a tower of glass, so the glamour of high politics has the potential to take prisoner those who fall prey to its charms. While Merlin may be the ideal model of the political magician, Merlin's downfall serves as a reminder of the price to be paid when magic becomes a political instrument.

BIBLIOGRAPHY

Adams, J. N., 'British Latin: The Text, Interpretation and Language of the Bath Curse Tablets', *Britannia* 23 (1992), 1–26.
Agrippa, H. C., *Opera*, 2 vols. (Lyon, 1530).
Aldhouse-Green, M., *Boudica Britannia: Rebel, War-Leader and Queen*, 2nd ed. (London: Routledge, 2014).
Almond, P. (ed.), *Demonic Possession and Exorcism in Early Modern England* (Cambridge: Cambridge University Press, 2004).
Anagnost, A. S., 'Politics and Magic in Contemporary China', *Modern China* 13 (1987), 41–61.
Archer, T. A. (rev. E. Hallam), 'Clifford, Rosamund' in *The Oxford Dictionary of National Biography* (Oxford: Oxford University Press, 2004), vol. 12, pp. 111–12.
Armitage, D., *The Ideological Origins of the British Empire* (Cambridge: Cambridge University Press, 2000).
Asprem, E., '*Logaeth, q consibra a caosg*: The Contested Arena of Modern Enochian Angel Magic' in E. Bever and R. Styers (eds.), *Magic in the Modern World: Strategies of Repression and Legitimization* (University Park, PA: Pennsylvania State University Press, 2017), pp. 91–118.
Aungier, G. J. (ed.), *Croniques de London depuis l'an 44 Hen. III, jusqu'à l'an 17 Edw. III* (London: Camden Society, 1844).
Bailey, S., 'From Sorcery to Witchcraft: Clerical Conceptions of Magic in the Later Middle Ages', *Speculum* 76 (2001), 960–90.
Baker, D. C., 'The "Angel" of English Renaissance Literature', *Studies in the Renaissance* 6 (1959), 85–93.
Bale, J. (ed. H. Christmas), *Select Works of John Bale* (Cambridge: Parker Society, 1849).

Barry, J., *Witchcraft and Demonology in South-West England, 1640–1789* (Basingstoke: Palgrave MacMillan, 2012).
Beal, P., 'Dicsone [Dickson], Alexander' in *The Oxford Dictionary of National Biography* (Oxford: Oxford University Press, 2004), vol. 16, pp. 131–2.
Belingradt, D. and Otto, B.-C., *Magical Manuscripts in Early Modern Europe: The Clandestine Trade in Illegal Book Collections* (Basingstoke: Palgrave MacMillan, 2017).
Bellany, A., 'Mistress Turner's Deadly Sins: Sartorial Transgression, Court Scandal, and Politics in Early Stuart England', *Huntington Library Quarterly* 58 (1995), 179–210.
'The Murder of John Lambe: Crowd Violence, Court Scandal and Popular Politics in Early Seventeenth-Century England', *Past and Present* 200 (2008), 37–76.
Bellany, A. and Cogswell, T., *The Murder of King James I* (New Haven, CT: Yale University Press, 2015).
Bevan, B., *Henry IV* (New York: St Martin's Press, 2004).
Bever, E. and Styers, R., 'Introduction' in E. Bever and R. Styers (eds.), *Magic in the Modern World: Strategies of Repression and Legitimization* (University Park, PA: Pennsylvania State University Press, 2017), pp. 1–16.
Biddle, M., 'The Painting of the Round Table' in M. Biddle (ed.), *King Arthur's Round Table: An Archaeological Investigation* (Woodbridge: Boydell, 2000), pp. 425–74.
Blake, E. O. (ed.), *Liber Eliensis*, Camden Third Series 92 (London: Royal Historical Society, 1962).
Blake, William, *Jerusalem: The Emanation of the Giant Albion* (London: William Blake, 1804).
Bloch, M. (trans. J. E. Anderson), *The Royal Touch: Sacred Monarchy and Scrofula in England and France* (London: Routledge and Kegan Paul, 1973).
Booth, C., 'Holy Alchemists, Metallurgists, and Pharmacists: The Material Evidence for British Monastic Chemistry', *Journal of Medieval Monastic Studies* 6 (2017), 195–216.
Booth, R., 'Standing within the Prospect of Belief: *Macbeth*, King James, and Witchcraft', in J. Newton and J. Bath

(eds.), *Witchcraft and the Act of 1604* (Leiden: Brill, 2008), pp. 47–68.

Bossy, J., *Giordano Bruno and the Embassy Affair* (New Haven, CT: Yale University Press, 1991).

Bray, G. L., *The Anglican Canons, 1529–1947* (Woodbridge: Boydell Press, 1998)

Brogan, S., *The Royal Touch in Early Modern England: Politics, Medicine and Sin* (Woodbridge: Boydell Press, 2015).

Brown, T., *The Fate of the Dead: A Study of Folk Eschatology in the West Country after the Reformation* (London: Folklore Society, 1979).

Burnett, C., 'Bath, Adelard of' in *The Oxford Dictionary of National Biography* (Oxford: Oxford University Press, 2004), vol. 4, pp. 339–41.

Butler, E. M., *Ritual Magic* (Cambridge: Cambridge University Press, 1949).

Byrne, G., *Modern Spiritualism and the Church of England, 1850–1939* (Woodbridge: Boydell and Brewer, 2010).

Cameron, E., *Enchanted Europe: Superstition, Reason, and Religion, 1250–1750* (Oxford: Oxford University Press, 2010).

Campion, N., *A History of Western Astrology Volume II: The Medieval and Modern Worlds* (London: Continuum, 2009).

Capp, B., *England's Culture Wars: Puritan Reformation and its Enemies in the Interregnum, 1649–1660* (Oxford: Oxford University Press, 2012).

Carey, H. M., *Courting Disaster: Astrology at the English Court and University in the Later Middle Ages* (Basingstoke: MacMillan, 1992).

Cesarino, L., 'How Social Media Affords Populist Politics: Remarks on Liminality based on the Brazilian Case', *Trabalhos em Linguística Aplicada* 59 (2020), 404–27.

Chardonnens, L. S., *Anglo-Saxon Prognostics, 900–1100: Study and Texts* (Leiden: Brill, 2007).

Clark, J. K., *Goodwin Wharton* (Oxford: Oxford University Press, 1984).

Clark, Stuart, *Thinking with Demons: The Idea of Witchcraft in Early Modern Europe* (Oxford: Oxford University Press, 1997).
Clayton, T. and Craig, P., *Diana: Story of a Princess* (New York: Atria Books, 2001)
Collins, D. J., 'Introduction' in D. J. Collins (ed.), *The Cambridge History of Magic and Witchcraft in the West: From Antiquity to the Present* (Cambridge: Cambridge University Press, 2015), pp. 1–14.
Collinson, P., *From Cranmer to Sancroft* (London: Continuum, 2006).
Comparetti, D., *Vergil in the Middle Ages*, translated by E. F. M. Benecke (Princeton, NJ: Princeton University Press, 1997).
Connolly, S. J., *Contested Island: Ireland 1460–1630* (Oxford: Oxford University Press, 2007).
Cook, J., *Dr Simon Forman: A Most Notorious Physician* (London: Chatto and Windus, 2001).
Copenhaver, B. P., *Magic in Western Culture: From Antiquity to the Enlightenment* (Cambridge: Cambridge University Press, 2015).
Crais, Clifton, *The Politics of Evil: Magic, State Power and the Political Imagination in South Africa* (Cambridge: Cambridge University Press, 2002).
Cressy, D., *Dangerous Talk: Scandalous, Seditious and Treasonable Speech in Pre-Modern England* (Oxford: Oxford University Press, 2010).
Crowley, A., 'Liber AL vel Legis', *Equinox* 1:10 (September 1913), 11–34.
Curry, P., 'Lilly, William' in *The Oxford Dictionary of National Biography* (Oxford: Oxford University Press, 2004), vol. 33, pp. 794–8.
Davies, O., *Witchcraft, Magic and Culture 1736–1951* (Manchester: Manchester University Press, 1999).
  Popular Magic: Cunning-Folk in English History, 2nd ed. (London: Continuum, 2007).
  A Supernatural War: Magic, Divination, and Faith during the First World War (Oxford: Oxford University Press, 2019).

Bibliography

De la Bédoyère, G., *Gods with Thunderbolts: Religion in Roman Britain* (Stroud: Tempus, 2002).

De Trokelowe, J. and De Blaneforde, H., *Chronica et annals, regnantibus Henrico Tertio, Edwardo Primo, Edwardo Secundo, Ricardo Secundo, et Henrico Quarto*, edited by H. T. Riley, 3 vols. (London: Longmans, Green etc., 1866).

De Yepes, D., *Historia Particular de la Persecucion de Inglaterra* (Madrid, 1599).

Dee, J. (edited by E. Fenton), *The Diaries of John Dee* (Charlbury: Day Books, 1998).

Devine, M., 'Treasonous Catholic Magic and the 1563 Witchcraft Legislation: The English State's Response to Catholic Conjuring in the Early Years of Elizabeth I's Reign' in M. Harmes and V. Bladen (eds.), *Supernatural and Secular Power in Early Modern England* (Farnham: Ashgate, 2015), pp. 67–94.

Duffy, E., *The Stripping of the Altars: Traditional Religion in England, c. 1400–c. 1580* (New Haven, CT: Yale University Press, 1992).

Dunn-Hensley, S., *Anna of Denmark and Henrietta Maria: Virgins, Witches and Catholic Queens* (London: Palgrave MacMillan, 2017).

Eamon, W., 'Technology as Magic in the Late Middle Ages and the Renaissance', *Janus* 70 (1983), 171–212.

Ekwall, E., *Studies on English Place-Names* (Stockholm: Wahlström and Widstrand, 1936).

The Concise Oxford Dictionary of English Place-Names, 4th ed. (Oxford: Oxford University Press, 1960).

Elmer, P., *The Miraculous Conformist: Valentine Greatrakes, the Body Politic, and the Politics of Healing in Restoration Britain* (Oxford: Oxford University Press, 2012).

Witchcraft, Witch-Hunting and Politics in Early Modern England (Oxford: Oxford University Press, 2016).

Elton, G. R., *Policy and Police: The Enforcement of the Reformation in the Age of Thomas Cromwell* (Cambridge: Cambridge University Press, 1972).

Erler, M. C., 'The Laity' in V. Gillespie and S. Powell (eds.), *A Companion to the Early Printed Book in Britain, 1476–1558* (Cambridge: D. S. Brewer, 2014), pp. 134–49.

Evans, W. D. (ed.), *A Collection of Statutes Connected with the General Administration of the Law*, 3rd ed., 10 vols. (London: Thomas Blenkarn, 1836).

Ewen, C. L., *Witchcraft and Demonianism: A Concise Account Derived from Sworn Testimonies and Confessions Obtained in the Courts of England and Wales* (London: Heath Cranton, 1933).

Fanger, C., 'Introduction: Theurgy, Magic and Mysticism' in C. Fanger (ed.), *Invoking Angels: Theurgic Ideas and Practices, Thirteenth to Sixteenth Centuries* (University Park, PA: Pennsylvania State University Press, 2012), pp. 1–33.

Favent, T., *Historia sive narracio de modo et forma Mirabilis Parliamenti*, edited by M. McKisak (London: Camden Society, 1926).

Feraro, S., 'Invoking Hecate at the Women's Peace Camp: The Presence of Goddess Spirituality and Dianic Witchcraft at Greenham Common in the 1980s', *Magic, Ritual, and Witchcraft* 11 (2016), 226–48.

Fisher, D., *The War Magician: The Man Who Conjured Victory in the Desert* (London: Weidenfeld and Nicholson, 2004).

F[isher], J., *The copy of a letter describing the wonderful woorke of God in delivering a mayden within the city of Chester* (London, 1565).

Fleming, J. V., 'The Round Table in Literature and Legend', in M. Biddle (ed.), *King Arthur's Round Table: An Archaeological Investigation* (Woodbridge: Boydell Press, 2000), pp. 5–30.

Foreman, P., *The Cambridge Book of Magic: A Tudor Necromancer's Manual*, edited by F. Young (Cambridge: Texts in Early Modern Magic, 2015).

Fortune, D., *The Magical Battle of Britain: The War Letters of Dion Fortune*, edited by G. Knight, 2nd ed (Cheltenham: Skylight Press, 2012).

Freeman, J., 'Sorcery at Court and Manor: Margery Jourdemayne, the Witch of Eye Next Westminster', *Journal of Medieval History* 30 (2004), 343–57.

Freeman, T. S., 'Demons, Deviance and Defiance: John Darrell and the Politics of Exorcism in late Elizabethan England' in P. Lake and M. Questier (eds.), *Conformity and Orthodoxy in the English Church, c. 1560–1660* (Woodbridge: Boydell Press, 2000), pp. 34–63.

'Foxe, John' in *The Oxford Dictionary of National Biography* (Oxford: Oxford University Press, 2004), vol. 20, pp. 695–709.

Fukuyama, F., 'The End of History?', *The National Interest* 16 (1989), 3–18.

Gaisser, J. H., *The Fortunes of Apuleius and the Golden Ass: A Study in Transmission and Reception* (Princeton, NJ: Princeton University Press, 2008).

Gaskill, M., *Hellish Nell: Last of Britain's Witches* (London: Fourth Estate, 2001).

Witchfinders: A Seventeenth-Century Tragedy (London: John Murray, 2005).

'Witchcraft, Politics, and Memory in Seventeenth-Century England', *The Historical Journal* 50 (2007), 289–308.

Between Two Worlds: How the English Became Americans (Oxford: Oxford University Press, 2014).

Geneva, A., *Astrology and the Seventeenth-Century Mind: William Lilly and the Language of the Stars* (Manchester: Manchester University Press, 1995).

Glickman, G., *The English Catholic Community 1688–1745: Politics, Culture and Ideology* (Woodbridge: Boydell and Brewer, 2009).

Goodare, J., 'Witch-Hunting and the Scottish State' in J. Goodare (ed.), *The Scottish Witch-Hunt in Context* (Manchester: Manchester University Press, 2002), pp. 122–45.

'The Scottish Witchcraft Act', *History* 74 (2005), 39–67.

Goodrich, P. H., 'Introduction' in P. H. Goodrich and R. H. Thompson (eds.), *Merlin: A Casebook* (London: Routledge, 2003), pp. 1–88.

Goodrick-Clarke, N., *Black Sun: Aryan Cults, Esoteric Nazism and the Politics of Identity* (New York: New York University Press, 2003).

Gordon, S., 'Necromancy and the Magical Reputation of Michael Scot: John Rylands Library, Latin MS 105', *Bulletin of the John Rylands Library* 92 (2016), 73–103.

Gosden, C., *The History of Magic: From Alchemy to Witchcraft, from the Ice Age to the Present* (London: Viking, 2020).

Gransden, A., *Historical Writing in England: c. 550–c. 1307* (London: Routledge, 1996).

— *A History of the Abbey of Bury St Edmunds 1257–1301* (Woodbridge: Boydell and Brewer, 2015).

Green, R. F., *Elf Queens and Holy Friars: Fairy Beliefs and the Medieval Church* (Philadelphia, PA: University of Pennsylvania Press, 2016).

Griffiths, R. A., 'The Trial of Eleanor Cobham: An Episode in the Fall of Duke Humphrey of Gloucester', in R. A. Griffiths (ed.), *King and Country: England and Wales in the Fifteenth Century* (London: Hambledon, 1991), pp. 233–52.

Gross, A., 'Ripley, George' in *The Oxford Dictionary of National Biography* (Oxford: Oxford University Press, 2004), vol. 46, pp. 1000–2.

Guerrero, J. R., 'Un Repaso a la Alquimia del Midi Francés en el Siglo XIV (Parte I)', *Azogue* 7 (2010–13), 75–141.

Gunther, R. T. (ed.), *Early Science in Oxford: Vol. XII: Dr. Plot and the Correspondence of the Philosophical Society of Oxford* (Oxford: Clarendon Press, 1939).

Hacking, R. D., *Such a Long Journey: A Biography of Gilbert Shaw, Priest* (London: Mowbray, 1988).

Hale, A., 'John Michell, Radical Traditionalism, and the Emerging Politics of the Pagan New Right', *Pomegranate* 13 (2011), 77–97.

Harkness, D., *John Dee's Conversations with Angels: Cabala, Alchemy, and the End of Nature* (Cambridge: Cambridge University Press, 1999).

Harmes, M., 'The Devil and Bishops in Post-Reformation England' in M. Harmes and V. Bladen (eds.), *Supernatural and Secular Power in Early Modern England* (Farnham: Ashgate, 2015), pp. 185–206.

Harms, D., Clark, J. R. and Peterson, J. H. (eds.), *The Book of Oberon: A Sourcebook of Elizabethan Magic* (Woodbury, MN: Llewellyn, 2015).

Harmsen, T., 'Weston, William' in *The Oxford Dictionary of National Biography* (Oxford: Oxford University Press, 2004), vol. 58, p. 314.

Harnischfeger, J., 'State Decline and the Return of Occult Powers: The Case of Propget Eddy in Nigeria', *Magic, Ritual, and Witchcraft* 1 (2006), 56–78.

Harris, R., *Politics and the Nation: Britain in the Mid-Eighteenth Century* (Oxford: Oxford University Press, 2002),

Harsnett, S., *A Discovery of the Fraudulent Practises of John Darrel* (London, 1599).

A Declaration of Egregious Popish Impostures (London, 1603).

Hart, V., *Art and Magic in the Court of the Stuarts* (London: Routledge, 1994).

Harvey, D. A., 'Elite Magic in the Nineteenth Century' in D. J. Collins (ed.), *The Cambridge History of Magic and Witchcraft in the West from Antiquity to the Present* (Cambridge: Cambridge University Press, 2015), pp. 547–75.

Henderson, L., 'Detestable Slaves of the Devil: Changing Ideas about Witchcraft in Sixteenth-Century Scotland' in E. J. Cowan and L. Henderson (eds.), *A History of Everyday Life in Medieval Scotland, 1000 to 1600* (Edinburgh: Edinburgh University Press, 2011), pp. 226–53.

Herzog, R., *Die Wunderheilungen von Epidauros* (Leipzig: Dieterich, 1931).

Heselton, P., *Doreen Valiente: Witch* (Nottingham: Centre for Pagan Studies, 2016).

Hinde, W., *A Faithfull Remonstrance of the Holy Life and Happy Death of Iohn Bruen of Bruen-Stapleford, in the County of Chester, Esquire* (London, 1641).

Hitchens, C., *For the Sake of Argument: Essays and Minority Reports* (London: Verso, 1993).
Hooley, D. M., *Roman Satire* (Oxford: Blackwell, 2007).
Howard, M., *Modern Wicca: A History from Gerald Gardner to the Present* (Woodbury, MN: Llewellyn, 2010).
— *Children of Cain: A Study of Modern Traditional Witches* (Richmond Vista, PA: Three Hands Press, 2011).
Hughes, J., *Arthurian Myths and Alchemy: The Kingship of Edward IV* (Stroud: Sutton, 2002).
— 'Politics and the Occult at the Court of Edward IV' in M. Gosman, A. MacDonald and A. Vanderjagt (eds.), *Princes and Princely Culture, 1450–1650: Volume Two* (Leiden: Brill, 2005), pp. 97–128.
— *The Rise of Alchemy in Fourteenth-Century England: Plantagenet Kings and the Search for the Philosopher's Stone* (London: Continuum, 2012).
Hutton, R., *The Pagan Religions of the Ancient British Isles: Their Nature and Legacy* (Oxford: Blackwell, 1991).
— *The Triumph of the Moon: A History of Modern Pagan Witchcraft* (Oxford: Oxford University Press, 1999).
— 'Valiente [née Dominy], Doreen Edith' in *The Oxford Dictionary of National Biography* (Oxford: Oxford University Press, 2004), vol. 56, p. 61.
— 'Witch-Hunting in Celtic Societies', *Past and Present* 212 (2011), 43–71.
— *Pagan Britain* (New Haven, CT: Yale University Press, 2013).
— *The Witch: A History of Fear, from Ancient Times to the Present* (New Haven, CT: Yale University Press, 2017).
Janacek, B., *Alchemical Belief: Occultism in the Religious Culture of Early Modern England* (University Park, PA: Pennsylvania State University Press, 2011).
Jarman, A. O. H., 'The Merlin Legend and the Welsh Tradition of Prophecy' in P. H Goodrich and R. H. Thompson (eds.), *Merlin: A Casebook* (London: Routledge, 2003), pp. 103–28.

Bibliography

Jenkins, R., *Black Magic and Bogeymen: Fear, Rumour and Popular Belief in the North of Ireland, 1972–74* (Cork: Cork University Press, 2015)

Jolley, D. and Paterson, J. L., 'Pylons Ablaze: Examining the Role of 5G COVID-19 Conspiracy Beliefs and Support for Violence', *British Journal of Social Sociology* 59 (2020), 628–40.

Jones, G. L., *The Discovery of Hebrew in Tudor England: A Third Language* (Manchester: Manchester University Press, 1983).

Jones, J. H. (ed.), *The English Faust Book: A Critical Edition based on the Text of 1592* (Cambridge: Cambridge University Press, 1994).

Jones, N., 'Defining Superstitions: Treasonous Catholics and the Act against Witchcraft of 1563', in C. Carlton (ed.), *State, Sovereigns and Society in Early Modern England: Essays in Honour of A. J. Slavin* (Stroud: Sutton, 1998), pp. 187–204.

Jones, W. R., 'Political Uses of Sorcery in the Middle Ages', *The Historian* 34 (1972), 670–87.

Kaczynski, R., *Perdurabo: The Life of Aleister Crowley*, 2nd ed. (Berkeley, CA: North Atlantic Books, 2010).

Kassell, L., *Medicine and Magic in Medieval London: Simon Forman: Astrologer, Alchemist, and Physician* (Oxford: Clarendon, 2005).

'"All was this land full-fill'd of faerie", or Magic and the Past in Early Modern England', *Journal of the History of Ideas* 67 (2006), 107–22.

Katz, D. S., *The Occult Tradition: From the Renaissance to the Present Day* (London: Pimlico, 2007).

Kavey, A., *Books of Secrets: Natural Philosophy in England, 1550–1600* (Champaign, IL: University of Illinois Press, 2007).

Kelly, H. A., 'English Kings and the Fear of Sorcery', *Mediaeval Studies* 39 (1977), 206–38.

Kelsey, H., *Sir Francis Drake: The Queen's Pirate*, 2nd ed. (New Haven, CT: Yale University Press, 2002).

Kieckhefer, R., 'The Specific Rationality of Medieval Magic', *The American Historical Review* 99 (1994), 813–36.
— (ed.), *Forbidden Rites. A Necromancer's Manual of the Fifteenth Century* (Stroud: Sutton, 1997).
— *Magic in the Middle Ages*, 2nd ed. (Cambridge: Cambridge University Press, 2000).
Kilroy, G., *Edmund Campion: Memory and Transcription* (Aldershot: Ashgate, 2005).
Kingsley, S. A., *God's Gold: The Quest for the Lost Temple Treasure of Jerusalem* (London: John Murray, 2006).
Kitch, A., 'The "Ingendred" Stone: The Ripley Scrolls and the Generative Science of Alchemy', *Huntington Library Quarterly* 78 (2015), 87–125.
Kittredge, G. L., *Witchcraft in Old and New England* (Cambridge, MA: Harvard University Press, 1928).
Klaassen, F., 'Ritual Invocation and Early Modern Science: The Skrying Experiments of Humphrey Gilbert' in C. Fanger (ed.), *Invoking Angels: Theurgic Ideas and Practices, Thirteenth to Sixteenth Centuries* (University Park, PA: Pennsylvania State University Press, 2012), pp. 341–66.
— *The Transformations of Magic: Illicit Learned Magic in the Later Middle Ages and Renaissance* (University Park, PA: Pennsylvania State University Press, 2013).
Knight, S. T., *Merlin: Knowledge and Power through the Ages* (Ithaca, NY: Cornell University Press, 2009).
La Fontaine, J. S., *Speak of the Devil: Tales of Satanic Abuse in Contemporary England* (Cambridge: Cambridge University Press, 1998).
Lachman, G., *Politics and the Occult: The Left, The Right, and the Radically Unseen* (Wheaton, IL: Quest Books, 2008).
— *Dark Star Rising: Magick and Power in the Age of Trump* (New York: Tarcher Perigee, 2018)
Láng, B., *Unlocked Books: Manuscripts of Learned Magic in the Medieval Libraries of Central Europe* (University Park, PA: Pennsylvania State University Press, 2008).

'Why Magic Cannot be Falsified by Experiments' in E. Bever and R. Styers (eds.), *Magic in the Modern World: Strategies of Repression and Legitimization* (University Park, PA: Pennsylvania State University Press, 2017), pp. 49–65.

Larner, C., *Witchcraft and Religion: The Politics of Popular Belief* (Oxford: Blackwell, 1984).

Larsen, E., *The School of Heretics: Academic Condemnation at the University of Oxford, 1277–1409* (Leiden: Brill, 2011).

Lawrence, D. R., *The Complete Soldier: Military Books and Military Culture in Early Stuart England, 1603–1645* (Leiden: Brill, 2009).

Lawrence-Mathers, A., *The True History of Merlin the Magician* (New Haven, CT: Yale University Press, 2012).

Leland, J., 'Witchcraft and the Woodvilles: A Standard Medieval Smear?' in D. L. Biggs, S. D. Michalove and A. Compton Reeves (eds.), *Reputation and Representation in Fifteenth-Century Europe* (Brill: Leiden, 2004), pp. 267–88.

'*Life* Goes to a Hex Party', *Life Magazine* 10:6 (10 February 1941), 86–9.

Liuzza, R. M., 'What Is and Is Not Magic: The Case of Anglo-Saxon Prognostics', *Societas Magica Newsletter* 12 (Spring 2004), 1–4.

Lloyd, James William, 'The West Country Adventures of Saint Augustine of Canterbury', *Folklore* 131 (2020), 413–34.

Lloyd Jones, G., *The Discovery of Hebrew in Tudor England: A Third Language* (Manchester: Manchester University Press, 1983).

Loar, C., *Political Magic: British Fictions of Savagery and Sovereignty, 1650–1750* (New York: Fordham University Press, 2014).

Lucie-Smith, E., *Joan of Arc* (London: Allen Lane, 1976).

Luhrmann, T., *Persuasions of the Witch's Craft: Ritual Magic in Contemporary England* (Oxford: Blackwell, 1989).

Luthman, J., *Love, Madness, and Scandal: The Life of Frances Coke Villiers, Viscountess Purbeck* (Oxford: Oxford University Press, 2017).

Mackinlay, J. M., *Folklore of Scottish Lochs and Springs* (Glasgow: W. Hodge and Co., 1893).
Marshall, P., *Beliefs and the Dead in Early Modern England* (Oxford: Oxford University Press, 2002).
Martin, M., *Literature and the Encounter with God in Post-Reformation England* (Farnham: Ashgate, 2014).
Maxwell-Stuart, P. G., *Satan's Conspiracy: Magic and Witchcraft in Sixteenth-Century Scotland* (East Linton: Tuckwell Press, 2001).
  'King James's Experience of Witches, and the English Witchcraft Act of 1604' in J. Newton and J. Bath (eds.), *Witchcraft and the Act of 1604* (Leiden: Brill, 2008), pp. 31–46.
  The Chemical Choir: A History of Alchemy (London: Bloomsbury, 2012).
  The British Witch: The Biography (Stroud: Amberley, 2014).
  'Magic in the Ancient World' in O. Davies (ed.), *The Oxford Illustrated History of Witchcraft and Magic* (Oxford: Oxford University Press, 2017), pp. 1–28.
McConnell, A., 'Lambe, John' in *The Oxford Dictionary of National Biography* (Oxford: Oxford University Press, 2004), vol. 32, pp. 296–7.
McKenna, J. W., 'How God Became an Englishman' in D. J. Guth and J. W. McKenna (eds.), *Tudor Rule and Revolution: Essays for G. R. Elton from His American Friends* (Cambridge: Cambridge University Press, 1982), pp. 25–44.
Mendelsohn, J. A., 'Alchemy and Politics in England, 1649–1665', *Past and Present* 135 (1992), 30–78.
Menghi, G., *Flagellum daemonum, seu exorcismi terribiles, potentissimi et efficaces* (Bologna, 1577).
  Eversio daemonum e corporibus obsessis (Bologna, 1588).
Michell, J., *Confessions of a Radical Traditionalist: Essays by John Michell*, edited by J. Godwin (Waterbury, VT: Dominion Press, 2005).
Mills, A. D., *A Dictionary of English Place-Names* (Oxford: Oxford University Press, 1991).

Monod, P. K., *Jacobitism and the English People, 1688–1788* (Cambridge: Cambridge University Press, 1989).
 Solomon's Secret Arts: The Occult in the Age of Enlightenment (New Haven, CT: Yale University Press, 2013).
Morpurgo, P., 'Scot [Scott], Michael' in *The Oxford Dictionary of National Biography* (Oxford: Oxford University Press, 2004), vol. 49, pp. 328–32.
Mulder, D., *The Alchemy of Revolution: Gerrard Winstanley's Occultism and Seventeenth-Century English Communism* (New York: Peter Lang, 1990).
Naudé, G., *The History of Magick, By Way of Apology, For All the Wise Men Who Have Unjustly Been Reputed Magicians, from the Creation, to the Present Age*, translated by J. Davies (London, 1657).
Neary, A., 'The Origins and Character of the Kilkenny Witchcraft Case of 1324', *Proceedings of the Royal Irish Academy: Archaeology, Culture, History, Literature* 83C (1983), 333–50.
Nicholl, C., *The Reckoning: The Murder of Christopher Marlowe*, 2nd ed. (London: Vintage, 2002).
Nicholls, M., 'Percy, Henry, Ninth Earl of Northumberland' in *The Oxford Dictionary of National Biography* (Oxford: Oxford University Press, 2004), vol. 43, pp. 711–13.
Nun-Ingerflom, C. S., 'How Old Magic Does the Trick for Modern Politics', *Russian History* 40 (2013), 428–50.
Nyndge, E., *A True and Fearful Vexation of One Alexander Nyndge* (London, 1615), reprinted in P. Almond (ed.), *Demonic Possession and Exorcism in Early Modern England* (Cambridge: Cambridge University Press, 2004), pp. 46–57.
O'Conor, N. J., *Godes Peace and the Queenes: Vicissitudes of a House, 1539–1615* (Oxford: Oxford University Press, 1934).
Oosthuizen, S., *The Emergence of the English* (Leeds: Arc Humanities Press, 2019).
Oppenheim, J., *The Other World: Spiritualism and Psychical Research in England, 1850–1914* (Cambridge: Cambridge University Press, 1986).

Osbern, Vita S. *Dunstani* in Eadmer of Canterbury, *Lives and Miracles of Saints Oda, Dunstan and Oswald*, edited by A. J. Turner and B. J. Muir (Oxford: Clarendon Press, 2006), pp. 41–159.

Otto, B.-C. and Stausberg, M., 'General Introduction' in B.-C. Otto and M. Stausberg (eds.), *Defining Magic: A Reader*, 2nd ed. (London: Routledge, 2014), pp. 1–15.

Page, R. I., 'Anglo-Saxon Runes and Magic', *Journal of the British Archaeological Association*, 3rd Series, 27 (1964), 14–31.

Page, S., *Magic in the Cloister: Pious Motives, Illicit Interests, and Occult Approaches to the Medieval Universe* (University Park, PA: Pennsylvania State University Press, 2013).

Magic in Medieval Manuscripts, 2nd ed. (London: The British Library, 2017a).

'Medieval Magic' in O. Davies (ed.), *The Oxford Illustrated History of Witchcraft and Magic* (Oxford: Oxford University Press, 2017b), pp. 29–64.

Parish, H., 'Magic and Priestcraft: Reformers and Reformation' in D. J. Collins (ed.), *The Cambridge History of Magic and Witchcraft in the West from Antiquity to the Present* (Cambridge: Cambridge University Press, 2015a), pp. 393–425.

(ed.), *Superstition and Magic in Early Modern Europe: A Reader* (London: Bloomsbury, 2015b), p. 16.

Parry, G., *The Arch-Conjurer of England: John Dee* (New Haven, CT: Yale University Press, 2011).

Patel, S. S., 'Treason, Plot, and Witchcraft', *Archaeology* 68 (2015), 23.

Paton, D., 'Witchcraft, Poison, Law, and Atlantic Slavery', *William and Mary Quarterly* 69 (2012), 235–64.

Pearson, N. G., *The Devil's Plantation: East Anglian Lore, Witchcraft and Folk-Magic* (London: Troy Books, 2015).

Pennecuik, Alexander, *The Works of Alexander Pennecuik* (Leith: A. Allardice, 1815).

Péporté, P., *Constructing the Middle Ages: Historiography, Collective Memory and Nation-Building in Luxembourg* (Brill: Leiden, 2011).

Perry, C., 'The Politics of Access and Representations of the Sodomite King in Early Modern England', *Renaissance Quarterly* 53 (2000), 1054–83.
Perry, M. (ed.), *Deliverance: Psychic Disturbances and Occult Involvement* (London: SPCK, 1987).
Peters, E., *The Magician, the Witch, and the Law* (Philadelphia, PA: University of Pennsylvania Press, 1978).
  'Political Sorcery at the Turn of the Fourteenth Century' in K. Jolly, C. Raudvere and E. Peters (eds.), *Witchcraft and Magic in Europe, Volume 3: The Middle Ages* (London: Athlone, 2002), pp. 218–22.
Petitpierre, R. (ed.), *Exorcism: The Report of a Committee convened by the Bishop of Exeter* (London: SPCK, 1972).
  Exorcising Devils (London: Robert Hale, 1976).
Porter, R., 'Witchcraft and Magic in Enlightenment, Romantic and Liberal Thought', in M. Gijswit-Hofstra and R. Porter (eds.), *Witchcraft and Magic in Europe: The Eighteenth and Nineteenth Centuries* (London: Athlone Press, 1999), pp. 191–254.
Power, M., *Roger Bacon and the Defence of Christendom* (Cambridge: Cambridge University Press, 2013).
Purkiss, D., *The Witch in History: Early Modern and Twentieth-Century Representations* (London: Routledge, 1996).
  Troublesome Things: A History of Fairies and Fairy Stories (London: Allen Lane, 2000).
Quaife, G. R., *Godly Zeal and Furious Rage: The Witch in Early Modern Europe*, 2nd ed. (London: Routledge, 2011).
Rattansi, M., 'Paracelsus and the Puritan Revolution', *Ambix* 11 (1963), 24–32.
Raiswell, R. and Dendle, P., 'Demon Possession in Anglo-Saxon and Early Modern England: Continuity and Evolution in Social Context', *Journal of British Studies* 47 (2008), 738–67.
Revolution Politicks: Being a Compleat Collection of All the Reports, Lyes, and Stories, Which Were the Forerunner of the Great Revolution in 1688, 8 vols. (London, 1733).

Richards, J., '"His Nowe Majestie" and the English Monarchy: the Kingship of Charles I before 1640', *Past and Present* 113 (1986), 86–94.

Richardson, A. (ed.), *Dancers to the Gods: The Magical Records of Charles Seymour and Christine Hartley 1937–1939* (Wellingborough: Aquarian Press, 1985).

Priestess: The Life and Magic of Dion Fortune (Wellingborough: Aquarian Press, 1987).

Rider, C., *Magic and Impotence in the Middle Ages* (Oxford: Oxford University Press, 2006).

Robinson, H. (ed.), *The Zurich Letters* (Cambridge: Parker Society, 1842).

Ryan, P., 'Shakespeare's Joan and the Great Whore of Babylon', *Renaissance and Reformation, New Series* 28 (2004), 55–82.

Saltman, K. J., 'Salvational Super-Agents and Conspiratorial Secret Agents: Conspiracy, Theory, and Fantasies of Control', *Simploke* 28 (2020), 51–63.

Saul, N., *Richard II* (New Haven, CT: Yale University Press, 1997).

Saunders, C. J., *Magic and the Supernatural in Medieval English Romance* (Cambridge: D. S. Brewer, 2010).

Sax, B., 'Medievalism, Paganism, and the Tower Ravens', *Pomegranate* 9 (2007), 62–77.

Sayles, G. O. (ed.), *Select Cases in the Court of King's Bench: Richard II, Henry IV and Henry V: Volume VII* (London: Selden Society, 1971).

Scholem, G., *Major Trends in Jewish Mysticism*, 3rd ed. (New York: Schocken, 1995).

Schuchard, M. K., *Restoring the Temple of Vision: Cabalistic Freemasonry and Stuart Culture* (Leiden: Brill, 2002).

Schwyzer, P., 'King Arthur and the Tudor Dynasty' in J. Parker and C. Wagner (eds.), *The Oxford Handbook of Victorian Medievalism* (Oxford: Oxford University Press, 2020), pp. 23–33.

Scot, R., *The Discovery of Witchcraft*, 2nd ed. (London, 1665).

Shamas, L. A., 'We Three': The Mythology of Shakespeare's Weird Sisters (New York: Peter Lang, 2007).

Sharpe, J., The Bewitching of Anne Gunter: A Horrible and True Story of Deception, Witchcraft, Murder, and the King of England (London: Routledge, 2000).

Simpson, J. Y., 'Notes on Some Scottish Magical Charm-Stones, or Curing-Stones', Proceedings of the Society of Antiquaries of Scotland 4 (1863), 211–24.

Skinner, S. and Rankine, D. (eds.), A Cunning Man's Grimoire: The Secret of Secrets, being Rawlinson MS. D. 253 (Singapore: Golden Hoard Press, 2018).

Smith, D. L., 'Politics in Early Stuart Britain, 1603–1640' in B. Coward (ed.), A Companion to Stuart Britain (Oxford: Blackwell, 2003), pp. 233–52.

Smith, S. B., Diana in Search of Herself: Portrait of a Troubled Princess (New York: Times Books, 1999).

Sneddon, A., Witchcraft and Magic in Ireland (Basingstoke: Palgrave MacMillan, 2015).

Spence, R. B., Secret Agent 666: Aleister Crowley, British Intelligence and the Occult (Port Townsend, WA: Feral House, 2008).

Stacy, W. R., 'Richard Roose and the Use of Parliamentary Attainder in the Reign of Henry VIII', The Historical Journal 29 (1986), 1–15.

Steible, M., 'Jane Shore and the Politics of Cursing', Studies in English Literature, 1500–1900 43 (2003), 1–17.

Stevenson, J. H. and Durie, B., Heraldry in Scotland (Glasgow: James Maclehose and Sons, 1914).

Stone, D., 'Nazism as Modern Magic: Bronislaw Malinowski's Political Anthropology', History and Anthropology 14 (2003), 203–18.

Stoyle, M., Soldiers and Strangers: An Ethnic History of the English Civil War (New Haven, CT: Yale University Press, 2005).

The Black Legend of Prince Rupert's Dog: Witchcraft and Propaganda during the English Civil War (Liverpool: Liverpool University Press, 2011).

Strathmann, E. A., 'John Dee as Ralegh's "Conjurer"', *Huntington Library Quarterly* 10 (1947), 365–72.

Stratton, K. B., 'Early Greco-Roman Antiquity' in D. J. Collins (ed.), *The Cambridge History of Magic and Witchcraft in the West from Antiquity to the Present* (Cambridge: Cambridge University Press, 2015), pp. 83–112.

Strmska, M. F., 'Pagan Politics in the 21st Century: "Peace and Love" or "Blood and Soil"?', *The Pomegranate* 20 (2018), 5–44.

Strong, R., *Henry, Prince of Wales, and England's Lost Renaissance* (London: Thames and Hudson, 1986).

Strype, J. (ed.), *Annals of the Reformation and Establishment of Religion*, 2 vols. (London, 1709).

Sturdy, D. J., 'The Royal Touch in England' in H. Duchhardt, R. A. Jackson and D. J. Sturdy (eds.), *European Monarchy: Its Evolution and Practice from Roman Antiquity to Modern Times* (Stuttgart: Franz Steiner, 1992), pp. 171–84.

Tacitus, *The Annals of Imperial Rome*, translated by M. Grant (London: Penguin, 1996).

Tebbe, N., 'Witchcraft and Statecraft: Liberal Democracy in Africa', *Georgetown Law Journal* 96 (2007–8), 183–236.

Thomas, A., 'Crown Imperial: Coronation Ritual and Regalia in the Reign of James V' in J. Goodacre and A. A. MacDonald (eds.), *Sixteenth-Century Scotland: Essays in Honour of Michael Lynch* (Leiden: Brill, 2008), pp. 43–68.

Thomas, K., *Religion and the Decline of Magic*, 4th ed. (London: Penguin, 1991).

Thomas, T., 'The Celtic Wild Man Tradition and Geoffrey of Monmouth's *Vita Merlini*: Madness or *Contemptus Mundi*?', *Arthuriana* 10 (2000), 27–42.

Thorndike, L., *Michael Scot* (London: Nelson, 1965).

Thornton, P., *With Love from Diana* (New York: Pocket Books, 1995).

Timbers, F., *Magic and Masculinity: Ritual Magic and Gender in the Early Modern Era* (London: I. B. Tauris, 2014).

The Magical Adventures of Mary Parish: The Occult World of Seventeenth-Century London (Kirksville, MI: Truman State University Press, 2016).

Tomás, E. G., 'Outside Bets: Disciplining Gamblers in Early Modern Spain', *Hispanic Review* 77 (2009), 147–64.

Tomlin, R., 'Cursing a Thief in Iberia and Britain' in F. M. Simon and R. Gordon (eds.), *Magical Practice in the Latin West: Papers from the International Conference held at the University of Zaragoza, 30 Sept.–1st Oct. 2005* (Leiden: Brill, 2009), pp. 245–73.

Toynbee, M. R., 'Charles I and the King's Evil', *Folklore* 61 (1950), 1–14.

Truitt, E. R., 'Celestial Divination and Arabic Science in Twelfth-Century England: The History of Gerbert of Aurillac's Talking Head', *Journal of the History of Ideas* 73 (2012), 201–22.

Turrell, J. F., 'The Ritual of Royal Healing in Early Modern England: Scrofula, Liturgy, and Politics', *Anglican and Episcopal History* 68 (1999), 3–36.

Van der Poel, M., *Cornelius Agrippa: The Humanist Theologian and his Declamations* (Leiden: Brill, 1997).

Van Patten, J. K., 'Magic, Prophecy, and the Law of Treason in Reformation England', *The American Journal of Legal History* 27 (1983), 1–32.

Von Franz, E. J.-L., 'Merlin in the Grail Legend' in P. H Goodrich and R. H. Thompson (eds.), *Merlin: A Casebook* (London: Routledge, 2003), pp. 273–88.

Wade, J., *Fairies in Medieval Romance* (Basingstoke: Palgrave MacMillan, 2011).

Walker, S., 'Rumour, Sedition and Popular Protest in the Reign of Henry IV', *Past and Present* 166 (2000), 31–65.

Walsham, A., '"Frantick Hacket": Prophecy, Sorcery, Insanity, and the Elizabethan Puritan Movement', *The Historical Journal* 41 (1998), 27–66.

'Miracles and the Counter-Reformation Mission to England', *The Historical Journal* 46 (2003), 779–815.

Warner, M., *Joan of Arc: The Image of Female Heroism*, 2nd ed. (Oxford: Oxford University Press, 2013).

Waters, T., 'Magic and the British Middle Classes, 1750–1900', *Journal of British Studies* 54 (2015), 632–53.

Cursed Britain: A History of Witchcraft and Black Magic in Modern Times (New Haven, CT: Yale University Press, 2019).

Watkins, C. S., *History and the Supernatural in Medieval England* (Cambridge: Cambridge University Press, 2007).

Watts, V., *The Cambridge Dictionary of English Place-Names* (Cambridge: Cambridge University Press, 2004).

Wesley, J., *Political Writings of John Wesley*, edited by G. Maddox (Bristol: Thoemmes Press, 1998).

Wertheimer, L., 'Clerical Dissent, Popular Piety, and Sanctity in Fourteenth-Century Peterborough: The Cult of Laurence of Oxford', *Journal of British Studies* 45 (2006), 3–25.

Weston, W., *William Weston: The Autobiography of an Elizabethan*, translated by P. Caraman (London: Longmans, Green and Co., 1955).

Westwood, J. and Simpson, J., *The Lore of the Land: A Guide to England's Legends, from Spring-Heeled Jack to the Witches of Warboys* (London: Penguin, 2005).

Wheeler-Bennett, J. W., *King George VI: His Life and Reign* (London: MacMillan, 1958).

William, O., 'Exorcising Madness in Late Elizabethan England: "The Seduction of Arthington" and the Criminal Culpability of Demoniacs', *Journal of British Studies* 47 (2008), 30–52.

Woolley, B., *The Queen's Conjurer: The Life and Magic of Dr Dee* (London: Harper Collins, 2001).

Yates, F. A., *The Occult Philosophy in the Elizabethan Age* (London: Routledge and Kegan Paul, 1979).

'Renaissance Philosophers in Elizabethan England: John Dee and Giordano Bruno' in *Lull and Bruno: Collected Essays* (London: Routledge and Kegan Paul, 1982), vol. 1, pp. 210–21.

The Art of Memory, 2nd ed. (London: Pimlico, 1992).

Giordano Bruno and the Hermetic Tradition, 2nd ed. (London: Routledge, 2002).

The Rosicrucian Enlightenment, 2nd ed (London: Routledge, 2002).

Yeates, S. J., *Tribe of Witches: The Religion of the Dobunni and Hwicce* (Oxford: Oxbow, 2008).

Young. F., 'Catholic Exorcism in Early Modern England: Polemic, Propaganda and Folklore', *Recusant History* 29 (2009), 487–507.

Young. *English Catholics and the Supernatural, 1553–1829* (Farnham: Ashgate, 2013).

A History of Exorcism in Catholic Christianity (Basingstoke: Palgrave MacMillan, 2016).

Magic as a Political Crime in Medieval and Early Modern England: A History of Sorcery and Treason (London: I. B. Tauris, 2017).

Edmund: In Search of England's Lost King (London: I. B. Tauris, 2018a).

A History of Anglican Exorcism: Deliverance and Demonology in Church Ritual (London: I. B. Tauris, 2018b).

'Sir Thomas Tresham and the Christian Cabala', *British Catholic History* 35 (2020), 145–68.

Zhao, X., 'Political Uses of Wugu Sorcery in Imperial China: A Cross-Cultural Perspective', *Magic, Ritual, and Witchcraft* 8 (2013), 132–61.

Zumthor, P., 'Merlin: Prophet and Magician' in P. H Goodrich and R. H. Thompson (eds.), *Merlin: A Casebook* (London: Routledge, 2003), 129–59.

Web sources

Armstrong, N., 'Coven ready: from Instagram to TV, why are witches so popular?', *The Guardian*, 15 September 2018, theguardian.com/tv-and-radio/2018/sep/15/witches-occult-dramas-tv-chilling-adventures-of-sabrina-strange-angel.

Fielding, J., 'Jimmy Savile was part of satanic ring', *The Sunday Express*, 13 January 2013, express.co.uk/news/uk/370439/Jimmy-Savile-was-part-of-satanic-ring.

Gibbons, F., 'Erdoğan's chief advisor knows what's behind Turkey's protests – telekinesis', *The Guardian*, 13 July

2013, theguardian.com/commentisfree/2013/jul/13/erdogan-turkey-protests-telekinesis-conspiracy-theories.

Hansard, 19 December 1988, publications.parliament.uk/pa/cm198889/cmhansrd/1988-12-19/Debate-4.html

.Hansard, 10 May 1990, publications.parliament.uk/pa/cm198990/cmhansrd/1990-05-10/Debate-2.html.

Hansard, 14 March 1991, api.parliament.uk/historic-hansard/commons/1991/mar/14/adjournment-easter-and-monday-6-may.

Kettley, S., 'Nostradamus 2019 prediction: Donald Trump assassination, war and hard Brexit', *The Daily Express*, 4 January 2019, express.co.uk/news/weird/1062497/Nostradamus-2019-predictions-forecast-donald-trump-assassination-war-brexit.

'Maoist cult leader sexually assaulted followers and kept daughter as slave for 30 years, court hears', *The Daily Telegraph*, 12 November 2015, telegraph.co.uk/news/uknews/crime/11990783/Maoist-cult-leader-kept-daughter-as-slave-in-south-London-for-30-years-court-hears.html.

Nash, C., '#Magicresistance: The Rise of Feminist Witchcraft', *Breitbart News*, 17 December 2017, breitbart.com/tech/2017/12/17/rise-feminist-witche.

Rankin, J., 'Britain accused of "magical thinking" over Brexit plan for Irish border', *The Guardian*, 25 August 2017, theguardian.com/uk-news/2017/aug/25/uk-accused-of-magical-thinking-over-brexit-plan-for-irish-border.

'Tower of London's "queen" raven Merlina missing', *BBC News*, 13 January 2021, bbc.co.uk/news/uk-england-london-55651104.

'Witches cast "mass spell" against Donald Trump', *BBC News*, 25 February 2017, bbc.co.uk/news/world-us-canada-39090334.

INDEX

Abbot, George, archbishop of Canterbury, 206
absolutism, monarchical, 22, 27, 111, 136, 191, 213, 223, 234, 264
Adelard of Bath, 65, 72–3
advisors, magical, 27–8, 92–7, 182, 250, 277, 302, 320, 331–4, 336–7, 341, 343
aeromancy, 95
Africa, 5, 21–2, 281, 319, 323, 325
Agrippa, Heinrich Cornelius, 144–5, 179, 239, 245
alchemy, 2, 5, 13, 21, 26, 28–9, 47, 49, 56, 64–70, 77, 82–3, 87, 92, 94, 100–5, 108, 110–13, 119–20, 128–30, 132, 158, 163–6, 168–70, 172–4, 185, 188, 195, 209–10, 231, 236–7, 240–4, 250, 252–4, 261, 263–5, 268–9, 272–3, 277, 287, 331, 333, 335, 339, 343
Alexander the Great, king of Macedon, 92, 109
Alexander VI, pope, 195
Alexis, Tsar of Russia, 20
Alfonsi, Peter, 72
Alighieri, Dante, 93
Al-Kindi, 48
Allen, William, 186
almanacs, 142–3, 228, 230–1, 250, 271
Almandal, 61

Ambrosius, 38–9
America, United States of, xvi, 287, 290, 292, 300, 302, 307, 311, 325, 328, 330
American War of Independence, 267
Amphitrite, 180
Amsterdam, Low Countries, 245–6, 262
amulets, 73, 107, 218, 248, 282
anarchism, 311, 314
Anarchy, the (1135-1153), 4, 72, 88, 91
Anderson, Edmund, 205
Andrew of Wyntoun, 193
angel (coin). *See* touchpieces
angel-conjuring, 61–2, 164, 171, 177, 261, 263, 277
angels, 96, 155, 182, 260–1, 268, 274
Anglesey, 32, 34
animals, allegorical, 79, 148
Anjou, duke of, 175, 182
Anne of Denmark, queen of England, 207
Anne, queen of Great Britain, 49, 234, 237, 275–6, 282
Antichrist, 112
anti-Sadducism, 249
Ap Gruffydd, Rhys, 148
Ap Owen, Madoc, 171
apocalypticism, 59, 112, 168, 174, 177, 244–7, 287, 324
Apollo, 36, 93
Apuleius, 48

369

Index

Aquinas, Thomas, 97
Arabic language, 46, 61, 68, 73, 93
architecture, 203, 211–12
Argentine, John, 100, 150
Aristotelianism, 48, 68, 74, 97, 169, 273
Aristotle, 109, 273
Armada, Spanish, 173, 298
Arnold of Villanova, 58, 66, 102, 112
Arran, earl of, 196
Arthur, king, 17, 27, 33, 37, 65, 67, 87, 158, 169, 174, 211, 239, 297, 306, 311
Arthur, prince of Wales, 139
Arthuret, Cumbria, 38
Arthurianism, 27, 69, 130, 138–9, 170–1, 175–6, 185, 188, 212, 332, 341–2
Ashdown Forest, Sussex, 299–300
Ashenden, John, 103–4
Ashmole, Elias, 17, 68, 228, 231, 241, 250, 332
astral magic, 48, 62, 73–5, 96, 100, 106
astrolabes, 74, 88, 111
astrology, 2, 13, 15, 17, 21, 26, 29, 31, 46, 56, 64, 69–77, 82–3, 87, 91–2, 94–6, 98, 103–4, 106–7, 111, 116–19, 125, 132, 134, 136, 141–3, 148–51, 163, 168, 172, 178–80, 185, 191, 228–30, 232, 236–7, 250–1, 277, 293, 297, 304, 320–2, 331–2, 339, 341, 343
  criticism of, 63, 95, 159, 181, 231
  horoscopes, 64, 71–3, 75, 98, 106–7, 109, 120–1, 126, 143, 145, 161, 182, 251, 298, 304
Atholl, countess of, 200

augury, 34, 36, 49, 76, 93
Augustine, archbishop of Canterbury, 157–8
Augustinianism, 68
Avalon, Isle of, 33
Awder, William, 184
Aylmer, John, bishop of London, 183

Bacon, Francis, 209, 240
Bacon, Roger, 27, 75, 94–5, 97, 115, 158, 165, 169, 331
Balakrishnan, Aravindan, 316
Bale, John, bishop of Ossory, 27, 154–8, 229
Balsom, Robert, 225
Balwearie, Fife, 93
bards, 37, 39
Barham, HMS, 304–5
Barons' War, 89
Bart, Jean, 274
Barton, Elizabeth, 152–3
basilisks, 55
Bath, Somerset, 36, 265
Baxter, Richard, 243
BBC, 295, 300
Beachy Head, battle of (1690), 269
Beaufort family, 126, 128, 135
Beaufort, Henry, bishop of Winchester, 126
Beaufort, Margaret, 130, 134, 138
Beaurevoir, France, 123
Becket, Thomas, archbishop of Canterbury, 89
Bede, 49–50, 153
Bedford, duke of, 107, 122, 124–5
Behmenism, 241
Ben Israel, Menasseh, 246–7
Bennett, Andrew, 318
Bensalia (fictitious island), 263–4

Index

Berkeley, Gloucestershire, 100
bewitchment, 16, 131, 206, 219, 250, 262, 331, 336–7
Bladud, king of Britain, 36, 41
Blake, Thomas, 132
Blake, William, 286–7, 315
Bletchley Park, Buckinghamshire, 315
Boccaccio, Giovanni, 93
Bodenham, Anne, 226
Boehme, Jacob, 241, 243, 245, 253, 283, 335
Boerio, John Baptista, 142
Bohemia, 94, 177, 182–3, 185, 210–11
Boleyn, Anne, queen of England, 27, 146–7, 189, 338
Bolingbroke, Roger, 125–6
Bologna, Italy, 93
Bolsonaro, Jair, 327
Boniface VIII, pope, 98
Bonner, Edmund, bishop of London, 161
Bonus, Petrus, 47
Boorde, Andrew, 143
Boreman, William, 234–5, 262
Bosworth, battle of (1485), 134
Boudicca, queen of the Iceni, 36
Boy (Prince Rupert's dog), 227
Boyle, Robert, 270, 273
Bradwardine, Thomas, 103
Brahe, Tycho, 172, 203
Bran the Blessed, 307
Brandeston, Suffolk, 224
Brandon, Suffolk, 86
Brest, France, 274
Brexit, 4, 306, 316, 329–30
Bricket Wood Coven, 300, 315
Bridlington, Yorkshire, 104, 128–9
British Israelism, 287, 314
Brittany, 40
brontology, 43, 76

Brothers, Richard, 285
Bruno, Giordano, 58–9, 178–83, 341
Buchanan, George, 191
buggery (crime), 147
Bulstrode, Whitlocke, 257
Burdett, Thomas, 132
Bury St Edmunds, Suffolk, 90, 128, 184, 224
Bury, Richard, bishop of Durham, 103
Butler, Pierce, 218

cabals, 1, 272
Cabot, John, 170
Cade, Jack, 127
Caerleon, Monmouthshire, 65
Caesarius of Heisterbach, 92
Calais, France, 111, 170
Calfhill, James, 160
California, 302
Calne, Council of, 158
Cambridge, Cambridgeshire, 258, 294
Camden, William, 167
Camilla, duchess of Cornwall, 320
Canterbury, Kent, 152
Carew, Thomas, 182
Carisbrooke Castle, Isle of Wight, 231
Carlism, 291
Carmarthen, Carmarthenshire, 39
Caroline of Brunswick, queen of the United Kingdom, 322
Carr, Robert, earl of Somerset, 213–14, 216
Cartimandua, queen of the Brigantes, 35
Casaubon, Meric, 291
Cashel, Co. Tipperary, Ireland, 93

Index

Cassius Dio, 36
Cassodorien, 92
Catholicism, 22, 140, 151–61, 180, 188, 197, 199, 222, 236, 256, 260, 271
Catilinet, Jean, 144
Cauchon, Pierre, bishop of Beauvais, 124
Cecil, Robert, earl of Salisbury, 216
Cecil, William, Lord Burghley, 149, 162–3, 166, 169, 174–7, 183, 185, 341
censorship, 29, 97, 143, 229, 231, 239, 248
cessationism, 156
Challenger (space shuttle), 317
chance, games of, 52
change, political, 4–5, 17–18, 24, 135–6, 140, 188, 232, 237, 325, 328
changelings, 89, 101, 127
Chaos Magick, 311
Chapman, George, 163
Chapuys, Eustace, 147
Charles I, king of England, 182, 191, 209, 211, 213, 218, 225, 229, 231–3, 243, 248, 264, 271, 334, 336, 343
  execution, 29, 235, 237–8
  personal rule, 220–2, 239
  trial, 228
Charles II, king of England, 228, 234, 236–51, 255, 261, 263, 272, 332, 334
  coronation, 250
  death, 260
  ghost of, 265
  interest in alchemy, 165, 252–4, 335
  restoration, 29, 235–6
Charles V, emperor, 106, 152
Charles V, king of France, 111
Charles VI, king of France, 111, 115
Charles VII, king of France, 123–4
Charles, prince of Wales (b. 1948), 320
charms, 3, 43, 45, 114, 117–18, 123, 151, 154, 156, 160, 186, 192, 198, 223, 248
Charnock, Thomas, 165
Chaucer, Geoffrey, 111
Cheyne, Thomas, 167
China, 22, 112, 237, 263, 302, 317, 323
chivalry, 17, 139
church courts, 127, 140, 149, 151, 157, 217
Churchill, Winston, 300–2, 305, 332, 342
Cicero, 178
Cinque Ports, 95
Civil War, English, 22, 28, 143, 213, 221–4, 233–4, 237, 239, 255, 277, 313, 338–9
Clary, Mary, 243
Clement VIII, pope, 182
Clifford, Rosamund, 89–92
Clifford, Walter, 89
climate change, 324
Climbié, Victoria, 319
Clinton, Edward, earl of Lincoln, 168
Cobham, Eleanor, duchess of Gloucester, 64, 125–6, 135, 338
Cochrane, Robert, 310
Coke, Edward, 215
Coke, Frances, viscountess Purbeck, 216–17
Colchester, Essex, 230
Cold War, 30, 307–8, 311, 340
Colet, John, 144

Index

colonialism, 21, 25, 34, 280–2, 322–3
Columbus, Christopher, 170
Communism, 241, 278, 293, 323
conservatism, political, 20, 30, 231, 235, 237, 256, 277, 290, 317
Conservative Party, 288, 290, 318
Copdock, Suffolk, 224
Copping, John, 184
Corbyn, Jeremy, 317
Cornelius de Lannoy, 166
coronations, 76, 95–7, 120–1, 123, 146, 162, 250
Cosin, John, bishop of Durham, 222
counterfeiting, 69, 119
Courtenay, John, bishop of Norwich, 120–1
courts, royal, 15–17, 19, 23, 27–8, 38, 63, 75–6, 84, 87–92, 95, 99, 102, 108, 110–11, 119, 123–4, 132–3, 135–6, 139, 141–51, 161, 164, 167, 169, 175, 177, 180, 182, 207, 210–18, 221, 223, 232, 238, 245, 250–3, 270, 281, 322, 331–2, 335–7, 343
Covenanters, 257
covens, 199, 298–300, 310–11, 315
Coventry, Warwickshire, 99
COVID-19, 4, 307, 329–30
Cradocke, John, 167
cramp rings, 129
Cranmer, Thomas, archbishop of Canterbury, 152
Crécy, battle of (1346), 103–4
Cromwell, Oliver, 227–8, 246, 255, 271
Cromwell, Thomas, 22, 146, 152, 188, 336

Crowley, Aleister, 30, 290–5, 299–303, 332
Crowley, Amado, 299
cryptography, 163, 181, 341
Cummings, Dominic, 336
Cummins, Geraldine, 296, 307
cunning-folk, 164, 187, 198, 213, 226, 232, 253, 286, 320
Cunningham, James, 283
Curry, John, 293
curse tablets, 36–7

Dalby, William, 102
Dalton, Thomas, 131
Dastin, John, 66, 102, 104
Davies, Eleanor, 219
Davies, John, 165
Davies, Mary, 294
D-Day, 305
De Wohl, Louis, 297
Dee, John, 17, 28, 139, 149–50, 161–9, 174–5, 179–81, 183–6, 188–9, 210–11, 228, 268, 273, 332
    influence on Aleister Crowley, 291
    theories of empire, 170–1, 176–8, 302
demonology, 5–6, 28, 52, 124, 127, 201–2, 231, 280, 308, 310
demons, 10, 12, 41, 44, 47, 51, 56–7, 60–3, 71, 76, 78–9, 81–2, 87, 92, 94, 98, 114–16, 120, 124, 130, 144, 153, 156–8, 164, 218
Denmark, 20, 41, 200, 203
Derby, William, 116
Despenser, Hugh, earl of Winchester, 100
Destiny, Stone of, 96
Devereux, Robert, 2nd earl of Essex, 187, 213

373

Index

Devereux, Robert, 3rd earl of Essex, 207, 213
devil-worship, 82, 99–100, 127, 157
Diana (goddess), 181
Diana, Princess of Wales, 30, 321, 343
Dickens, Geoffrey, 318
Dickinson, Edmund, 252
Dicsone, Alexander, 179, 182
Diggers, 241–2
dissenters, Protestant, 236, 256, 265, 271, 283
distillation, 165, 253
divination, 3, 34–5, 43–6, 52, 60, 63, 70–1, 76–8, 95, 97, 111, 192, 343
Dorchester, Dorset, 158
Doughty, Thomas, 174
Douglas, Jane, Lady Glamis, 194–5
dragons, 38, 66, 109, 130, 139, 173
Drake, Francis, 173–4, 342
Drayton, Michael, 212
dreams, 96, 101, 110–11, 155, 177, 182, 193
Drogheda, Ireland, 227
druids, 32–5, 39, 212
  modern, 314
Dudley, John, duke of Northumberland, 154
Dudley, Robert, earl of Leicester, 162, 174–7, 182–4
Dunbar, battle of (1650), 227
Duncan, Helen, 30, 303–7, 340
Dunkirk, France, 274, 297
Dunstan, archbishop of Canterbury, 49–50, 66, 157
Dutch Revolt, 174, 176
Dutch Wars, 250

Earls Colne, Essex, 222
Earth Mysteries, 313–14

Edinburgh, Lothian, 190, 192, 203
  Arthur's Seat, 192
  Castle, 194
  Holyrood Palace, 192
Edmund, king of East Anglia, 110
Edward I, king of England, 96, 98, 107, 244
Edward II, king of England, 91, 98–9, 104, 107
Edward III, king of England, 65–7, 75, 102–7, 109
Edward IV, king of England, 91, 108, 129–30, 134–5, 138, 147, 162, 331, 335
Edward of Westminster, prince of Wales, 127
Edward the Confessor, king of England, 49, 107, 110, 130
Edward V, king of England, 19, 132, 134
Edward VI, king of England, 141, 149, 154, 159, 162
Edward VII, king of the United Kingdom, 319
Edward, the Black Prince, 109
Edwards, Susanna, 257
Edwin, king of Northumbria, 49
effigies, magical. *See* images, magical
Egypt, 47, 58–9, 95, 156, 181, 224, 285, 301
Eleanor of Aquitaine, queen of England, 101, 135
elixirs, 2, 67, 100, 105, 131, 253, 335
Elizabeth I, queen of England, 18, 27–8, 108, 139, 141, 147–8, 161–71, 174–7, 180–4, 186–9, 200, 204, 209, 244, 248, 268, 311, 332–4, 336, 342

accession, 160
coronation, 162
experiments with alchemy, 163, 165–6, 185–6
images of, 23, 185
Elizabeth of York, queen of England, 138, 143
Elizabeth, queen of Bohemia, 210
Elkes, Thomas, 176
Ely, Cambridgeshire, 85, 127
empire, idea of, 28, 158, 169–78, 185, 211, 281–2, 287, 302
Enlightenment, 6, 21, 201, 234, 266, 279–86
epilepsy, 130
Epiphany, 17, 110
Episcopi, canon, 44
Erbery, William, 243
Erdoğan, Recep Tayyip, 327
Erghome, John, 100, 104, 108
Erskine, James, 280
espionage. *See* spying
Ethelbert, king of Kent, 157
European Union (EU), 316, 327, 329
Everard, William, 241
Evola, Julius, 313, 315, 328
Exclusion Crisis, 236, 256–7, 271
Exeter, Devon, 257
exorcism, 47, 63, 83, 151, 155, 234, 250, 278, 294, 309–10, 317
explorers, 164, 168, 170, 172–3
Eymerich, Nicholas, 119

Faber, Albert Otto, 252
Fabri, Fabri de Dya, 66, 102
fairies, 42, 62, 101, 127, 167–8, 192–4, 221, 260, 268–9, 274, 312
Fall, the, 55, 58
familiars, 123, 153, 225, 227
fascism, 19–20, 290, 295, 301, 313

Fastolf, John, 107
Fates, 193
favourites, royal, 15–16, 100, 213, 215–16, 218, 232
Fayed, Dodi, 321
feminism, 9, 290, 311
Fénelon, François, 284
Ferguson, Sarah, duchess of York, 320
Ficino, Marsilio, 57–8, 129, 144
Firebrace, Roy, 303–4
Firmicus, Julius, 71–2
First World War, 291–3, 323
Fisher, Geoffrey, archbishop of Canterbury, 308
Fisher, John, bishop of Rochester, 149
Fleming, Ian, 300
Flete, John, 96
Flitcham, Norfolk, 320
Fludd, Robert, 208–9
folklore, 91, 93, 108, 174, 298, 320, 336
Forman, Simon, 187–8, 193, 213–14, 228
Fortune, Dion (Violet Firth), 296, 302, 306
Foxe, John, 162
Framlingham, Suffolk, 336
France, 40, 103, 105–7, 114, 124–5, 236, 265, 284, 287, 297, 334
Franckwell, Millicent, 165
Frank, Debbie, 320
fraud, magic as, 45, 119, 124, 155–7, 206, 232, 271, 304
Frazer, James, 8
Frederick II, emperor, 93
Frederick of the Palatinate, king of Bohemia, 210
Freemasonry, 59, 180, 202–4, 208–9, 233, 272, 284–5, 288–9

French Prophets, 283
French Revolution, 30, 267
friars, 62, 100, 108, 113, 117, 119, 121, 123, 154, 178
Frobisher, Martin, 171, 173, 176
Frodsham, Humphrey, 217
functionalism, 9, 11, 14
Fusoris, Jean, 120–1

Gadbury, John, 251, 271
Galen, 263, 273
Gardner, Edward, 309
Gardner, Gerald, 290, 298, 300, 309, 315
Geffroy de Lestainx, 119
Geoffrey of Monmouth, 3, 17, 36, 38–41, 49, 65–6, 73–4, 77–9, 86–7, 120, 170, 211, 287, 331
Geoffrey, count of Anjou, 88–9
geomancy, 77, 87, 95, 97, 104, 110–11, 125, 343
George I, king of Great Britain, 276
George II, king of Great Britain, 276
George III, king of the United Kingdom, 285
George IV, king of the United Kingdom, 322
George V, king of the United Kingdom, 292
George VI, king of the United Kingdom, 282
George, duke of Clarence, 132–3, 162
George, prince of Denmark, 275
Gerald of Wales, 88–9
Gerard of Hereford, archbishop of York, 72
Gervase of Tilbury, 74
ghosts, 265, 288, 305
Gilbert, Humphrey, 164, 168–9, 174, 273

Gilbert, John, bishop of Bangor, 109
Gildas, 39
Glanvill, Joseph, 273
Glastonbury, Somerset, 66, 286, 296, 306, 314
Gloucester, Gloucestershire, 131
Glyndŵr, Owain, 120, 135, 335
Goddess Spirituality, 311
Godstow, Oxfordshire, 90
Golden Dawn, Hermetic Order of the, 289–91, 293
Goldwell, James, bishop of Norwich, 133
Gordon, John, 212
Gove, Michael, 330
Grace, Pilgrimage of, 153
Grail, Holy, 287, 292
Greatrakes, Valentine, 249, 252
Greek Fire, 168
Green Ribbon Club, 272
Greene, Robert, 158
Greenham Common, Berkshire, 311
Greenwich, Kent, 125
grimoires, 133, 163, 165
Grindal, Edmund, archbishop of Canterbury, 160
Grosseteste, Robert, bishop of Lincoln, 75, 115
gunnery, 172, 339
gunpowder, 105, 269
Gunpowder Plot, 217
Gunter, Anne, 206

Hacket, William, 184–5
Hagia Sophia, Istanbul, 95
Hailes Abbey, Gloucestershire, 117
Hajdu, Emma, 308
Halesworth, Suffolk, 224
Hall, John, 240
Hall, Thomas, 243

Index

Halley's Comet, 128
Hampton Court, Surrey, 145, 165
Hariot, Thomas, 172
Harley, Robert, earl of Oxford, 272
harm, magical, 4–5, 10–11, 56–7, 64, 80, 84, 88, 108, 115, 140, 158, 175, 188, 194, 197, 205, 217, 248, 288, 319, 335
Harrison, William, 158, 200
Hartley, Christine, 296
Hartlib, Samuel, 240
haruspicy, 34
heliocentrism, 178, 271
Hengrave, Suffolk, 167
Henri III, king of France, 179–80
Henry de Grosmont, 106
Henry I, king of England, 18, 78, 87
Henry II, king of England, 63, 72, 88–91
Henry III, king of England, 93–7, 107, 135, 331
Henry IV, king of England, 18–19, 75, 115–20, 135, 138, 270, 335, 343
Henry of Avranches, 93
Henry the Young King, 89
Henry V, king of England, 120–2, 124
Henry VI, king of England, 64, 124–7, 129, 335, 343
Henry VII, king of England, 130, 134, 138–9, 141–3, 165, 197, 332
Henry VIII, king of England, 22, 27, 79, 138–41, 143, 145, 147–8, 158
  accession, 143
  marriages, 146
  reformation under, 152–4, 160, 169, 188

Henry, prince of Wales (1594-1612), 209–10
Hepburn, James, earl of Bothwell, 200
heraldry, 79, 139, 143, 184, 195
herbalism, 55–6
heresy, 113, 122, 127–8, 160, 180, 182, 324
Hereward the Wake, 85–6
Hermeticism, 23, 57–9, 96, 129, 144, 163, 178–9, 185, 189, 203, 209–10, 233, 238, 332
Hess, Rudolf, 299–300
Heydon, John, 251
Heywood, Thomas, 229
Himmler, Heinrich, 296
Hitchens, Christopher, 321
Hitler, Adolf, 20, 295–7, 299–302
Hobbes, Thomas, 249, 273
Holinshed, Raphael, 192–3
Holme, Norfolk, 145
Holt, John, 257
homosexuality, 147, 217
Honorius III, pope, 93
Hooper, John, bishop of Gloucester, 159
Hopkins, Matthew, 224, 226, 228
Horace, 34, 60
Hounslow Heath, Middlesex, 260, 266
Howard, Frances, countess of Essex/countess of Somerset, 213–15
Howard, Henry, 3rd duke of Norfolk, 146
Howard, Henry, 4th duke of Norfolk, 166, 168, 181
Howard, Lord Henry, 181
Howard, Robert, 217
Howe, Geoffrey, 318
Hubert de Burgh, 95
Hues, Robert, 173

Hugh of Avalon, bishop of Lincoln, 90
Humphrey, duke of Gloucester, 124–5
Humphrey, John, 230
Hundred Years' War, 102–9, 134, 170, 334, 339
Hungarians, 308
Hungerford, Walter, 147, 338
Huntly, countess of, 197
Hutchinson, Francis, 259
Hven, Denmark, 203
Hwicce, 42
hydromancy, 95

Iceland, 20
Illtud, 39
images, magical, 23, 48, 57, 62, 74, 100, 106, 108, 131, 146, 175–6, 178–9, 183–4, 189, 215, 292, 322
impotence, 213
imps. *See* familiars
incubi, 38, 40–1, 69, 73, 92, 146
Inglewood, John, 119
inquisitors, 82, 119
intelligence, government, 178, 279, 291–3, 295, 299, 308, 311–12, 315, 339, 341
Interregnum, 23, 29, 83, 139, 235, 237–50, 254–5, 273, 287, 332, 338
Ipswich, Suffolk, 251
IRA, 312
Iraq War, 333
Ireland, 25–6, 93, 98–100, 154, 187, 193–4, 209, 211, 226, 249, 327
Irish Republic (1916), 293
Northern Ireland, 30, 312–13, 327, 340
Isabella II, queen of Spain, 291
Isabella of England, empress, 93

Isabella of France, queen of England, 91, 100–1, 135
Isabella of Valois, queen of England, 111, 115
Iscanus, Bartholomew, bishop of Exeter, 45
Isidore of Seville, 44
Islam, 46, 60, 65
Islamic world, 2, 40, 50, 65, 73, 77, 87
Islington, Middlesex, 175
Italy, 40, 128, 144, 150, 200

Jacobites, 237, 266, 269–71, 280, 282–5
Jacquette of Luxembourg, 131, 134
Jamaica, 280
James I, king of Scots, 195
James II, king of England (VII of Scots), 29, 234, 236, 251, 254, 259–67, 269, 275, 284, 332, 336–7
James III, king of Scots, 190–1, 194
James IV, king of Scots, 195
James V, king of Scots, 194, 196
James VI and I, king of Scots/ king of England, 23, 28, 191, 213–16, 218, 233, 239, 248, 332
  alleged murder, 218, 227
  assassination attempts, 200–1
  birth, 200
  demonological writings, 201–2
  English reign, 204–12
  interest in Freemasonry, 202–12
Jamestown, Virginia, 281
Jargeau, battle of (1429), 123
Jay, E. G., 307
Jerusalem (hymn), 286
Jews, 60, 72, 144
  expulsion from England, 62

Index

return to England, 29, 59, 244–7
Joachim of Fiore, 168
Joan of Arc, 122–4, 339
Joan of Navarre, queen of England, 121, 135
John de Montfort, 106
John de Rupescissa, 47, 112
John de Walden, 102
John of Bridlington, 153
John of Gaunt, duke of Lancaster, 113, 116, 126, 138
John of Nottingham, 99–100
John of Powderham, 101
John of Salisbury, 63
John XXII, pope, 99–100
John, king of England, 92, 158
Johnson, Boris, 336
Jones, Inigo, 211, 332, 335
Joseph of Arimathea, 66–7, 287
Jourdemayne, Margery, 127
Joyce, William ('Lord Haw-Haw'), 300–1
Jung, Carl, 9, 321

Kabbalah, 26, 59–61, 84, 144–5, 163, 179, 209, 212, 244–7, 272
Katharine of Aragon, queen of England, 146, 152
kawannah, 246–7
Kelley, Edward, 177, 183, 185, 210, 268
Kelly, David, 333
Kendal, John, 142
Kilkenny, Co. Kilkenny, Ireland, 98–9
Kilwardby, Robert, archbishop of Canterbury, 97
Kirkeby, John, 128
Knaresborough, Yorkshire, 221
Knole House, Kent, 206

Knox, John, 197
Kratzer, Nicholas, 143
Küntzel, Martha, 295
Kymer, Gilbert, 129
Kyteler, Alice, 98–9

Labour Party, 278, 317–18
Lacy, Edmund, 121
Lake, Thomas, 216
Lambe, John, 217–20, 222–3, 226, 232, 337
Landguard Fort, Suffolk, 224
Lang, Cosmo Gordon, archbishop of Canterbury, 303
Langton, Stephen, archbishop of Canterbury, 93
Langton, Walter, bishop of Coventry and Lichfield, 97–8
Latimer, John, 113
Laud, William, archbishop of Canterbury, 217, 222–3, 271, 337
Laudianism, 21, 222–4
Laurence of Oxford, 90
Layamon, 40
Le Fèvre, Nicolas, 252
Le Poer, Arnold, 99
legitimacy, political, 11, 18–21, 23, 27, 87, 92, 116, 138, 199, 207, 238, 259, 276, 282, 323
legitimism, 290–1
Leland, John, 139
Leofnoth, 71
leprosy, 105
Levellers, 241, 261
Levi, Eliphas (Alphonse-Louis Constant), 289
Lewis of Caerleon, 134, 332
ley lines, 278, 294, 313
Lilly, William, 21, 228–33, 332, 338

lithomancy, 56, 196
Lloyd, Temperance, 257
Llull, Ramon, 66, 102, 108, 178
Llwyd, Morgan, 243
Lollardy, 112–13, 116, 119, 151, 154
London, 29, 51, 114, 120, 142, 144, 146, 193, 204, 211, 213, 219, 228–9, 245, 249, 253, 265, 272, 280, 284, 289, 298, 308
  Buckingham House, 219
  Lambeth Palace, 307
  legendary foundation, 36
  Metropolitan Police, 319
  Old Bailey, 305
  Salisbury Court, 179
  Somerset House, 166
  St James's Palace, 252
  St Katherine's Hospital, 102
  St Paul's Cathedral, 115, 144, 223, 283
  Tower of, 66, 102, 105, 108, 173, 270, 306
  Westminster, Palace of, 250
  Whitehall, Palace of, 254
Louis VIII, king of France, 92
Louis XIV, king of France, 15, 250
Louvain, Low Countries, 129, 150, 191
love magic, 16, 23, 131, 140, 175, 213, 215–16
Lovetot, John, 97
Low Countries, 150, 168, 174, 176, 179, 190, 236, 263, 267
Lowes, John, 224–5, 233, 267
Lucan, 60
Luria, Isaac, 246–7
Lydgate, John, 128
Lyle, Felix, 320
Lyme Regis, Dorset, 225, 262

Macbeth, king of Scots, 192–3
Magdalene, John, 115–17, 331
Magi, the, 17, 46, 110
Magic Circle (organisation), 304
magic, definitions of, 8–14
magic, varieties of. *See* astral magic; Chaos Magick; harm, magical; love magic; natural magic; necromancy; ritual magic
magical thinking, 4–5, 9, 18–19, 323, 327–8, 330
magnetism, animal, 322
magnets, 55
Malinowski, Bronislaw, 328
Malleus maleficarum, 205
Maltby, Edward, 299
Mannyng, Robert, 40
Maoism, 316
Mar, Violat, 200
Marcelline, George, 212
Marner, Robert, 119
Marston Moor, battle of (1644), 227
Marxism, 9, 316
Mary I, queen of England, 130, 149, 159, 161, 196, 336
Mary II, queen of England, 29, 236, 259, 266–70, 273, 275, 277, 332
  death, 274
Mary of Guise, queen of Scots, 196
Mary of Modena, queen of England, 254, 264, 268, 275
Mary of Teck, queen of the United Kingdom, 282
Mary, queen of Scots, 162, 166, 181, 196, 200
Maryland, 300
Maskelyne, Jasper, 296
masques, 23, 167, 182, 207, 211, 221, 233, 281, 332, 335, 343
mass, 27, 113, 154–6
Massachusetts, 281

Mathers, Samuel Liddell
  MacGregor, 290–1
Matilda, empress, 4, 88
Maximilian II, emperor, 168
Maxwell, Lord, 168
medicine, 100, 125, 214, 217,
  228, 234, 254
  alchemical (iatrochymistry),
    100, 243, 252–4, 263–4, 335
  astrological, 56, 112, 129, 142,
    150, 187, 190–1, 203, 208,
    213, 229, 333
Medley, William, 169
Melusine, 131
memes, 328
memory, artificial, 178–81, 341
Merciless Parliament, 114
mercury (metal), 66, 68–9, 130,
  195, 209, 242, 252
Merlin, 1, 3, 18, 26, 33, 50, 66,
  77, 92–3, 109, 128, 137, 139,
  175, 239, 297, 311, 336, 342,
  344
  alchemist, 69
  artificer, 3, 138, 211
  astrologer, 73–4
  grave, 204
  magician, 40–1
  occult advisor, 17, 27–9, 92,
    139, 188, 277, 302, 331–3
  origins, 37–9
  prophet, 3, 24–5, 39–40, 78–9,
    86–7, 120, 130, 153, 158,
    228, 232, 283, 341
Merlina (raven), 306
messianism, 116, 184, 186, 246,
  285
metric system, 316
MI5, 279, 299, 303–10, 315, 341
MI6, 296, 299, 341
Michel de Castelnau, 179
Michell, John, 313–16
Mint, Royal, 108, 270

misogyny, 101
Moldwarp prophecy, 120, 153
Montgomery, Ernesto, 303
More, James, 224
More, Thomas, 153
Morley, Daniel, 65
Mortimer, Anne, 130
Mortimer, Robert, bishop of
  Exeter, 310
Mortimer, Roger, 100
Mortlake, Surrey, 175, 177, 183
Morton, earl of, 200
Morton, John, archbishop of
  Canterbury, 142
Moscow, Russia, 278
Moses, 47, 59, 244
Muggleton, Lodowick, 243
Muggletonianism, 249
Murray, Margaret, 292
mysticism, 20, 53, 179, 243, 278,
  315–16, 322, 335

Nandyke, Thomas, 142
Napier, John, 203–4
Napier, Richard, 203
Napoleon I, emperor, 298
Naseby, battle of (1645), 225,
  229, 233
National Front, 315
nationalism, mystical, 30, 286,
  313
Native Americans, 34, 281
natural magic, 3, 6, 17, 26, 29,
  54–60, 68, 71, 73–4, 83, 96,
  107, 135, 158, 169, 178, 231,
  237, 241, 247–8, 284, 332,
  334
Naudé, Gabriel, 51
Navy, Royal, 175, 251, 269, 301,
  304
Nazism, 19–20, 295–6, 299–300,
  303, 333, 340
neo-Nazism, 315

necromancy, 35, 41, 49, 57, 60–1, 63–4, 94, 97, 115, 117, 119, 125, 127, 132, 142, 147, 155, 157, 164, 173, 186, 193, 197, 222, 227, 241, 266–7, 287–8, 312
Nectanebus, 109, 225
Nennius, 38
Neofolk movement, 314
Neopaganism, 290, 298, 310–11, 313–15, 317
Neoplatonism, 57, 185, 211, 238
Neville, Charles, 6th earl of Westmoreland, 168
Neville, George, archbishop of York, 129
Neville, Isabelle, duchess of Clarence, 132
Neville, Richard, earl of Salisbury, 107
Neville, Richard, earl of Warwick, 131
Neville's Cross, Co. Durham, 103
New Age movement, 290, 313, 321
New Forest Coven, 300
New Forest, Hampshire, 298–9
New World, 23, 34, 171, 174, 176, 180
New Zealand, 282
Newbury, battle of (1643), 225
Newmarket, Suffolk, 251
Newton, Isaac, 258, 266, 270, 273
Night, School of, 186
Nixon, Robert ('Old Nixon'), 79, 283, 342
Nonjurers, 283
Norman Conquest, 86–7
Norns, 42, 193
North Berwick, East Lothian, 200
Northampton, Northamptonshire, 104
Norton, Samuel, 170
Norton, Thomas, 67, 129, 131, 170
Norway, 20
Norwich, Norfolk, 175
Nostradamus, 267, 329
numerology, 77, 94, 212, 245

obeah, 280–1
occult, definition of, 2, 5–6
Olga, grand duchess of Russia, 320
Orléans, France, 123
Osborne, Ruth, 282
Oswald, king of Northumbria, 157
Outlaw, Roger, 99
Outlaw, William, 99
Overbury Plot, 23, 28, 213–16
Overbury, Thomas, 213–15
Oxford, University of, 97, 112, 125, 128, 179, 206, 258

pacts, Satanic, 81, 99–100, 215, 227
Pagan Federation, 315
paganism, 41–6, 55–6, 58, 73, 167, 294
Palermo, Italy, 93
Palko, Betty, 321
palmistry, 250, 286
Paracelsianism, 241, 243, 264
parapsychology, 288
Paris, France, 117
  University of, 97
Paris, Matthew, 74
Parish, Mary, 253–4, 260–3, 265, 268–9, 273–5
Parker, George, 271
Parliamentarians, 225–7, 229–34, 239, 244, 340

Parron, William, 142–3
Parry, Hubert, 286
Parsons, Robert, 186, 189, 336
Partridge, John, 271–2
Pausyl, river, 204
Pearl, The (poem), 47
Peasants' Revolt, 113
Pellitus, 49
Pendragon, Uther, 128
penitentials, 43, 45
Penshurst, Sussex, 127
Percy, Henry, 9th earl of Northumberland, 172–3
Percy, Thomas, 7th earl of Northumberland, 168
Perrers, Alice, 108–9
Persia, 3
Persians, 34–5, 50
Perth, Perthshire, 201
Peterborough, Cambridgeshire, 90
Petitpierre, Max, 309–10
Philadelphianism, 283
Philip II, king of Spain (king of England 1554-58), 161, 176–7
Philippa of Hainault, queen of England, 108
Philippe de Mezières, 117
Philippe VI, king of France, 106
Philosophers' Stone, 65–7, 102, 104, 165, 171, 174, 183, 185, 243
Pico della Mirandola, Giovanni, 144
Pimlico, London, 306
Pinnell, Henry, 243
Plato, 144
Pliny the Elder, 3, 34, 45
Plot, Robert, 263–4, 332
poaching, 167
poisoning, 23, 56, 86, 91, 95, 118–19, 132, 142, 148–9, 177, 187, 190, 194–5, 200, 214–16, 218

Poisons, Affair of, 15, 252
polemic, anti-magical, 22–3, 156, 233
Poor Law, 286
Pope, Alexander, 275
Popish Plot, 236, 251–2
populism, 20, 327
Pordage, John, 21, 241, 338
Portsmouth, Hampshire, 305
Portugal, 176, 245
Pregnani, Abbé, 250–1
Prestall, John, 166, 168
Preston, battle of (1715), 284
Prestonpans, East Lothian, 280
printing, 75, 142–3, 150, 239
Privy Council, 175, 186, 285
    Scottish, 198, 259
projection, astral, 303
propaganda, 5, 9, 19, 23, 76, 84, 101, 112, 127, 143, 167, 199, 223, 227–8, 231, 233, 266, 271, 292, 301, 337, 339–40
prophecy, 5, 14, 25, 39–40, 59, 78–9, 84, 87, 112–13, 117–18, 120, 128, 130, 143, 148, 153–4, 167–8, 170, 174, 177, 181, 183, 186, 193, 204–5, 219, 228–9, 232, 237, 243, 257, 267, 274, 283, 285, 306–7, 318, 321, 323, 331, 341–2
protection marks, ritual, 206
psychics, 31, 294, 296, 320–1
Punk Rock, 311
Puritans, 21–2, 59, 83, 183–4, 213, 220, 222–3, 225–6, 231, 233, 239, 243, 245, 249, 255, 337
pyromancy, 95

quadrants, horary, 110
Quakers, 243
quietism, magical, 112, 331, 342–4

quintessence, 65, 105
Qur'an, 65

Rabbard, Ralph, 129
radicalism, political, 20, 23, 29, 112, 135, 230, 236–7, 240–1, 244, 276, 285, 290, 311, 313–14, 338
Raimondin, count of Poitou, 131–2
Raleigh, Walter, 172, 186, 253
Ralph of Coggeshall, 60
Ramsay, Andrew Michael, 284–5
Ranters, 271
Raymond of Marseilles, 88
Raymund of Tallega, 103
Razielis, Liber, 61
Razin, Stepan, 20–1
Ré, Île de, France, 218
rebellions, 1, 16, 19–21, 120, 142, 153, 167, 187, 221, 232, 250, 256, 261, 267, 281, 291, 332
Reeve, Thomas, 250
Reformation, 27, 59, 71, 141, 183, 229, 240, 334
  Edwardian, 141, 154
  Elizabethan, 141, 159–60
  Henrician, 27, 140–1, 152–4, 169, 188
  Scottish, 27, 141, 160, 191, 196–204
Rehoboam, 112
religion, relationship with magic, 8, 13–14, 33–5, 46, 50, 52–4
Renaissance, 26, 52, 57–9, 142, 144–5, 150, 185, 209–10, 244
Restoration of the Monarchy, 23, 29, 83, 232–3, 235, 238, 247, 250–5, 263, 332, 338
Reuchlin, Johann, 59, 209
Revolution, Glorious, 29, 265–7, 273, 339–40

Rhases (Mohammed ibn Zakariya al-Razi), 69
Richard de Ledrede, bishop of Ossory, 99
Richard I, king of England, 92
Richard II, king of England, 18–19, 27, 109–18, 135–6, 168, 188, 331, 342–3
Richard III, king of England, 19, 134, 138, 142, 147, 332
Richard, Brother, 123
Richard, earl of March, 128
Richmond, Surrey, 126, 210, 283
Right, Claim of, 259
rings, magical, 64, 108, 145
Ripley, George, 17, 27, 67, 128–9, 165, 170, 331
Ritual Abuse, Satanic, 317–19
ritual magic, 26, 30, 46, 56, 59, 71, 75, 82–3, 103, 114, 133, 145, 155, 162, 164–5, 169, 228, 273, 285, 288, 290, 308, 317
Roach, Richard, 283
Robert de Vere, duke of Ireland, 117
Robert I, king of Scots, 105
Robert III, count of Artois, 105–6
Robert of Chester, 72
Robert of Ketton, 65
Robert, earl of Leicester, 88
Robins, John, 143
Rochester, Kent, 168
Rogers, Rita, 320–1
Roman Britain, 32–7
Ros, Lady, 216
Rose, Tudor, 138–9
Roses, Wars of, 124–35
Rosicrucianism, 195, 208, 210, 251, 272
Rouen, France, 122
round table, King Arthur's, 138–9

Rous, John, 102
Rowling, J. K., 32
Royal Society, 240, 263, 273
Royalists, 222–31, 233–5, 237, 239, 241, 248–50, 255, 272, 332, 338, 340
Rudolf II, emperor, 183, 185, 210
runes, 43
Rupert of the Rhine, 224, 227, 253
Russia, 20–1, 278, 302, 307
Ruthven, John, earl of Gowrie, 201

Sackville, Thomas, earl of Dorset, 206
sacrifice, 45, 98, 294
  human, 33, 35, 38, 298
Salisbury Plain, Wiltshire, 212
Salisbury, Wiltshire, 112, 226
Salmon, Pierre, 115
Salomon de Caus, 210
Sanders, Alex, 290
Sandringham, Norfolk, 319
Satanism, 294, 312, 318
Saul, king, 117
Saunders, Richard, 250
Savile, Jimmy, 319
scepticism, 28, 153, 184, 201, 206, 231, 244, 254, 256, 259, 276
Schaw, William, 203
Scheves, William, archbishop of St Andrews, 191
Scholasticism. *See* Aristotelianism
Scone, Perthshire, 96
Scot, Michael, 92–4, 133, 331
Scot, Reginald, 6–7, 151, 184, 201, 276
Scotland, 1, 4, 15, 23–5, 27–8, 38, 59, 82–3, 93, 105, 140, 159–60, 190–204, 209, 221, 227, 232, 257–60, 275, 299–300, 316, 337

Scott, James, duke of Monmouth, 250, 261–3, 336
scrying, 164, 168, 177, 183, 296
Seabrook, William, 300
second sight, 192, 202
Second World War, 30, 279, 292, 295–307, 323, 333, 340–1
sects, Commonwealth, 186, 226, 231, 235, 238, 243, 247, 249–50, 273
Sedgemoor, battle of (1685), 262
Seymour, Charles, 296, 298
Seymour, Edward, duke of Somerset, 149, 154
Seymour, Frances, countess of Hereford, 187
Shakespeare, William, 192
  Henry VI Part 1, 123
  Macbeth, 192
  The Tempest, 162, 207
Shaw, Gilbert, 278, 294, 302, 308–10
Shelley, Jane, 186
Shipton, Mother, 79, 342
Sibly, Ebenezer, 133
Sibyl, Roman, 47
Simmons, Simone, 320
Simon de Montfort, 90
Skipper, Mary, 224
Snowdonia, Wales, 278
Solomon, king, 1, 17, 47, 60–2, 111–12, 135–7, 203–4, 208, 223, 233, 334
  seal of, 96
South Africa, 21–2
Southgate, Troy, 315
Southwell, Thomas, 125–6
Spain, 40, 60, 180–1, 186, 218–19, 225, 245, 291
Spanheim, Germany, 162
Sparrow, Anthony, bishop of Norwich, 271
Sparrow, John, 243

385

Spenser, Edmund, 185, 209
Spiricus, 191
Spiritualism, 30, 287–8, 292, 296, 303–5, 323, 340
spying, 30, 174, 179, 181, 183, 341
St John, Henry, viscount Bolingbroke, 272
Stacy, John, 132
Stafford, Humphrey, duke of Buckingham, 127, 142, 148
Stapleton, William, 145–6
Staunton, Edmund, 223
Stearne, John, 226
Stephen, king of England, 4, 72, 88
Stewart, Henry, Lord Darnley, 200
Stoke Newington, London, 311
Stonehenge, 33, 40, 128, 211
Story, Edward, bishop of Carlisle, 131
Strathclyde, kingdom of, 39
Strike, General, 278
Stuart, Henry Benedict, cardinal, 282
Stuart, James Edward ('Old Pretender'), 275–6
succubi, 89, 92
Suetonius Paulinus, 32
sundogs, 229
superstition, accusations of, 33–5, 43, 130, 141, 149, 151, 157, 159–61, 188, 197, 235, 257, 266, 277, 280–1, 285, 323
Surlingham, Norfolk, 145
swords, magical, 262
Swynford, Katherine, 126, 138
Sylvester II, pope (Gerbert of Aurillac), 74, 115
Symon de Phares, 106, 119
Syon, Abbey of, 153

Tacitus, 32, 34–6
Taillebois, Ivo, 85
Taliesin, 39
talismans, 55, 178–9, 207, 211, 221, 228, 262, 292, 328
Tanner, John, 98
Tany, John, 245–6
Tattershall, Lincolnshire, 167
Tempier, Etienne, archbishop of Paris, 97
Templar, Knights, 285
Tenison, Thomas, archbishop of Canterbury, 259
Teversal, Nottinghamshire, 42
Thabit ibn Qurra, 73
Thacker, Elias, 184
Thames, river, 181, 219, 254, 319
Thelema, 291, 293–5
Theodora, empress, 100
Theosophy, 289, 309
theurgy, 57, 61, 144, 210, 247
thief detection, magical, 140
Thirty Years' War, 210
Thomas de Pizan, 106
Thomas of Woodstock, duke of Gloucester, 117
Thomas the Rhymer, 153, 204
Thoresby, John, 132
Thornton, Penny, 320
Tideman, Robert, bishop of Worcester, 117
toads, 90–1, 117–18, 200
Toledo, Spain, 65, 93
toleration, religious, 210, 236, 240, 265, 284
Tomson, John, 254
Tonge, Israel, 252
Tories, 256, 263, 271, 280, 290
torture, 113, 132, 161, 190, 194, 338
touching, royal, 17, 29, 49, 107–8, 129, 220, 236, 247–9, 275–7, 282, 313, 334

touchpieces, 108, 282
touchpieces1, 207
tournaments, 167
transubstantiation, 113, 154–6
treason, magical, 15, 26, 75, 98, 106, 109, 113–14, 119, 121, 125, 132, 134, 136, 140, 147–9, 152–3, 166, 176, 182, 186, 194, 200–1, 216, 229, 232, 237, 251, 261, 321–2, 331, 337–9
treasure-hunting, magical, 64, 140, 145, 172, 254, 261, 268
Trembles, Mary, 257
Tresham, Thomas, 245
Tresilian, Robert, 114–15, 135
Trithemius, Johannes, 162, 171, 209
Troubles (Northern Ireland), 30, 312, 340
Trump, Donald, 325, 328
Turner, Anne, 214
Turner, George, 214
Turner, Robert, 239
Tutankhamen, 295
Tweed, river, 204
Twynho, Ankarette, 132

unicorns, 195
Uniformity, Act of (1559), 240
Union of Crowns (1603), 28, 139, 190, 204, 229
Union, Treaty of (1707), 24, 196, 258
Usk, Adam, 116–17
utopianism, 244

V for Victory sign, 300–1
Vagrancy Act (1824), 286, 294, 304–5
Valiente, Doreen, 315–16
Van der Post, Laurens, 321
Van Helmont, John Baptist, 264

Vaughan, Thomas, 239
Venutius, king of the Brigantes, 35
Vergil, Polydore, 139
Vigna, Piero della, 93
Vikings, 43
Villiers, George, 1st duke of Buckingham, 28, 216–20, 222–3, 336–7
Villiers, George, 2nd duke of Buckingham, 251
Villiers, John, viscount Purbeck, 216
Villiers, Mary, countess of Buckingham, 218
Vincennes, France, 120
vitalism, 55
Vitruvianism, 211
vodun, Haitian, 19
Vortigern, king, 38, 66, 130

Wake, Thomas, 131
Walcher, prior of Great Malvern, 72
Wallace, Colin, 312
Walsingham, Francis, 181, 183, 341
Walsingham, Thomas, 117
Walter de Istlip, 99
Waltham Abbey, Essex, 250
Wardour Castle, Wiltshire, 225
Wareham, William, archbishop of Canterbury, 152
warfare, 6–7, 26, 28, 30, 36, 63, 76, 86, 88, 102–9, 122–4, 134–5, 208, 222–8, 233, 250, 279, 291–2, 295–307, 313, 323, 331, 339–40
Warner, Walter, 172
Warwick, Warwickshire, 131–2
Watkins, Alfred, 294
Webster, John, 243
Weird Sisters, 42, 192–3

Weldon, Anthony, 201
Westminster Abbey, 95–7, 118, 126, 301
Westminster, Synod of (1102), 45
Weston, Richard, 214
Wharton, George, 229–30, 250
Wharton, Goodwin, 29, 254, 260–1, 263–77, 332, 337
Whigs, 29, 234, 237, 256–7, 260, 266, 270–2, 276, 280, 283, 337, 340
White Ship disaster, 18, 88
White, Ronald, 310
Whitelocke, Bulstrode, 229
Whitgift, John, archbishop of Canterbury, 183
Whittaker, Alexander, 281
Whorewood, Jane, 231
Wicca, 290, 298, 311, 314
Wildman, John, 241, 261–3
Wilhelm II, Kaiser, 292
Wilkins, John, 244
William Adelin, 87
William I, king of England, 85–6
William III, king of England, 29, 236, 259, 266–9, 273, 275, 277, 332, 336, 340
William of Malmesbury, 71, 74
William of Newburgh, 79
Williams, Thomas, 253
Williamson, Cecil, 298–9
Wilshire, David, 318
Wilton Diptych, 110
Winchester, Hampshire, 138
Windsor, Berkshire, 126
Winstanley, Gerard, 241–3, 338
witchcraft, 1, 5–7, 15, 26, 28–9, 34, 42, 48, 56, 80–3, 91, 100, 118, 123–4, 141, 147, 151, 153, 155, 157, 159–60, 174, 176, 186–91, 193–5, 198–201, 204–8, 214, 216–17, 220–2, 231–2, 234, 237–9, 250–1, 266, 281–3, 286, 288, 292, 298–9, 318, 324, 330, 335–7, 339–40
  African, 21–2, 319, 325
  decline of, 254–60, 277
  Jamaican. *See obeah*
  Neopagan. *See* Wicca
Witchcraft Acts
  1542, 140, 148–9
  1563, 140, 197
  1563 (Scottish), 140, 156, 194, 197–8
  1604, 140, 205
  1735, 30, 279–80, 286, 305, 309
Witchcraft, Museum of, 298
Wolsey, Thomas, cardinal, 27, 145–6, 336
Wood, Edward, Viscount Halifax, 288
Woods, Mary, 213–14
Woodstock, Oxfordshire, 89–90, 161
Woodville, Elizabeth, queen of England, 91, 131, 134–5, 147
Worcester, battle of (1651), 227
Worcester, Worcestershire, 139
Wynkyn de Woorde, 142

Yeats, W. B., 290, 293
York, Yorkshire, 43, 72
Yves de Saint Branchier, 106